SHIP OPERATIONS AND MANAGEMENT

INSTITUTE OF CHARTERED SHIPBROKERS

OUR WORD OUR BOND

Published by the
Institute of Chartered Shipbrokers
85 Gracechurch Street
London
EC3V 0AA
United Kingdom
Telephone: +44 20 7623 1111
Email: books@ics.org.uk
www.ics.org.uk

Published 2017
ISBN 978-1-911328-05-6

Terms of use

While the advice given in this book *Ship Operations and Management* has been developed using the best information currently available, it is intended purely as guidance to be used at the user's own risk. No responsibility is accepted by the Institute of Chartered Shipbrokers (ICS), the membership of ICS or by any person, firm, corporation or organisation (who or which has been in any way concerned with furnishing of information or data, the compilation or any translation, publishing, supply or sale of the book) for the accuracy of any information or advice given in the book or any omission from the book or for any consequence whatsoever resulting directly or indirectly from compliance with or adoption of guidance contained in the book even if caused by a failure to exercise reasonable care.

Printed and bound in the UK by Cambrian Printers
Design and book production by Jacamar (www.jacamar.co.uk)
Front cover image: Portpictures.nl

ACKNOWLEDGEMENTS

First and foremost, we would like to thank Mark O'Neil for his inspirational support in the revision of this book. We must also acknowledge the contribution of several industry professionals, among them Dr K E Harrington, Mike Powell and Jae Sundaram who have shared their wealth of knowledge and experience with the Institute.

Special thanks are due to Tony Addison and Nick de Spon for their efforts in the review of this book. Acknowledgement must also go to Costas Lambrou for his assistance in the updating of this book and to Dinah Bromwich and Philip Moore for their efforts in improving the quality of the text.

The illustrations have been sourced from across the industry but particular thanks go to Danny Cornelissen of Portpictures.nl. The artistry of these images raises the stakes in the appearance and presentation of our maritime textbooks.

CONTRIBUTING EDITOR

Tony Addison

Tony Addison has spent a lifetime in the shipping industry. He attended the London Nautical School from the age of 11 before going to sea as a cadet and deck officer in the British Merchant Navy.

He came ashore as operations superintendent for a Japanese shipowner in their London office and attended vessels calling at UK ports. He then moved to a small Greek shipowner as operations manager. Tony immediately began studying for Institute examinations and he qualified as a Fellow in 1986.

Tony then joined Mitsui OSK Lines where he worked in London and Rotterdam for almost 30 years in every aspect of the business including nine years as operations manager for car & ro-ro division and 11 years as general manager. Tony left in 2015 and is now a freelance business consultant.

TECHNICAL REVIEW

Nick de Spon

Nick de Spon is an ex-master mariner who, after 14 years on general cargo ships, bulk carriers and tankers, worked in ship and cargo surveying and marine operations for 30 years. Recently retired, Nick continues to lecture on shipping operations and is an examiner for the Institute of Chartered Shipbrokers.

Foreword

Mark O'Neil

President, Columbia Shipmanagement Ltd

Since the beginning of civilisation, shipping – or the 'maritime adventure' – has been at the heart of international trade and commerce. And what an adventure it has been: navigating the practical and physical minefields between shipper and consignee, the fixing of the vessel for the shipment in question, insuring the same, the vagaries of local and international contract and shipping laws, inconsistent competencies of vessels' crews, perils of the sea, pirates, wars, cargo and vessel damage. Nothing much has changed and the adventure continues as much today as it ever did.

International trade is changing. Global internet sellers, such as Amazon, are becoming all-consuming and supremely dominant in the marketplace, and are increasingly looking to logistics, vertical supply chains and technology to bridge (and control) the gap between seller and buyer. Shipping will always be an important element in that logistics framework and vertical supply chain, but will be regarded as an *element* only, as opposed to a separate and stand-alone function. This difference of perception is of vital importance, and will shape the shipping industry going forward. To play our part in this new age, and to take full advantage of the benefits offered, we must ensure that we deliver ever greater efficiencies and efficacies, and embrace technological advances via eco-friendly vessel design and consumption and digitalisation of processes.

Shipping will remain a profoundly human endeavour. The seafarer is both potentially the weakest and the strongest link in the maritime adventure. No amount of technological advance will change that, given the unpredictability of the natural environment in which ships operate. Whilst crewless vessels remain a possibility for coastal trade, we are very far away indeed from contemplating crewless vessels for oceangoing vessels. The quality of the seafarer, his values, culture, initial and ongoing training, specialisation and his well-being and that of his family, have never been more important than they are today.

As an industry facing revolutionary change in technological advances and business organisation, the challenge for all of us in our respective fields is to stay *relevant* and stay *compelling*. Achieve that and we will continue to reap our just rewards and enjoy fulfilling and successful careers in shipping. The information contained within the covers of this latest edition of *Ship Operations and Management* will equip you with the necessary knowledge to assist you on this road, and will serve as an invaluable *aide-mémoire* whatever your level of experience.

Contents

Appendices Contents

Chapter 1

Shipowners, operators and managers

1.1 THE SHIP MANAGER

There is much more to shipowning than simply buying a ship, finding the right cargoes and carrying them, as many have found to their cost. Historically, a shipowner would undertake all the functions required in owning and operating a ship in-house, although in times before international communications were possible, the ship's Master would have full power to act on the owner's behalf.

Today, traditional shipowners may still carry out all the functions of ownership and operation themselves but there also exists a whole sector of organisations offering their services as ship managers. This practice can be traced back to the 1960s, when the major oil companies discovered tax incentives available to them if they owned the ships that carried their cargoes. Later, in the crises provoked by the rapid rise in oil prices of the following decade, many shipowners found it economically impossible to operate profitably. As a result, hundreds, if not thousands, of vessels were abandoned to the owners' creditors, usually banks or finance houses.

The resultant increase in the number of organisations that owned ships but did not have the know-how or experience to operate them, led to a business model that delegated the management of day-to-day operations to independent ship managers. Ship management is a complex business involving registration with a country or flag of choice, manning, insuring, maintaining and operating in an international arena with many laws, rules and conventions to comply with.

The first decision that a shipowner has to make, therefore, is who to use for this work. The first thought would be to hire the necessary personnel and create all the requisite departments. This in-house approach has much to commend it. The obvious one is close control by owners of all aspects of the management activity. The amount of money tied up in owning a ship makes the idea of having day-to-day contact with all those involved in its care appear such an advantage that the decision seems obvious.

That was often the view until the question of cost was considered. Skilled managers and support staff command high salaries. If an owner has very few ships, the cost to be allocated against each to cover the management function becomes uneconomical. This is not a problem for the owners of large fleets, where the management costs are spread over more units and thus will be at an acceptable level. Moreover, the higher income will permit the engagement of top-class managers and support staff, all of whom are likely to be fully employed.

For small-scale owners or organisations that do not see ship operating as a core business, the common response is to employ the services of an independent ship management company. There are now many such companies based in different parts of the world. These contain all the different departments needed to provide an efficient service for which they charge a fee or they can subcontract the services of specialists for certain aspects of the operation. Because of their size, they are usually able to attract top-class executives and the large numbers of ships under their management enable them to enjoy economies of scale.

There is, of course, a dilemma for the medium-sized shipowner, which will have to consider the benefits of using its own staff over which it has direct control and balance this against the economies in using a third party to manage its ships. Sometimes that problem is solved by subcontracting only a part of the management function, which is possible in view of the clear demarcation between the different activities in ship management. Crewing is a prime example of this partial subcontracting and will be covered later.

For financial and legal reasons, some large shipowners will have their fleet owned by several paper shipowning companies based in open registry countries. These are then bareboat or time chartered in, and managed by either in-house or independent management companies.

Another device that has successfully overcome the lack of economies of scale for the medium- sized shipowner has been contracting to manage other owners' ships by using personnel employed in caring for the owner's own vessels. This is different from the pooling arrangement adopted by many owners adopt for commercial employment of their vessels since, under that type of arrangement, the real management of the ship remains with the owner.

1.1.1 The management agreement

In view of the large amounts of money and capital assets involved, a very clear written agreement is essential if disputes and misunderstandings are to be avoided. Each management agreement is probably unique, but the Baltic and International Maritime Council (BIMCO) has compiled a printed standard ship management agreement (known as SHIPMAN) and crew management agreement (CREWMAN) which, even if not used in their entirety, provide a first-class checklist of all the matters that should be considered in making such a contract.

The SHIPMAN agreement has evolved over time and it is probably true to say that the 1998 version is the most popular, although a new version of the agreement was developed in 2008 and released as SHIPMAN 2009. This new version reflects changes in the shipping industry in general and to international conventions and codes. In that respect, it may be considered more relevant, but many managers would have been making their own unique amendments to the earlier contract and may prefer to work using that version rather than the new agreement.

Whichever version is used, the agreement identifies (in the boxes in Part I of the form) all the different duties that may be subcontracted by the shipowner to a ship manager and these headings are a useful index to the duties that must be carried out if the management is handled in-house. Each actual management agreement will be individual because the shipowner may choose to handle some of the activities itself or use a different manager, for example, to handle crewing.

The clauses in Part II of the agreement relate to the way in which the management contract itself will be carried out. For example, clause 6.3 in the 1998 version (clause 10(c) of the 2009 form) is most important as it provides that all insurance policies will be in the names of both owners and managers. This means that both parties have the benefit of the protection, and in the chapter on insurance it will become clear how important this is.

1.2 STRUCTURE OF SHIPOWNING AND MANAGEMENT ORGANISATIONS

A number of issues dealt with in this introductory chapter will be dealt with later in much greater depth. The purpose at this stage is to give a general overview of all those matters that fall within the overall responsibility of the ship operator whether as an owner or as a manager.

At the top of any shipowning or operating corporate structure will be a board of directors headed by a chairman or president and a managing director. It is their task to determine the overall policy of the business and future direction that the company will take.

Policy areas which will be decided by the top management might include:

- the philosophy of the company's strategy;
- the type and size of vessels used;
- fleet replacement policy such as owning and chartering options;
- flag policy;
- the trades or routes that the company will serve;
- in-house ship management or contracted out;
- financial performance.

Having established the policies, the board will delegate the management of these functions to various in-house departments or contract them out as appropriate. However, as ultimate owners of the ship, the board (or, very occasionally, an individual owner) will be held responsible and liable for the proper management of the ship under most international conventions.

1.2.1 The structure of ship management

The way in which these practical services are dealt with, and especially how the various functions are grouped together, will vary according to the company concerned. However, all these different activities will need to be provided either from within the company or by contracting out to independent ship management or crewing companies.

Acquisition of vessels

Before the company can operate it must have some vessels under its control.

1. Outright purchase

   The traditional way of procuring ships is to buy them outright. The company will either use its own cash resources to buy the vessel, or more likely, obtain a loan or mortgage secured on the vessel. In times when finance is scarce or shipyards are not busy, cash-rich owners are in the best position to obtain tonnage on favourable terms. For instance, following the financial crisis in 2009 many such owners were able to purchase new vessels from shipyards at prices almost half that at which they were initially contracted, owing to the original owners defaulting on contracts.

   The very largest companies may employ their own naval architects and design staff to create the type and size of newbuilds they want for the future, or this function may be delegated to independent naval architects. More commonly, companies may buy vessels built to a pre-existing shipyard design that may be modified to their needs.

   Other companies may concentrate on building up their fleet by buying secondhand tonnage and will use the services of a sale and purchase broker for this purpose.

2. Finance-based long-term chartered

   Increasingly, shipowning companies are using more innovative ways to procure new ships through intermediaries. This is because either the company does not have sufficient borrowing capability to purchase all the ships it wants to operate, or an intermediary is in a better position to obtain tax benefits from purchasing ships than the operating company. The shipowner may still be heavily involved in the design of the ship and may have the lifetime use of the vessel, sometimes with an option to purchase after a specified period for a nominal sum.

   A typical tax-driven approach is the German KG scheme, whereby German individuals or companies which own vessels can secure favourable tax treatment, part of the benefit of which they can pass on through competitive charter rates to operating companies. Ships under these arrangements can be bareboat chartered, where the charterer is responsible for crewing, maintenance and so on, or time chartered, where the actual owner performs these functions.

   The popularity of the KG model has declined quite severely since 2009 owing to a collapse in operating income as both freight for liner services and hire rates for time-charter vessels have fallen from the record levels set just before the economic crash of 2008 and soaring fuel costs in the same period. Far from receiving income from their investments, the KG fund investors are now frequently being called upon to provide additional income to keep the ships operating at or below breakeven levels.

3. Time charters

   Other companies will time charter suitable tonnage from other shipowning companies. Time charters are also used to acquire tonnage to meet short-term commitments or fluctuations in the fleet, perhaps to replace tonnage during a drydock programme or to meet a seasonal spike in demand. The fall in the hire rate for time charter vessels since 2008 (referred to above) has caused some operators to rethink even this long-established form of securing tonnage.

The time charter contract locks the charterer in for the duration of the contract to paying a fixed daily sum which may have been economic at the time it was entered into but has become less so as freight rates in general have fallen.

4. Bareboat and demise charters

The last type of employment is that of a bareboat arrangement. Here, a shipowner, on the basis of a long-term charter from a charterer, builds a ship mainly to their or a shipyard standard design but possibly with some modifications needed by the charterer. The charterer provides the crew and treats the ship in many ways as its own, maintaining the vessel, keeping it classed, insured and so on but paying a daily bareboat hire for the vessel as in a time charter but at a reduced rate. Often, the bareboat charterer will also paint the ship in its own livery.

In return, it pays the owner a monthly bareboat hire. Thus the owner is paid for initially funding the ship and earns a profit. The period of the charter varies. It is probably uneconomic to take a ship for a short period of a year or two. Most vessels are financed over a period of seven to 10 years, so a bareboat charter will usually last for as long as or longer than this period. The main advantage for the charterer is that it is spared the initial financing costs of the ship, but nevertheless gains the advantage of an addition to its fleet without a large capital expenditure. In addition, the charterer maintains a skilled workforce within its shipping department, enhancing its shoreside operations over time.

If the ship is bareboat chartered for its whole trading life, the charter is called a demise charter.

1.2.2 The technical departments

A ship requires constant supervision of its structure and its machinery, much of which needs a regular programme of maintenance. A merchant ship which is not kept in a seaworthy condition will be unemployable and subject to official sanctions.

Seaworthiness does not just mean that there is no danger of a ship sinking (although that is obviously a vital element): the term can also be considered to cover its cargo-worthiness. No matter how sound the hull of the ship is against springing a leak, and how good the engine is to propel the ship to its destination, if the cargo tanks are not sound, if the hatches let water into the holds, or the ventilation is inadequate so that cargo becomes damaged, then a merchant ship is considered unseaworthy.

Maintenance of the physical structure of the ship falls neatly into two distinct sections which are usually referred to as deck and engine room. The term 'engine room' is easily understood as there is no difficulty in visualising the compartment of the ship that contains the main engine plus auxiliary machinery such as electricity generators and pumps. It does, of course, extend a little farther than the actual engine room as the term naturally includes the propeller shaft and the propeller at the end of it.

It is perhaps better to think in terms of 'deck' as meaning all the rest of the ship which is not covered by the expression 'engine room' because that is the responsibility of the deck department.

The engine room department will usually employ shore-based marine engineers, customarily referred to as engineering superintendents. They have to oversee the routine operation of the ships' main and auxiliary machinery, keeping a close watch on routine servicing, maintenance and replacement of those parts which wear out and need regular renewal. A small but vital element of their job is to ensure that the correct grade and quality of bunker fuels and lubricants are supplied to the ships.

Superintendents have to be ready to react without delay with advice or physical presence in the event of a breakdown and to oversee major repairs, inspections and overhauls.

The deck department is also often staffed by ships' officers who have decided to work ashore and they are usually referred to as marine superintendents. Their duties, like their engineering colleagues, are concerned with maintaining the structure of the ship, from overseeing major surveys and repairs to ensuring the paintwork is kept in good condition.

Failure to ensure efficiency in the technical departments will quickly result in the ships being in trouble. It is the responsibility of classification societies to provide an independent check on the condition of the vessel and if a vessel is found to be substandard, then a temporary suspension or withdrawal of class can have very serious consequences for the vessel's ability to trade. Unchecked it could lead to a major catastrophe with human lives as well as goods being placed at risk. As a result of international conventions initiated by the International Maritime Organization (IMO), which is a division of the United Nations, most of the world's maritime countries have enacted laws which permit port state control inspection and detention, a device which enables a ship to be detained until substandard items are put right. Such detention is one of the risks owners run if their technical departments are inadequate.

1.2.3 IMO Conventions

The two most important conventions are the International Convention for the Safety of Life at Sea (SOLAS) and the International Convention for the Prevention of Pollution from Ships (MARPOL). These conventions have spawned a number of subsidiary conventions and codes which have also been enacted into national laws albeit with varying degrees of acceptance by signatory countries so that not all codes and conventions apply to every ship afloat.

The SOLAS Convention in its successive forms is generally regarded as the most important of all international treaties concerning the safety of merchant ships. The first version was adopted in 1914 in response to the Titanic disaster. The 1974 version is the fifth version and includes the tacit acceptance procedure, which provides that an amendment shall enter into force on a specified date unless, before that date, objections to the amendment are received from an agreed number of parties. As a result, the 1974 convention has been updated and amended on numerous occasions since it came into force in 1980. The convention in force today is sometimes referred to as SOLAS, 1974, as amended.

The main objective of the SOLAS Convention is to specify minimum standards for the construction, equipment and operation of ships, compatible with their safety. Flag states are responsible for ensuring that ships under their flag comply with its requirements, and a number of certificates are prescribed in the convention as proof that this has been done. Control provisions also allow contracting governments to inspect ships of other contracting states if there are clear grounds for believing that the ship and its equipment do not substantially comply with the requirements of the convention – this procedure is known as port state control, which is discussed in chapter 3.

Ensuring that ships are properly maintained is one of the aims of the International Safety Management (ISM) Code, or to give it its full title, the International Management Code for the Safe Operation of Ships and for Pollution Prevention. Like other IMO codes such as FSS Code (fire safety systems) and LSA (life-saving appliances) Code, the ISM Code is part of the SOLAS Convention.

The operators' safety management systems (SMS) should ensure compliance with mandatory rules and regulations, taking into account applicable codes, guidelines and standards recommended by the IMO.

Although the ISM Code is not confined to technical management, it is usually one of the superintendents that takes on the role of designated person ashore (DPA), the only role actually described in the code, and becomes the link between ship's personnel and the shore management and directors.

MARPOL is the main international convention covering prevention of pollution of the marine environment by ships from operational or accidental causes. The MARPOL Convention was adopted on 2 November 1973 at IMO. The Protocol of 1978 was adopted in response to a spate of tanker accidents in 1976–77 and absorbed the 1973 MARPOL Convention, which had not yet entered into force. In 1997, a protocol was adopted to amend the convention and a new Annex VI was added which entered into force on 19 May 2005. MARPOL has been updated by amendments through the years.

The convention includes regulations aimed at preventing and minimising pollution from ships – both accidental pollution and that from routine operations – and currently includes six technical Annexes:

Annex I Regulations for the Prevention of Pollution by Oil (entered into force in 1983). This covers prevention of pollution by oil from operational measures as well as from accidental discharges. The 1992 amendments to Annex I made it mandatory for new oil tankers to have double hulls and brought in a phase-in schedule for existing tankers to fit double hulls.

Annex II Regulations for the Control of Pollution by Noxious Liquid Substances in Bulk (entered into force in1983). Some 250 substances were evaluated and the discharge of their residues is allowed only to reception facilities unless certain concentrations and conditions are complied with. In any case, no discharge of residues containing noxious substances is permitted within 12 miles of land.

Annex III Prevention of Pollution by Harmful Substances Carried by Sea in Packaged Form (entered into force in 1992). This contains general requirements for the packing, marking, labelling, documentation, stowage, quantity limitations, exceptions and notifications of 'harmful substances', which are those substances identified as marine pollutants in the International Maritime Dangerous Goods Code (IMDG Code) or which meet the criteria in Annex III.

Annex IV Prevention of Pollution by Sewage from Ships (entered into force in 2003). This contains requirements to control pollution of the sea by sewage. The discharge of sewage into the sea is prohibited, except when the ship has in operation an approved sewage treatment plant or when the ship is discharging comminuted and disinfected sewage using an approved system at a distance of more than three nautical miles from the nearest land; sewage which is not comminuted or disinfected has to be discharged at a distance of more than 12 nautical miles from the nearest land.

Annex V Prevention of Pollution by Garbage from Ships (entered into force in 1988). This deals with different types of garbage and specifies the distances from land and the manner in which they may be disposed of. The most important feature is the complete ban on the disposal into the sea of all forms of plastics.

Annex VI Prevention of Air Pollution from Ships (entered into force in 2005). This sets limits on sulphur oxide and nitrogen oxide emissions from ship exhausts and prohibits deliberate emissions of ozone-depleting substances.

Perhaps the most important aspect of Annex VI is the establishment of emission control areas (ECAs) and sulphur emission control areas (SECAs). In these areas, only fuel with a low sulphur content can be used, meaning the ship has to carry different grades of fuel and switch between them as appropriate. Low sulphur fuel is more expensive and currently has about a 50% premium over intermediate fuel oil (IFO). The price is such that some owners are fitting systems known as scrubbers that remove the sulphur oxides from the ships' exhaust emissions.

Also under Annex VI, emissions of nitrogen oxides are controlled at various levels depending upon the date a ship was built. Complying with the requirements of the NOx Code, which governs this aspect, can be achieved in a number of ways. The most simple of these involves running the engine only within parameters laid down by the engine maker. That is reasonably simple but involves the ship being permitted to use only original equipment manufacturer (OEM) spare parts, which may not always be readily available.

In 2004, IMO adopted another convention which is aimed at controlling the management of ballast water. In 2016, the IMO Ballast Water Management Convention received sufficient ratification and it is in force as of 8 September 2017. Under the convention's terms, ships are required to manage their ballast water to remove, render harmless, or avoid the uptake or discharge of aquatic organisms and pathogens within ballast water and sediments. Meanwhile, the USA proceeded with its own similar regulation, which is now in force, meaning that ships trading to US waters will be required to fit a ballast water treatment system according to a rolling programme, based on the age of the ship and its ballast water capacity.

1.2.4 Storing

In addition to the purchasing needs of the technical departments there are other requirements for equipment, maintenance materials and spares. The officers and crew have to be housed and fed, and worldwide purchasing requires specialist skills, especially to achieve maximum economy without skimping. Food can be a particular problem because different nationalities have different eating habits, some of which have to be strictly adhered to. Stores department personnel have to be aware of this and to be sure that adequate supplies of the appropriate foods are bought, particularly if the ship is trading to an area where such items are difficult to obtain.

Food can be a particular problem because different nationalities have different eating habits, some of which have to be strictly adhered to

1.2.5 Insurance

Perhaps surprisingly, insurance is a shipowner's second biggest item of cost, meaning that the efficient administration of it is very important. This includes war risk insurance, although these premiums are low.

Insurance for ships falls into two distinct categories and the most obvious is the insurance against loss or damage to the ship itself – referred to as hull and machinery (H&M) insurance. The most famous provider of this type of insurance is Lloyd's of London, an organisation which started in the City of London in 1687. Insurance with Lloyd's is provided by individuals known as underwriters, who get their name from the way each person accepted a part of the risk by writing his name, one under the other. This system of personal risk exists to this day but the individuals tend to join together into syndicates. Access to the underwriters is only possible through a Lloyd's broker, who acts on behalf of the shipowner in seeking the best cover possible at the lowest premium, which is the money paid by the shipowner to secure the insurance cover. When the broker has obtained sufficient cover, it is possible for the contract to be drawn up (and this is referred to as the insurance policy). The insurance broker's income is a small percentage of this premium, while the rest is shared among the underwriters in proportion to the amount of the risk each one has accepted.

Marine insurance is by no means the monopoly of Lloyd's, and many of the bigger insurance companies now include this type of cover among their activities. Such companies may cover the entire risk, although it is by no means unusual for marine insurance brokers to arrange a policy which is partly covered by Lloyd's underwriters and partly by companies. The London insurance market is international in its scope but there are many insurers based around the world catering to international and domestic needs.

Should there be a casualty (which could range from a small scrape against a rock to total loss of the ship), a claim will usually be made against the underwriters, who, once again, have to be approached via the insurance broker through whom the cover was arranged.

The other type of insurance can best be summed up under the heading of third-party insurance. This includes such things as claims against the ship by a port authority for damage done by the ship hitting the jetty, claims by crew members for personal injury when negligence is alleged against the shipowner and claims by cargo owners when their cargo is not delivered in the same apparent good order and condition as it was when it was loaded. In other words, any claim made against the ship by another person or company. The biggest source of claims is for oil pollution. Injury and cargo damage are expensive but, compared with an oil spill, they pale into insignificance.

For reasons which go back a long way, the London underwriters were reluctant to offer this sort of cover. As a result, the shipowners joined together into self-insuring groups and formed associations formally titled Protection and Indemnity Associations but which to this day are still referred to as P&I Clubs. Protection involves the legal help that the clubs give to fight against unfair claims, while indemnity covers the repayment to the owners for any third-party claims that have been legitimately made and settled.

Outside the UK it is not unusual for insurers to provide both H&M and P&I cover.

Both these types of insurance need constant attention, as most shipowners inevitably have several claims outstanding or in the pipeline. This means there is always work to be carried out by the ship manager's insurance department.

1.2.6 Operations

Having covered the essential tasks of maintaining the ship in a seaworthy and commercially sound condition, the ship managers need to have a department which can provide the organisation to ensure the ship carries out the tasks to which it has been committed by the commercial staff who arranged its employment. Employment can involve carrying in-house cargoes, operating in the spot market or may even involve operating on a liner service.

The operations department will know from the technical departments that the ship is ready to carry out revenue-earning work and the commercial staff will have explained what the commitment is. It is then up to the operations staff to carry out all the many tasks needed to fulfil this commitment. For example, an essential job is to ensure that the ship is sent to the right place at the right time and then told where to go next. Decisions have to be made as to how much bunker fuel will be the ideal quantity and where this should be taken on board. Similarly, it needs to be ensured that the agents at all ports of call are advised and their responses acted upon is essential. Crew changes have to be organised at the appropriate intervals and careful planning can avoid expensive air travel for crew members leaving or joining the ship. Routine drydocking is another major activity which has to be harmonised with commercial commitments. While many specialist tasks can be passed to the appropriate departments, the operations staff have to co-ordinate it all.

1.2.7 Commercial

Many shipowners subcontract all the management of their ships with the exception of the actual arranging of the ships' commercial activities. Thus the contact with brokers and the fixing of the charters or, in the case of liners, the marketing and documentation, are under the owners' total control.

As mentioned above, there has to be very close liaison between staff in the commercial and the operations departments to ensure such things as having the right amounts of bunkers available at suitable times and places, to organise crew changes and to harmonise routine drydocking with commercial commitments.

When the management includes the commercial work as well, or in the case of the management being carried out by the owners themselves, this close liaison between the operations staff and the commercial department is far simpler. In some companies this has developed into such a close tie that it is difficult to see where the precise divisions lie. It is the commercial department's job to decide what business to go for and to authorise the brokers accordingly, but such decisions should only be made with the advice of the operations staff that what is proposed is physically and conveniently possible.

Given that a particular piece of business is workable, the commercial staff are given the task of ensuring that it is as profitable as possible. Hence an understanding of the market conditions, much of this learnt from the brokers, is an essential element of this decision-making process. Skill at producing voyage estimates to enable viability and comparison with other business to be checked is an important part of this process.

Each voyage cannot be looked at in isolation, and an eye must be kept on where the ship will become empty and what sort of following business may be available. For example, it could be worth ignoring a cargo nearby and sailing in ballast to a further port if the business there takes the ship in turn to an area where there is the prospect of good follow-up business.

While all the departments in a ship manager's office are vital, the responsibility for the eventual success of the venture rests with the commercial department.

1.3 SHIP'S PERSONNEL

Even with first-class departments in the ship manager's office, and despite all the technological advances made over the last century, a ship's eventual success or failure will depend on its officers and crew. This in turn makes it imperative for the ship managers to have a well-run crewing department.

Many different (and sometimes opposing) factors have an influence on crewing matters, the first of which, regardless of any external pressures, is one of safety. Safety, first of all, in its obvious humanitarian sense, is not risking the lives of the people on the ship or on any other ship with which it might collide. Safety also in the material sense of not risking an enormous financial outlay in the hands of incompetent workers.

Safety will also be dictated from external sources, which, in the case of responsible maritime countries, will be in the form of statutory manning levels where the precise number and competency of the officers and crew will be laid down according to the size and type of ship and will be enforced by the law of the country of registration. The precise number and rank of seafarers for a specific ship may well be fixed but is more likely to vary depending on the area of operation and possibly even the cargo.

The flag of registration of the vessel is important because minimum safe manning levels will be set and enforced by the law of the country of registration, as indeed may be the nationality of the crew. Crews from some countries are very much cheaper to employ than others. For example, the wage levels in Europe are several times higher than those in the Philippines. Some maritime countries insist on the employment of nationals of the flag of registry. Others, while retaining many of the safety aspects of ship manning, are more relaxed about the nationality of the crew. This has given rise to companies which undertake to provide entire crews. Many such crewing contractors directly supervise the training of the required personnel and ensure that they are replaced at the appropriate times.

Manning levels will also form part of any labour agreements in countries where trade unions are able to negotiate minimum standards. These standards are principally focused on the safety of the union's members, although they have on occasion also had an impact on manning levels and wider employment rights for their members. In the case of the traditional maritime nations, agreement is usually negotiated between the national union and either the individual owners or with an association representing all the owners in that country.

Despite all the technological advances made over the last century, a ship's eventual success or failure will depend on its officers and crew

Where there is no tradition of shipowning, one may encounter agreements negotiated by the International Transport Workers' Federation (ITF), which is a body to which many of the world's transport unions, dealing with sea, road, rail and air transport, are sometimes affiliated. The ITF is dedicated to ensuring that shipowners do not, in its opinion, exploit seamen from poorer nations by paying them low wages and placing them in substandard ships. There is a blue card system. This documentation demonstrates that the conditions of pay and employment are equal to, or better than, the ITF requirements. In the main this has involved boycotts against ships belonging to targeted owners, some of whom in turn have taken legal action to prevent the ITF's actions from impacting on their shipping operations.

In early 2008, a long-running dispute involving Viking Line (a Finnish ferry operator) and the Finnish Seamen's Union came to an end in an out-of-court settlement. The dispute concerned the ship operator's intention to reflag the vessel and alter the conditions of crew employment. The ITF became involved in the dispute and legal actions took place in the UK and the European Court of Justice. It is generally accepted that the unions were likely to lose the case because, under European Union law, companies and organisations have a right of freedom of movement. The out-of-court settlement probably saved the union side from being forced to pay damages and legal costs. As a result of the legal dispute, the power of the ITF to disrupt work on vessels in Europe has been diminished.

The ITF focuses its campaigns mainly against those ships which are registered under flags of countries which have no real maritime tradition and exert very loose control, if any, upon the manning levels or other matters of crew competency. These are the ships operating under open registries. The attraction for shipowners to register under such flags is a combination of this lack of regulation of personnel, lower crewing costs and little or no taxation demands on earnings. These attractions have to be balanced against the risk of attracting the disapproval of such bodies as the ITF, which, through its affiliated national trade unions, is able to immobilise a ship by the withdrawal of all shore labour in countries where secondary picketing by workers not involved in the dispute is allowed.

As well as actual flags of convenience, some of which have earned a poor reputation, some countries have recognised that the strictness of their maritime laws might tempt local owners to register ships abroad. These countries have, therefore, agreed to the formation of second registries, sometimes referred to as offshore or international registries.

Belgium, Denmark, France, Germany, Norway, Spain and the United Kingdom all have second registries, many of them specifically formed for political reasons. In the case of the UK, the Isle of Man register developed as a result of the peculiar semi-independence of certain off-shore islands around the British Isles. Several UK-owned ships have re-registered in the Isle of Man because, according to the owners, simply avoiding the requirement to deduct and collect income tax and social security contributions on behalf of the government, has reduced staff in the crewing department such that it represents the difference between profit and loss. The shipowner's decision as to where to register its ships will, therefore, have a significant effect on the work of the crewing department.

While retaining many of the safety aspects of ship manning, open registers are more relaxed about the nationality of the crew. Crewing contractors also, therefore, provide entire properly trained crews for ships on open registers.

The International Convention on Standards of Training, Certification and Watchkeeping for Seafarers (STCW) is an international convention established by the IMO. It sets out the minimum levels of training and administration and has been adopted by most of the maritime countries of the world. The original convention came into being in 1978 but was updated in 1995 and again in 2010 when the so-called Manila amendments were adopted by a diplomatic meeting in the Philippines. The latest version includes these amendments and is referred to as STCW 2010.

The amendments adopted include the following:

- improved measures to prevent fraudulent practices associated with certificates of competency and strengthen the evaluation process (monitoring of parties' compliance with the convention);
- revised requirements on hours of work and rest, and new requirements for the prevention of drug and alcohol abuse, as well as updated standards relating to medical fitness standards for seafarers;
- new certification requirements for able seafarers;
- new requirements relating to training in modern technology such as electronic charts and information systems (ECDIS);
- new requirements for marine environment awareness training and training in leadership and teamwork;
- new training and certification requirements for electro-technical officers;
- updating of competence requirements for personnel serving on board all types of tankers, including new requirements for personnel serving on liquefied gas tankers;
- new requirements for security training, as well as provisions to ensure that seafarers are properly trained to cope if their ship comes under attack by pirates;
- introduction of modern training methodology including distance learning and web-based learning;
- new training guidance for personnel serving on board ships operating in polar waters;
- new training guidance for personnel operating dynamic positioning systems.

All countries with seaports have the power to check that seamen on visiting vessels have the appropriate certificates and training required under the convention. This is enforceable under port state control.

The International Convention on Standards of Training, Certification and Watchkeeping for Seafarers (STCW) sets out the minimum levels of training and administration

1.4 ACCOUNTING

There are two good reasons why a clearly defined agreement on accounting procedures is reached between the owners and the managers. The first is the obvious fact that the owners are not only entrusting to someone else the management of capital assets, probably worth tens of millions of dollars, but also allowing that third party to commit significant sums of money daily in the running of the ships.

The second is that shipowners need to know whether or not the sort of business in which the ships are engaging is covering costs, and preferably making a profit. Whenever a new piece of business is being contemplated the commercial department makes a voyage estimate. As the name implies, this is an estimate of the financial outcome of the voyages or period being considered. To make this estimate, three cost areas have to be combined. The first are the fixed costs. A major item here would be amortisation or depreciation, which is the term used to cover the need during the working life of the ship gradually to write off the initial cost of the ship. Frequently, a ship is paid for with money borrowed from a bank or other financial institution and the cost of the instalments repaying the loan plus the interest charged by the lender is also treated as a fixed cost. These acquisition costs occur whatever the ship is doing, whether it is sailing on a voyage, working in port or simply lying idle waiting for business.

Then there are operating costs, which are only incurred if the ship is active, but have to be paid whether the ship is earning money or not (such as crews' wages).

Fixed costs and operating costs are provided to the commercial staff by the managers and it is essential that they have accurate budgets of all anticipated expenses which they, or the owners themselves, break down to a cost per day.

This is taken into the calculation of the voyage estimate, which, in turn, will calculate the voyage costs, which will be those expenses directly resulting from undertaking that voyage (such as bunker fuel and port expenses). The voyage estimate will also provide an estimate of how many days the voyage will occupy, including any distance (and therefore time) which may have to be covered in ballast to reach the first loading place. The distance involved divided by the ship's average speed will tell how many days at sea are required, while the ship's fuel consumption will indicate how much fuel will be used at sea. The rates of loading and discharge proposed during negotiations will provide an idea of the number of days in port but experience of the trade will make this part of the estimate more accurate.

It is common practice for several voyage estimates to be carried out simultaneously to compare one piece of business with another before entering into serious negotiations. The outcome of one particular voyage is not the only factor to be considered, as one always has to take into account where the ship will end up (that is, in a place where follow-up business is available or whether a long ballast run is necessary to get the next business).

This is not the end of the accounting dialogue between managers and owners because the actual financial outcome of each voyage made during the accounting period has to be produced and compared with the original estimate. It is only in this way that all relevant staff in the company develop a bank of experience so that future voyage estimates benefit from lessons learnt and are thereby more accurate than mere guesses.

While all managers have to be able to calculate voyage estimates, it is more usual these days for the information to be fed into a software program that will produce the final estimate. The attraction of such software is that it frequently contains a database of distances so that only the port names need be entered. Such software can also be programmed to contain details of ECAs allowing provision to be made for different fuel types needed during the voyage.

1.5 THE MANAGER IS STILL AN AGENT

It is important to remember that under a ship management contract the principal is the shipowner and that the ship manager is their agent. This may sometimes be difficult for the outside world to see when the only contact the agent or broker has is with the ship manager. It is not unusual for shipowners with several vessels to register each ship in an individual owning company, possibly even in different flag countries. This is for good accounting or legal reasons and should not necessarily be a cause for concern. The ship manager, who may be part of that shipowner's organisation or may be independent, will generally look after the whole fleet.

Unfortunately, but rarely, there are occasions when this can be a problem. Ship managers can plead their agency relationship with the owner to avoid responsibility for the owner's debts, when they are actually part of the same business. The test must always be whether or not the management company has a good reputation and a track record in the marketplace.

1.6 EMPLOYMENT OF PORT AGENTS

Wherever a ship goes in the world it will need an agent at every port of call to make the necessary arrangements for it to enter and leave that port, to discharge or load cargo, to comply with local regulations and to pay for services rendered and taxes or dues payable. In theory, it is possible for the Master to handle all such matters but, except for some small coasters trading on regular routes, this is not practical.

It is usually the ship manager's responsibility to choose and appoint the port agent. However, it has to be recognised that in the case of voyage charters, many charterers will wish to nominate the agent to be used by the owner in respect of their business. The reason for such nomination may be that the charterer wants an agent who has particular experience of the cargo or terminal used, or to protect its commercial confidentiality. Whatever the reason, it is a negotiated clause in the charter and it must be remembered that the nominated agent is legally the agent of the ship, not the charterer, and is paid for by the shipowner.

When a port agent is appointed, it is that agent's responsibility to act at all times in the best interest of the vessel. The shipowner will need to keep the agent advised as to a ship's movements and expected time of arrival (ETA). The agents will know from the schedule when the next vessel is due at their port. The owner and agent will be in constant communication by telephone, fax or email regarding changes to the schedule and all the other anticipated requirements for the ship.

The ship's Master will also contact the agent to advise them of the ship's requirements. It is obviously necessary to give the agent as much advance warning as possible, although this is not always feasible (as with an emergency due to damage or illness, for example).

The agent will contact the ship with any information of which the Master should be aware. Equally, agents will contact their counterpart at the next port of call, as a ship leaves, to advise the agent there of any requirements about which there is not the time or the need to contact the principal.

The following is a list of some of the routine matters that are handled by an agent, before, during and after a ship calls at their port:

i) Before arrival

- arranging a berth and discussing the cargo-handling programme with the terminal operators/stevedores, and any special cargo matters;
- booking a pilot, tugs and other services such as watermen to handle mooring lines;
- arranging attendance by the customs and immigration authorities;
- arranging for a doctor to attend, either for routine matters (such as inoculations) or in respect of illness;
- arranging for the delivery of supplies of food, water, bunkers and stores of all kinds;
- preparation of the required ship's papers (for example, inward and outward clearance,

light and port dues and other charges);

- collecting mail for the ship ready to be taken on board;
- arranging for a government official or consular officer to be present if crew are to sign on or off;
- arranging for transportation to and from airports and railways stations, and possibly hotels, for crew arriving and leaving.

ii) On arrival

Board the ship immediately on arrival and meet the Master and perhaps other officers to discuss their various requirements. These may consist of:

- arranging for cash to be brought on board for distribution to the crew. A large amount of cash may be needed if a crew is to sign off and, in some parts of the world, this may necessitate the use of security guards;
- arranging for crew needing medical or dental treatment to visit a doctor or dentist;
- finalising precise details concerning the cargo work, involving discharge or loading of, for example, livestock, hazardous goods, heavy lifts and valuables;
- arranging for the reporting to the principal of any details concerning insurance and general average claims;
- arranging for the attendance of surveyors for either cargo or ship damage, or both.

iii) During the ship's call

- daily liaison with the ship's personnel and cargo superintendent on continuing cargo work;
- towards the end of the call, arranging the signing of mate's receipts and bills of lading;
- payment of bills/invoices for goods and services supplied to the ship;
- frequent and regular communication with the principal concerning the ship's progress and sailing prospects;
- arranging pilot, tugs, etc for departure.

iv) On departure

- obtaining from the Master the ETA at the next port and the ship's requirements on arrival there.

v) After departure

- advising the agent at the next port of the ETA and all the requirements of the ship on arrival (for example, water and bunker needs, which may be urgent after a long voyage). The ship may have to wait at anchor for a berth, and bunkers, stores and provisions might need to be delivered by boat;
- any special medical or crew welfare needs should be advised so that there is sufficient time to make the necessary arrangements.

Having listed all the duties of the appointed agent it will be clear that it will be the responsibility of the ship manager to instruct the agent in respect of all these matters in a timely manner. It is very important that any discretion given to the agent (for example, to order overtime or stores, or to advance cash to the Master) is clearly set out both as to the circumstances and the amount of money that can be expended.

Chapter 2

The ship

2.1 INTRODUCTION

The purpose of this chapter is to describe the different kinds of ships that are in common use, the employment they are engaged in, the kind of equipment that can be found on board and the criteria employed by shipowners in deciding what sort and size of vessel to buy. It also looks at the ship management function in context by relating it to the vessel, its crew, its owners and those who use its services, namely, charterers, shippers and passengers.

2.2 THE SHIP

It is important to understand the different ways of describing a ship's size and dimensions so that one vessel can be compared against another or the suitability of a vessel for a particular trade can be assessed. Different measurements are more appropriate to some ship types than others. For example, a bulk carrier would normally be referred to by its deadweight tonnage while a container ship would be measured by its capacity in twenty-foot equivalent units (teus).

There are several different types of measurement used for different purposes.

2.2.1 Tonnages

These are the actual weights of the ship and its cargo.

Total displacement tonnage

The total displacement is the total weight of the vessel at any particular time and includes the light displacement of the ship plus the weight of everything on board including any cargo, fuel constant and ballast. It is the weight of the water that the vessel displaces and is important when berthing alongside a jetty or terminal where there is a limit on the strength of the structure, that is, the maximum loading of the jetty. Displacement tonnage is also used with reference to warships.

Deadweight

Deadweight is the amount of cargo, stores, fresh water and oil that can be put into the vessel such that it is at its appropriate loadline. The summer deadweight tonnage (sdwt) is the one that is normally quoted in the ship's particulars. It closely approximates to the maximum cargo that the vessel can load. It does not include the weight of the vessel although this is obviously a component of the draught.

Constant

The ship's constant is the difference between a vessel's design lightship and its actual displacement when empty. The ship's constant is normally determined by a draught survey. A draught survey will take account of fresh water, ballast or fuel but, because the measurement of these is often difficult and inexact, a draught survey will often indicate that some other weight that is not identifiable is on board. This may be fuel residues in the bottom of the bunker tanks, ballast remaining in the bottom of tanks and lines, an accumulation of stores on board, rust and sediments in ballast tanks, fouling on the hull, a build-up of paint coatings or measurement error due to sag. The ship's constant will vary over the life of the vessel. Having determined the constant, this will often be used at future draught surveys.

2.2.2 Space tonnages

Although these two measurements are called tonnages they are actually mere numbers based on an international formula (International Tonnage Convention) for comparing the overall size of ships. These tonnages are frequently used by ports and statutory bodies as the basis of levying dues or taxes on vessels.

Gross tonnage – the old register tonnages (gross registered tonnage (grt) and net registered tonnage (nrt) of 100 cubic feet) were replaced under the Tonnage Convention 1969 (which came into force in 1994) with a new figure calculated to a set formula. Like the old register tonnage, the new figure is intended as a measure of all the enclosed spaces on a ship including the superstructure, but the new formula includes a sliding scale element so that the exact size of a gross ton will vary slightly between 95 and 105 cubic feet depending on the ship's design. Gross tonnage is widely used to describe the size of passenger vessels and ferries, and it is possibly the most common basis of port charges for all ships. This is because a ship's gross tonnage will not change unless there is a significant alteration to the vessel. With a known and fixed gross tonnage it is easy for a port authority to determine what charges to apply. As the gross tonnage does not change whether the ship is loaded with one tonne of cargo or fully laden, it encourages owners to enter or leave port with the largest cargo possible.

Net tonnage – the gross tonnage less those spaces such as engine room and crew accommodation that cannot be used for commercial (that is, revenue-earning) purposes.

(Note that many people, particularly the media, frequently refer to the size of a vessel as being 'X tons' without specifying what sort of tons. Passenger ships in particular are often described as 'weighing X tons', when the figure being quoted is usually gross tonnage.)

2.2.3 Measurements

These are the important dimensions of the vessel which must be known to determine whether the vessel can safely enter locks, canals, docks and so on.

Length overall (LOA) – the length of the ship from the foremost point on the bow to the most aft point on the stern.

Beam – the overall width of the ship, often referred to as breadth. This is important for transiting locks and canals

Moulded depth – the height of the ship from the bottom of the keel to the top of the main deck.

Draught (sometimes also spelt draft) – the distance from the waterline to the bottom of the keel. This determines the minimum depth of water the ship needs to be afloat.

Freeboard – the distance from the waterline to the ship's main deck.

Keel to top of mast (KTM) – this is the measurement of the height of a ship from the bottom of the keel to the highest point.

Air draught – the distance from the waterline to the highest point on the ship's superstructure, usually the top of the mast. This is important when making passage under bridges or overhead power cables. As this is measured from the waterline, the air draught will vary depending on the ship's draught at the time.

In some ports where shore loading or discharging gear can only operate between certain fixed limits, air draught is sometimes used also to describe the maximum height available between the waterline and the top of the hatchcovers. In oil tankers it is sometimes used to describe the distance from the waterline to the centre of the cargo manifold. This can lead to confusion and it would be better if this term was not used in such circumstances and the term 'waterline to manifold height' was used instead.

Cargo measurements and capacities

Grain cubic capacity – the measurement in cubic metres or cubic feet of the internal capacity of all cargo spaces when they are filled with a free-flowing material such as bulk grain. This measurement includes such spaces as the recess between the frames of the ship's hull.

Tanker cubic capacity is usually expressed as 98% of the total cargo tank volume and may include the slop tanks, which will be stated.

Bale cubic capacity – the measurement in cubic metres or cubic feet of the internal capacity of all accessible cargo spaces if the holds are full of baled cargo. The smaller spaces and recesses, for example, between the frames and the ship's hull, are excluded.

Lane-metres – many roll-on/roll-off (ro-ro) ships have their cargo spaces divided into lanes in which vehicles will be stowed one behind the other. The total length of all the lanes in metres is used to describe the cargo capacity of the ship.

Teu – container ships are usually described in terms of the number of containers they can carry. The abbreviation teu stands for twenty-foot equivalent unit and is the customary way of referring to a container ship's size.

Some of these dimensions and some additional measurements are shown here.

Basic ship dimensions

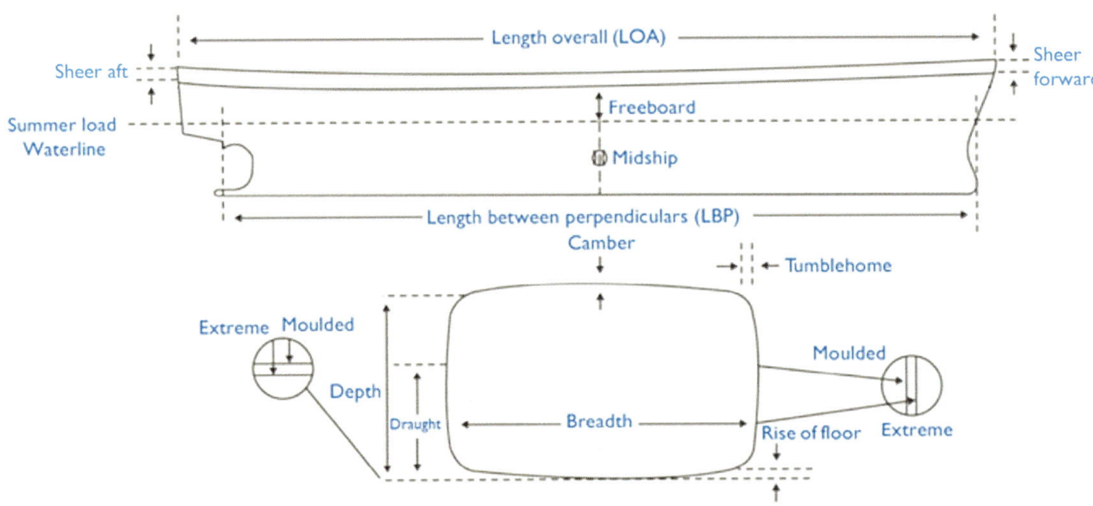

2.2.4 Ship plans

Three different types of plans will be commonly encountered in day-to-day dealings with ships.

General arrangement plans

These are just what the name implies – they show the main parts of the ship from a side view as well as a plan view for each deck. They usually include one or more cross-sections. Simplified general arrangement plans are used in some of the descriptions of ships which follow. The general arrangement plan will also indicate the features of the loadline and the vessel's displacement scale – that is, a scale showing the distance by which the vessel will sink into the water for each tonne loaded on board.

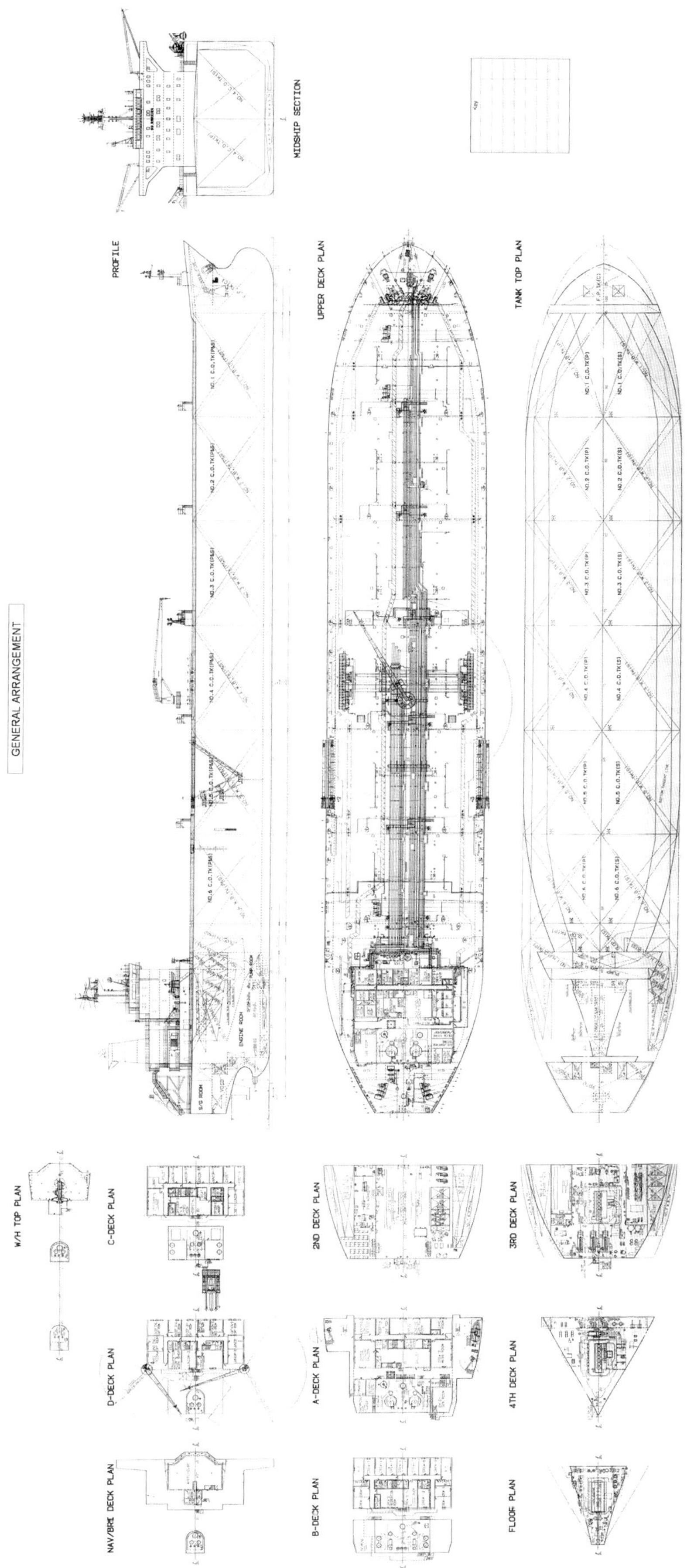

The general arrangement plan shows the main parts of the ship

Capacity plans

These are similar to general arrangement plans but, in particular, show full details of the hatches, cargo-carrying spaces, bunker, ballast and fresh water tanks.

Stowage plans

These are plans which are created as the ship is loaded to show where each parcel of cargo is placed in the vessel and the ports between which it is moving. The importance of the stowage plan and its relationship to a vessel's stability is discussed later.

Tanker plans

These are plans which show the tank layout and the position of the pumps, loading and discharge lines and the cargo manifolds. It also shows tank volumes and has a deadweight scale.

2.3 BASIC SHIP LAYOUT

A basic knowledge of how ships are generally laid out will also assist in understanding the operational and commercial aspects of the shipping business. Below is a typical commercial vessel layout and this layout is, with only a few exceptions, universal for some very fundamental reasons.

Until the advent of vessels powered by steam or motor, all vessels were at the mercy of the wind. To take full advantage of this, commercial vessels which relied on speed more than their armaments were built with long narrow hulls to allow easy passage through the water. This was particularly true on long voyages. Space on board was at a premium, which normally mandated small high-value cargoes such as spices, precious metals and stones, silks, tea, sugar and opium.

The powered vessel changed this and led to a massive expansion of trade in all commodities, especially in bulk. This in turn led to the development of the commercial ship form we know today. In simple terms, a commercial vessel is a rectangular box carrying the cargo. Virtually all commercial vessels trading today have this layout. There are some exceptions, but these are due to other factors which will be explained. The purpose of the vessel is to carry cargo and therefore the cargo compartment forms the main part of the hull of the vessel and takes up at least 75% of the length of the vessel. In most vessels, this cargo compartment is surrounded on at least both sides and underneath with a double hull, which is used for the storage of ballast water and as a buffer between the cargo and the sea in the event of hull damage. In addition, the front end of each cargo compartment may also be protected in a similar way with a void or empty space called a cofferdam. Only on the top of the cargo compartment is there a single skin, the main deck of the vessel. See Figure 1, which shows this and the double bottom.

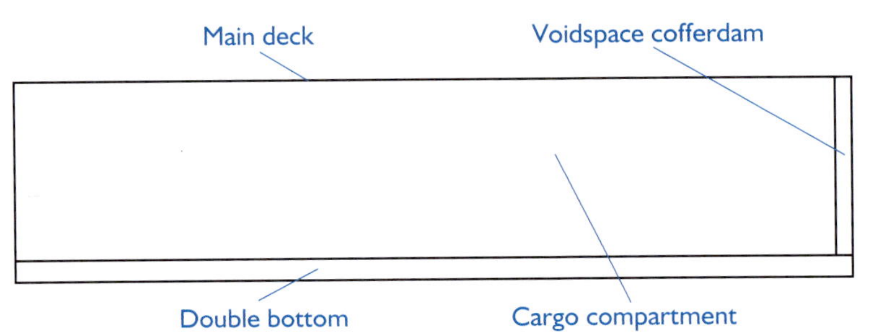

Figure 1

Some vessels, particularly tankers, may have a similar compartment at the after end of the cargo compartment as a buffer between the volatile dangerous cargo and the engine space. This is often used as a pump room. See Figure 1a.

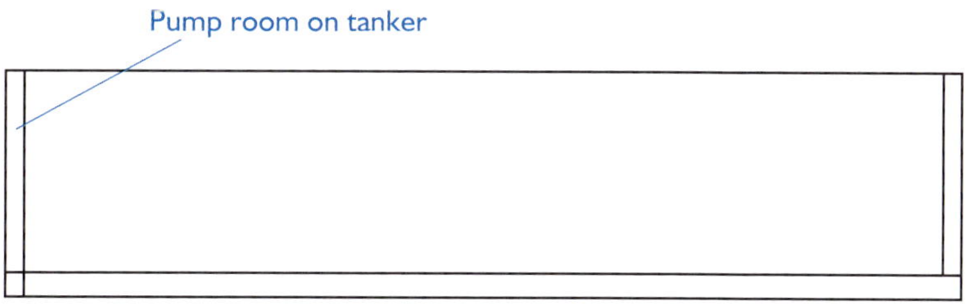

Figure 1a

A transverse arrangement of a tanker is shown in Figure 2. This shows the double hull of the vessel from the deck level on one side across the bottom and up to the deck on the other side. This U-shaped compartment will be split into at least two sections with a centreline bulkhead creating two L-shaped tanks as a minimum. This is to prevent water running from one side of the vessel to the other when filling or emptying tanks which could easily lead to the vessel's capsize. These tanks in the double hull are used for ballast.

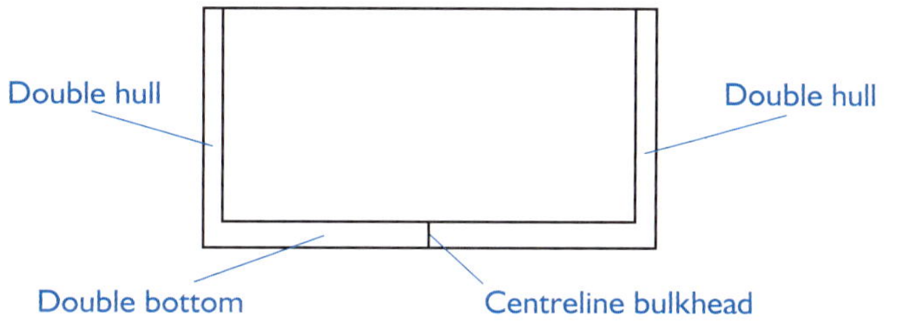

Fig 2

For obvious reasons, a box is not going to move easily through the water on its own. To help it, some form of propulsion is needed and for most ships, this will be placed at the back or stern of the box to push it through the water. In most vessels this takes the form of a single large low-speed diesel main engine about the size of a small house for any vessel over about 15,000dwt. This will be sited on the top of the double bottom with extra strengthened plating called the bedplate. Surrounding this engine will be an enclosed space called the engine room, which will reach from the double bottom up to the main deck level and even further in an enclosed space in the accommodation block. This engine room will, in addition to the main engine, house most of the auxiliary equipment used to run the engine, pumps, fans, turbo-chargers, fuel systems, heaters, etc, as well as generators or alternators to provide electrical power for all the systems on the vessel, and an engine control room. This whole box forms an integral part of the hull of the vessel. See Figure 3.

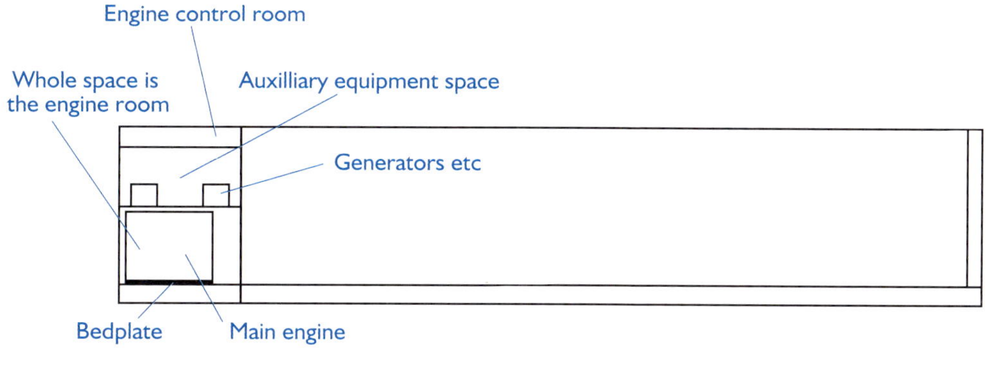

Figure 3

The accommodation, as mentioned previously, will be sited on top of the main deck and may surround the upper parts of the engine room, which generally house the exhaust piping and associated systems to take the exhaust gases to the funnel (see Figure 4). On larger vessels this may all be contained in a separate block behind the accommodation to reduce associated noise and vibration. See Figure 4a.

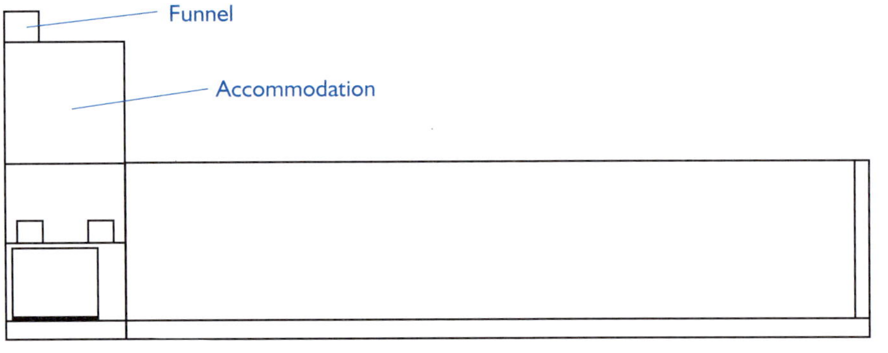

Figure 4

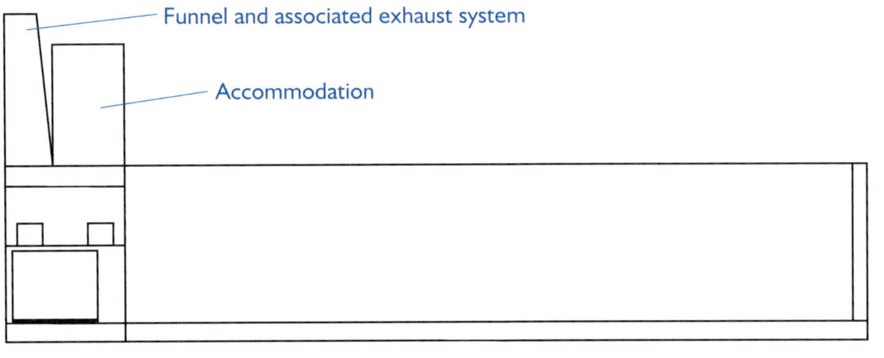

Figure 4a

The accommodation is the main living area of the vessel with the mess rooms, galley, recreation room, cabins for officers and crew, storerooms, offices and ultimately the bridge or wheelhouse at the top for navigating the vessel. The bridge needs to be at the top to provide a clear view all around. On top of the bridge is an open deck called the monkey island, where there will be a main mast holding navigation lights, radars, satellite communication equipment, radio aerials and flag hoists. The funnel will also be up here on most vessels. See Figure 5.

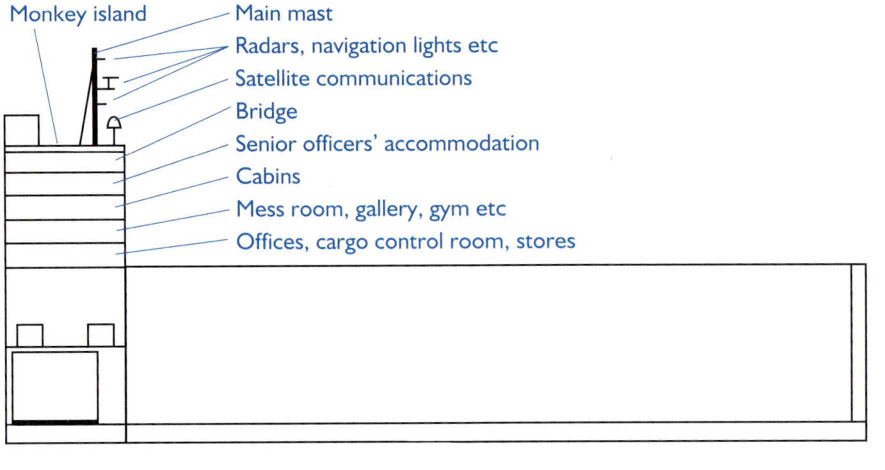

Figure 5

The stern of the vessel is a very important area and must be clearly understood. To show this it is necessary to add another box to the aft end of the engine room at approximately half the height of the engine room. See Figure 6. This will be explained shortly.

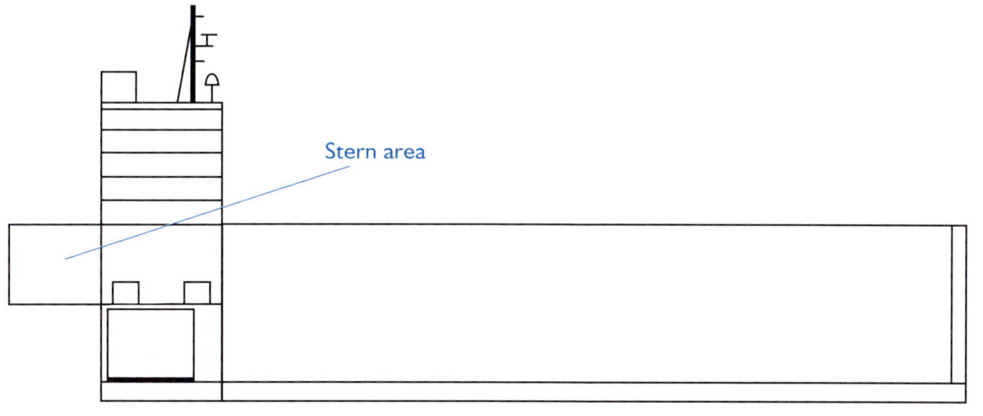

Figure 6

An engine needs to have some way to transmit its power and this is normally using a propeller. This will be connected externally via a shaft to the main engine to push water and move the hull through the water. To do this it will need to be housed in a tube, the stern tube, to avoid water ingress. The engine and the auxiliary machinery will also need fuel or bunkers. These are often stored in large tanks forward of, and on both sides of, the engine room. See Figure 7.

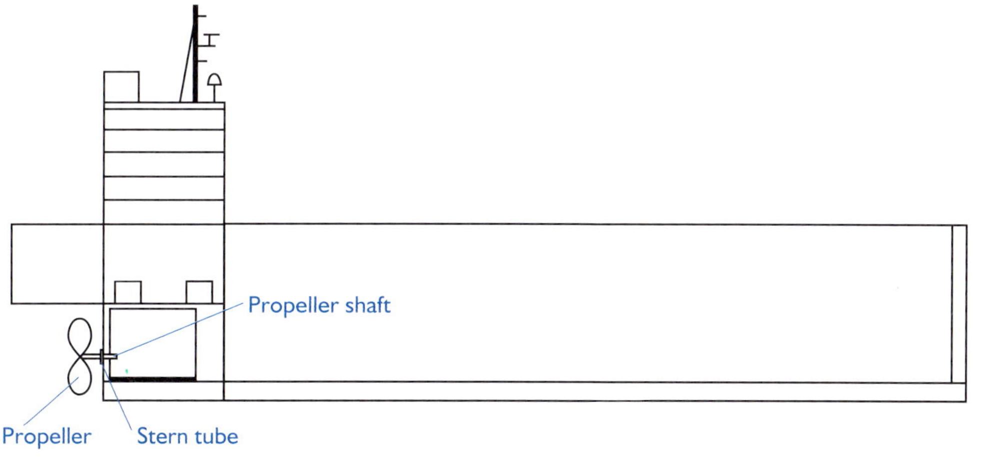

Figure 7

The hull of the vessel is for much of its length still a box shape but, at the stern, the sides will come together and narrow down to come to a point where the propeller is sited. This allows the flow of water to be drawn to the propeller and be driven backwards making the vessels hull move forward. To direct this flow and allow the vessel to steer in different directions a rudder is set right behind, or abaft, the propeller. See Figure 8.

Figure 8

Now to return to the box in Figure 6. Obviously, this is only a representation of the actual layout of the vessel but it serves to explain its placing. A number of important spaces in this area can be identified.

1. First, the rudder needs to be controlled and turned by using some machinery which is connected electronically with the ship's steering system on the bridge. This machinery, a series of hydraulic rams, is housed in a compartment above the rudder called the steering gear room, often abbreviated to just the steering gear.

2. Second, is a ballast tank located at the aft end of the vessel called the afterpeak. In some vessels this may be used for the storage of fresh water but in most others it is used for ballast. It may be quite small in comparison to other ballast tanks but its position at the aft end of the vessel has a greater leverage than a larger tank closer to the longitudinal centre of gravity of the vessel. Why should it be necessary? Many vessels when fully loaded have a tendency to take up a position in the water where the forward draught is greater than the aft draught. It is called being trimmed by the head. This is not really satisfactory as this may allow heavy head seas to break more easily over the fo'c'sle head, which might be unsafe. It may also have some effect on the vessel's speed. To counteract this filling, the afterpeak thereby raises the bow a little.

3. Third, a vessel when in port needs to tie up to the berth using a combination of ropes and wires, mainly from the bow and stern. Some of these may be stored on mooring winch drums but most will not. When heading out to sea these ropes will need to be stored below deck in a secure space. Therefore a rope store space is needed at the stern of the vessel for this storage, normally just under the aftdeck, or poop as it is known. A mooring winch, or two, one on each side depending on the size of vessel will therefore be located on the afterdeck.

Adjacent to these spaces may be some additional storerooms for the engine department, an emergency fire pump compartment and refrigeration spaces. This is not a full list. All ships have minor differences dependent on the space available but all will have 1, 2 and 3. See Figure 9.

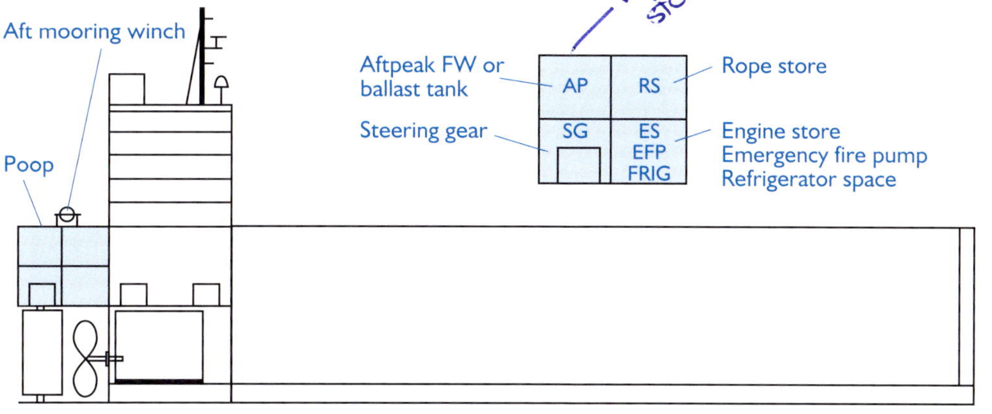

Fig 9

All vessels will also have at least one lifeboat. Until recently most vessels had two lifeboats, one on each side of the accommodation. In the event of disaster, and the need to abandon the vessel, these would each be manually launched using a pair of gravity davits. Each boat, capable of taking the entire crew, would then be boarded and lowered to the water, manually disconnected and moved away from the vessel. A boat each side was mandatory in case a severe list might make one of the boats unusable. This type of arrangement is shown in Figure 9a. Recently, many new vessels, in particular, bulk carriers and tankers, have been fitted with a single, stern launched, freefall lifeboat placed on the centreline. This boat, resting on a sloping slipway, is boarded by all the crew, who strap themselves into the seating provided. The boat, which is provided with its own air supply, is sealed shut, the engine is started and then it can be launched from inside and slides down the slipway, dropping into the water below at an angle of about 45 degrees. This method, although quite dramatic, has the benefit of giving the crew the chance to get off a fast-sinking vessel, particularly a bulker, and avoid the danger of fire on the water from an oil tanker's cargo. This type of arrangement is shown in Figure 9b.

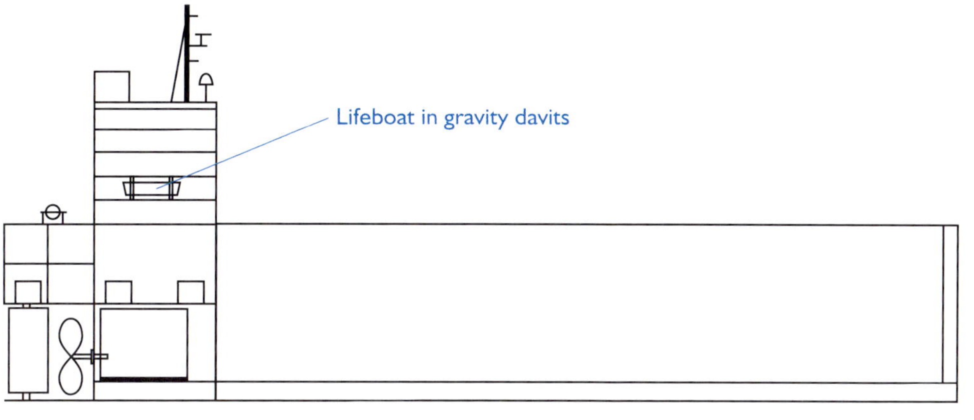

Figure 9a

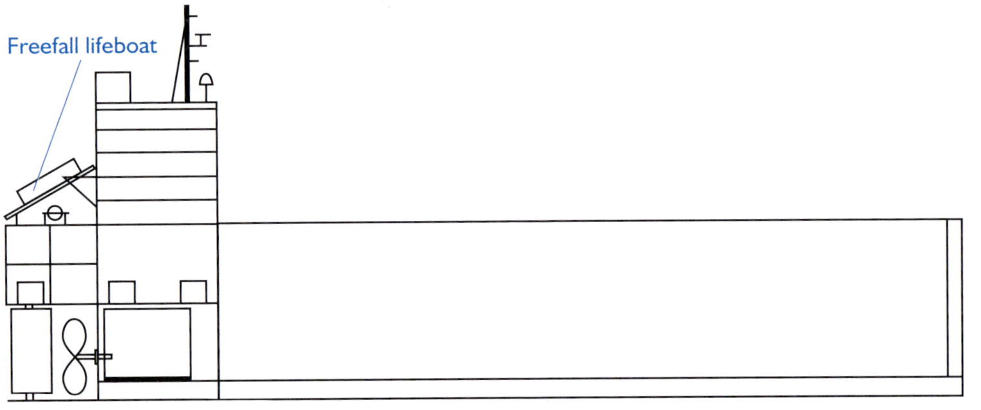

Figure 9b

This, then, describes the stern arrangement of the vast majority of the world's commercial vessels. Now to look at the for'd, or forward, end.

At the front of the cargo box, the vessel tapers to a point to push the water aside and aid free movement through the water. Of course, vessels are more sophisticated than this but understanding the layout and the reasons why will help to improve your knowledge. This area of the vessel is of vital importance as it needs to be very strong and in this region, extra transverse framing reduces the available cargo space so it is used predominantly for the carriage of ballast, the equipment and machinery for mooring and anchoring the vessel, and for storage. Until about 60 years ago, a vessel's bow was formed by tapering the sides of the vessel together in the bow as shown in Figure 10.

Figure 10

However, this idea was refined, extending the top part forward and splaying out the sides slightly to push the water aside and prevent it going over the fo'c'sle head. A small number of passenger liners and warships adopted a form of bulbous bow in the 1920–30s because the design proved that ships so equipped were faster and reduced the bow wave produced, but few others followed as they were expensive to fabricate. From the 1960s, however, bulbous bows have become almost the rule due to improved design and more advanced welding technology. The main exception is in icebreaker vessels, where a sharp cutting bow shape is required.

With the increased size and length of vessels, and the move of the accommodation and engine room to the afterend, this has meant that when, empty of cargo, the vessel's bow or bulbous bow would be out of the water. Even with full ballast in the double hull the bow would still be high in the water, which would not be safe or manageable. A large ballast tank is needed at the forward end, and this tank, called the forepeak, takes up most of the bow space and will often include the bulbous bow as well. Above the forepeak, often as a continuation of the main deck to the bow, the vessel has a large storeroom called the fo'c'sle. This store will be used for the stowage of mooring ropes, a paint store and some machinery. All the above are shown in Figure 11.

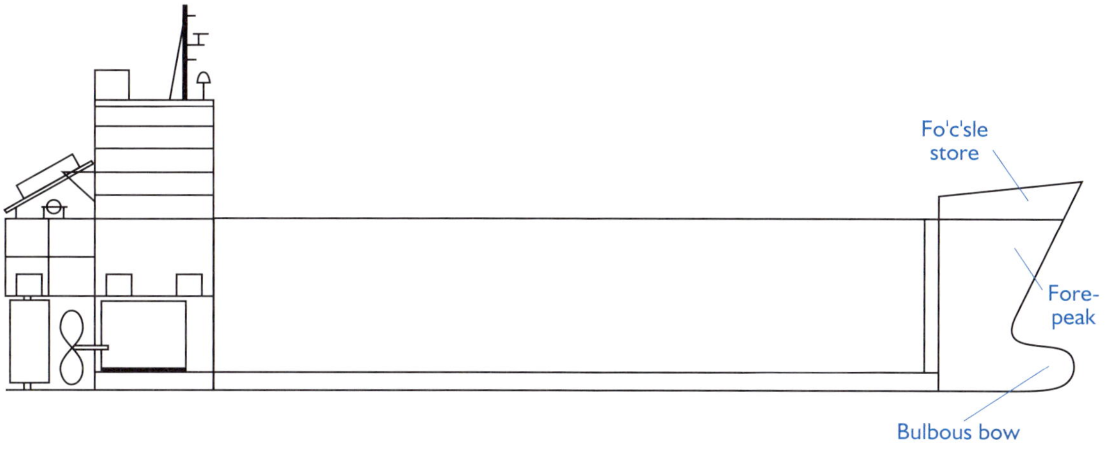

Figure 11

Above the fo'c'sle is an open deck area called the fo'c'sle head. This open deck, often slightly sloping upward towards the bow, is sheltered behind the top of the bow shell plating such that persons working there will gain a measure of protection from the seas and spray. However, the aft end of the fo'c'sle head is open so that water shipped over the bow will quickly drain off onto the deck and back to the sea. The top of the bow shell plating is pierced with strengthened holes called fairleads, allowing ropes and wires to be sent ashore for mooring. In the centre is a large piece of machinery which is a windlass. This is used both for raising and lowering the anchors, one on each side, but can also be disconnected from these and used as a winch for wires and rope moorings. The anchor, when stowed, partly protrudes from the bow plating but with its stock drawn up by the anchor chain into a pipe called the hawse pipe, leaving the flukes protruding. From this, the chain is led over a shaped drum (called a gypsy) on the windlass and thence down another pipe called the spurling pipe, into the chain locker. The chains for each anchor, which are each over 300 metres in length, are stored in the chain lockers, which are two large circular silos in the forepeak tank. Finally, at the afterend of the fo'c'sle head there will be the foremast, which carries navigation lights, the whistle and a bell. See Figure 12.

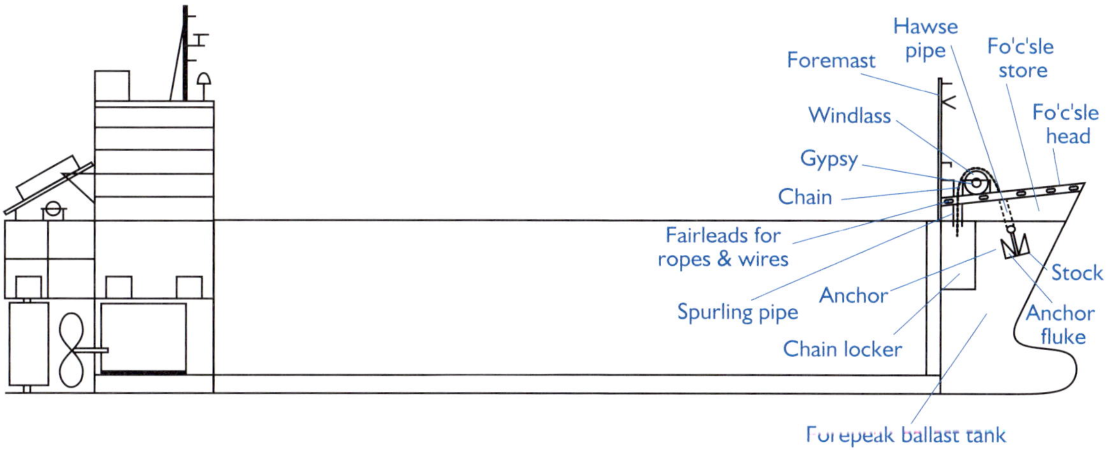

Figure 12

At this point you should be able to visualise the basic form for most modern commercial bulk carriers, tankers and container ships. The large long compartment for the cargo will be subdivided into a number of smaller compartments, depending on the size and type of vessel. The first subdivisions will be transverse, or across the vessel, dividing the cargo space into a number of similar sized compartments called holds or tanks and numbered from forward. The divisions are made by steel watertight walls or bulkheads. These are primarily a safety measure; one long cargo compartment, if breached by the sea, would quickly flood and the vessel would sink. The size of each hold/tank will be as large as possible, depending on the size of the vessel and the need to prevent the ship sinking if a single hold is flooded. Given that at each end of the vessel the hull sides start to taper together, this decreases the capacity of the most forward and after holds or tanks. Generally, most of the intervening holds or tanks are of almost the same capacity. This will be shown in the later drawings.

What then about the exceptions? We are only considering ships that carry cargo, so passenger ships are excluded. But so are ro-ro vessels, freight ferries and some very large modern container vessels. This is because the design of the ro-ro and ferry is dictated by the requirement for cargo to be loaded and discharged as quickly as possible by driving the cargo on and off the vessel. This is facilitated by internal ramps and massive watertight doors in the hull at a variety of locations but often at the bow and stern. As for the very large container vessels, the reason is different. In many ways, they are like conventional vessels but some have an accommodation block and navigation bridge located nearer the bow in an attempt to improve the visibility for those on the bridge and allow containers to be stacked higher throughout the vessel length.

Going back to Figure 12, it is now necessary to put some further detail on the vessel to show the three basic types of vessels.

Bulk Carriers

There are two basic types, geared and ungeared. Handysize and handymax are normally geared as they carry more varied cargoes and may trade to ports where there is no infrastructure for handling cargo. Most of the smaller vessels have a maximum of five holds and hatches. They will be equipped with four cranes of up to max 30t safe working load (SWL) placed between the hatches. Hatches will be hydraulic, stacking vertically at each end of the hatch coamings. Tank tops will be strengthened for grab discharge and the vessel will have its own grabs for use where needed. Decks and hatchcovers will be suitable for carrying a limited number of containers. Figure 13 shows a geared handysize vessel which is currently working cargo with its cranes.

Hatch 1 is closed; hatch 2 is open and the covers are stowed at each end as cranes 1 and 2 work the hold together; hatch 3 is closed; hatch 4 is open, covers stowed each end and being worked by crane 3; hatch 5 is open, covers are still stowed at each end but cargo is finished and crane 4 is in the stowed position.

Handysize and Handymax

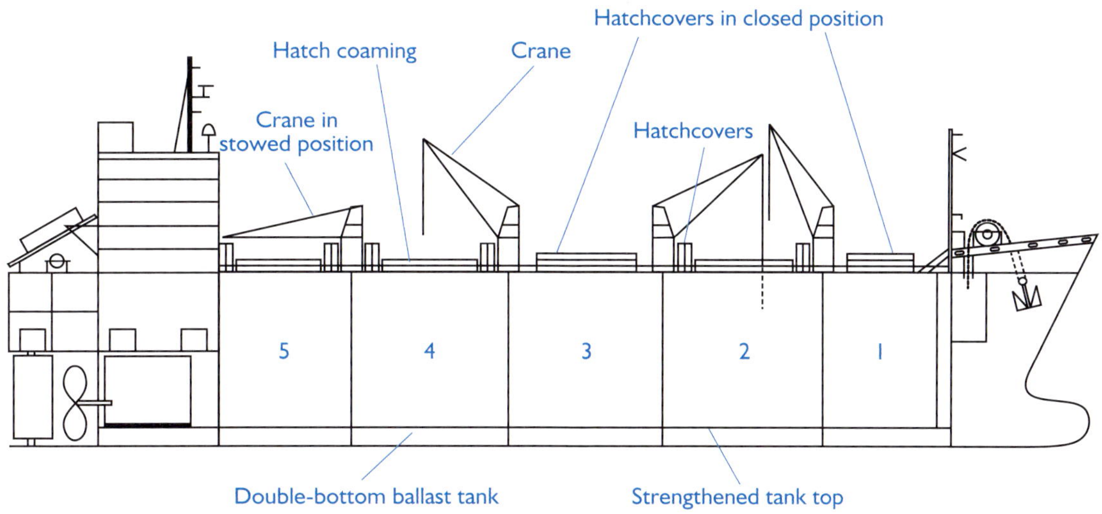

Figure 13

Larger bulk carriers, Panamax and Capesize are not geared. Large bulk carriers tend to carry limited cargoes such as iron ore, coal and bauxite, and generally trade to and from ports that have equipment for bulk loading and discharge.

Panamax vessels may have either side rolling or fore- and aft-rolling hatches although the latter is more common. They will generally have seven holds and hatches. Capesize vessels generally have nine holds and nine side-rolling hatches. Some of the largest Vale vessels only have seven. They do not have gear. See Figure 14, which shows a Panamax vessel with no gear. In this drawing hatches 1, 2, 3 and 7 are closed while 4, 5 and 6 are open and stowed at the fore and aft end of the hatch coaming.

Panamax

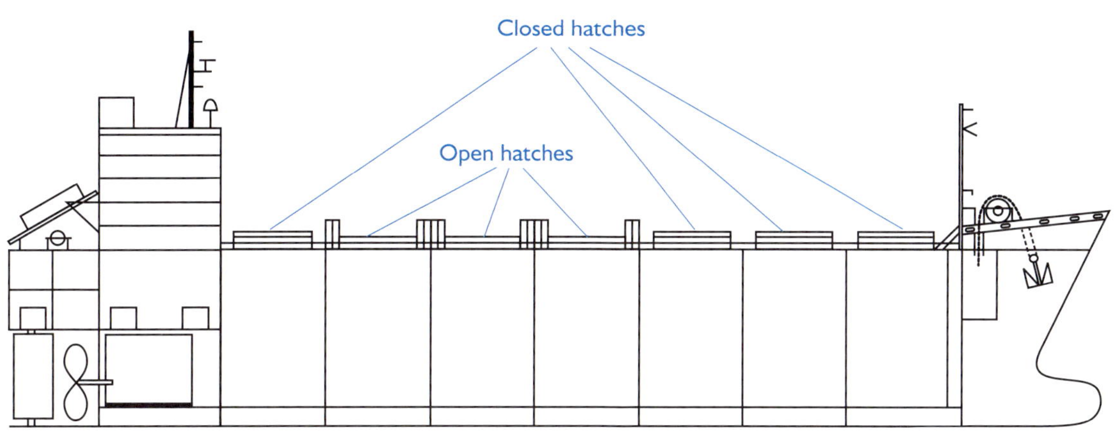

Figure 14

It is now time to look at the transverse arrangements for vessels shown in Figure 2. There will also be some differences in the internal structure of the holds of bulk carriers which are designed to make the carriage of bulk cargoes safer and the discharge of all the cargo easier.

This can best be shown using the cross-section of the vessels which now shows the front view of a typical vessel's accommodation with the bridge or wheelhouse above and then the monkey island, main mast and funnel. On small vessels, the accommodation will generally go right across the vessel to use all available space (see Figure 14a), but on bigger vessels with similar sized crews this is not necessary and the bridge will be extended out on an uncovered area called the bridge wing on each side to allow proper observation of the ship's side, particularly when berthing in port (see Figure 14b).

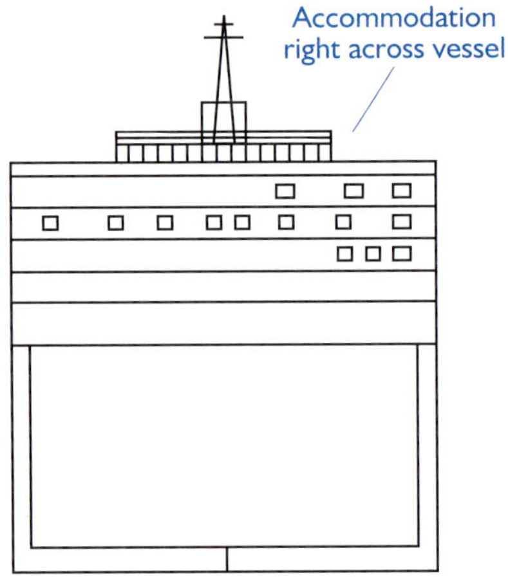

Figure 14a

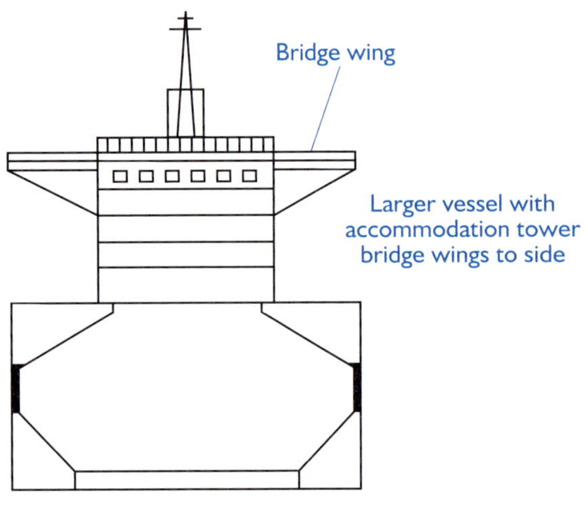

Figure 14b

All bulk carriers will have hatches through which to load and discharge the cargo. On smaller specialised vessels these hatch openings may be wider and longer but, for most vessels above about 20,000dwt, the hatch size may be of varying length, dependent on their number and the length of the vessel, but their width will normally be slightly under half the breadth of the vessel to maintain the vessel's strength. This large rectangular opening in the deck will be strengthened around all four sides by a raised bulkhead which extends above and below the deck level, providing strong reinforcement. This is called the hatch coaming and may extend as much as 2m above the deck necessitating ladders or raised steps to be used to look into the hold. It also forms the base for the hatchslabs or hatchcovers which are placed on top. These will normally be raised and lowered onto the top of the coaming or rolled into place using hydraulic rams or chain drives. On smaller vessels these are mostly stowed at the front and back end of each hatch coaming when the hatch is open.

Figure 15 shows this arrangement with the hatchcovers in closed condition. Also shown is the arrangement of the internal structure of the cargo holds, which does not actually resemble a box but is more like a hexagon. The hold is shaped in this fashion for safety and convenience. First, the safety aspect should be considered. Most dry bulk cargoes are loaded by grab or some kind of loader and are poured from a height into the hold. These commodities will form a pyramid shape which will fill the bottom of the hold as the top rises up towards the open hatch. The upper side part of the hold is therefore shaped with an upper hopper tank to accept this pyramid shape such that, when the cargo fills the hatch coaming area, it is against the underside of the upper hopper tank and therefore cannot move. If the hopper was not there the cargo could move when the ship sails into bad weather and this could be catastrophic. The lower hopper has a similar shape but its role is to guide the cargo towards the centre of the hold when the cargo is being discharged. The angled slope will allow the cargo to slide to the centre, where it will be reachable by grabs being lowered through the hatch opening without need for men or machines to go into the hold to move the cargo into reach.

Smaller bulk carriers will be geared as mentioned. This will normally be a series of cranes on the centreline of the vessel on a raised pedestal above the decks clear of the hatchcovers. Figure 15a shows this with the hatch in the closed position and Figure 15b shows the hatch in the opened position stowed at the forward and aft end of the hatch. As already stated, Capesize vessels and some Panamaxes will have side-rolling hatches but are not geared. This is shown in Figure 15c.

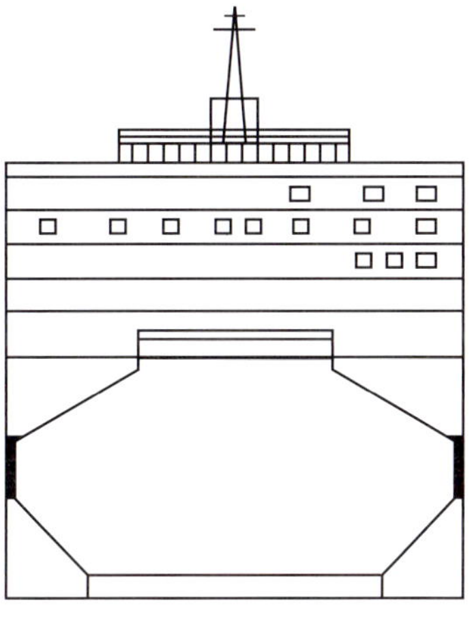

Figure 15

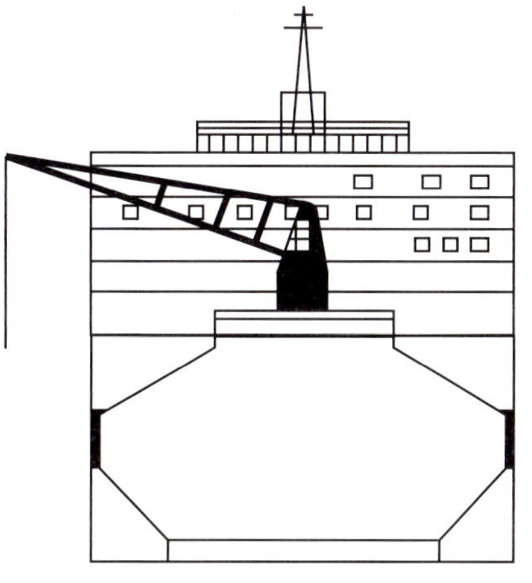

With crane in working position. Hatch closed

Figure 15a

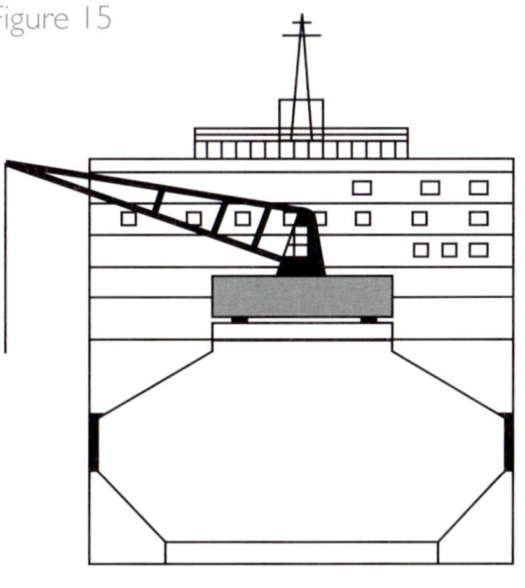

Hatch open and covers stowed at forward and aft end of hatch

Figure 15b

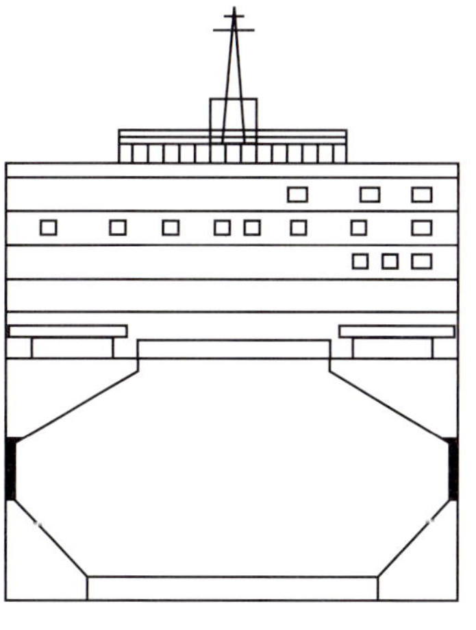

Side-rolling hatchcovers open on Capesize and some Panamaxes

Figure 15c

Container Ships

The purpose of the majority of container vessels, apart from the smaller geared feeder vessels, is to transport containers from one container crane equipped port to another and for this reason, few have gear. The box-like shape of the cargo space is still divided transversely into a number of holds but these will be equipped to take a stack of containers of limited size differences and these will be stowed both under the deck and above up to a height just below the bridge. This height will be reduced towards the forward end to allow a view ahead of the vessel's bow. As hatches take up valuable space, the hatch slabs will normally be removed by shore cranes when necessary and be stacked on the shore. Some container vessels have no hatches, with containers in a continuous stack from the bottom through the hatch coaming and up above the deck. In the hatches, vertical guide rails allow easy and fast placing of the containers into the stacks. Above deck these rails are continued on many hatchless vessels. Figures 16 and 17 show the profile and cross-section of a typical container vessel. Most container vessels have a protective breakwater at the forward end of the container area to provide some protection from seas coming over the bow in bad weather.

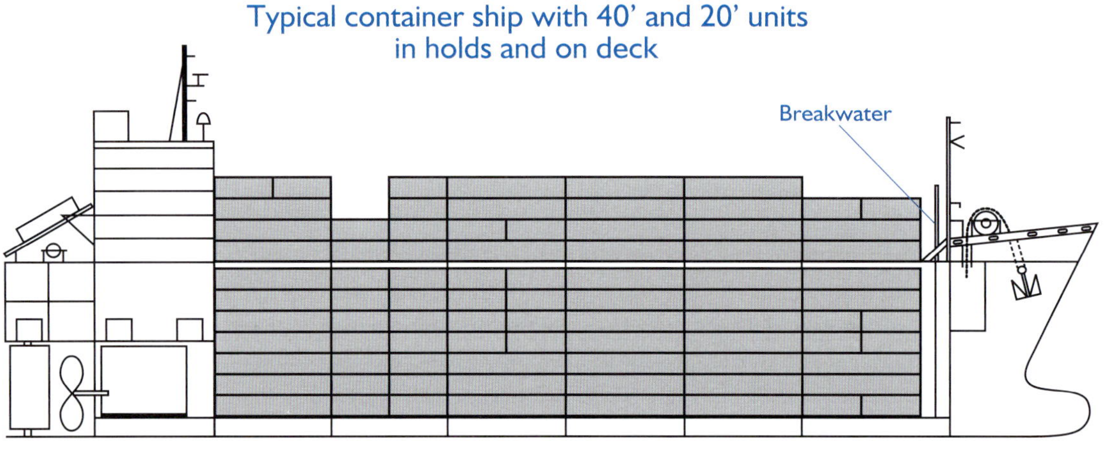

Figure 16

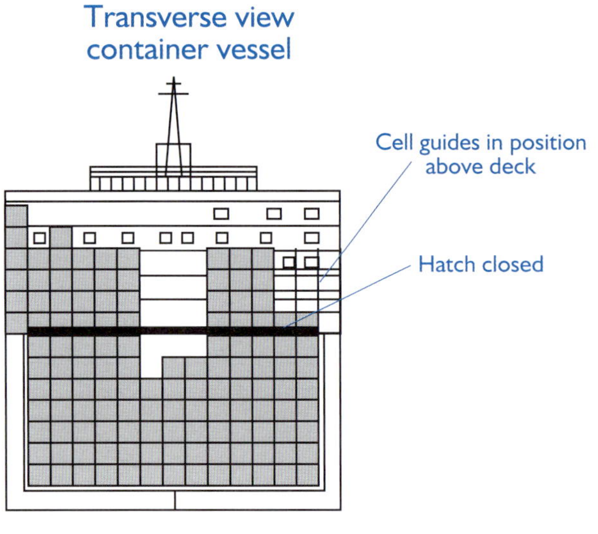

Figure 17

Tankers

Oil tankers generally fall into two types: smaller vessels up to Panamax which carry products, and larger vessels which generally carry crude, but both of these share a lot of common characteristics. All oil tankers are double hull with segregated ballast tanks, manifold systems, hose-handling cranes and venting systems, and all over 20,000dwt are fitted with inert gas (IG) systems. Most modern vessels are fitted with cargo heating systems consisting of heating coils in the bottom of the tank, and most will have a freefall life boat, so any drawing of them can use a single template, but there are a couple of exceptions to this rule. The cargo compartment of the majority of tankers is, like the bulk carrier, divided by a series of transverse bulkheads into cargo tanks numbered from forward. It is very common for tankers to have the cargo compartment divided into six parts, as shown in Figure 18, which shows the profile of a typical conventional larger tanker, which may be used for large parcels of products but normally is in the crude oil trade, the Aframax, Suezmax and VLCCs.

Conventional tanker profile

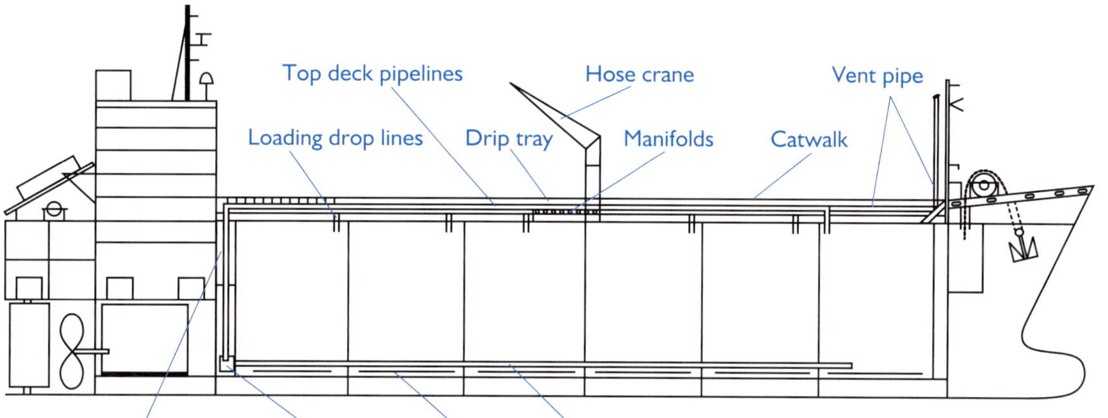

Figure 18

These vessels have a simple system of three pumps and three lines, providing the vessel with three totally segregated cargo systems but which can be interconnected through crossover valves when carrying a single homogenous grade. The pumps will be situated at the bottom of a pump room just forward of the engine room and will draw cargo from their own bottom line or from other lines through a series of crossovers in the pump room. The cargo will be pumped up to the deck through three top lines and along the deck to the manifold area, where it will be delivered to the manifolds on both sides for going ashore. Often, the pipes will have a catwalk structure built above them to allow access in relative safety to the forward end of the vessel when loaded and in bad weather.

The deck pipes (top lines) will also be used for loading the tanks so will continue forward of the manifold to the forward tanks. Underneath the manifolds at each side will be a drip tray to prevent any leaks spilling on the deck. As tanks are loaded the gases and vapours in the tanks are pushed out by the rising cargo. This is carried by separate venting pipelines to raised vent pipes, often at the forward end of the vessel.

Smaller tankers up to Panamax size may have a different arrangement of pumps and associated piping and manifolds. Here, each individual cargo tank will have its own in-tank submerged cargo pump called a deepwell pump as the suction at the bottom is in a small well at the bottom of the tank. This means that the cargo tank can be emptied completely during discharge. The pumps are driven by electrical or hydraulic power from the deck above and the cargo is pumped up a pipe to the deck and will be led to its own manifold. Often, the port and starboard tanks of each section (1P and 1S for example) will share a common manifold but this will be segregated from all other tanks so allowing more flexibility with the number of different types or grades of cargo that can be carried. This is shown in Figure 18b.

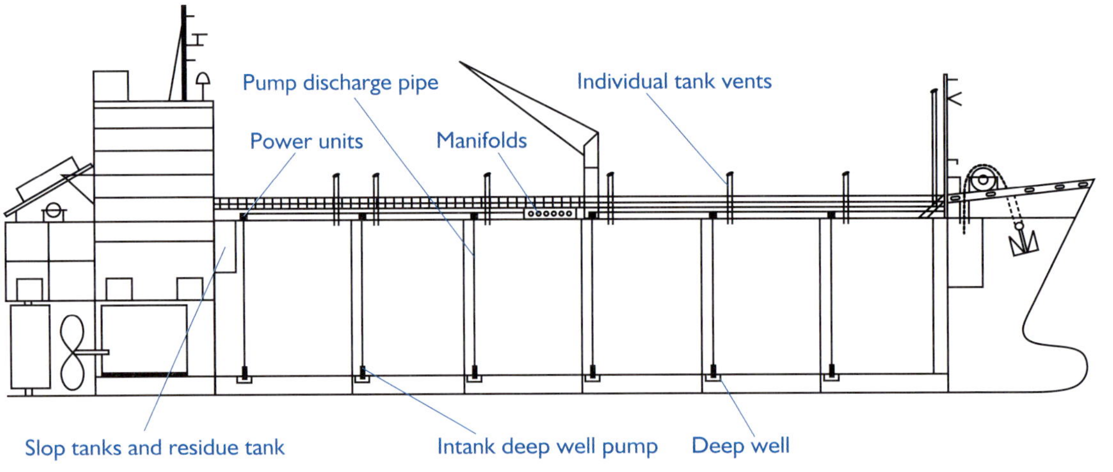

Figure 18b

Unlike the bulk carrier holds, the cargo tanks are further divided longitudinally into port and starboard tanks with a longitudinal corrugated watertight (w/t) bulkhead, which is first, a safety measure to reduce the danger of free surface arising but it also aids cargo flexibility. This in effect means that there are twelve cargo tanks named 1–6 P&S. In most vessels, the port and starboard tanks in each of the six sets are connected and are looked on as a common system but not in all. See Figure 19.

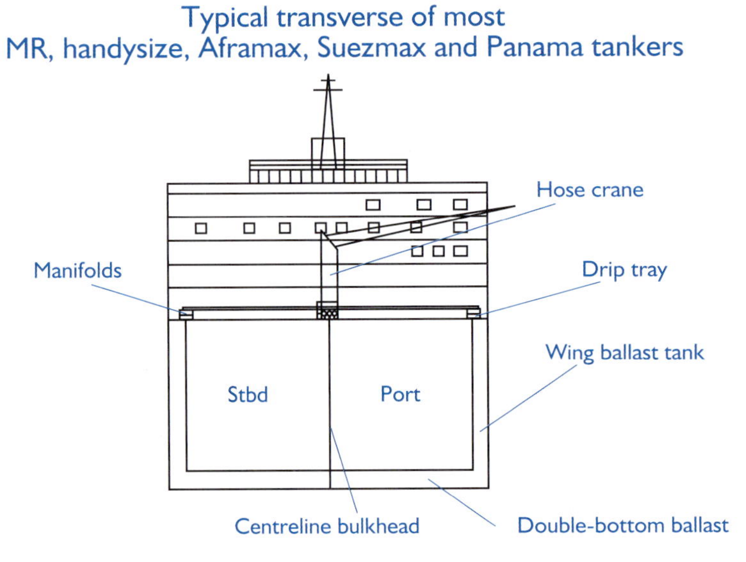

Figure 19

In VLCCS, given the size of the vessel and the corresponding size of the tanks, the tanks may be divided into three: Port, Centre and Starboard and may have a crane at each side. This layout is shown in Figure 19a.

Typical layout of cross-section VLCC

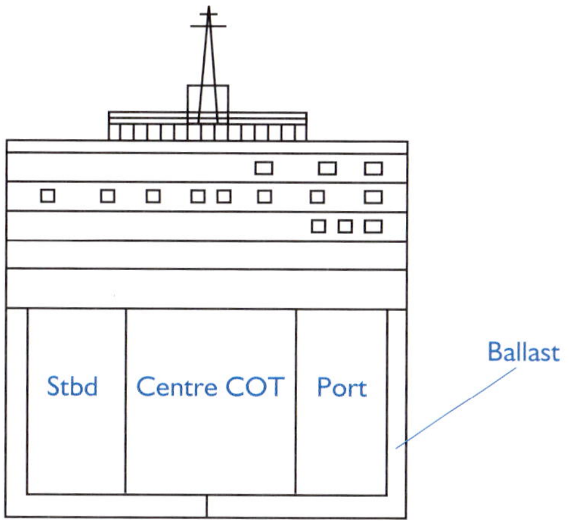

Figure 19a

Reference has been made to loadlines. Each vessel is allocated, on construction, a loadline, which is basically a mark, known as the Plimsoll mark, on the ship's side which indicates the maximum draught to which the vessel can be loaded. Because a vessel can be loaded with safety to a deeper draught in calmer weather, different marks are allocated to different seasons and also to allow for loading in fresh water (which is less buoyant than salt water). To determine the vessel's draught, draught marks are painted on the vessel's hull at the bow, stern and amidships by the loadline.

2.4 PROPULSION

Although a few large older ships and many of the liquefied natural gas (LNG) carriers are powered by steam turbine, the overwhelming majority of vessels are today powered by either slow-speed or medium-speed diesel engines. Particular attention is paid in modern ships to the fuel preparation equipment, enabling vessels to burn low-cost residual intermediate fuel oil (IFO) and heavy fuel oil (HFO) bunker fuels efficiently and without harm to the engines.

Some older vessels may also consume marine diesel oil (MDO) (a fuel of better quality) or a blend of IFO and diesel in the auxiliary engines used to power the generators and also in the main engine when the vessel is entering or leaving port, or while manoeuvring in confined waters. This is because the response of an older engine design to a change of throttle position is very slow when burning IFO bunkers. As this fact could jeopardise the safety of the ship when an instantaneous response by the engine is required, the fuel will be switched from IFO to MDO where the response will be almost instantaneous.

Mention has already been made of the requirement for ships in certain areas to burn low sulphur fuel oil and as the permissible sulphur content is further reduced by legislation. As the global limit for sulphur content is expected to be limited to 0.5% from 2020, some expect that newbuild ships may in future be required to run only on MDO and the even cleaner low sulphur gasoil (L S gasoil).

MDO and MGO are not the correct technical terms for particular types of fuel as specified by the universal standard ISO 8217, it is called distillate fuel. In addition, ships operating in the various ECAs could not use any of the distillate fuels in the standard. They would have to use an LSGasoil for a prolonged period in the main engine. New products are now available to meet the market for this with low sulphur and volatility, and higher viscosity, density and flashpoint characteristics.

A very small number of ships have been fitted with dual-fuel engines that can run on both oil fuels and LNG, and an even smaller number are fitted with engines that only burn LNG. So far, these ships have been almost exclusively those that operate in Norwegian waters, where financial incentives to burn such fuels exist.

A modern term that has become popular is that of an eco-ship. As bunker fuels have become more and more expensive, shipbuilders offered what they called eco-ships with changed hull shape and altered bow and stern profiles to give a cleaner movement through the water. More economical engines are available and such things as the provision of shaft generators were fitted to enable ships' alternators to be shut down at sea. Some car carrier vessels have solar panels on their top decks.

The overwhelming majority of vessels are today powered by either slow-speed or medium-speed diesel engines

2.5 EMPLOYMENT OF SHIPS

In simplistic terms, ships are employed either as liners or as tramps. What defines a ship as a liner is that it trades according to a schedule, on a designated route, and its cargo is made up of very many different consignments from numerous shippers, generally manufactured or semi-manufactured goods. Freight rates are usually published in a tariff and may vary according to the commodity. The trading area will determine the type of vessel, which may be a container ship, a ro-ro or a combination of two types. General purpose ships are still used in a very few liner trades. The normal document covering the contract of carriage will be a bill of lading or waybill.

The name 'tramp' refers to the fact that the ship trades where the market takes it. This form of operation is also referred to as the spot market. Its cargo is usually all one commodity, although there may be different grades, is generally a raw material and there is normally only one shipper. The contract of carriage will be a charter party and this can be on a voyage basis when the charterer pays so much freight per tonne of cargo for an agreed quantity, usually a full cargo from A to B. Alternatively, the contract can be a time charter when the ship charterer pays hire per day for the use of the ship for an agreed period, which can be just a few weeks, or months or years. In either case, the rate of freight or hire will be freely negotiated and its level will depend on the strength or weakness of the shipping market at the time.

Tramps have tended to be mainly general purpose ships, but today there is a high degree of specialisation.

2.6 TYPES OF SHIPS

Ships can be divided into three main categories:

- dry cargo;
- tankers;
- miscellaneous.

2.6.1 Dry cargo

As the name suggests, these vessels are designed to carry dry, non-liquid cargo, and can be further subdivided into bulk carriers, multipurpose, container ships, ro-ro ships and refrigerated ships.

2.6.1.1 Bulk carriers

Bulk carriers are the unsophisticated travelling boxes of the oceans. They range in size from the smallest coaster of about 250 tons deadweight up to the largest ore carriers of 400,000dwt. Names have been given to various categories of bulk carrier reflecting their size and, in some cases, the maximum size of vessel that can enter certain important ports or navigational areas. The following table gives details of some of the names used and typical dimensions. The penultimate three ship types are named after ports and the Seawaymax is the largest vessel size that can transit the St Lawrence River to reach the Great Lakes from the North Atlantic.

Capesize is a term given to a bulk carrier of about 170,000dwt upwards. Most Capesize bulk carriers will go round the Cape of Good Hope but many of them can go loaded through the Suez Canal. Capesize vessels in excess of about 200,000dwt are known as very large ore carriers (VLOCs).

Typical dimensions for bulker types

Type	Deadweight	LOA	Beam	Draught
Handysize	20–40,000	113–180m	19–29m	8–10m
Handymax/ Supramax	40–59,000	150–200m	23–32m	10–12.8m
Panamax	60–80,000	225m	32.3m	12.04m
New Panamax*	120–130,000	366m	49m	15.2m
Capesize	80–400,000	225–300m	32–50m	12–22m
Kamsarmax	82,000	229m	32.3m	14.4m
Dunkirkmax	175,000	289m	45.05m	18m
Newcastlemax	185,000	-	47m	-
Seawaymax	30,000	225.6m	23.8m	7.92m

*New Panamax is the term given to the largest vessels able to transit the Panama Canal since its expansion in 2016

Very large ore carrier bulker

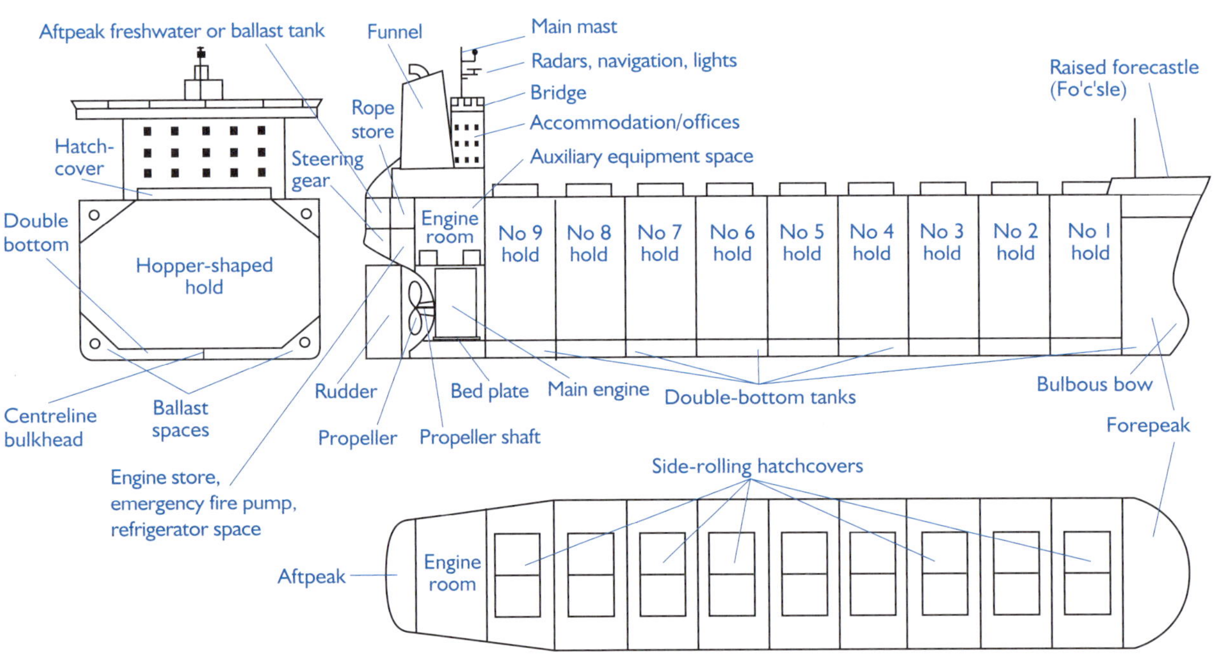

Typical vessel specifications

Typical size	200–400,000dwt
Typical length	320 metres
Beam	60 metres
Draught	22 metres
Holds/hatches	Nine holds/nine hatches
Main engine	30–40,500kWh

Capesize vessel

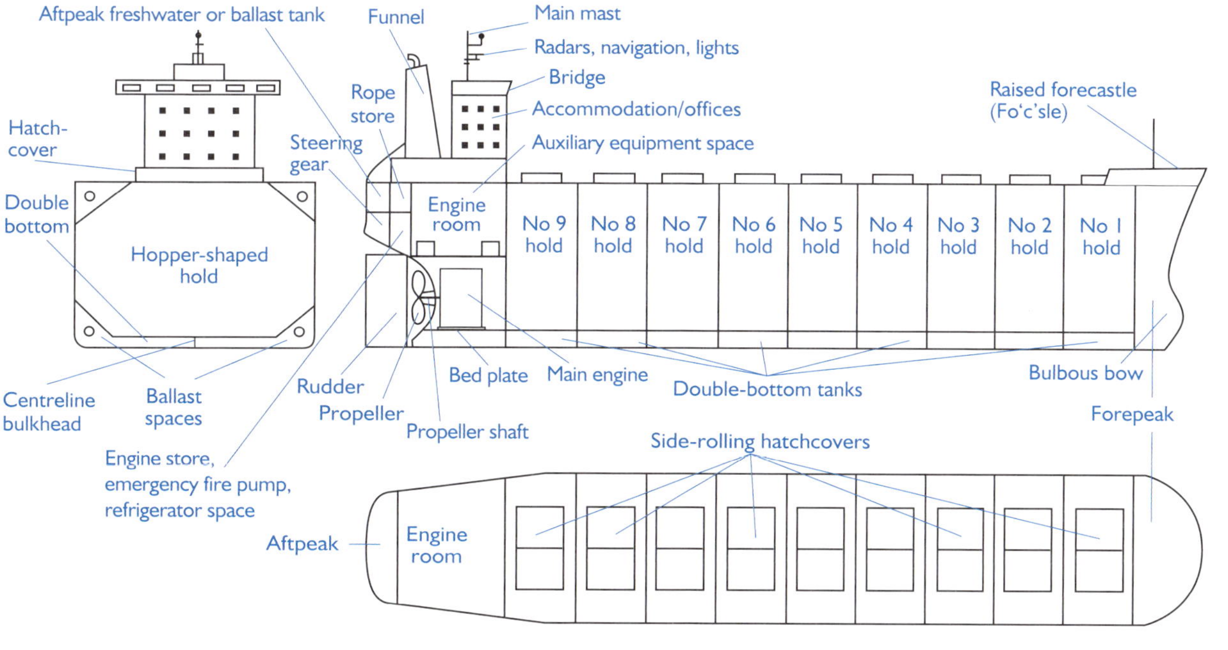

Typical vessel specifications

Typical size	180,000dwt
Typical length	290 metres
Beam	45 metres
Draught	17.5 metres
Holds/hatches	Nine holds/nine hatches
Main engine	23–25,000kWh

New Panamax bulker

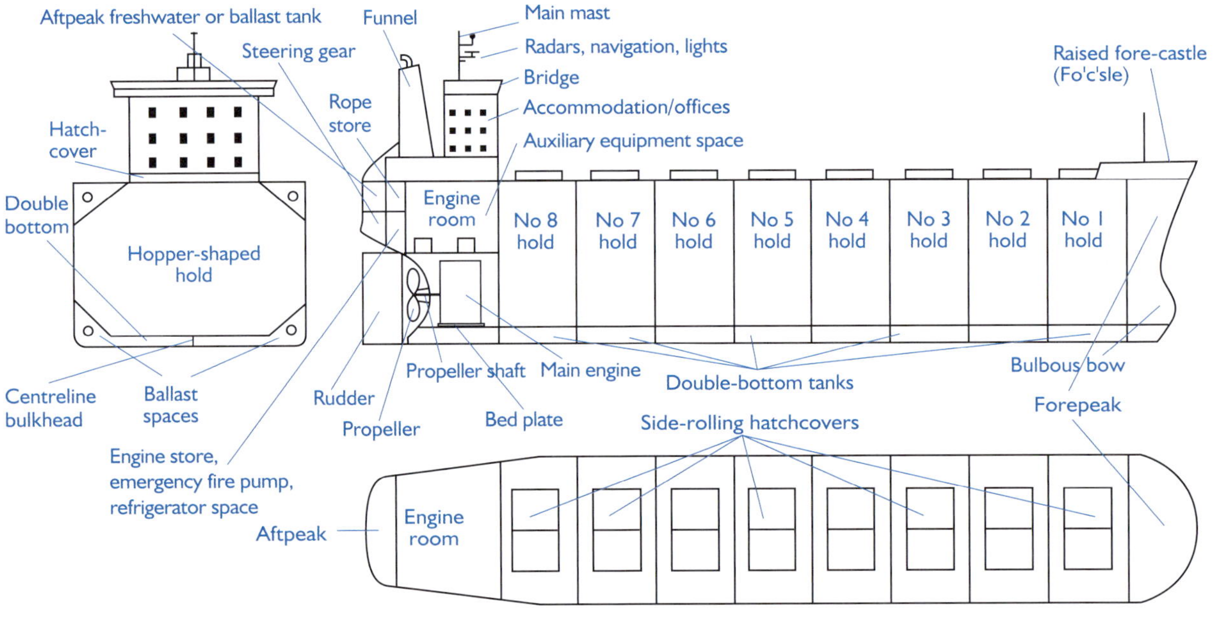

Typical vessel specifications

Typical size	120,000dwt
Typical length	250 metres
Beam	43 metres
Draught	14.5 metres
Holds / hatches	seven–eight holds / seven–eight hatches
Main engine	20,000kWh

Handymax/Supramax bulker

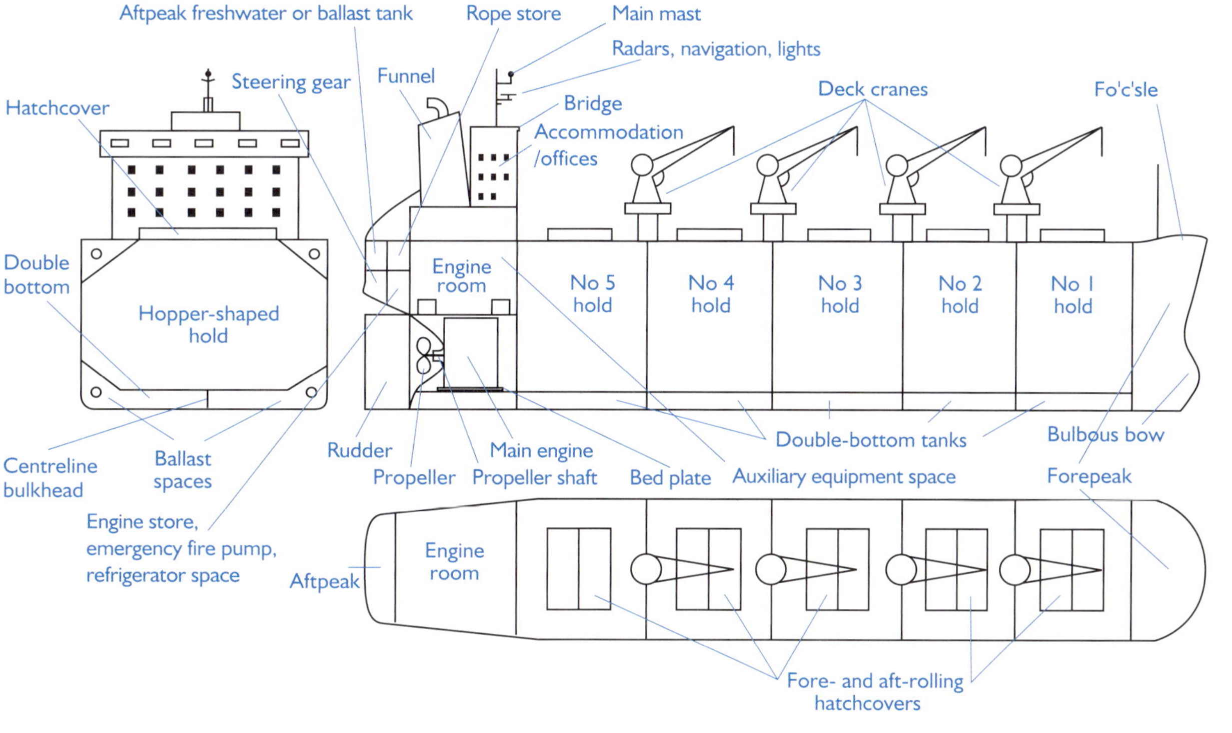

Typical vessel specifications

Typical size	40–60,000dwt
Typical length	190 metres
Beam	32.2 metres
Draught	11.5 metres
Cranes	40 tonne swl x 4
Holds/hatches	Five holds/five hatches
Main engine	12,500kWh

Handysize bulker

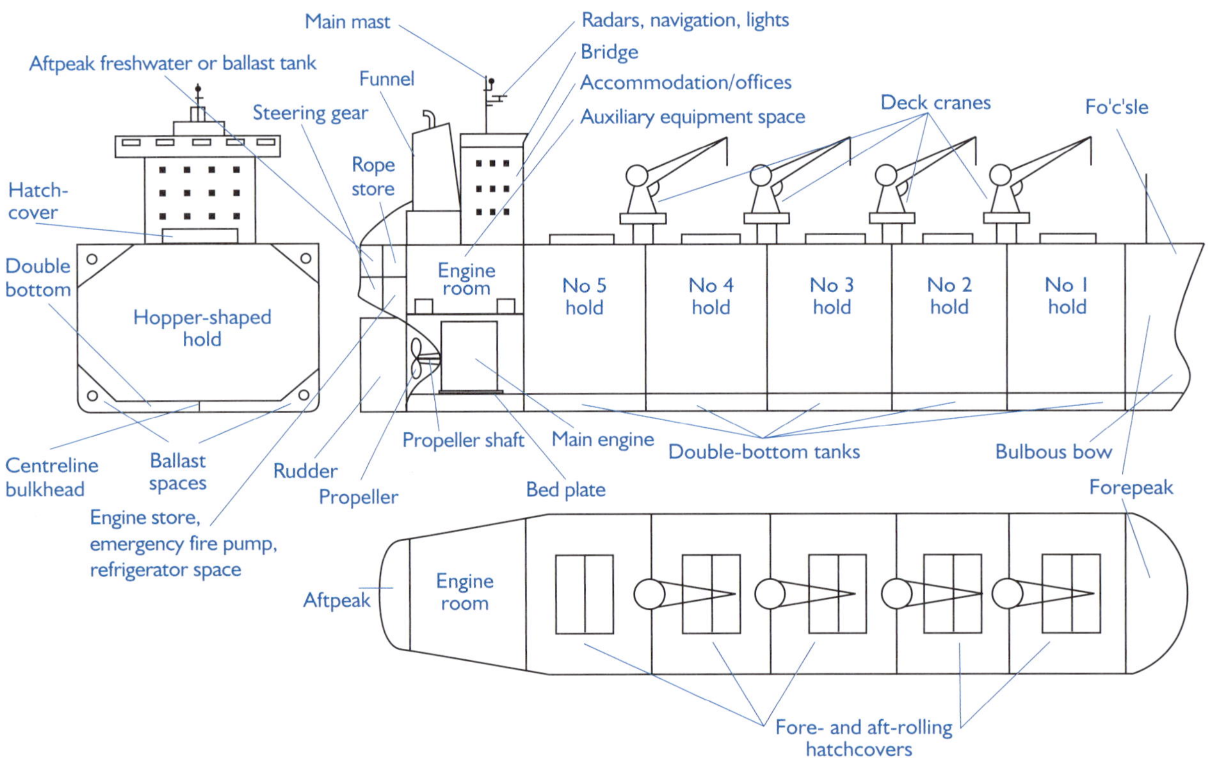

Typical vessel specifications

Typical size	25–40,000dwt
Typical length	180–200 metres
Beam	24–30 metres
Draught	9.5–10.5 metres
Cranes	20–30 tonnes swl x 4
Holds/hatches	Five holds/five hatches
Main engine	9–11,000kWh

Access to the generally unrestricted holds is by way of hatches of the largest size commensurate with the vessel's structural integrity, to allow for rapid loading and discharge of cargo. The vessels are primarily designed for the carriage of bulk cargoes, such as ores, grains, coal and fertilisers, and consequently the holds are constructed to be self-trimming (that is, shaped in such a way that when loaded into the holds, the cargo will trim itself evenly over the area of the hold without requiring any manual labour).

Such even distribution is necessary for two reasons. First, to ensure maximum utilisation of the ship's holds. Were the ship to be loaded through a small hatch, the cargo would adopt a conical shape. The shape of that cone would be dictated by the natural angle of repose of the material concerned. Angle of repose differs widely from commodity to commodity on this scale in just the same way as simple substances behave in a domestic kitchen. For example, quite different shapes are formed when pouring out sugar, flour, lentils and so on. In most cases, it will be easy to visualise the point of a cone of cargo protruding through the hatchway long before the hold is full.

The second reason for trimming the cargo across the whole of the hold is one of safety. Even distribution of cargo is always important, not only to ensure that the ship rides on an even keel but also to avoid uneven stresses on the structure of the ship.

Therefore, the first requirement of a self-trimmer is to have the largest hatch size commensurate with safe construction. This allows for the loading appliance to spread the cargo evenly and you will sometimes encounter, in charter parties, a clause requiring the shipper to ensure that the cargo is spout-trimmed.

Self-trimming design does not only apply to loading because grabs are almost invariably used to discharge such ships, and grabs would not be able to reach right into the angle between the vertical side of the ship and the bottom of the hold. This is overcome by constructing a sloping section at an angle of about 45° running fore and aft for the whole length of the hold, known as a wing tank. This trims the cargo into the square of the hatch within reach of the grab, thus minimising the amount of shovelling, by hand or with a bobcat, required to reach the last few tonnes of cargo. That wing tank serves a second purpose in that it houses ballast spaces which can be filled with water to take the ship more deeply into the water for greater stability when the ship is sailing without cargo.

Reverting back to the angle of repose, it is important to remember that different substances also vary in their stability and it is easy to imagine a cone of cargo, if left untrimmed, quite quickly collapsing as soon as the ship was subjected to any buffeting. If the cargo simply settled down to a level surface, all well and good, but if it settled when the ship was heeling to one side, then the ship could quickly assume a dangerous list. This is another reason for the cargo to be at least spout-trimmed at the loading port although, for some commodities, it does not end there.

Some materials, such as grain especially, tend to shift about almost like a fluid. This would mean that buffeting could cause a dangerous list even if the cargo had been levelled carefully at the time of loading. In days gone by, this problem was overcome by the use of shifting boards – vertical wooden partitions which divided what would otherwise be one large free surface into a number of smaller ones so that cargo movement would not cause a list.

If one encounters some older grain charter parties, especially in the shortsea trades, reference will even be found to the shippers having to provide up to 10% of a grain cargo in bags for safe stowage. The bagged cargo would be laid on top of the bulk to stop it shifting as an alternative to shifting boards.

Modern bulk carriers approach this problem differently by having a deeper hatch coaming and shaping the hold to reduce the free surface at the top of the cargo. This is achieved by again having plating at a 45° angle but this time along the angle between the deck and the side of the ship. This shape has the effect of reducing the free surface within which the fluid-like movement can take place. The compartments constructed in this way are also used for ballast water when required. The ability to put some ballast above the waterline instead of all of it in the bottom of the ship also makes for a much more comfortable ballast passage for both the ship and those in it by raising the centre of gravity. With all the weight at the bottom of the ship a pendulum effect is set up when the ship encounters any sort of heavy weather and you will hear seafarers referring to such a condition as the ship being 'very stiff ', which is not only uncomfortable but sets up dangerous stresses on the structure of the ship.

It is also worth noting that if the reverse occurs and there is too much weight at the top of the ship, its rolling movements become exaggerated and the crew will refer to it as being 'tender'.

Medium and smaller bulk carriers refer to carriers from about 20,000dwt to about 40,000dwt, known as handysize. They are also equally suitable for the carriage of steel, packaged lumber and bagged cargoes. An important consideration for owners of bulk carriers is to decide whether or not to equip the ship with cargo gear, usually cranes mounted on deck to load and discharge the vessel. On medium and small bulk carriers, cargo gear increases their flexibility by enabling them to trade to places where shore facilities are not adequate. By no means do all small bulkers have such equipment but many certainly do. For example, some modern 40,000 tonners have cranes capable of at least 30t swl . Larger vessels seldom have their own gear as such ships tend to trade between modern cargo installations where loading is by shore gantry cranes with purpose-built devices (such as spouts) and discharge is by grabs or some other equipment designed for rapid unloading. At such places, cargo gear mounted on the ship would simply prove a hindrance to rapid loading and discharging.

In certain dedicated trades, vessels are fitted with integral conveyor systems, so-called self-unloaders.

Ore carriers

To some owners, the large bulk carrier was too specialised while to others it was not specialised enough. Among the latter were those shipowners who wished to commit themselves to the iron ore trade. Some of these were divisions of the large iron and steel conglomerates, and the ore carriers were designed and built for them or for shipowners with long-term charters to these conglomerates. One may well ask why they were not content with a normal bulk carrier. The reason is that a bulk carrier is built with enough cubic capacity to carry cargoes such as grain and coal, which require at least 1.27 cubic metres (45 cubic feet) per tonne weight of cargo. This is far too much space for a heavy commodity such as iron ore. Not only does a dense material such as iron ore (which only occupies the bottom half of the holds) make a normal bulk carrier very stiff, but the owner of such a bulk carrier has simply acquired far more ship capacity than is required. Ore carriers are therefore constructed with large double bottoms and wing tanks which increase the strength of the ship to cope with the stresses of carrying such dense cargo.

2.6.1.2 Multipurpose

These vessels are the modern successors to the conventional cargo ships of 20 years ago, and are designed to be able to take bulk cargo, bagged cargo, containers and general cargo with equal ease and, if necessary, at the same time. They exist within the narrow size range of 5,000–25,000dwt. They usually have two decks (known as a tweendecks) with large hatches and with some cargo gear of sufficient capacity to lift containers and other heavy pieces of cargo of up to 40 tonnes. Some have huge cranes with 200–300 tonne capacity. There have been few newbuilds of this type in recent years as, in the main trades, they have been replaced by container or ro-ro vessels.

Multipurpose vessel

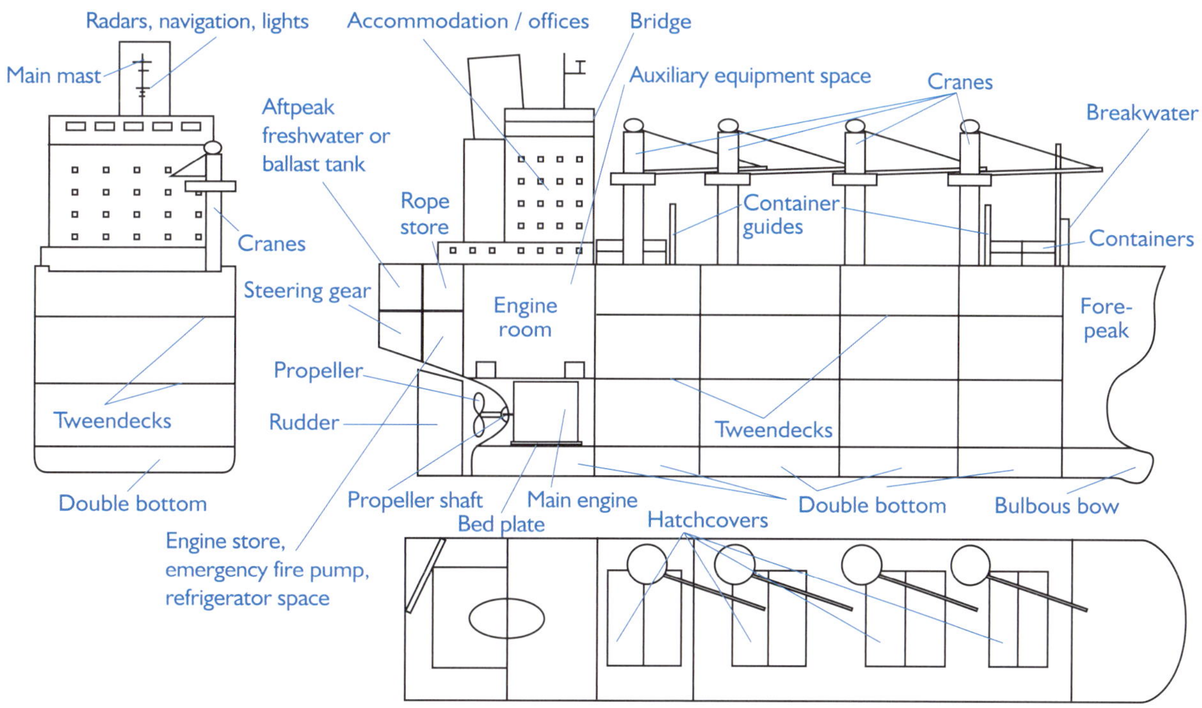

Typical vessel specifications

Typical size	30,000dwt
Typical length	192 metres
Beam	28 metres
Draught	11.2 metres
Holds/hatches	Four to five holds/eight to 10 hatches
Capacity	30-35,000 cubic metres
Teu	1,500
Cranes	40–300 tonnes swl
Main engine	21,000kWh
Speed	18–20 knots

2.6.1.3 Container vessels

These vessels are designed to take containers only and range in size from the small coasting container vessels up to the large and fast oceangoing container vessels. Their holds are cellular, that is to say, they have vertical frames or guides into which the containers are slotted. They are able to handle containers of International Organization for Standardization (ISO) dimensions, generally 20 or 40 feet in length. The size of the vessels is expressed by the number of twenty-foot equivalent units (teus) they will be able to carry. Many small and medium-sized container vessels are self-sustained, meaning they have cargo gear on board with which they can load and discharge containers.

All large container vessels cater for refrigerated containers by supplying electric power to which the containers with integral refrigeration systems can be connected. Highly specialised container ships for trades where there is a high demand for chilled cargo are equipped with centralised refrigeration machinery which delivers cooled air to insulated containers through portholes in the units, although this system is now being phased out.

An important feature of container ships is the arrangement of the holds. They are completely open-hold ships, which means that the hatches give access to the whole of the hold area. This means that there is no need for any stowage work and, as the cell guides are erected in the holds, no lashings are required below decks. The pontoon hatchcovers are fitted to carry containers up to six or seven tiers high on deck. Below deck, the boxes are secured by the cellular arrangement but on the hatchcovers, the containers are lashed to prevent movement.

The modern deepsea gearless container ship carries between 3,000teu and up to about 20,000teu. It will have a service speed of 22–26 knots. Panamax vessels are the largest that can navigate the Panama Canal. Traditionally, these were about 4,500teu, less than 295 metres LOA, 32.2 metres beam and 12 metres draught on tropical loadline. With the expansion of the Panama Canal, opened in June 2016, new Panamax (or neopanamax) vessels are up to 13,000teu, 366 metres LOA, 49 metres beam and 15.2 metres draught. Post-Panamax vessels are those too large for such transit.

Many large modern container ships are hatchless vessels. The cell guides are extended above main deck level so that on-deck lashing is also unnecessary. In another type, there is also a heightened and streamlined fo'c'sle with a wave-breaking device intended to keep water away from the main deck of the vessel. In both cases, the intention is to avoid the additional labour and delay involved in removing and replacing hatchcovers as well as the tedious securing of the containers carried on deck.

Post-Panamax container ship

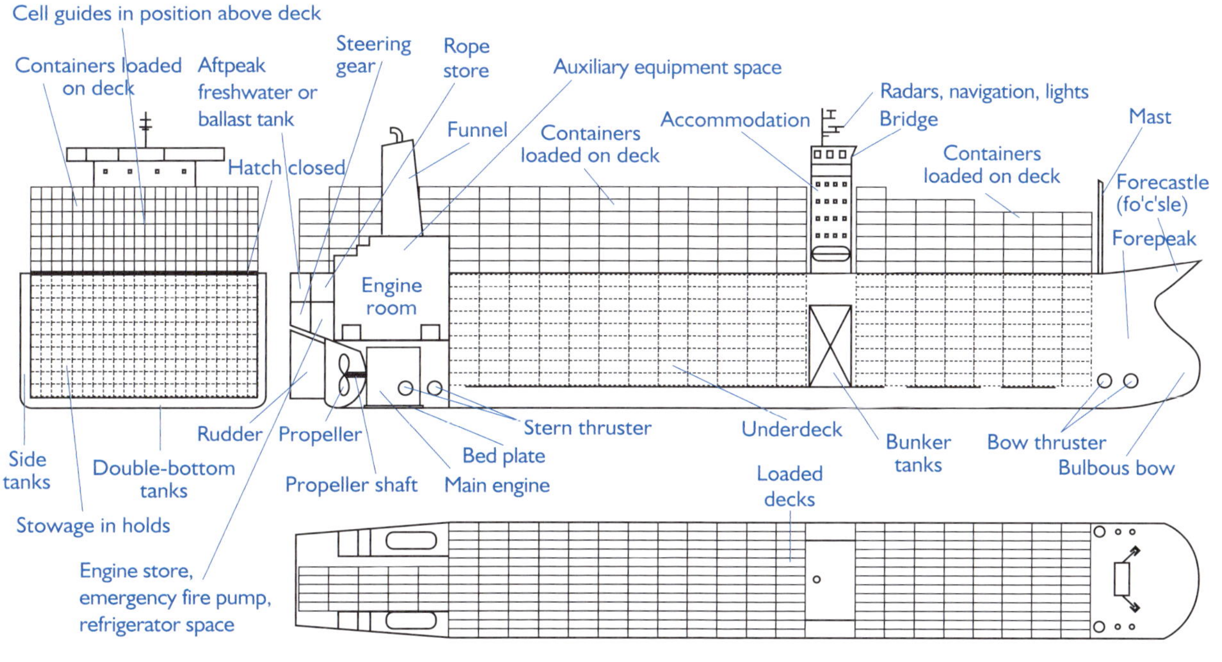

Typical vessel specifications

Typical length	400 metres
Beam	57 metres
Draught	15.5 metres
Teu	14,500
Main engine	80,000kWh
Speed	Up to 22 knots

New Panamax container ship

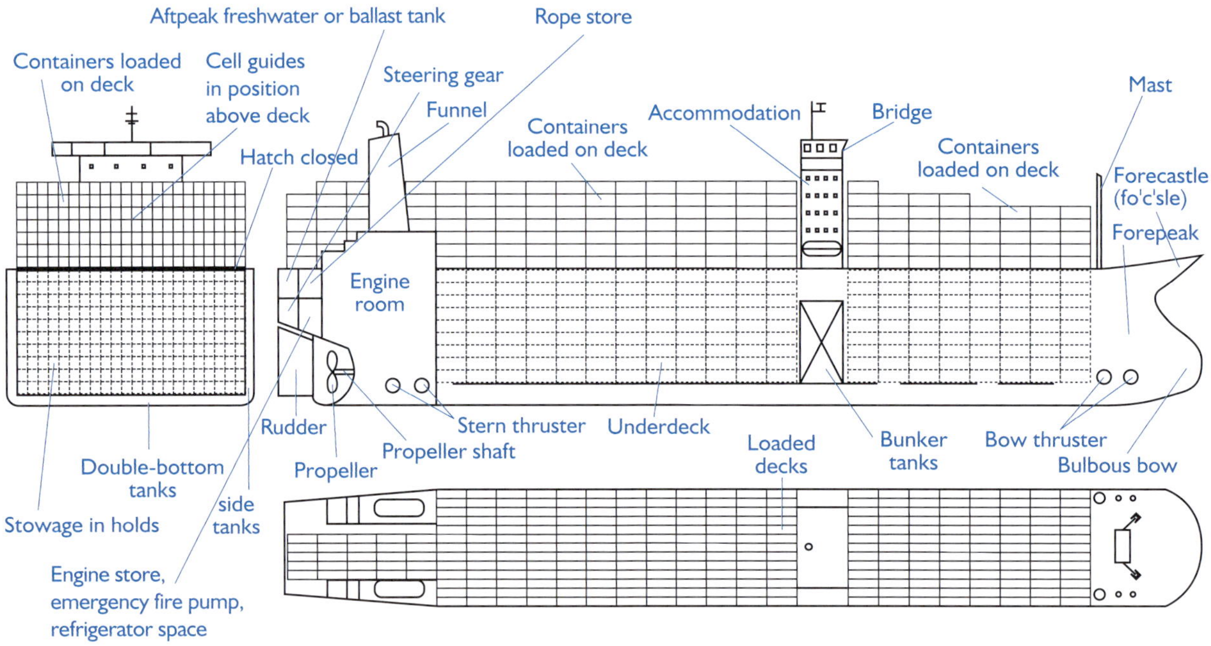

Typical vessel specifications

Typical length	366 metres
Beam	49 metres
Draught	15.2 metres
Teu	10,000–14,500
Main engine	55,000kWh
Speed	Up to 20 knots

2.6.1.4 Roll-on/roll-off vessels (ro-ro)

These vessels are suitable only for cargo that can be driven on and off the ship, such as cars, lorries and cargo on trailers, which can be either road trailers or 'Mafi' trailers designed solely for shipborne use, being loaded and unloaded in dockside terminals.

Pure ro-ros are most common although, on certain trades, vessels which are part container vessel, part ro-ro can be found. The size of a ro-ro is measured in lane-metres, which indicate the total length of the marked parking lanes of 3.5m wide that are available on board. The size and safe working load of the entrance ramp, the width and height of the openings leading into the hull and the number of liftable decks are all important factors for the type and size of vehicles which a ro-ro vessel can carry. Pure car carriers (PCC) and pure car and truck carriers (PCTC) also fall into this category.

Ro-ro vessel

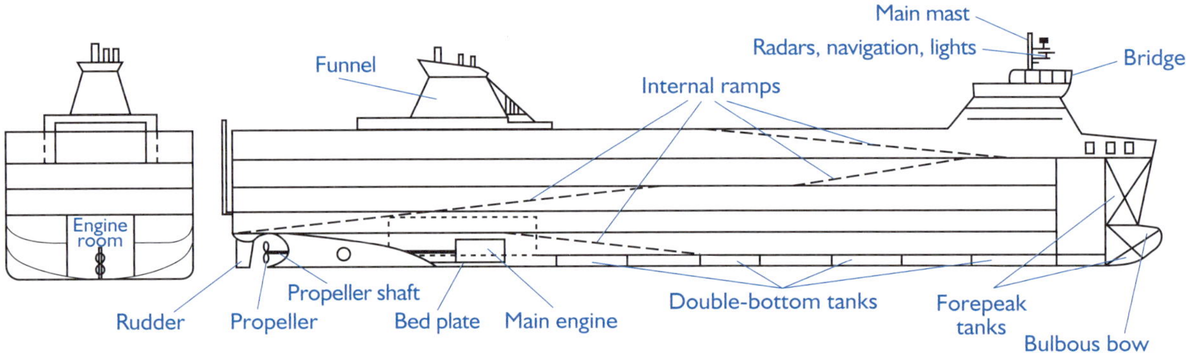

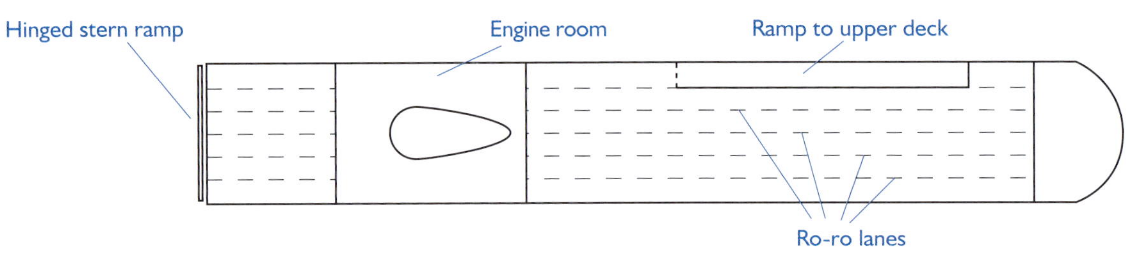

Typical vessel specifications

Typical length	200 metres
Beam	26 metres
Draught	7 metres
Capacity	4,000 lane-metres
Ramp load	100 tonnes
Main engine	40,000kWh
Speed	19 knots on 90 tonnes fuel oil per day

2.6.1.5 Refrigerated vessels

These vessels, customarily known as reefers, are very specialised ships. They have two or more decks and, as the name implies, are basically oceangoing fridge freezers. The holds are insulated and they have an extensive compressor system with which they keep the temperature in the holds down at the required level (as different cargoes require different temperatures). They are usually very fast, up to 22 or 23 knots, thus reducing the transit time for the frozen or chilled cargo. They also have small hatches and cargo gear designed to operate speedily, thus limiting the time the cargo is exposed to the elements.

The size of a reefer vessel is usually expressed by the volume of the vessel's holds and expressed in cubic feet or sometimes in cubic metres.

2.6.2 Tankers

This category encompasses any vessel designed to carry liquid cargoes and ranges from the ULCC (ultra-large crude carriers) of about 350–500,000dwt down to the smallest estuarial tank barge. Not only do these tankers carry crude oil but also, provided they are suitably equipped, are capable of carrying refined or semi-refined petroleum products or a wide variety of other liquid cargoes including chemicals and such liquids as wine in bulk. In describing oil cargoes, the term 'dirty' refers to crude oil cargoes and residual fuels while 'clean' refers to more refined or semi-refined products. It should, however, be noted that within the product trade itself petroleum spirit, kerosene and so forth, are naturally described as clean, while products at the other end of the refining scale, such as heavy fuel oil, bitumen and asphalt, are referred to as dirty.

Whereas a crude carrier will only take a very limited number of grades of oil, clean products or chemicals tankers, might well have the capability of taking a large number of different products at one time. This parcelling of clean cargoes is a common feature, particularly of chemical tankers designed to take several different (and often incompatible) liquids carried in separate tanks. This demands an elaborate pumping and pipework system to prevent the intermingling of cargoes. Also, bearing in mind that some liquid chemicals react with steel, chemical tankers will have some of their tanks made of stainless steel or coated with special paints such as epoxy or even with rubber. A chemical tanker operator will always keep a careful note of which particular chemical can be carried in which particular tank. The wrong chemical in a tank with an incorrect coating could have disastrous results.

Given that the range of liquids now carried in bulk covers everything from liquid sulphuric and hydrochloric acid to vegetable oils and wine, the range of capabilities of chemical tankers has to be wide.

Into the tanker category can also be placed the liquid petroleum gas (LPG) tankers carrying, for example, butane, propane and ammonia; and the liquefied natural gas (LNG) tankers carrying methane.

All tankers are equipped with pumps by which they discharge their cargoes. They are also equipped with sophisticated cargo tank cleaning apparatus. Unlike dry cargo ships, where all that is needed to clean the cargo holds is a pressure water hose and brooms, liquid cargo tanks need elaborate cleaning. In the case of oil tankers, to avoid the risk of explosion, it is important to reduce the oxygen and the oil vapour content of the tanks before cleaning takes place. This is done with an inert gas system (IGS) by pumping inert gas (usually the exhaust gases from the main or auxiliary engine) or from an inert gas generator into the tanks prior to the commencement of cleaning. Modern crude oil tankers employ a crude oil wash system (COW), which reduces the clingage of cargo to the tank tops and sides. In the case of chemical tankers, cleaning can be even more complicated, with high pressure steam being necessary in some cases.

Other equipment which can be found are cargo heating coils, which are located on the bottom of the tank and are used for heating the cargo to prevent it from becoming too viscous to pump or even solidify at ambient temperatures. In some product tankers equipped with deep-well pumps, special deck-heating systems replace the in-tank coils. To heat the cargo the deep-well pumps pump the cargo through the exchange heater, a box with heating coils in it, which then recirculates back to the tank.

At the other end of the scale is refrigeration for LPG and LNG. The latter has to carry cargoes loaded at minus 162°C. These have insulated tanks and pipework constructed of special steels to cope with the very low temperatures and have either compressors or pressurised tanks to maintain the cargo in a liquid state.

The final piece of equipment found on tankers is a crane for handling the loading and discharging hoses. This is located by the cargo manifold amidships.

Type of tanker	Deadweight	Comment
Crude Oil Carriers		
ULCC	350–500,000	Ultra-large crude carrier
VLCC	270–320,000	Around 2m barrels
Suezmax	140–170,000	One million barrel capacity
Aframax*	80–120,000	Around 600,000 barrels
Clean Product Carriers		
Large range 2 (LR2)	95–120,000	Tanks coated for clean cargoes
Large range 1 (LR1)	65–75,000	Tanks coated for clean cargoes
Panamax	55–80,000	New Panamax size changed in 2016
Medium range (MR)	35–55,000	Usually carry clean cargoes
Handy	15–35,000	Clean or dirty cargoes
Chemical tankers	10–38,000	Coated or stainless steel tanks

*The AFRA sizes are used as a rate system within the trading world but, in the real commercial world, most of the cargo parcel sizes dictate the size of the vessels

Here are the AFRA sizes in deadweight tonnes capacity:

General purpose tanker	10,000–24,999
Medium-range tanker	25,000–44,999
LR1 (large range 1)	65,000–75,000
LR2 (large range 2)	95,000–120,000
VLCC (very large crude carrier)	160,000–319,999
ULCC (ultra-large crude carrier)	320,000–549,999

Aframax. Now loosely applied to tankers from 80,000dwt up to about 120,000dwt. Its origins go back to a committee formed at the behest of the major oil companies called the London Tanker Brokers' Panel, which periodically calculated average freight rate assessments (AFRA). These rates were used for a variety of purposes including long-term contracts in which the parties agreed to relate the freight rate to the current AFRA in some way.

One category of size for which an AFRA was calculated was 45,000–79,999dwt and there was a big drop in rate after that for the 80,000–159,999dwt size. It was, therefore, sensible for owners having ships built of around 80,000dwt to ensure that they did not exceed 79,999dwt. The panel still exists but is now independent of the oil companies and it calculates AFRAs commercially for anyone wishing to use the service.

Suezmax. A large tanker capable of transiting the Suez Canal fully loaded where there is a draught restriction of about 20m salt water dependent on the beam. They are designed to carry 1m barrels of cargo.

Very large crude carrier (VLCC). A crude oil tanker of between 270,000–320,000dwt. These are designed to carry 2m barrels of cargo.

Ultra-large crude carrier (ULCC). A crude oil tanker in excess of 450,000dwt, of which only two are currently trading.

The term ULCC is also sometimes encountered with regard to container carriers, particularly those over 14,000teu capacity, but then stands for ultra-large container carrier.

Aframax tanker

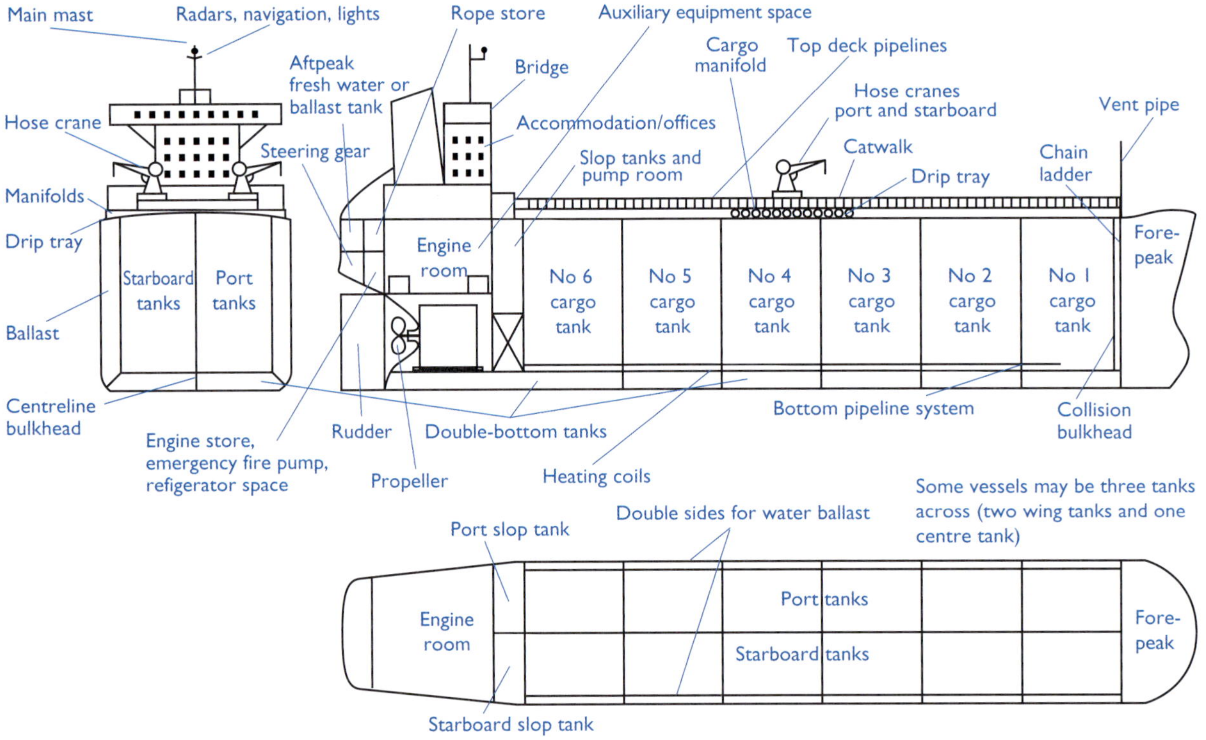

Typical vessel specifications

Size	95–120,000dwt
Length	250 metres
Beam	44 metres
Draught	14.6 metres
Cargo tanks	12
Slop tanks	2
Cargo pumps	4
Ballast pumps	2
Main Engine	17,000kWh

Large Range 1 (LR1) tanker

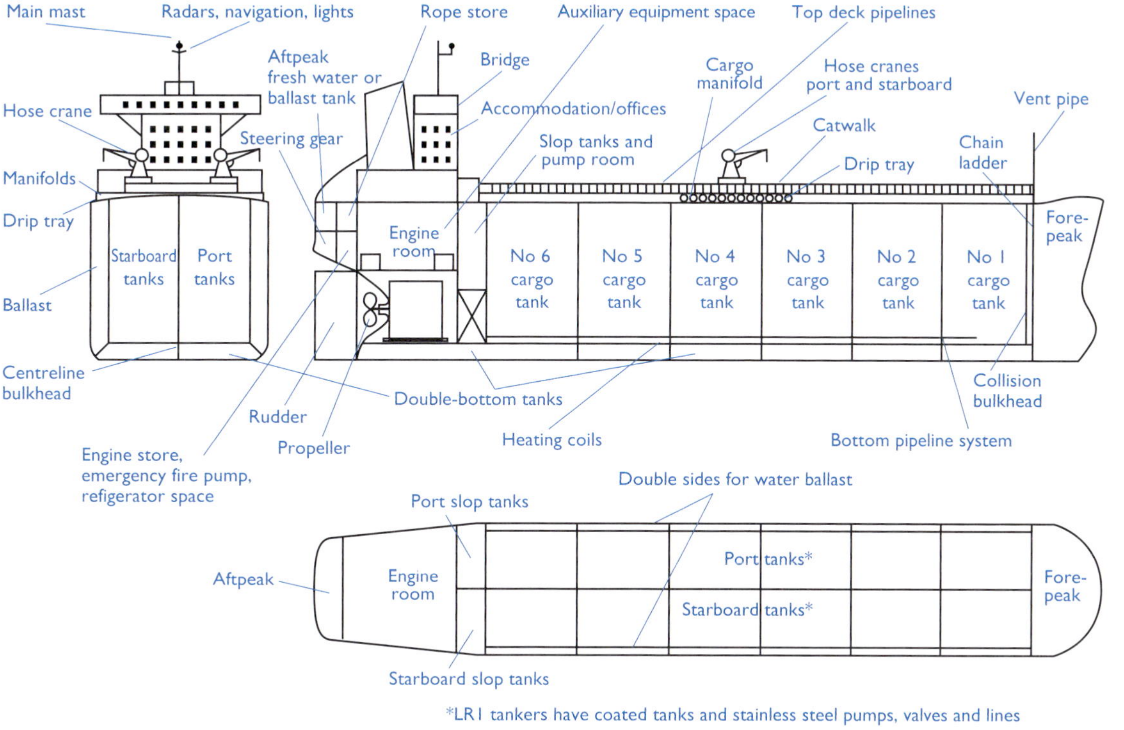

*LR1 tankers have coated tanks and stainless steel pumps, valves and lines

Typical vessel specifications

Size	65–75,000dwt
Length	229 metres
Beam	32.2 metres
Draught	14 metres
Cargo tanks	12
Cargo pumps	4
Ballast pumps	2
Slop tanks	2
Main engine	15,500kWh

Large Range 2 (LR2) tanker

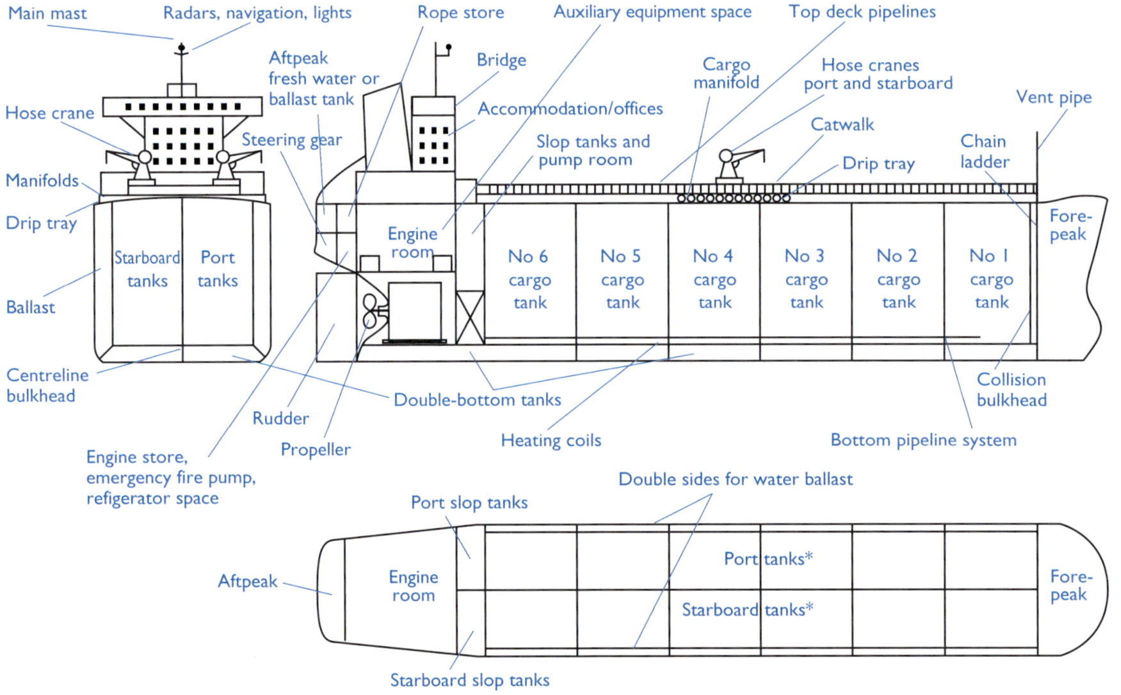

*LR2 tankers have coated tanks and stainless steel pumps, valves and lines

Typical vessel specifications

Size	95–120,000dwt
Length	250 metres
Beam	44 metres
Draught	14.6 metres
Cargo tanks	12
Cargo pumps	4
Ballast pumps	2
Slop tanks	2
Main engine	17,000kWh

Medium-range tanker

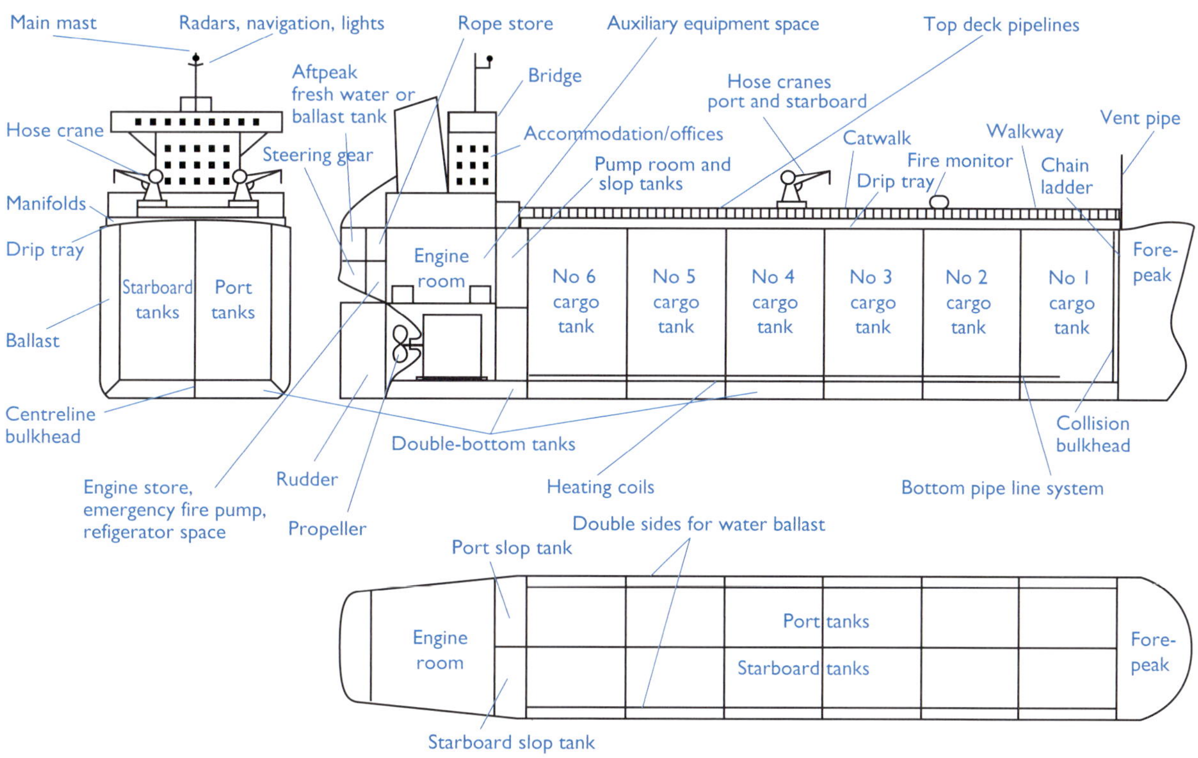

Typical vessel specifications

Size	32–50,000dwt
Length	189 metres
Beam	32 metres
Draught	13 metres
Cargo tanks	12
Slop tanks	2
Cargo pumps	4
Main engine	9,000kWh

Very Large Gas Carrier (VLGC)

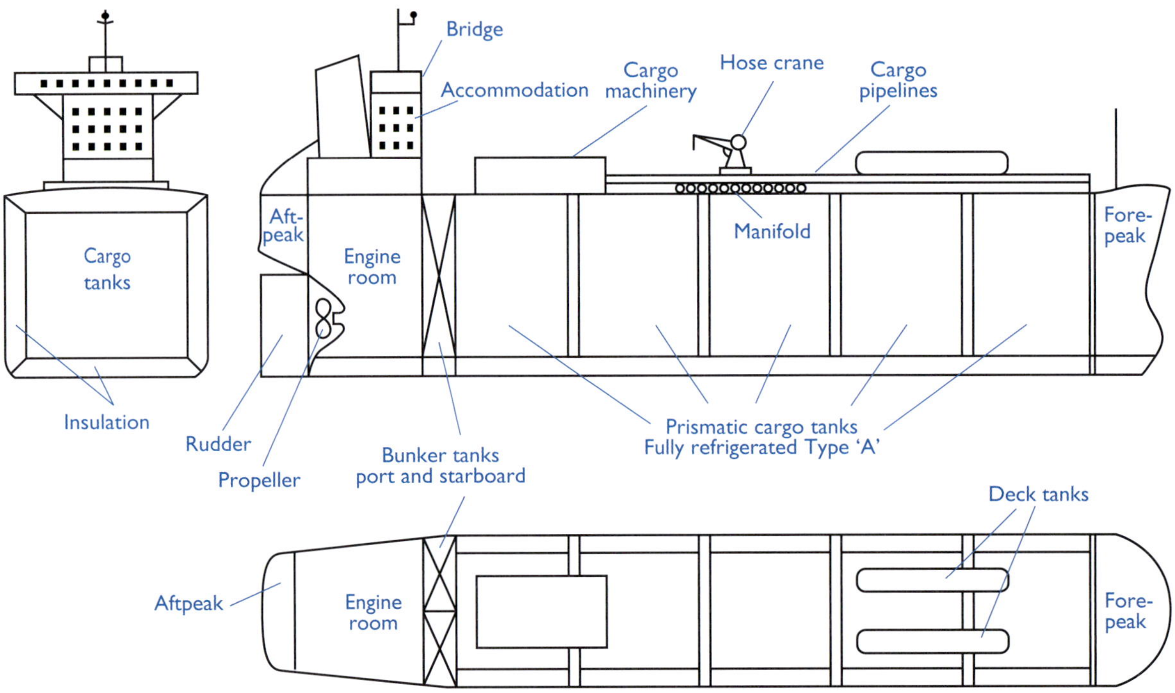

Typical vessel specifications

Size	50–70,000dwt
Length	226 metres
Beam	35 metres
Draught	11 metres
Capacity	660,000m^3
Cargo temperature	down to -50°C
Main engine	16,500kWh
Speed	17 knots

Typical cargoes

Propane -42°C Butane -5°C Ammonia -33°C

Pressurised LPG large gas carrier

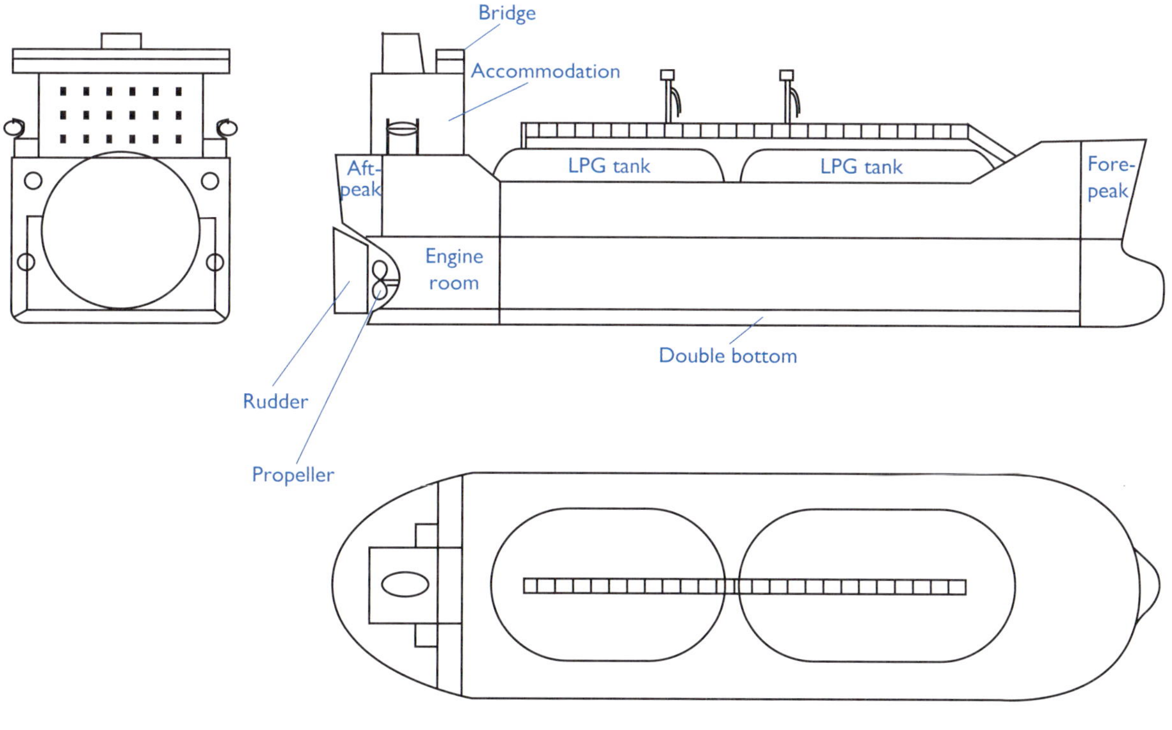

Typical vessel specifications

Size	4,800dwt
Length	93 metres
Beam	17.6 metres
Draught	4.2 metres
Capacity	3,500m^3
Cargo types	Butane, butadine, propane, propylene, VCM

LNG ship with Moss spherical tank design

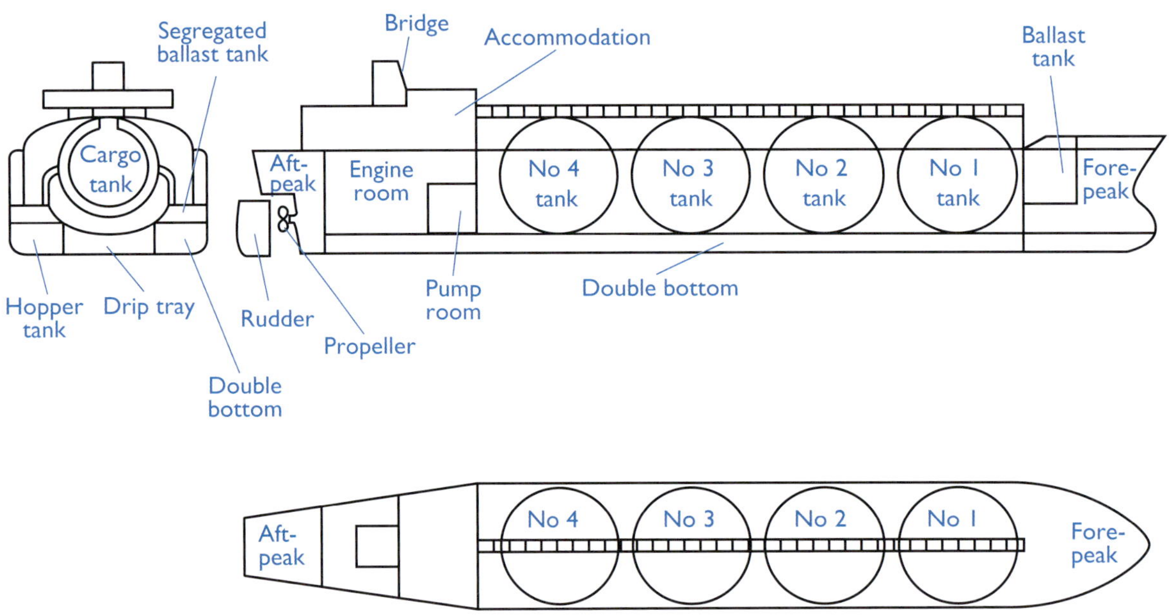

Typical vessel specifications

Size	66,500dwt
Length	290 metres
Beam	42 metres
Draught	10.7 metres
Capacity	130,000m³
Cargo tanks	Four refrigerated tanks
Pumps	10 x 1,100m³ (two pumps per tank)
Main engine	30,000kWh

LNG with prismatic tank design

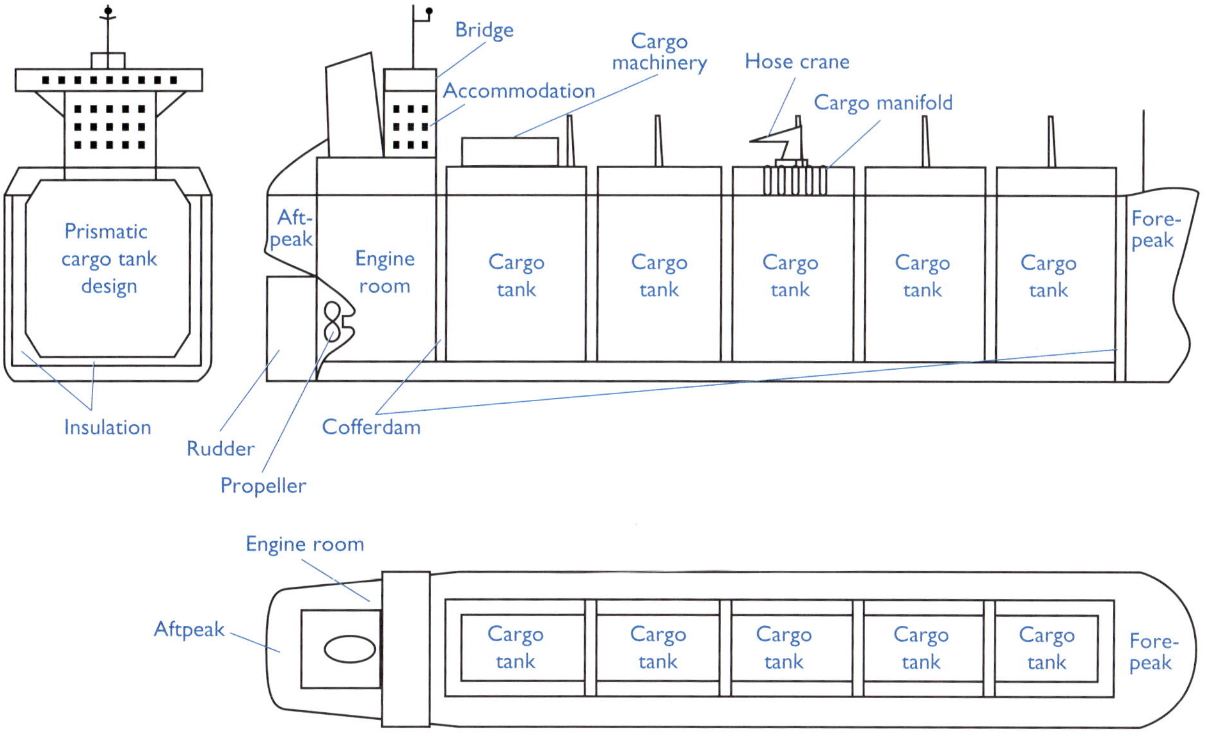

Typical vessel specifications

Size	100–130,000dwt
Length	277–345 metres
Beam	44–53 metres
Draught	11.4–12 metres
Capacity	140–260,000m^3
Cargo temperature down to	-166°C
Main engine	30,000kWh
Speed	19 knots

2.6.3 Miscellaneous vessels

The scope for this heading is enormous, covering as it does everything else that floats except warships and private yachts. The main types of vessel in this category are:

Tugs. These range from the large oceangoing salvage tugs, which are also used to tow oil rigs around the world, to the small harbour tugs. The power of these tugs can either be expressed by the brake horsepower (bhp) of their engines or (more usually) by the bollard pull they can exert.

Tugs range from the large oceangoing salvage tugs to the small harbour tugs

Oil rigs. These are seldom self-propelled and are used in offshore oilfields. They are usually divided into two categories, drilling and production platforms. In deep water, these are not anchored but rely on powerful azimuthing thrusters for accurate position keeping.

Oil rigs are seldom self-propelled

Offshore supply vessels. Such vessels are easily recognised by their large flat cargo-carrying platform aft-built specifically to service oil rigs. The more powerful vessels are described as anchor-handling tug supply vessels and as such can sometimes double as tugs.

Offshore supply vessels are easily recognised by their large flat cargo-carrying platform aft-built specifically to service oil rigs

Cruise/passenger liners. The glamour vessels of the oceans are nowadays designed with short seven-to-14-day voyages in mind with as many ports of call as possible inserted into the schedule. They are usually of a very shallow draught, which enables them to enter or get as close as possible to as many exotic ports as possible.

Cruise ships are usually of a shallow draught to enable them to enter as many exotic ports as possible

Ferries. Designed to ply between the same two ports as quickly as possible and as often as is economically viable. They are almost all ro-ros, with the occasional train ferry, and are designed for the rapid loading and unloading of passengers, cars and lorries. They range in size from the super ferries with facilities that would not shame a cruise liner (in fact, some ferries advertise themselves as mini cruises) to the humble cross-river or harbour ferry.

Several other names are used to describe types of ships and often the name relates to size or employment limitations. Some examples are:

Laker. A vessel capable of trading into the Canadian/US Great Lakes, where there is a beam restriction in the St Lawrence Seaway locks of 23.15m and a draught restriction of 26ft in fresh water, up to about 30,000dwt part loaded because of the draught limitation to about 19,000dwt fully laden.

Panamax. The largest type of vessel capable of transiting the Panama Canal. Traditionally, this was a beam restriction of 32.2m, length of 289m and a draught of about 12m fresh water. The Panama Canal Authority has extended the size of the locks, so since June 2016, the Panama restrictions increased to beam of 49m, length of 366m and draught of 15.2m. Vessels which have been designed to meet these new Panama Canal restrictions have inevitably been labelled 'new Panamax'.

Post-Panamax. A vessel, particularly a container carrier or passenger ship, too large to transit the Panama Canal.

2.7 DECISIONS REGARDING THE SIZE OF VESSEL

Measured on the cost per tonne/mile basis, by far the cheapest form of transport is by sea. It is also true that the larger the ship, the cheaper the transportation cost per tonne will be. Therefore, the shipowner will wish to acquire the largest possible ship to be able to reap the benefit of the economy of size. Against this are two restraints. First, the owner will want a vessel which is as flexible as possible and able to enter and operate in as many ports as possible. This is important because the vast majority of ports in the world have some kind of restrictions as to the dimensions of vessels. The second is that because of trade patterns, shippers may only be able to ship their cargoes in certain restricted sizes. Thus, while a VLCC might be ideal for shipping crude oil from the Middle East to Rotterdam, it would be unlikely to be used for carrying oil from the Netherlands to Great Britain. Likewise, up to 20,000teu container vessels are employed on the Far East to Europe trade but not on intra-Mediterranean routes. Consequently, a shipowner will wish to acquire the largest possible vessels commensurate with the company's projected trading patterns.

2.8 SHIP MANAGEMENT

So far, we have examined and reviewed some of the common ship types and have identified in broad terms the ways in which they may be employed. These are all areas for decision by the shipowner. Having reached a decision on type, size and trade, the owner must then consider how the ship will be managed. The job of the ship manager is simple – to translate the owner's ideas into reality, so that the vessel can perform the tasks set by the owner efficiently, safely and profitably.

In some cases, ship management will be carried out by the shipowner's own organisation, and in others, an independent organisation will be employed under contract. In either event, the functions are basically similar.

Ship management includes registration and documentation of the ship as required by national and international authorities. It also covers crewing, victualling, stores, spare parts, maintenance and repairs, and extends to arranging insurance and the handling of claims and recoveries, and the appointment of surveyors and a host of other tasks designed to keep the ship running properly. In short, it is the ship manager's responsibility to ensure that the ship is 'tight, staunch and strong, and in every way fitted for the voyage.'

2.9 SHIPBOARD-HANDLING EQUIPMENT

2.9.1 The derrick

The simplest form of cargo-handling equipment used on board a ship is the derrick, which was developed from the spars of sailing vessels as a means of lifting and transferring cargo from ship to quay and vice versa. It is essentially just a mast and a swinging boom which allows a load to be lifted and moved sideways. A refinement of this was developed using two derricks, one on each side of the vessel at each hatch. One derrick plumbed over the hatch square while the other was set over the shore. By connecting the two cargo wires together to a hook, cargo could be lifted quickly from the ship and swung across to the shore without moving the derrick booms themselves, which were fixed in place. This rig, called 'union purchase', was very efficient for the bulk load or discharge of bagged or baled goods. While there are some improved modern versions of derricks in use, they have largely been replaced by cranes or gantries on modern vessels.

2.9.2 Deck cranes

Although cranes existed in ships from the beginning of the 20th century, it was not until the late 1960s that more vessels started to operate with them. At the beginning, cranes were expensive compared with derricks, slower to operate, capacity and outreach was limited and they required highly skilled drivers.

With the increase in the carriage of unitised cargo, the practical value of the cranes' accurate spotting ability became more apparent. Thus cranes, often having a capacity of 25–40 tonnes and sufficient outreach to plumb two holds, as well as overside, are now commonly found on ships.

Placed between two hatches, the crane can slew around 360° and so can operate over two hatches without changing the rig. Bulk carrier cranes are often now fitted with grabs and are lashed down on the main deck when not in use.

Heavy-lift ships are, as the name suggests, fitted with much higher capacity cranes than are typically found on most vessels. Cranes of 100 tonnes or more lifting capacity are common and it is not unusual to find ships with cranes capable of lifting well over 1,000 tonnes. The record for capacity is constantly being broken but now comfortably exceeds 3,000 tonnes. Ships' cranes can sometimes operate in tandem, with two cranes being used with a lifting beam to lift a single heavy or awkward load.

Heavy-lift ships are fitted with much higher capacity cranes than are typically found on most vessels

2.9.3 Gantry cranes

Certain types of container and ro-ro ships and barge carriers are equipped with travelling, portable gantry cranes which straddle the full width of the ship and move along the weather deck on rails situated outboard of the hatch coamings.

Such gantries can only be effectively employed in full-form ships with extensive parallel body because the rails on which they run must be parallel with each other.

The hoist can be slewed to port and starboard and plumb over any part of the area under the gantry, and with the gantry being able to move fore and aft, all of the weather deck can be utilised for stowing cargo. Once the cargo (for example, a container) has been lifted clear of the deck, it is either discharged onto a trailer on the quay or placed on a trailer on board and driven off the ship via a ramp.

Containers are usually handled by shore terminal equipment but gantry cranes can be seen occasionally, either in large ships as an interim measure while port facilities are still being developed or in smaller ships for self-sufficiency when operating in less well-equipped ports.

2.9.4 Self-discharging equipment

Cranes and gantries are not the only equipment carried to facilitate discharge. With greater specialisation of vessels for particular commodities or trades, a range of highly individual systems have been created to discharge bulk cargoes into dedicated shore installations. These include conveyor systems, elevators based on Archimedes screws and suction systems.

2.9.5 Cargo Pumps

Most large tanker vessels have a simple system of three pumps and three lines providing the vessel with three totally segregated cargo systems but which can be interconnected through crossover valves when carrying a single homogenous grade of cargo. The pumps will be situated at the bottom of a pump room just forward of the engine room and the pumps will draw cargo from their own bottom line or from other lines through a series of crossovers in the pump room. The cargo will be pumped up to the deck through three top lines and along the deck to the manifold area, where it will be delivered to the manifolds on both sides for going ashore.

Smaller tankers and product tankers may have a different arrangement of pumps and associated piping and manifolds. Here, each individual cargo tank will have its own in-tank submerged cargo pump called a deep well pump as the suction at the bottom is in a small well at the bottom of the tank. This means that the cargo tank can be emptied completely during discharge. The pumps are driven by electrical or hydraulic power from the deck above and the cargo is pumped up a pipe to the deck and will be led to its own manifold so allowing more flexibility with the number of different types or grades of cargo that can be carried.

2.10 RO-RO ACCESS EQUIPMENT

2.10.1 Ramps – bow/stern doors

As mentioned earlier, the characteristic features of ro-ro vessels are the ramps. Ramps are used externally to convey wheeled vehicles between the quay and the ship and internally to provide access from deck to deck. External ramps can take three forms:

- axial bow and stern ramps;
- angled quarter ramps;
- slewing ramps.

Internal ramps can either be fixed or moveable, serving two or more decks.

An axial stern ramp can also act as a stern door where the ramp is short. Alternatively, when the axial ramp is long, then a separate watertight door is used, closing prior to the ramp being raised. Bow openings allow access to cargo spaces through the forward end of the ship and there are two types commonly in use: bow visors and bow clamshell doors. A bow visor is a portion of the ship's bow which is hinged at the weather deck level and is raised upwards when entry is required. A separate inner watertight door is provided along with an axial ramp.

The twin bow clamshell doors are located in the plating around the stem and are hinged to open outwards from the centreline. The operation, sealing and securing arrangements are similar to that of a bow visor and also have an internal watertight door and axial ramp.

The characteristic features of ro-ro vessels are the ramps

2.10.2 Internal ramps and lifts

In ships with several vehicle decks, internal fixed or moveable ramps are used as less space is wasted. As an alternative to ramps for transferring vehicles from one deck to another, elevators or lifts are employed.

The advantages of elevators over ramps are:

- they require less internal space;
- cargo can be stowed on them.

Disadvantages of elevators over ramps are:

- positioning of elevators within a ship must be carefully chosen;
- they are more complicated in terms of electrical and mechanical equipment and hydraulics;
- if too close together when serving different decks, manoeuvring space is likely to become restricted;
- they have interrupted cycles of operation unlike ramps which can be used continuously.

There are various forms of elevators:

Wire-operated – which is the simplest form. These elevators can have a lifting capacity of approximately 50 tonnes. The overall cycle to load a vehicle, lower, discharge and rise again would be about three minutes.

Chain-operated – uses heavy roller chains to lift its platform. This type of elevator can provide a weathertight means of closing the deck when stowed at its upper limit.

Scissor lifts – have a platform supported by a system of levers and hydraulic ramps. They do not need guides and are stowed in the double bottoms of vessels. The upper openings must therefore have a separate hatchcover to close.

2.10.3 Side loaders

Side loaders, side doors or side ports are found in some ro-ro vessels and frequently on reefer ships, and their purpose is to augment the main cargo access areas.

Side doors are most useful on a vessel when its draught remains fairly constant. It would be no use to have side doors on a ship where its draught varies greatly and the doors at times are below quay level or way above. There are numerous designs of side doors and the design depends on the type of vessel and cargo expected to be carried. Forklifts are used to convey cargo to the door for loading, then it is transferred to the hold by another forklift working inside the vessel.

- Side-swinging door is hydraulically operated. It opens outwards and stows along the ship's side.

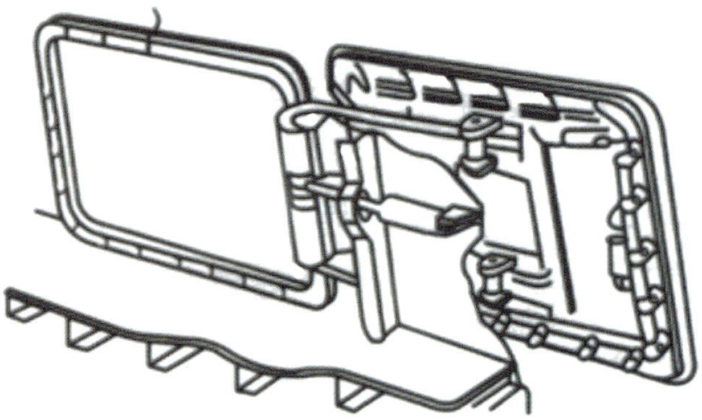

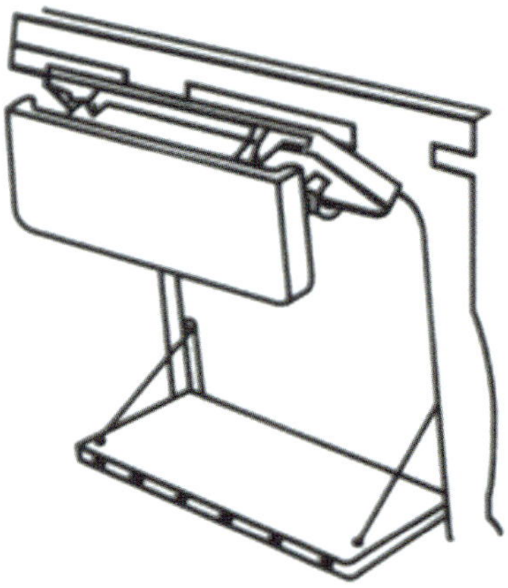

- Upward-folding door is usually supplied with a loading platform.
- Side door – hatchcover has the benefit of being able to handle cargo that was too high for the previous design.
- Side port conveyor and elevators facilitate the transfer of cargo to the lower deck.
- Side door/ramp for forklift trucks has an external loading platform so forklift trucks can drive up ramps and place cargo on board.
- Side door/ramp for ro-ro operation comes in two or three sections and, when folded, becomes a weathertight door. Side ramps are used mainly in car carriers and vessels that use trailers or forklift trucks to stow directly.

Chapter 3

Registration and classification

3.1 REGISTRATION

All ships, regardless of type and purpose, have to be registered as belonging somewhere in the world. As a ship will spend most of its life in international waters, trading between nations, it cannot be said to belong automatically to a particular country in the same way as a factory or other similar static plant. However, a ship cannot be stateless. It has to belong to one particular country to be subject to that country's laws, which should incorporate the various international conventions for ships and, in time of difficulty, to be able to claim the protection of that country. Within that country the vessel will be registered at a particular port, the Port of Registry, which is an important item of information in a ship's details.

The United Nations Convention on the Law of the Sea 1982 (UNCLOS) requires every ship to sail under one flag according to article 92, and also, under article 91, confers a right to every country, whether littoral or landlocked, to have ships flying its flag.

If a country exercises this right, it must also assume an obligation to ensure that the ships are subject to its effective jurisdiction and control under article 94. This means that the country may offer a workable environment for ship operators, for instance, in the following areas:

- fiscal regimes, such as tax exemption, foreign exchange controls and fees;
- legal regimes which include limitation of liability, mortgage laws and litigation laws;
- ownership requirements;
- bilateral or multilateral agreements which accord special rights to its ships, which might include cargo-sharing, taxation and right of entry;
- manning requirements, nationality, recognition of certificates, manning scale and wage scales.

More onerously, it also means that the country must ensure that:

- the ship is subject to its exclusive jurisdiction on the high seas;
- it has jurisdiction under its internal law over each ship and its Master, officers and crew in respect of administrative, technical and social matters concerning the ship.

It is therefore in pursuance of this obligation that a flag country has laws and regulations covering:

- standards of construction, equipment and survey of its ships;
- the manning of ships, labour conditions and the training of crews;
- safe navigation of ships;
- reduction and control of marine pollution;
- investigation of casualties involving its ships.

A significant amount of influence in connection with ship registration is exercised by the International Maritime Organization (IMO), which is part of the United Nations, with its headquarters in London. It is responsible for regulating the use of the seas by the agreement of international conventions. Its main activities relate to safety at sea, protection against pollution and the settlement of international law of the sea disputes.

However, the provisions under UNCLOS are of a general nature. UNCLOS also provides that there must be a genuine link between the ship and the flag country but is silent on what constitutes the link.

The United Nations Convention on the Conditions for the Registration of Ships, which was adopted in 1986, was intended to fill the vacuum left by UNCLOS, but it has yet to come into force and has so far attracted only 14 of the 40 countries needed to have it ratified. It is intended to lay down the obligations that a flag country must assume in relation to the registration of ships in that country. Its main provisions are as follows:

- it applies only to self-propelled seagoing ships of 500grt and above, which are used in international seaborne trade for the transport of goods or passengers;
- the flag country must have an adequate and competent maritime administration and shall implement applicable international rules and standards such as those of the IMO and the International Labour Organization (ILO);
- owners or operators are adequately identifiable for the purpose of ensuring their full accountability;
- a country of registration has an option to comply with either the provisions on ownership or manning or with both.

  On ownership – a flag country must provide in its law and regulations appropriate provisions for participation by that country or its nationals as owners of ships flying its flag or in the ownership of such ships and for the level of such participation.

  On manning – a country of registration shall observe the principle that a satisfactory part of the complement consisting of officers and crew of ships flying its flag be nationals or people domiciled or lawfully in permanent residence in that country, either on a ship, company or fleet basis;
- a country of registration must ensure that the shipowning company or its subsidiary company or its principal place of business is established within its territory. Otherwise there must be a representative or management person who shall be a national of that country;
- a country may register vessels chartered-in by a charterer in that country in conformity with the convention.

In 2005, Liberia was the last signature added to the convention and the only one of the 14 to have a significant number of ships sailing under its flag. It is therefore unlikely that the convention will come into force at any time in the immediate future.

3.1.1 Registering a ship

To register a ship, the new owner needs to produce evidence of title. For a newbuilding, title to ownership is proved through a builder's certificate or, in the case of a secondhand vessel, a bill of sale issued by the former owner. A British bill of sale form, XS 79A, is often used for ship transfers between international corporations, even if no British company is involved. Also used is the all-purpose BIMCO bill of sale form. For sales between individuals or partnerships there is the British XS 79 form.

The owner, whether a person or a corporation, also needs to show proof of entitlement to register the vessel under the desired flag. For a person, such proof should be merely a matter of providing satisfactory nationality or residential documentation, but company requirements are more involved.

First, it will be necessary to prove the existence and currency of the corporation by providing such documents as a valid certificate of incorporation, and perhaps proof that corporate taxes and fees have been paid up to date.

Second, it is possible that the registrar will want to see a legally attested copy of a resolution, signed by a majority, if not all, of a company's officers or shareholders, to show that agreement has been reached to acquire the ship.

Finally, whoever is claiming to represent the corporation will have to prove their identity, perhaps by producing a power of attorney document that gives them the right to act on the corporation's behalf. The document will spell out the limits of their powers, which will include the power to sell a vessel.

...d be mentioned that although the bill of sale evidences a change of ownership, it does ... guarantee clean title. There is a need for a transcript of registry in a secondhand sale from ...e former owner, which will offer greater security to a buyer of clean title. This transcript will show registered mortgages on the vessel and a buyer's registry will definitely wish to have the original of this before issuing new registration to a buyer on delivery of the vessel.

Registration of merchant ships can be a complicated procedure and there is no margin for error, since it is necessary to act swiftly before a vessel is delivered and to ensure registration is correctly accomplished immediately upon delivery. A prospective owner should thoroughly investigate the requirements of the intended registration authority well before the day of handover. The owner will need to keep that authority informed of the expected date and time of registration and have all the necessary documents prepared well ahead of time. It is far simpler if the transfer of ownership takes place under the same flag. However, there may still be a delay in obtaining approval for the change of ship's name, which has particular consequences when arranging charters, and changing markings for a newly acquired ship. It is unrealistic to arrive at a registrar's office unannounced and unexpected, hoping for immediate attention.

Each maritime country maintains ship registry offices in most of its main commercial centres and ports, often closely linked to customs authorities. If the owner is outside the flag country, then registration can also be arranged through a commercial attaché at the country's consulate or embassy. Such foreign registrations are commonplace, especially for open registry countries where few of the owners are resident. It is also a frequent occurrence in major maritime centres, such as London, which see a high volume of sale and purchase transactions between foreign parties. Nevertheless, if it is necessary to register a ship abroad, even more care should be taken, given the distances and time differentials involved.

Seemingly mundane tasks should not be overlooked. It is important to check that the registrar will permit the use of the chosen name. Most authorities will not permit the use of a name that has already been entered on that country's register of shipping, or even a name that could be confused with an existing entry. It is important to leave enough time for the consulate-based commercial attaché to contact the responsible registrar in his home country to receive authority for the intended use of the new name.

Wherever the registration operation is enacted, each place maintains its own register book and enters the following details of the vessel:

- names and addresses of the owners, and their shareholding if more than one owner;
- details of the vessel, including a brief description of its type, age, builder and dimensions;
- gross and net tonnage;
- record of any mortgages on the ship;
- the vessel's name, its official number (allotted by the registrar), port and date of registry.

Having entered these relevant details in the register, the registrar will issue a certificate of registry containing the basic information above. As this is the owner's evidence of the registration of the ship under the flag of choice, the document must be kept in a safe place aboard the vessel, together with its other trading certification.

3.2 TYPES OF SHIP REGISTRIES

There are, broadly speaking, four types of registries:

- **The traditional or closed registries** – these generally have more stringent criteria for ownership, mainly that only citizens and companies incorporated in the country can qualify. The degree of closeness varies because foreigners can still get in by way of companies unless there are stringent criteria also for company ownership. Examples of such registries are most of the European countries, except the international registries. The original registries still belong to the traditional category.

- **Open registries** – established as a service to the international shipping community. The most notable examples are Liberia and Panama.
- **Offshore or international registries** – these registries are set up by the countries with traditional registries to stem the exodus of ships from their original registries. These are designed to lower the operating costs of owners and some are also designed to attract foreigners. Examples are the Norwegian, Danish and German international registries and the UK Isle of Man registry.
- **Bareboat registries** – these registries allow bareboat-chartered ships to be registered. Examples of countries that allow this form of registration (after the original registration has been suspended) are Germany, Australia, Liberia, Panama and the Philippines.

3.3 CHOOSING A FLAG

In the past, the choice of the country of registration was easy. The owners registered and crewed their ships in the country where they lived and conducted their business. This state of affairs lasted until the 1920s when some US owners found that the high cost of running ships under the US flag, with crew wage levels particularly high, made it impossible for them to compete in the international shipping market. They therefore searched for a country which:

1. would permit a company owned and controlled by non-nationals to operate ships under its flag. Most traditional maritime countries insisted that the owning company was registered, owned and controlled by its own nationals only;
2. would permit the beneficial owners to reside and operate elsewhere and to maintain all accounting and banking operations and keep all profits in a different country;
3. would permit the employment of crew of any nationality and at any wage scale the owners wished. Most countries insist that a significant number of the crew are its own nationals, employed at nationally agreed wage scales;
4. would demand minimal taxation.

They found the country they were looking for in Panama and later, in the 1940s, Liberia. With ships registered under either of these flags, the US owners were able to compete on the international tramp (both dry and tanker) markets and in the non-protected liner runs. In the 1990s, the private company running the Liberian registry had a disagreement with the country's then leader, Charles Taylor, and set up a new operation in the Marshall Islands.

3.3.1 Flag competition

In the same way, traditional European and Japanese tramp owners have found it increasingly difficult to participate in an increasingly competitive shipping market. Whereas it is probably true that a shipowner would, all things being equal, prefer to register their ship under the flag of their own country and crew it with their fellow nationals, increasing labour costs and operational regulations and restrictions have made this economically unfeasible in many cases.

These owners too have taken refuge under the Panamanian, Liberian and Marshall Islands flags as well as others around the world. The three flags mentioned attract business from operators in all corners of the globe and it is fair to say that more than half of the newbuildings delivered each year to the world's leading shipowners will be registered in one or other of these registries.

At the other end of the scale, there are open registries which cater for old and decrepit tonnage that would probably not find acceptance elsewhere. The ships registered under these flags are generally those that give the concept of open registries a bad name. As a consequence, ships under those flags are often singled out for special attention and scrutiny from port state control (PSC) inspectors.

3.3.2 Supporting national flags

Nevertheless, there are several ways in which a national government, if it so wishes, can assist its own national fleet:

- facilitating loans at a low rate of interest;
- assistance with social security payments for the crews;
- preference for the national fleet for government cargoes and for cargoes controlled by the major industrial concerns in the country. Such flag discrimination was particularly apparent in the liner trades during the 1980s and 1990s but active policing of the 40/40/20 UNCTAD Rule has made it almost irrelevant today;
- exclusive employment of national flags in certain protected trades, such as coasting or cabotage;
- advantageous taxation schemes so that profits gained from shipowning activities bear little or no tax.

If a shipowner or ship manager does operate in a country which actively encourages shipowning by its nationals, has domestic wages which enable crews to be employed at competitive salary levels and has a pool of experienced seamen, it will be attractive to register ships under that flag. A good example of such a country is India. Greece encourages its highly entrepreneurial shipowners by permitting them to register the shipowning companies abroad (usually Panama or Liberia) while the ships themselves are registered in Greece – thus combining the best of both worlds.

3.3.3 Changing registry

Failing any active encouragement from its government, many traditional shipowners feel they have no alternative but to register their ships abroad. The choice of registry will be influenced by:

- cost – registration fee and annual tonnage tax;
- acceptability – not every flag is welcomed in every country;
- port state control targeting – some PSC regimes target vessels according to stringent criteria which frequently include the flag.

The shipowners therefore have two choices. They can either use an offshore registry or an open registry.

Offshore registries are established with favourable taxation regimes and flexible employment regulations but retain links to the established maritime country from which they draw the majority of their tonnage. They also demand some commercial presence from the shipowner in the territory.

Examples of these offshore registries are:

Great Britain	Isle of Man and Bermuda
Norway	Norwegian International Ship Register
Netherlands	Netherlands Antilles

Open registries have already been described. They have no connection with established maritime countries and most of them only demand the most cursory presence from shipowners on their territory. As noted, the best-known examples of open registries are Liberia and Panama, both with a large number of ships entered in their registers. There are now many more countries offering similar facilities with varying degrees of success.

In selecting which flag the vessel will fly, the shipowner or ship manager will consider if there are any commercial or political reasons why a particular flag vessel should be used in a particular trade, or whether there are any reasons, political or commercial, why a particular flag vessel should not be used. For example, a Liberian-flagged vessel would be refused entry into Syria and difficulties can be experienced with both Liberian- and Panamanian-flagged vessels in Australia, New Zealand and Scandinavia.

Having selected the country whose flag the vessel will fly, and established, if necessary, the shipowning company there, the owner will apply to have the vessel registered in that country.

This entails the authorities, or more usually an authorised classification society acting on behalf of the authorities of that country, inspecting the vessel:

1. to ensure that the vessel complies with both national and international rules and regulations;
2. to measure the vessel to ascertain its dimensions and gross and net tonnages.

On receipt of all relevant information, and a fee, the authorities will issue:

a) a certificate of registry, confirming that the vessel is registered in that country. It will also give the vessel's official number and radio call sign;

b) international tonnage certificate, giving the gross and net tonnage;

c) licence to operate the vessel's radio station.

The ship is now registered.

Panama has a large number of ships entered in its register

3.4 CLASSIFICATION

The first thing which must be said is that while a ship must be registered it does not, in theory, have to be classed. However, bearing in mind the very nature of classification (that is, an independent check on the condition of the vessel) it is not difficult to see how an unclassified ship will be handicapped in obtaining both insurance and employment. The fact is that the vast majority of shippers and charterers, together with underwriters and P&I Clubs, all insist that the vessel has to be classed.

This independent check is carried out by classification societies, which are autonomous bodies structured in different ways. Some are limited liability companies with shareholders. These include Det Norske Veritas Germanischer Lloyd and Bureau Veritas. Some enjoy an unusual charitable status such as Lloyd's Register and some are state-owned or licensed and include RS, IRS and CCS.

Regardless of the type of corporate structure, classification societies have strong links with shipbuilders and marine underwriters, and employ naval architects, engineers and metallurgists. The majority also have IT specialists who can produce software programs for ship design, strength and stability calculations.

Many classification societies are also delegated with the task of surveying and issuing flag country certificates but it is important to understand that they do this as agents for the country or flag concerned and are acting under its authority and not as direct contractors to the shipowner.

The principal and internationally recognised classification societies are those that are members of the International Association of Classification Societies (IACS), namely:

Members	Symbol
American Bureau of Shipping	ABS
Bureau Veritas	BV
China Classification Society	CCS
Croatian Register of Shipping	CRS
Det Norske Veritas Germanischer Lloyd	DNV GL
Indian Register of Shipping	IRS
Korean Register	KR
Lloyd's Register	LR
Nippon Kaiji Kyokai (Class NK)	NK
Polish Register	PRS
Registro Italiano Navale	RINA
Russian Maritime Register of Shipping	RS

Classification societies draw up detailed specifications of all material used in the construction of ships and rules concerning not only the construction of all equipment on board but also the ship itself. To assist them in enforcing their rules and regulations, they maintain a network of exclusive and part-time surveyors throughout the world.

In April 2006, members of IACS introduced two sets of common structural rules, one for tankers and one for bulk carriers over 150 metres in length. These rules were developed jointly by IACS members after consultation with other interested parties. In effect, all new ships contracted to come into service after 1 April 2006 were to be built to the same rules regardless of which IACS member is going to accept them for classification.

Common structural rules

It has to be said that there was a great deal of scepticism concerning the introduction of the new rules. Some owners complained that they would inflate the cost of new ships, while other owners believed that the rules would not lead to more robust vessels. As with all changes to the status quo, only time will tell which view was correct. Early experience of the new rules has highlighted some differences in the standards between the two ship types in areas that many believe should be common to both types. As a result, IACS has embarked on a programme to harmonise the rules and a new set of common structural rules (CSR) was unanimously adopted at the 69th session of the IACS council meeting held in London in December 2013.

The new rules apply to all oil tankers over 150m in length and bulk carriers over 90m in length contracted for construction on or after 1 July 2015 and became compulsory for newbuilding contracts signed on or after 1 July 2016.

Ship designers will be able to work to one common standard applicable to both ship types with more comprehensive structural analyses, including finite element method (FEM) calculations covering fore and aft parts and new rule checks including new buckling, fatigue and ultimate strength criteria. All this aims to enhance the safety and reliability of the structure.

Following a significant container ship casualty in 2013, the IACS council has also decided to take a proactive approach to structural safety of container ships, following a comprehensive review of existing technical requirements for hull structural design, construction and survey. IACS decided to expand the scope of current IACS unified requirements for post-Panamax container ships. These requirements will cover two important areas: scope of hull girder strength assessment and specific loading cases that will provide more comprehensive safety margins.

Classification societies will consider any vessel as a candidate for classification but not all will be accepted. To ensure acceptance, most owners will opt to have their ship built under survey. For that to happen, and the ship to be awarded the coveted Maltese cross or star mark on its notation, the following sequence of events will take place:

- The plans are scrutinised and, if found satisfactory, will be approved by the society.
- The building of the vessel will be supervised by a surveyor from the society, who will maintain a programme of constant spot checks and examinations to ensure that the rules of the society are being met. They will also ensure that all material used is of a quality approved by the society.
- The final sea trials of the newbuilding will be attended by the surveyor. Provided everything is satisfactory, the vessel will then be formally entered as classed with the society and a certificate of class will be issued.

Occasionally, a shipyard will build vessels speculatively, or a ship started for one customer may be completed for another (for example, in circumstances such as bankruptcy of the first customer), and it may well be that the new owner wants the ship classed with a different classification society. Under such circumstances, the chosen classification society, presented with a half-built or even completed ship, would not classify it as being built under survey. It would insist on inspecting the plans and carrying out a thorough inspection of the ship before accepting it. Ships like this would not be given a cross or star notation.

To maintain its classification, each vessel will have to enter a programme of surveys. This programme will ensure that everything on board the vessel which is material to the safety of the vessel is surveyed in rotation according to a predetermined timetable.

These surveys are scheduled so that every item will have been inspected at the end of a four-year cycle. Once this cycle has been completed satisfactorily the vessel will have completed its first special survey (SS), whereupon the entire cycle of surveys begins all over again. Inserted into this programme is a requirement that the vessel is drydocked twice during the survey cycle.

However, societies give themselves the power to grant an extension of one year; a year of grace in a survey cycle bringing it up to five years in certain cases where warranted by the progress of survey items and the condition of the vessel warrants it.

Special surveys

Although even their own rules may state that the survey cycle is four years, virtually every classification society has extended this to a five-year period. The IMO has accepted this state of affairs, and in most of its documents, special survey intervals are listed as five, 10 or 15 years. In a new development, many classification societies now allow the intermediate surveys to be carried out with the ship afloat provided an underwater inspection is possible, so drydocking may now occur only every five years. Some societies have extended the interval even further to seven-and-a-half years for newly built vessels satisfying certain conditions regarding service and hull coating.

It is also a requirement of classification societies that in the event of any accident happening to the ship or its equipment, a class surveyor must be called in to examine the damage, to advise if the repair has to be done immediately or whether it can be postponed, and, if so, for how long. If a postponement is granted, full details are entered in the vessel's records as a recommendation. The eventual repair will have to be done under the supervision of the class surveyor.

It is normal for a ship, once it has been built under the rules of a particular society, to remain with that society for its life. There is, however, nothing to stop an owner from transferring from one society to another, always providing that the two societies' building rules are compatible and subject to a full survey by the new society. The societies within IACS have a special agreement regarding transfer between themselves known as the transfer of class agreement (TOCA). Under this agreement, ships with overdue surveys or outstanding recommendations will probably not be accepted by the owner's chosen new society.

The classification societies keep full survey records of all ships that they classify. These records will list all the surveys passed with the date during the current cycle, together with all surveys yet to be passed with the dates when they fall due. The records will also list all repairs done under class requirements and all current recommendations for future repairs. Additional certificates are issued in respect of special characteristics such as the ship's ability to carry refrigerated cargo.

These records are of great importance to a potential buyer of any secondhand ship and are usually inspected at quite an early stage in negotiations.

3.4.1 Certification

To trade and, more importantly, to get customs' clearance at each of its ports of call, the vessel will have to maintain and carry on board at all times a complete set of certificates.

Certificate of registry. This is issued by the government of the country whose flag the vessel flies. It is valid until the vessel is sold and states the name of the vessel, its official number, its call sign, its principal dimensions and the name of the owners.

International tonnage certificate. This is issued by the government of the country whose flag the vessel flies, usually from measurements made by an authorised classification society. It is valid until the vessel is sold and it states the vessel's gross registered tonnage (grt) and net registered tonnage (nrt).

Certificate of class. This is issued by the classification society confirming that the vessel is classed by them. If the vessel is equipped for the carriage of refrigerated cargo, the refrigeration installation is certificated separately.

Radio station licence. This is issued in compliance with the International Telecommunication Union Convention to certify the vessel to operate its radio station.

In addition to these four certificates issued during registration as described in the previous section, there are other certificates that are always needed to show the vessel's compliance with international regulations and conventions.

Minimum safe manning certificate. This is issued by the government whose flag the vessel flies and states the minimum number, and appropriate ranks of that number, of crew the vessel can sail with. This is issued based on the type and size of the vessel, and the sophistication of the automation equipment on board.

Loadline certificate. Valid for five years, subject to an annual survey, giving details of the vessel's freeboard measurements.

Safety construction certificate. Valid for five years, subject to an annual inspection and an intermediate survey at either two or three years.

Safety equipment certificate. Valid for five years, subject to annual survey and intermediate survey as above, confirming that the vessel's lifesaving equipment (such as lifeboats and liferafts, pyrotechnics, firefighting equipment and emergency radios) is all in good working order and meets international regulations. The surveyor will also want to examine the vessel's charts and nautical publications such as pilot books, lists of lights and nautical almanacs, or its electronic chart display and information system (ECDIS) and backup arrangements if used instead.

Safety radio certificate. Valid for five years, subject to an annual validation survey. The first page is the certificate confirming that the vessel's radio and radar equipment meet international regulations. The other pages give the details of the equipment required and available.

International Oil Pollution Prevention certificate (IOPP). Valid for five years, subject to an annual survey and an intermediate survey at either two or three years confirming that the vessel is equipped with machinery to remove oil from ballast and/or bilge water being pumped overside.

International Safety Management certificate (ISM). This shows compliance with the ISM Code. This is dealt with in greater detail later.

International Ship Security certificate (ISSC). This shows compliance with the International Ship and Port Facility Security Code. This is dealt with in greater detail later.

The four 'safety' certificates above are required under the IMO Safety of Life at Sea Convention (SOLAS). The IOPP certificate relates to the MARPOL Convention. All these are usually issued by an authorised classification society on behalf of the government whose flag the vessel flies. The surveys needed to issue or renew these certificates are totally independent of the classification surveys.

Lifting appliance certificate. If the vessel is going to load or discharge with its own gear, this gives details of the cargo gear survey and the relevant safe working loads.

Ship sanitation certificate. Previously called the deratisation certificate, this confirms that the vessel is free from all traces of rats. It is issued by a port health authority and is valid for six months.

Dangerous goods certificate. This shows that the vessel meets the requirements and gives details of the separations available for the carriage of dangerous goods.

Grain book. If the vessel is going to load bulk grain it must carry a book giving details of the vessel's stability calculations when loading bulk grain, and which is authenticated by the government of the country whose flag the vessel flies.

Deadweight scale. This scale, often included in the ship's capacity plan, shows the immersion of the vessel, that is, draught at any degree of loading.

International ballast water certificate. Valid for five years, subject to an annual survey and an intermediate survey at either two or three years. Ships also need to have a ballast water management record book.

3.5 PORT STATE CONTROL

In 1978, following a series of high profile accidents, the IMO produced the 1978 Protocol that amended the annex to the 1974 SOLAS Convention. Regulation 19 of the amended annex was subtitled simply 'Control' and introduced the concept of port state control. Control provisions allow contracting governments to inspect ships of other contracting states if there are clear grounds for believing that the ship and its equipment do not substantially comply with the requirements of the Convention.

Earlier that year, a group of western European countries, equally concerned about substandard ships, was about to introduce the Hague Memorandum. This document was designed to bring about a joint effort to enforce provisions contained in the ILO Convention. However, following the IMO action, the European countries drew up a new document incorporating the new provisions of the 1978 SOLAS Protocol.

Fourteen nations signed the document entitled *'The Paris Memorandum of Understanding on Port State Control'* (Paris MOU) in January 1982. Six months later, in July 1982, the document came into force and the first regional group aimed at ridding the seas of unsafe substandard vessels was formed.

Today, there are many regional port state control groupings covering the majority of world ports. PSC inspectors make random inspections of ships calling at their ports to check compliance with international conventions and gauge the vessel's threat to safety and the environment. Ships that fail an inspection will usually be required to rectify deficiencies before being allowed to put back to sea. Some deficiencies may be deferred until the next port of call.

3.6 NATIONAL INSPECTIONS

The authorities of the vessel's flag country will reserve the right to board a vessel flying its flag and hold a full inspection along the lines of the port state control survey. The more careful register will maintain an active worldwide network of surveyors to ensure moderately frequent inspections of the vessels which fly its flag. Some outsource this to classification societies.

3.7 CONDITION SURVEYS AND INSPECTIONS

P&I Clubs are now conducting their own independent condition surveys of vessels over 10 years old entered with them. They have no power to stop the vessel but, should they note any deficiencies, they may limit the vessel's P&I cover until the deficiency is corrected. For example, if they note that the vessel's hatches are not watertight they will limit the cover for cargo claims until the hatches are repaired. This may invalidate the charter party, which requires the vessel to be seaworthy and cargo worthy.

Increasingly, in recent years, charterers are requiring their own inspections to be carried out which extend far beyond the more customary hold or tank inspections. This is particularly the case with the major oil companies.

There exists the Ship Inspection Report (SIRE) system which records ship inspections. The SIRE inspection system was started by the Oil Companies International Marine Forum (OCIMF) and is a unique tanker risk assessment tool of value to charterers, ship operators, terminal operators and government bodies concerned with ship safety. Charterers can investigate the condition of ships before accepting them as suitable for chartering. The consulting of this system by charterers has led to an astonishing increase in the quality of vessels, their management and crews. Large dry bulk charterers have also begun to rely on SIRE reports.

3.8 OTHER SURVEYS

There are several other surveys that relate to the commercial operation of the vessel.

On- and off-hire surveys – when a vessel is operating on time charter, the owner and charterer will wish to agree the extent of any damage, particularly in the cargo areas at the time of commencement and again on completion of the charter.

Bunker surveys – also in the case of time charter, the owners and charterers must agree the quantity of bunkers on board.

Pre-loading surveys – all voyage charters require the vessel to be in a clean condition to receive the cargo but many charters today provide that this shall be to the satisfaction of the charterer's surveyor.

Vetting surveys – carried out by inspectors to ensure that tankers are suitable for a certain trade in terms of quality.

Draught surveys – made generally before and on completion of loading or discharging, to confirm cargo quantity loaded or discharged.

Port state control inspections – carried out by government-appointed inspectors to ensure that vessels comply with certain standards as laid down in the Paris MOU.

Terminal inspections – carried out by terminal inspectors to ensure that the vessel is of the correct type and quality to discharge at its facility.

3.9 CONCLUSION

Safety and efficiency must be at the top of a professional shipowner's list of priorities. The condition of a ship will reflect the manager's attitude to these important factors. A ship manager should treat all surveys and inspections as an opportunity of showing how careful and attentive they are to the needs of running a safe ship and not as a game of 'cat and mouse' to see how much can be hidden from a surveyor and got away with. Likewise, a professional ship manager should lose no opportunity to motivate the crew in the constant battle to maintain the very highest degree of safety.

3.10 ISM CODE

The International Management Code for the Safe Operation of Ships and for Pollution Prevention (ISM Code) is also part of the SOLAS Convention. The background to the introduction of the Code was a series of very high profile maritime losses during the 1980s and early 1990s. In particular, the total loss of the Dover-Zeebrugge ferry *Herald of Free Enterprise* in 1987 with a large passenger death toll was almost entirely the result of a lack of safety management procedures. This was followed shortly after by the loss of the ferry *Estonia* in the Baltic and, although there was more doubt about the proximate cause, safety management was certainly a factor. There were other ferry incidents, not only in Europe but around the world.

However, although many of the total losses that occurred during this period were less high profile, a significant number were bulk carriers seriously damaged or lost, sometimes without trace of vessel or crew. These were mostly large bulk carriers but there were also some new and well-maintained container ships and a maiden voyage barge carrier. In some of these cases, there was little doubt that a lack of maintenance played a large part in the tragedy. In particular, there were failures of side shell plating owing to corrosion, particularly in the areas of side shell frames. In other cases, the losses were because of failures in risk recognition and subsequent management.

3.10.1 Objectives

The stated objectives of the ISM Code are set out in the preamble, paragraph 1:

'The purpose of this code is to provide an international standard for the safe management and operation of ships and for pollution prevention.'

Section 1.2 (objectives):

1.2.1 The objectives of the code are to ensure safety at sea, prevention of human injury or loss of life and avoidance of damage to the environment, in particular to the marine environment and to property.

1.2.2 Safety management objectives of the company should, *inter alia:*

- 1.2.2.1 provide for safe practices in ship operation and a safe working environment;
- 1.2.2.2 establish safeguards against all identified risks, and
- 1.2.2.3 continuously improve safety management skills of personnel ashore and aboard ships, including preparing for emergencies related both to safety and environmental protection.

1.2.3 The safety management system should ensure:

- 1.2.3.1 compliance with mandatory rules and regulations; and
- 1.2.3.1 that applicable codes, guidelines and standards recommended by the organisation, classification societies and maritime industry organisations are taken into account.

3.10.2 ISM and crew training

There is nothing new in shipowners having to employ competent crew. However, the ISM Code now requires that records of the recruitment of key personnel be kept and that training records are up to date. Crew training is a requirement of the International Convention on Standards in Training, Certification and Watchkeeping for Seafarers (STCW), which is another IMO convention relating to training standards.

In respect of the Master, section 6.1 of the code states:

'The company should ensure that the Master is properly qualified for command, fully conversant with the company's safety management systems (SMS) and given the necessary support so that the Master's duties can be safely performed.'

There is a further requirement that senior ships' officers should have a working knowledge of the code's requirements, while the crew must certainly be aware of the basic safety drill requirements.

The ship must carry on board all relevant documents necessary to comply with the code. These must include an ISM manual and a record of training in safety management.

3.10.3 ISM and the charterer

Actual compliance with the code is the responsibility of the shipowner and the ship manager to whom the owner has entrusted the vessel. There are, however, some significant implications for the charterer.

The introduction of the code was intended to create a new culture of safety at sea, whereby accidents, and particularly pollution incidents, would not be tolerated. When an accident happens in high profile waters, the public want someone made accountable. In the case of the loss of the tanker *Erika* off the coast of France in 2000, much of the blame for the serious oil pollution of the French holiday beaches attached to the charterer, the French oil company *TotalFinaElf,* because, unlike the owners, it had a very obvious public image.

3.10.4 Implementation of the ISM Code

Initially, the major maritime countries, including the USA, members of the EU, Norway, Australia, Canada and Japan, embraced the code wholeheartedly while others, especially some minor maritime countries in the Far East, were less enthusiastic. More recently, the doubters have seen the benefits and today, the code is enforced by most flag and port countries.

3.10.5 Procedures

The code requires formal procedures for all activity relating to the safe management and operation of the vessel, both in the offices ashore and in the ship afloat. In the same way as in other quality systems, the procedures need to be fully documented. While documented ship and safety management systems can be bought off the shelf, these will still need to be substantially tailored to the requirements of the individual company, the types of vessels it operates and even the trade routes with which it is involved. The best practice is to write the procedures in-house so that they reflect the best actual practice used in the company. All employees, both ashore and afloat, need to be inducted into the system, although the degree of involvement will vary greatly with seniority and areas of responsibility.

The ISM Code recognises that all ship-operating companies differ in their organisation and size and so does not seek to lay down specific tasks. It does, however, require all companies to nominate a designated person ashore (DPA), who will be the link between each ship and the highest authority within the company. In a very large company there might be many DPAs or a single person may cover the role. Usually, the DPA will be a senior superintendent, but other than their role as the link with the directors or owners of the company, the ISM Code itself is silent on what experience is needed to perform the task. According to some legal opinion, it is not necessary for the DPA to even have seagoing experience.

An important aspect of any management system is identifying and reporting non-conformities. This is particularly the case with accidents, near misses and navigational discrepancies which may be seen to bring into question a particular officer's competence. These may occur because the system is not being followed, in which case corrective action needs to be taken to prevent reoccurrence. However, non-conformance is often the result of a badly written procedure which does not reflect the reality of the activity. In such cases, the procedure needs to be changed to reflect the reality. Reporting and investigation of non-conformance is at the heart of systems' improvement.

When a safety management system has been approved for the first time, the company is issued with a document of compliance (DOC) for its whole system and, as each ship is audited and approved, it is issued with a safety management certificate (SMC). The ship's SMC becomes invalid immediately the ship is either sold or the management of it is entrusted to a new manager.

3.10.5.1 The role of the DPA

As stated above, the DPA is responsible for being the link with the ship and shore and will have direct access to very senior management. They shall be properly resourced and supported. The role is important as it is key in the development and implementation of the SMS within the company so as to ensure safety at sea, the prevention of injury and death and avoiding environmental damage, in particular the marine one.

The DPA occupies a unique position in the company, so does not report to any particular department head, which prevents their role being subordinate to that department's requirements.

They can intervene at any point to stop something happening or ensure that something does happen if, in their judgement, this is necessary for the proper operation of the SMS.

Although this is not mandatory, the person chosen to be the DPA should preferably have seagoing experience as a certified ship's officer and at a senior rank. They should have operational experience in ship management at a senior level and some shore-based qualification relevant to the role and the marine industry. As their role will be to report direct to senior management, they should have the necessary skills to do this while having a hands-on attitude to dealing with the officers and crew who look to them for guidance. They should have a good technical or operational knowledge of safety management and appropriate knowledge of shipping and shipboard practices. They should be familiar with carrying out an audit of the safety management system.

As their responsibilities include the development of the SMS, they should be fully familiar with the ISM Code and should be able to determine if the SMS meets the requirements. They should be able to assess its effectiveness by a process of audits and reviews and keep a proper record of this. They should fully endorse the safe practices recommended by the different organisations such as Class, IMO and other international bodies and see that these have been included within the SMS.

They should also analyse information and data from accidents, hazardous situations, near misses and incidents to apply the lessons learned from these.

- Communication and implementation of safety and environmental policies.
- Carry out internal audits of both the office and the vessels on a six-monthly basis or more frequently if required to ensure that, through visits to the vessels and the offices, all personnel are following the requirements of the SMS and are monitoring this.
- Arrange external audits by Flag, Class or recognised organisation (RO) annually or at specified intervals.
- Follow up on shipboard recordings of safety audit reports and familiarisation with recording these.
- Monitoring and periodic tests of ships' safety equipment.
- Organise safety and training meetings.
- Ensure that orders for spares and stores for SMS are properly followed up.
- Review Masters' reports and internal audits.
- Continuous monitoring and review of the SMS.
- Reporting and analysis of non-conformities, accidents and hazardous occurrences.
- Make appropriate revisions to the SMS and ensure that adequate resources and shore-based support is provided to achieve all the above.

3.10.5.2 Documents

Every vessel should have the following documents to show compliance with the ISM.

An SMC (Safety Management Certificate) and a copy of the DOC (Document of Compliance) appropriate for the type of vessel are mandatory and they signify that the management system for the vessel and for the company meets the requirements of the ISM Code and the vessel is operated under its precepts.

The SMC and DOC are issued by the flag state or a by an organisation recognised by the government or by another contracting government at the request of the flag state administration. They are issued under the authority of the IMO.

The SMC will be issued to the ship by the flag state after verifying that the manager and ship operate in accordance with approved safety management systems. It is valid for five years but with an intermediate verification after approximately 2.5 years to ensure the vessel is still compliant or more frequently if there is reason to do so as, for example, a number of reported non-conformities. The SMC loses validity if the vessel is sold.

The DOC will be issued to every manager whose SMS has been audited and complies with the ISM Code. It will be issued by the flag state or by an organisation recognised by Flag. A copy of the DOC will be kept on board for production by the master. It is valid for five years with annual verification to show that it remains compliant. A DOC is required for each type of vessel the manager operates. If it has a mixed fleet of tankers, gas tankers and chemical tankers it would require three DOCs, one for each type.

In addition to the above, the vessel and the manager will need to be able to show the following during a verification and inspection to show that the SMS is in operation as envisaged.

Records of audits. As it says, a complete record of the audits, which should show objective evidence that the SMS is being implemented by the shipping company and its vessels. The objective evidence is based on observations, measurements or tests that are made during an audit and which can be verified.

Records of non-conformities. When objective evidence indicates that a specific requirement stated by the SMS is not being fulfilled, it is considered that a situation of non-conformity has occurred. An audit or inspection may reveal a number of minor non-conformities which will require remedying in a short time period. A major non-conformity is an extremely serious situation which poses a serious threat to the safety of personnel, the ship or the environment. It will require immediate corrective action to be taken by the ship's management. It indicates a major lapse in effective and systematic implementation of the ISM Code.

Details of officers' training. This will be as required by STCW and all officers will need to be fully certificated as necessary; their certificates must be revalidated at regular intervals.

Continuous synoptic record (CSR). A form of logbook that stays with the vessel for its whole life, and records all changes of owner, class, flag, name, ISM, etc. A ship must keep its copy of the whole CSR aboard whatever changes, even its management, and the original documents must not be modified, deleted, erased or defaced. It will always be inspected by auditors and port state inspectors

3.10.6 ISM audit

The object of the code is safety management coupled with continuous improvement. There has to be an audit trail to prove this and the management office is audited annually by external auditors authorised by the flag country. Each vessel must be audited twice every five years. Between these external audits the managers must undertake internal audits to ensure that there is continuing compliance and must retain the documentary evidence of the internal audits. The audits have to show that what is written in the procedures actually takes place in practice and that there is evidence to support this.

Every aspect of these external and internal audits must be in accordance with the ISM manual.

Shipboard and office procedures are linked so that, for example, Masters' or chief engineers' reports become quality records to support the vessel maintenance which the office has planned or has ordered.

3.10.7 ISM and port state control

The proper knowledge and application by the ship's command of the vessel's safety management systems is subject to port state control inspection. The inspector's role in this case is not to cancel the vessel's safety management certificate (that is a matter for the flag country), but the ship can be detained until any breaches of the SMS are corrected.

As one wise commentator has observed: 'Safety is a culture but if you think safety is expensive, try accidents!'

3.11 THE ISPS CODE

The full name is the International Ship and Port Facility Security Code. This is a part of the SOLAS Convention devised by the IMO as a response to concerns over security and terrorism.

The ISPS Code is very much a reaction to the terrorist attacks in New York in September 2001 but it does include elements of two other problems, piracy and stowaways, that have been of concern for many years.

As the full name suggests, the ISPS Code works on two levels: ships over 500gt and ports. Governments and maritime administrations have appointed recognised security organisations (RSOs) to certify the security arrangements that have been made in ports, on ships and in the shore offices of shipping companies. Exactly what sort of organisation can become an RSO is entirely at the discretion of national governments. Within the UK, only the Maritime and Coastguard Agency (MCA) has the power to vet ships, but many flag countries have delegated the work to classification societies.

To comply with the code, ships and ports have to be subjected to a risk assessment, after which a security plan is drawn up. The plan is then reviewed by the RSO and, after a successful inspection and audit of the port or ship, a certificate is issued. On a practical level, both ports and ships operate on a three-stage security alert with the precautions taken dependent on the security threat assessed. This means that, for the most part, both operate at the lowest level, Level 1, until some intelligence received makes a higher level desirable.

Ship operators are obliged to nominate a company security officer ashore who is responsible for implementing the code throughout the company and its fleet. Each ship must have a ship security officer responsible for implementing the approved ship security plan on board. Specialist security training should be given to any person being given special security roles.

As well as the duties for some staff, ships also have to install some extra equipment. Under the terms of the code all vessels must be fitted with a ship security alert system (SSAS) which can be used to send an alarm to shore if the ship's security officer believes it is warranted.

In addition, a system of daily reporting has to be initiated, although virtually all efficient ship operators have done this as a matter of routine in any case. As with all international regulations, there are some countries that feel that the ISPS Code does not go far enough and have introduced other measures. For example, the USA requires all ships destined to discharge at a US port to lodge a manifest of cargo to be loaded 24 hours before it is put on the ship at the foreign port. Any carrier which loads cargo that was not included in the manifest risks being denied entry to US ports and may have to return to the loading port with all cargo remaining on board. It is also likely that they will be treated as a non-compliant ship for future calls to US ports.

The USA has also ended the block visa system whereby all members of a ship's crew would be covered under a single visa and it now requires each seafarer to apply for their own visa. Because of the lengthy procedures this involves, many crew members are not able to obtain a visa and are, in effect, confined to their ship while in US ports.

As well as the ISPS Code, another reaction of the IMO to the growing threat of terrorism was the establishment of long-range identification and tracking (LRIT) of ships. This was approved by the IMO in resolution MSC202(81) which amends chapter V of SOLAS, regulation 19-1, and binds all governments that have contracted to the IMO.

Ships affected by LRIT (all passenger vessels and cargo ships over 300gt) must report their position to their flag administration at least four times a day. This is generally done using the ship's satellite communications systems set to automatically make the reports. The information is stored and may be released by the flag country to any government requesting details of a ship's movements.

3.12 THE IEEC

IEEC stands for International Energy Efficiency Certificate. It is a newly introduced certificate that is mandatory for all vessels of 400gt and above. Contrary to most statutory certificates, the IEEC is not connected to a survey scheme and does not have an expiry date. For new ships, the certificate will state both the attained and required energy efficiency design index (EEDI) of the vessel.

For new ships, an IEEC is to be issued at the vessel's initial survey, provided the EEDI has been verified for applicable vessels, and the ship's energy efficiency management plan (SEEMP) is on board. For existing ships, the IEEC is to be issued on the first intermediate or renewal survey for the International Air Pollution Prevention (IAPP) Certificate, whichever comes first, on or after 1 January 2013, provided the SEEMP is on board.

Additionally, the IEEC must be reissued in the case of a major conversion. The latter applies to new ships and the IMO has ruled that existing ships need an IEEC after any type of major conversion.

Chapter 4

Marine insurance

4.1 THE MANAGEMENT OF RISK

One way of managing risk is by purchasing insurance, by which means the risk is transferred away from the assured allowing it to operate without the burden of a catastrophic financial loss had it been uninsured. This in turn enhances commerce by allowing entrepreneurs to expand their activities, as part of the financial risk is now spread between them and insurers.

Risk management is a fundamental tool for both assureds and insurers in identifying and evaluating their exposure and thus trying to minimise the same by active steps within the assured's operations.

Alleviating the loss by spreading it among other parties, such as the insurers, was the original notion under Rhodian law, the forefather of modern general average, as it introduced the notion of sharing the loss among the participants of the common adventure, being the first insurance-related principle in recorded history.

Today, insurance cover is usually arranged with an insurance company or mutual association. In shipping in particular, several underwriters may share the risk of insuring one vessel due to the risk profile, insurer's appetite and values involved.

A ship operator, be it the operator, owner or charterer, has to consider the types of risks, including loss of or damage to a vessel's hull and machinery, third-party protection and indemnity risks and a number of ancillary risks such as war risks, loss of hire, cost of strikes, delay and kidnap for ransom among others.

Insurances for hull, third-party liabilities and their ancillary risks can be placed through many channels, including but not limited to:

- syndicated markets, in particular through Lloyd's of London;
- subscription through commercial insurance companies and/or Lloyd's syndicates;
- mutual associations including hull but mostly alluding to P&I Clubs;
- fixed premium P&I Clubs;
- general average, where the risk of a specific venture (voyage) may be shared by those involved under certain circumstances.

4.2 HULL AND MACHINERY INSURANCE

This cover provides compensation for loss of or damage to a ship arising out of insured perils under the hull policy taken out by the assured. The policies reflect the Marine Insurance Act (MIA) 1906. The listed perils focus on covering the main marine perils arising, as described below, and also naming in particular perils that the market has seen have led to losses throughout the centuries.

'"Maritime perils" means the perils consequent on, or incidental to, the navigation of the sea, that is to say, perils of the seas, fire, war perils, pirates, rovers, thieves, captures, seizures, restraints, and detainments of princes and peoples, jettisons, barratry, and any other perils, either of the like kind or which may be designated by the policy.' (Marine Insurance Act 1906, s 3(c))

As an example, we can refer to the most commonly used hull policy in the market, namely, the Institute Time Clauses Hulls (ITCH) 1983, whereby, under clause 6, it lists the perils that the policy will cover the assured for and which can be seen are the ones the act above refers to. This policy is the widest, with various others available for other options depending on the vessel type, waters navigated and adventure undertaken – for example, a voyage to the demolition yard, justifying a lesser cover than usual. Following this policy, the market has introduced various other options offering broadly similar cover. The latest is the International Hull Clauses (IHC) 2003, which is the market's effort to encapsulate all the existing clauses most commonly used in marine policies to date and to add new clauses that reflect principles and developments that under older versions are added through ancillary clauses and thus do not form part of the main body of the policy wording, such as under the 1983 version.

It is important to bear in mind that, apart from the London Institute Clauses, there are several different versions such as the American Institute Hull Clauses, the Nordic, the German DTV and various others less widely used. Some large shipping companies have been able to negotiate modifications to the standard conditions. It is important that ship operators are aware of the various types of cover available in the market and of the main differences between them. It should also be remembered that London conditions are subject to the UK Marine Insurance Act of 1906, in part amended by the Insurance Act 2015 as discussed below.

In this chapter we shall be using either of ITCH 1983 or IHC 2003 and will identify them accordingly.

Most hull and machinery insurance covers are arranged or placed by insurance brokers. Especially in the case of Lloyd's of London, only an accredited broker is permitted to place business. It is the broker's job to find the best suitable deal for their client based on their client's demands and needs. It is normal practice for a large risk such as a fleet of ships or an FPSO (floating production storage and offloading) or an expensive specialist vessel to be spread widely over the market, since each participating market has a limited capacity to offer for each risk (line size). Also, the risk appetite may not justify each market's commitment of their full line, thus making the broker look and find in the market, both Lloyd's and non-Lloyd's, the necessary capacity to cover the risk 100%.

A risk can be exclusive to one broker or it can be split and placed by two or more brokers. This is not ideal as not all brokers have adequate access to markets that want to write the risk or they may want to approach markets that the other placing broker(s) will approach. This is because in an orderly placement, that is, when the client instructs, for example, two brokers, they will ask the brokers to each approach a specific list of markets. Otherwise the client will simply advise two brokers to place their respective order for the risk, for example, 50% of the risk each, and let them compete in the market to find the best carriers/insurers on a first come, first served basis that the market operates under. This leads to confusion and it is not the usual way to do business.

If the client wishes to test their current broker, they can instruct another broker to obtain quotes to compare them with the existing rates and perhaps either ask the incumbent broker to obtain the same, if they are more competitive, or ask the prospective broker to place some or all of the risk. This is the case when the client is not satisfied with the incumbent broker's services but it does not happen lightly as the market may not know this. It will see another broker trying to place the risk and this raises concerns that the client is volatile and may replace the markets under their programme as well as the broker. This is a concern as the new broker may use different markets from the incumbent broker or partly replace some from the programme.

This is not satisfactory, not only because of the loss of business by the markets being replaced but also because they may have paid for losses, thus they would anticipate to be on the programme on renewal and try to make up some of the paid loss by earning the respective premium. The client should also recognise the value of continuity and of building up a good relationship with underwriters in the longer term. This brings advantages such as possible discounted terms and loss payments being paid out quicker than if the client were a new one, where the claims team needs to ascertain how and why the loss arose, which requires time and expense.

4.2.1 Placing the insurance

We briefly saw how a broker deals with an enquiry. We shall also examine how Lloyd's and the London market are structured and expand on the markets and how they operate.

There are various types of market depending on their security and structure. The most notable and famous one is that of Lloyd's of London. The rest are the London markets, as colloquially known, and the international markets.

The Lloyd's market is a market and not an insurance company in its own right. A Lloyd's broker has access to various syndicates, as the insurance companies writing business on Lloyd's paper, or else with Lloyd's security, are called. These syndicates may be strictly Lloyd's syndicates, therefore not having another company outside Lloyd's writing business on non-Lloyd's paper, or they may be Lloyd's syndicates which are part of an insurance group that has Lloyd's and non-Lloyd's companies writing insurance.

For example, we may have XYZ syndicate, identified by its own distinct four-number code such as 1234, while at the same time having a company market XYZ writing business on non- Lloyd's paper.

There are differences between the two, despite both being under the XYZ group of companies. The first is that they are different companies in their own right. This means that they have their own balance sheets and liabilities for the business they write and the liability cannot pass from one to the other.

The next is that a Lloyd's syndicate is supervised by the Lloyd's Corporation as not all insurance companies are eligible to write business as a Lloyd's syndicate. This is because the requirements to set up a syndicate, manage it and finance it, have to follow specific rules set out by Lloyd's. Once a company applies and satisfies Lloyd's requirements, it is allowed to write business with Lloyd's security. This security is rated as A+ and all Lloyd's syndicates have the exact same rating. On the slip the syndicate can be identified by its four-number code, no name is added, and there will be an anchor next to it, which is how syndicates at Lloyd's originally started writing marine business.

The management of the syndicate is undertaken by a managing agency which, again, has been approved by Lloyd's.

In the past, and until the late 1980s and early 1990s, Lloyd's syndicates could be set up by a group or individuals with a lot of money to invest. This they put into a syndicate. With the many losses that occurred, a large number of these syndicates went bankrupt and this led to some of the Names, as these individuals are called, becoming bankrupt as well. This was because Lloyd's always pays its losses, even if that means having to wind up the syndicate. The result of these losses was a restructuring of Lloyd's, whereby it minimised the entry of Names to a bare minimum. Hence only a very few Names are part financiers of Lloyd's syndicates. Most of the syndicates are companies in their own right.

Lloyd's still operates the old mode of operation, whereby the brokers meet in person with the underwriters and transact business and present their submission. This is the information gathered on the risks to be presented and negotiated with the underwriters. They will then decide if they like it or need more information. They will then either write a line, or all of it if the limits are low, and the business is attractive to the underwriter, who has the line size to commit, or they can decline it.

Usually, the risks are based on a subscription basis, hence there are several underwriters covering the risk. The broker therefore has to obtain lead terms from a number of underwriters that he knows can offer the terms the client wishes, send them to the client and explain the differences, advantages and so forth to the client and then the client will order the broker to proceed with one set of lead terms. The broker will then try to fill the slip for up to 100% with follow markets that will follow the leader. This is where the name 'underwriter' comes from as they write under the leader's line. Once he has committed 100% of the risk or even more, the broker will liaise with the client and the respective policy documents will be issued. The skill of the broker is to select lead underwriters who are respected in the market to set a premium and terms appropriate to the risk, otherwise it may be difficult for the broker to find sufficient underwriters willing to follow the lead and fill the slip.

Lloyd's is based in a building where the trading floor is open-plan and thus a broker can easily locate the underwriters with whom he wishes to hold discussions, see if they are busy and thus go elsewhere if possible instead of queuing. Therefore, Lloyd's still operates as it started at Edward Lloyd's coffee shop, where brokers and underwriters started meeting and transacting business.

Nowadays, of course, technology assists in expediting transactions by emailing, confirming cover until the actual slip is stamped, or 'scratched' as it is called. Equally, systems for processing premiums, claims' notifications, loss payments, endorsement issuance and so on are in place so as to facilitate trade and insurance business.

Another market that can be accessed by a broker, not necessarily a Lloyd's broker this time, is the London market which is sometimes referred to as the company market, that is, non-Lloyd's. This is not solely London-based companies but can be based in the Channel Islands, Bermuda or other countries and can be both direct or reinsurance.

The International Underwriting Association (IUA), which evolved from the merger of the Institute of London Underwriters (ILU) and the London Insurance and Reinsurance Market Association (LIRMA), represents the non-Lloyd's insurance and reinsurance. It also represents non-Lloyd's insurers and issues policy wordings for marine, aviation and other types of risks that are used by the market, be it Lloyd's or non-Lloyd's.

The broker who wishes to place insurance would approach insurance companies for lead terms, as with a Lloyd's placement. If the risk is large or complex and thus more than one market is required, he will expand his contacts. He will be armed with the full particulars of the risk to be placed, namely, the submission. As an example, in hull insurance it will be about the ship's specifications, the values, management and loss record.

As with all insurances, the doctrine of utmost good faith applies in the marine market. A full disclosure of all material facts is, therefore, essential. Prior to the passing of the Insurance Act 2015, the only remedy for non-disclosure/misrepresentation under sections 17–20 of the MIA 1906 was to void the contract of insurance. Section 14 of the Insurance Act 2015 repeals the second part of the sentence of section 17 of the MIA 1906, to leave the bare statement that 'A contract of marine insurance is a contract based upon the utmost good faith.' This effectively means that in the event of a breach of the 'duty of utmost good faith', the insurer must seek damages as the remedy of avoidance for material non-disclosure is no longer available.

Section 21(2) of the Insurance Act 2015, repeals sections18–20 of the MIA 1906. Section 3 of the Insurance Act 2015, seeks to modify the duty of utmost good faith that underpins insurance contracts by introducing a new duty of 'fair presentation of the risk'. Section 3(1) to (5) of the Insurance Act 2015 now effectively replaces sections 18, 19 and 20 of the MIA 1906. The duty of fair presentation requires the insured to either i) disclose to insurers 'every material circumstance' which the insured knows or ought to know, or ii) provide the insurer with 'sufficient information' to put a prudent insurer on notice that it needs to make further enquiries into those 'material circumstances'.

As with the Lloyd's practice, the broker negotiates with the leading underwriters to obtain their terms, negotiates with the client on which set is favourable to him and then, if he is successful, gets the order to place it and then finds follow markets to complete the slip.

Each underwriter under the policy is solely responsible for their own line size, and liability from other underwriters cannot be spread to other participating underwriters. Thus we have a several liability regime. Even if an insurer fails, goes bankrupt or will not agree to pay, their line equivalent of the loss will simply not be paid and the assured will receive the balance by the remaining participants in the policy.

Outside the London market a broadly similar procedure applies, although, particularly in Scandinavia, much hull insurance is arranged with mutual associations.

For clients not residing in an insurance centre it may be preferable to place the insurance with a local insurance broker, who will in turn place the risk through their correspondent on the London or another leading market.

In some countries, the client will be obliged by law to place the risk with a local, often national, insurance company, which might or might not then reinsure the risk with a leading market. If this is the case, it is important to ensure that, in the event of a casualty, the claim is payable in hard currency as the chances are that the vast proportion of an owner's expenses resulting from a casualty will be incurred overseas. Quite often in these cases, the risk is reinsured by fronting it in another market outside that country. This is a lawful practice and has been used for years.

In the insurance policy there can be several parties as assured and co-assureds, for example, having the respective vessel's registered owner as the main assured (each vessel having a separate owner as registered due to the one-ship companies' set up for limitation of liabilities purposes), and having the beneficial owner of all vessels named as the operator (who, in fact, is the same for all vessels in a fleet) as well as the technical, operations and crewing departments as co-assureds.

4.2.2 The premium

The cost of insurance, or premium, is normally expressed as a percentage of the agreed valuation of the risk, in our case, the vessel's value. The agreed value should in total never be less than the reasonable market value of the ships concerned. This valuation generally represents the limit of the underwriters' indemnity. The premium rating is negotiable depending on a number of factors. These include the valuation, the type and size of the particular ship or fleet, the reputation and experience of owners and operators and their loss record over previous years, together with the general state of the insurance market that affects market appetite and rating levels.

In the past, overcapacity resulted in a general softening of the market, with more entrants coming in and prospective markets waiting to join, either via Lloyd's or non-Lloyd's, both direct or reinsurance or both. Whereas cut-price insurance helps owners in the short term, underwriters do need to build up a reasonable reserve against the inevitable bad years with heavy losses. The amount that a shipowner is prepared to accept for their own account, or the deductible, is also taken into consideration. The deductible amount is normally applied to each and every loss, but sometimes annual aggregate deductibles are also used.

As the secondhand values of ships fluctuate, it is common for individual ships to be rated with a base value on full conditions. Thereafter, if the ship's price goes up, an increased value insurance can be taken out for total loss only (TLO) risks at a lower premium rating. The London market limits increased value (IV) to 25% of the agreed value, as seen under the disbursements warranty in IHC 2003, but other mechanisms (such as anticipated earnings) also exist to allow for additional TLO cover. The IV assists to the fact that, at the time of the loss, the value of the vessel may be higher than the agreed value under the policy, as can be the case with fluctuating vessel values; and since the insurance policy is a contract of indemnity, by agreeing to the IV the insurer ensures the indemnity principle is fulfilled on its part and the assured is properly indemnified. Thus fluctuations in ships' values can be economically catered for, the important consideration being always to ensure that the aggregate valuation for insurance exceeds the reasonable market value of the asset but not being unreasonably higher than what the market values are, as this may seem to the insurer to be fraud or moral hazard, which may lead to a total loss allowing the assured to claim more than what the reasonable value at the time of the loss is.

The method of assessing ships' values is a matter of choice. Some owners look at market resale prices only, while others prefer to enhance this with an element of newbuilding replacement cost. Frequently, if a ship is subject to a mortgage, the lender stipulates a minimum value, thus introducing the loan-to-value ratio protecting the mortgagor from sudden and long-lasting vessel downside valuations, and their interest will be endorsed on the policy. Ship operators should monitor the sale and purchase market, and consult with owners as values fluctuate to ensure that their ships are properly covered. The consultation of expert sales and purchase brokers is a normal practice.

The challenge for having the vessels' values up to date at all times is the triggering of the loan-to-value ratio stipulations that affect the repayment of the mortgage in that usually the mortgagee has to pay higher instalments or renegotiate the mortgage or even repay the mortgage in one balloon payment. This is a critical development as, when values decrease, this means that the freight market has been descending for months, if not years, in advance, as the vessels' values delay in following the freight market, since the latter fluctuates more greatly and more easily than the valuations.

Therefore an owner will be very apprehensive in revaluing their fleet when the values reduce substantially as this will be an admittance that they are losing money in the freight market; their assets devalue and thus the mortgage's relevant stipulations may require that they pay higher instalments, as an example. But, as the market has already deprived them from lucrative freight rates, lack of liquidity may be an issue and may cause the owner to default.

Equally, if the vessels' value reduces they have to be amended in the insurance policy accordingly so as to follow the principle of indemnity, meaning that the assured owes to earn the loss incurred and no more, thus the valuations should reflect a reasonable market value at all times.

On occasion, the values will not be amended on the policy or in the mortgage if the market trends are rapid and it is suspected that such downturns are temporary, but this is on a case-by-case basis for each owner, each mortgage lender and the insurance market participants.

4.2.3 Total loss

Total loss can be either actual or constructive. We have an actual total loss (ATL). This takes place when the vessel, in our case, *'is destroyed, or so damaged as to cease to be a thing of the kind insured, or where the assured is irretrievably deprived thereof'* (MIA 1906, s 57).

The constructive total loss (CTL) scenario is when the ship is not actually destroyed or lost but where it becomes so badly damaged that the cost of repair exceeds its insured value (MIA 1906, s 60). In such circumstances, the vessel may be declared a CTL, which is covered by IHC clause 21. This must be done clearly in full consultation and agreement with the underwriter, in which event the owners have the option to tender a notice of abandonment (NOA) of the vessel to the underwriters involved (MIA 1906, s 62) but they are not obliged to accept it for various reasons. Some reasons may be that there will be nothing to be salvaged to recoup part of the loss paid out or when there is a wreck and the cost of removal and resulting liabilities will be so great that they would not want to accept the abandonment. Nonetheless, they will pay the loss under the policy if it is insurable. If the underwriters accept the NOA, what is left of the ship becomes the property of the underwriters who have the responsibility for wreck removal, liabilities incurring as and when they arise. The policy wording will normally allow for the insured value of the ship to be substituted for the repair value to determine when the vessel can be considered a CTL.

4.2.4 Particular average

Particular average (PA) means a partial loss caused by a peril insured against as distinct from total loss or general average. In this context, the word 'average' does not have its everyday meaning and its origins are somewhat obscure, although perhaps a little easier to understand when general average is covered later. Average in this sense is deemed to mean loss.

Particular average is the most common type of claim under a marine insurance policy and occurs when a ship sustains damage as a result of one of the perils insured against where the cost of repairs is less than the level of indemnity or value allowed for in the policy. The perils insured against in the policy are clearly laid down, as can be seen, for instance, under IHC 2003, clause 2. Additionally, most owners elect to extend their policy by means of an additional perils clause, IHC 2003, clause 41, which gives them greater flexibility and scope to submit claims. This was formerly known as the Inchmaree Clause and owes its name to a case which went to the House of Lords in 1887 when it was held that damage done to the SS *Inchmaree* owing to inadvertence on the part of a member of the crew, when the donkey boiler blew up, was not a peril insured against under the normal marine insurance policy of the day. Under ITCH 1983, section 6(2) the damage to the vessel by the broken shafts or boilers is covered but not the repair of such shafts and/or boilers, even though an additional clause can be added to cover that. Under IHC 2003, clause 41 such additional perils clauses form part of the policy and thus both the damage to the vessel and the boiler/shafts are covered.

When dealing with particular average, the normal criterion is the reasonable cost of repairs to the ship, assuming that the shipowner had acted as a prudent uninsured thus trying to minimise the loss. Reasonable cost of repairs could include the cost of removing a ship to a repair yard including bunkers consumed and relevant port charges, drydocking and repair accounts, spare parts supplied and transport thereof, superintendence, surveyors' fees and wages, and maintenance of the crew during the removal. In certain circumstances, and in particular when liner vessels are concerned, temporary repairs can also be recovered, although it needs to be demonstrated that by carrying out temporary repairs the owners were able to save the underwriters money. Unrepaired damage under IHC 2003, clause 20 can also form part of a PA claim on the grounds that there would have been a depreciation of the ship's value by virtue of the damage not being dealt with. In such cases, the underwriters' surveyor must agree the estimated cost of unrepaired damage and an allowance is then negotiated in full and final settlement with the insurers, perhaps 60% or 70% of the estimated cost.

A very important consideration for both total loss and particular average loss is that there is an exclusion protecting public policy in that no one can benefit from one's own wrong and thus the application of MIA 1906, section 55(2), whereby, if a loss occurs owing to the wilful misconduct of the assured, then the loss is not covered.

4.2.5 Collision

The hull and machinery insurance policy will also cover expenses and liabilities incurred by an operator if their ship comes into collision with another vessel. Whereas normal US and Scandinavian conditions permit full recovery of such cost and liabilities, the London market has, for historical reasons, taken a somewhat different approach.

It must be assumed that before the days of steamships, collisions between two sailing vessels competently handled and subject to the same natural influences of wind, tide and current were comparatively rare. But, during the first half of the 19th century, the London market underwriters became increasingly concerned regarding the number of occasions when steamships ran down or collided with sailing ships, which on occasion may have been down to wilful misconduct. They may also have wanted to increase the risk awareness and prudence of the operators, thus requiring them to operate as a prudent uninsured and bear the first one quarter of the liabilities incurred through collision. They therefore introduced what was called a 'running-down clause' into their policies issued to steamship owners whereby the underwriters would only pay three-quarters of the liability arising out of such collisions. This three-quarters collision liability provision carries through to the present day under London conditions, IHC 2003, clause 61. It was a direct result of the imposition of the running down clause that led to British shipping companies during the mid-1800s banding together to form mutual protection and indemnity associations. These were originally specifically set up to provide mutual insurance cover for the remaining one-quarter collision liability.

In any event, the question of the division of liability for a collision is almost invariably the subject of those in Trinity House, who are experienced mariners. They advise the judges in Admiralty court on how navigation standards and rules ought to have been observed before the collision took place and accordingly apportion the liability to the parties involved, as it is rarely the case that one party alone was 100% responsible for the collision. Policies also provide (under a sister ship clause) for the situation where two vessels under the same ownership collide with one another. They allow the owner of the two vessels to recover under the policy as if the vessels belonged to different owners, subject to no wilful misconduct being proven on behalf of such assured owner.

4.3 GENERAL AVERAGE

General average (GA) is a peculiarity of marine insurance tracing its origins back over many centuries when the concept of the common venture incorporating both the shipowner and cargo owner began. In simplistic terms, however, it is another example of the sharing or spreading of risk for the preservation of ship and cargo in a common adventure when facing a peril insured against. Thus the parties involved in the common adventure, who have vested interests in the successful execution of the venture, will contribute to the reasonable, extraordinary losses suffered by the other parties involved in the adventure, as seen in the definition of general average under MIA 1906, section 66(2) and (6) referring to the perils faced that have to be insured against.

It is important to remember that general average exists regardless of insurance, although, in practice, the insurers of the various interested parties do become heavily involved, be they marine hull insurers, P&I Clubs or cargo underwriters.

General average only arises in certain very special circumstances. As mentioned, in English law a general average act takes place only when an extraordinary sacrifice or expenditure is voluntarily and reasonably made in time of peril insured against for the purposes of preserving property involved in a maritime adventure. The important words in that definition are that the sacrifice must be extraordinary, must be voluntary and reasonable and must be incurred in time of peril. Examples of such situations would be:

- where cargo is jettisoned for common safety;
- where a vessel suffers a fire and cargo is damaged by efforts to extinguish the fire such as a hold being flooded;
- where a ship is in difficulty and requires the assistance of a salvage tug to remove the ship from danger.

A further type of allowable general average expenditure would be the costs of making for a port of refuge, including the cost of cargo handled at the port of refuge specifically to enable repairs to the ship to be carried out for the safe prosecution of the voyage.

In the majority of cases, the procedures for defining and dealing with general average are as laid down in a document called the York-Antwerp Rules. The York-Antwerp Rules are held under constant review and occasionally new versions are introduced. The last three editions are dated 1994, 2004 and 2016. Each of the sets of rules contains varying provisions and it is generally accepted that the 2004 version was less favourable to shipowners in some areas than the earlier editions. Exactly which set of rules applies is determined by mutual agreement when negotiating shipping contracts. Given the opportunity, most owners tended to opt for the 1994 version. On 5 May 2016, a new version of the York-Antwerp Rules was settled at a conference convened by the Comité Maritime International. Having been approved by the shipowners' association, BIMCO, for inclusion in BIMCO charter parties, bills of lading and waybills, these rules stand a good prospect of being adopted in place of the York-Antwerp Rules 1994 which are currently most commonly incorporated by reference into charter parties and bills of lading. In so doing, York-Antwerp Rules 2016 will fill the gap created by the failure of the 2004 rules.

Whenever a potential general average situation arises, it is important that the ship operators quickly consult an experienced average adjuster, who will advise on arrangements for collecting security from cargo interests.

It is important to mention that if the York-Antwerp Rules are not agreed then the law of the state where the general average act ceases, namely, where the vessel is brought in safely, applies and may be different from English law. Even if the York-Antwerp Rules apply, they may be interpreted differently in that jurisdiction if, for example, they are incorporated in that state's law or if the policy is subject to another jurisdiction. For the application of this principle see IHC 2003, clause 8.

Average adjusters are firms of specialists which undertake the painstaking task of determining what expenses may justifiably be included in the general average settlement. They also have to calculate the value at the material time, usually just before the accident, not only of the ship itself but of every piece of cargo it is carrying. This is a formidable task when one realises that in a modern container ship the number of separate consignments can run into several thousands. In such cases it can be more cost effective for the insurers to pay the claim rather than declaring general average.

When a 'general average act' is declared, a decision taken by the operator after consultation with their insurers, there are several tasks which have to be undertaken immediately, even though the average adjustment process can take months or years to complete.

If the operator has appointed an average adjuster soon after the incident, they will arrange through the operator's agents or their own correspondents at the destination for the cargo interests or consignees to be contacted so that the necessary documents can be arranged.

However, if the owner delays the appointment of an adjuster, which is quite common, then almost all the work in collecting the documents will be delegated to the operator's local port agent.

The documents that must be collected are, first, an average bond signed by each of the consignees and then either an average guarantee signed by the cargo insurers or the payment of a general average deposit where cargo is uninsured. A copy of the commercial invoice for the cargo in question will also be necessary to show the value. In time, perhaps a year or more later when all costs and values have been analysed, the adjusters will prepare a general average statement. This will split the total allowable general average expenditure into shares in proportion to the value of ship, cargo and bunkers involved.

Each party is then called on to pay its share or general average contribution to the general average fund, which is, in turn, redistributed to the parties who incurred the sacrifice, usually the shipowner and those cargo interests whose cargo may have been lost or damaged in the common interest. Many owners' hull policies contain a partial waiver clause whereby hull underwriters agree to pay the general average contribution due from the cargo interest up to a certain amount. This is designed to speed up the adjustment process when relatively small sums are involved.

4.4 SALVAGE

Salvage expenses are frequently dealt with in a similar manner. The requirements for salvage are that the property must be in danger, the salvage services offered have to be voluntary and that the services are based on a no cure-no pay principle. This is to encourage best endeavours from the salvor to salvage the property. It has to be mentioned that no salvage awards are due for saving of life. Therefore, in bygone days, salvage was not under contract but simply voluntary and on a no cure-no pay basis. This has changed with the introduction of Lloyd's open form (LOF) in 1892 and standardised in 1908, thus introducing contractual salvage but still on a no cure-no pay basis. There are other salvage contracts besides LOF, but LOF has been used for almost 50% of the recorded salvage cases. LOF is being revised continuously so as to follow developments in commerce and law, and the latest version is LOF 2011.

LOF is closer to pure salvage principles as reflected under MIA 1906, section 65, but there are other contracts that stipulate the terms and conditions and may not be on a no cure-no pay principle. Instead they are based on a fixed rate for the services rendered irrespective of the outcome or based on a combination of what the rates will be but in any scenario, namely, in a successful or unsuccessful outcome. Therefore the rates are fixed and thus will not resort to the arbitration panel, as an LOF would do, to calculate the salvage award upon a successful salvage.

Where a ship receives salvage services either from a professional salvor or another commercial vessel, the salvage costs are shared between both ship and cargo interests and, under current marine policies, such as IHC 2003, clause 8, they tend to fall under general average. To avoid the risk of a rapidly deteriorating situation when a ship is clearly in distress, Masters are empowered and should be encouraged to engage salvage services without delay. In signing a Lloyd's open form, Masters are acting on behalf of both ship and cargo as an agent of necessity. Their position is fully protected under international law and the Master and owner of the vessel have a duty to co-operate fully with the salvor during the course of salvage operations. Equally, the salvor has a duty of care to the owners of the vessel and cargo owners in danger so as to exercise due care to prevent unnecessary damage to the vessel and/or cargo and also to try to minimise any damage to the environment. To have a full view, look at the Salvage Convention 1989, article 8. Once more, it is customary practice for an average adjuster to be involved in salvage cases, preparing the necessary adjustment when all costs are finalised.

If we have an LOF, then the salvage award is calculated based on the salved values of ship and cargo. The salvor will therefore receive a proportion of the salved value that will vary depending on the salvor's best endeavours to save the ship and cargo, freight, bunkers and any other value that was salved and will contribute to the award. In particular, the salvor's award is calculated on the basis of the salved value of the vessel, cargo, freight and bunkers; its skill and efforts; measure of success; the degree of danger faced; the expenses, time and losses incurred; and any investment the salvor may have put into tugs and other salvage material; and risk of liability to the salvor during salvage. Apart from the LOF, a good overview of how a salvage award is fixed can be gained by looking at articles 13 (salvage award) and 14 (special compensation) of the Salvage Convention 1989.

It is worth noting that the current Lloyd's open form salvage agreement provides a mechanism whereby salvors may be granted an enhancement on the salvage award to cover the reasonable costs of preventing or alleviating pollution damage where their activities involve laden tankers. This particular provision was introduced in 1980 and is a departure from the no cure-no pay principle. It was brought about following pressure from the International Salvage Union after a number of cases where tankers were so badly damaged that salvors were obliged to tow them out to deep water and sink them. Under the old regime, salvors got nothing for their pains in such circumstances because there was no cure, and this was clearly a highly unsatisfactory state of affairs. At present, discussions are taking place with a view to introducing a new salvage convention extending this principle to cover not only laden oil tankers but also other types of pollution prevention activity.

Currently, salvage is carried out and governed under the Salvage Convention 1989. The previous 1910 convention was based on the traditional principle of no cure-no pay. The intention of the Salvage Convention 1989 was to encourage salvors to act in all cases involving a threat to the environment, even when the traditional salvage award may not have covered their expenses in full. Under the 1989 convention, the main salvage award is still based on no cure-no pay, but the award will take into account 'the skill and efforts of the salvors in preventing or minimising damage to the environment', as well as the traditional factors of salved value, danger, out-of-pocket expenses, success, time and skill.

This basic no cure-no pay award is dealt with under article 13. The Salvage Convention also introduces a safety net where salvors who have worked on a ship or cargo which threatens damage to the environment have failed to earn, under article 13, an award sufficient to cover their costs.

In such circumstances, they are entitled to special compensation under article 14, based on the cost of personnel and equipment used and out-of-pocket expenses incurred to the extent that they exceed any article 13 award. In addition, if they have prevented or minimised environmental damage, the article 14 award is subject to an uplift of 30–100%, the 100% to be allowed if it is fair and just to do so. Hull and cargo underwriters continue to pay article 13 awards, even if these are increased because of environmental factors, but P&I Clubs cover article 14 awards. Special compensation is payable in excess of the salvage award and is taken out of the salved value of the properties in question: vessel, cargo, freight and bunkers. If the salved value is not sufficient to pay for the special compensation, then an excess payment, as calculated by the arbitrators, will be paid to the salvors.

Attention has to be paid to the fact that if a salvor is negligent in the discharge of its duties during salvage operations and fails to prevent or minimise pollution, or their actions may even result in an increase in pollution, then the salvor may be deprived of any expenses due to it, and may also be liable for compensation for clean-up costs and any damage to the vessel and or cargo, subject to the universal limitation afforded to it under the LLMC (Limitation of Liability for Maritime Claims Convention) 1976/96.

The Salvage Convention came into force in1996 but had already been introduced into the 1990 and 1995 versions of LOF. There have been a number of problems about the workings of articles 13 and 14, some of which have concerned shipowners and P&I Clubs and others have concerned salvors. The clubs were worried that the safety net gave salvors an incentive to extend salvage work as long as possible, allowing underwriters to delay the decision as to whether a ship would be accepted as a constructive total loss.

Salvors were concerned that article 14 only applies if there is a threat to the environment, which has to be proved, and that article 14 is not relevant outside coastal or inland waters. They were also concerned by a decision of the English courts in the *Nagasaki Spirit* case that the rates for equipment and personnel cannot include any element of profit. Profit is limited to one uplift, which only applies if damage to the environment is minimised or prevented. All these issues led to costly arbitrations involving article 14. Consequently, negotiations took place with a view to agreeing a simplified framework for special compensation which would promote fast responses to casualties but reduce the potential for legal disputes. As a result of these discussions, the SCOPIC (Special Compensation P&I Club) clause has been developed as an alternative to article 14 for dealing with special compensation. The clause has been revised from time to time, with the latest version being referred to as SCOPIC 2011.

The main changes brought about by the SCOPIC clause, introduced in 1999, are that the salvor has the option of invoking the special provisions whenever they choose, regardless of the circumstances. They do not have to prove environmental threat and no geographical restriction applies. If the clause is invoked, the shipowner must provide security within two working days. If, thereafter, the shipowner thinks that the security is too high, or the salvor thinks it is too low, each is entitled to require the other to reduce or increase the security. If the shipowner does not provide security within two working days, the salvor can withdraw from the provisions of the SCOPIC clause and revert to their rights under article 14.

The salvor can terminate the services if they reasonably anticipate that the total cost of past and future services will exceed the value of the property capable of being salved plus their SCOPIC remuneration.

Shipowners can terminate the SCOPIC agreement subject to five days' notice. The shipowner has the right to send on board a special casualty representative (SCR) and hull and cargo underwriters each have the right to send on board one special hull and special cargo representative.

Before leaving the subject of general average and salvage, some mention should be made of the question of seaworthiness. In these litigious days, it has become increasingly prevalent for cargo interests to raise objections when called upon to make general average contributions. Cargo owners, on behalf of their insurers, may in some cases engage lawyers and seek ways of proving unseaworthiness of the vessel at the commencement of the voyage, thereby obviating their obligation to contribute to general average or salvage. Human error or misjudgement is a major factor in most accidents at sea and elsewhere, a fact fully recognised by insurers.

Thus crew negligence and faulty navigation are both long-standing and acceptable defences acknowledged by courts of law. On the other hand, lack of due diligence on the part of an owner is not. Recent cases clearly place a heavy responsibility on the ship operator to select the crew with utmost care and to supervise the operation of the vessel meticulously.

4.5 SUE AND LABOUR

In all insurance policies the assured has a duty to sue and labour – that is to say, that the assured has to take all reasonable steps to avert or minimise a loss from a peril insured against and the sum incurred is in addition to the amount of loss of the vessel.

Therefore, if there is a loss with sue and labour expenses incurred for the avoidance or minimisation of a loss, the sue and labour expenses will be paid separately from what the underwriter pays for the loss and the supplementary sum recoverable as sue and labour is limited to the amount paid for the loss by the underwriters. Hence the assured will receive the indemnity for the loss and a separate amount for its sue and labour expenses that cannot be more than the amount paid as the indemnity for the loss. IHC 2003, clause 9 reflects the provisions of sue and labour as seen in MIA 1906, section 78. General average and salvage charges are not recoverable under sue and labour as the principles behind them are different.

For instance, when a ship suffers damage at a berth to which it has been ordered by a charterer who has warranted that it is safe, the costs incurred should be recoverable from the charterer by reason of the safe berth clause in the charter party. Similarly, repair costs may be recovered from repairers owing to negligent workmanship and cross-liabilities must be pursued from the other party following a collision. The underlying principle is that the shipowner ought to behave as a prudent uninsured and protect the underwriters' interests at all times.

4.6 NAVIGATING LIMITS, WAR RISKS AND SANCTIONS

The London market and other markets lay down certain navigational restrictions, both permanent and seasonal, principally for the Arctic, Antarctic, Baltic and St Lawrence Seaway, which are deemed particularly hazardous, chiefly owing to ice at certain seasons of the year. These are known as navigating limits to which IHC 2003, clause 32 refers to. It is a condition that the vessel will not trade in the designated areas at proscribed seasons. However, it is usually possible to apply to underwriters for permission to breach navigating limits against payment of an additional premium (AP), which is normally charged on a voyage-by-voyage basis.

All standard marine policies specifically exclude damage resulting from wars and hostile acts, and capture, seizure, arrest or strikes are covered in IHC 2003, clauses 29–33. From time to time, marine underwriters declare certain ports and areas of the world, where hostilities are taking place or threatened, as war zones, as areas where normal marine policy cover is suspended. Other market underwriters, however, specialise in providing specific cover for war zones for which an AP is charged.

In practice, an operator obtains an annual war-risk policy and will pay the annual premium. If during the policy period it will have one or more of its vessels breaching a war-risk area, as listed in the Joint War Committee's war-listed areas, issued and revised periodically – usually once a year unless sudden changes occur – then it will pay a pre-agreed breach war AP. The current version is the JWLA022 listing the countries deemed as war-risk areas and includes countries that are not at war but have the risk of war-related risks such as war, civil war, revolution, insurrection, civil strife, capture or seizure, arrest or detainment as seen in Institute War and Strikes Clauses (Hulls-Time) 1983, clause 1, for example.

It is important to note that such breaches must be declared in advance of the entry into the breach areas otherwise suspension of cover may be the result as this is usually a breach of warranty. A held covered clause is usually inserted but the assured has to observe the policy and not rely solely on the held covered clause, unless if the omission to advise the breach was inadvertent, whereby the underwriter will exercise its discretion.

The exit from the war-risk area should also be advised as the AP is based on the time in the breach area and usually calculated on seven-day periods, unless otherwise agreed with underwriters, namely, pro rata, on 14-day periods or otherwise.

As of late, the introduction of financial and trade sanctions on a number of countries for a number of reasons have been introduced and the market has introduced standard sanctions clauses, such as LMA3100, whereby they exclude cover under a policy where there is a sanctioned assured and/or when the vessel trades in a sanctioned country and/or carrying sanctioned cargo.

Thus the brokers and insurers have to exercise due diligence and have their compliance offices enquire details on risks that may relate to any sanctioned person, country or cargo and accordingly either decline to quote or bind a policy, or even cancel the policy if, after binding, it is proven that the assured, cargo or countries of residence of the assured or trade of the vessel are sanctioned.

4.7 CLAIMS HANDLING

While no two casualties are ever the same, there are always a number of common elements to which attention should be paid to ensure a prompt and flawless settlement. Within the ship operator's organisation, close liaison and understanding between the insurance claims department, the technical superintendents and the accountants is most important so that the flow of information once the claim arises is efficient. Co-operation is also needed during the claims handling/negotiation to assist with expertise and further information, thereby shedding light on their side of the claim, either defending or claiming as seen under IHC 2003, clause 45. This will lead to the quick settlement of the claim and reach an optimum loss amount.

Under the old provisions of the MIA 1906, a breach of a warranty in a marine insurance contract would have entitled the insurer to avoid all claims under the policy from the date of breach. This position has now been modified by the Insurance Act 2015, through the introduction of sections 9, 10, and 11, which lessen the severity for the breach of a warranty.

But, of course, when a casualty occurs, the onboard personnel from the Master downwards will have to deal with the problem as best they can. Seagoing personnel are very practical and will be the most qualified to deal with an emergency since they know more about the vessel than anyone else, apart from shore-based personnel who liaise with them, such as the designated person ashore, the superintendents and the captains in the operations departments.

The first person ashore to learn about the accident will usually be the duty superintendent. They should promptly pass details to the company's insurance manager, who will in turn alert:

a) the insurance broker so that the underwriters can be advised and arrangements made for the underwriters' surveyor to attend the vessel to inspect any damage;

b) the P&I Club, if it relates to a P&I insured loss such as crew claim, cargo, collision, pollution, contact with fixed and floating objects (FFO), damage to hull or charter party dispute, the latter being an extension of any physical damage resulting to loss of hire claim under a time charter, for example;

c) the average adjuster to liaise with all interests, such as the surveyor, cargo interests for collection of security when necessary, and start gathering information;

d) the owner and charterer, continuing to keep both informed as the situation develops;

e) an appropriate lawyer, possibly in conjunction with the P&I Club;

f) cargo interests should also be kept informed.

In the meantime, the technical departments will be in contact with the vessel, trying to assess the extent of the damage and formulating plans for dealing with the immediate situation and for temporary/permanent repairs. The classification society will have to be informed if the damage pertains to class, such as in a collision, fire/explosion in the machinery room or cargo holds, or cracks to the plating due to bad weather among others.

The ship's crew should ensure that full records of their actions relating to an incident are carefully maintained. Photographs illustrating any damage are frequently useful. Logbooks, course recorders, echo sounder printouts and similar documentary information must be preserved. It is vitally important that such documents are only made available to owners or their proper representatives, not to charterers, their solicitors, foreign port authorities, or to the press or others not directly involved. IHC 2003, clause 45, reflects the duties of the assured at the beginning of and during the claims handling.

In due course, the vessel will arrive at the repair port as agreed with the underwriters, since the underwriters will have a list of repair ports they approve of, where work, possibly including drydocking, will have to be undertaken. The operator's superintendent will be in attendance, together with the insurer's surveyor and classification society surveyors. A P&I surveyor, in addition to a hull surveyor, may also be necessary if cargo has been damaged. Following IHC 2003, clause 46 provides a good sequence of what has to be done, by whom and that the hull insurer's surveyor must certify the cost of any repairs as being fair and reasonable and the underwriter must allow the repairs to proceed. Of course, there are circumstances where urgent repairs are needed and the assured owner/operator may proceed to the closest dock that can accommodate the vessel and effect such repairs, and then advise the insurers. If this is the case, the promptness of notification of insurers and despatch of the surveyors on site is of fundamental importance.

In short, the assured has to comply with the claims notification (IHC 2003, clause 43) and tender clauses (IHC, clause 44) in the policy, the latter being the one stipulating that the insurer may have the authority to decide which ports can be used for the vessel to sail for repairs or veto other ports that the assured proposes that may be closer. In this case, the insurer will pay additional voyage costs to the approved yard of its choice. If no approved yards exist in the area where the loss took place, then the insurer will require the assured to receive tenders by local yards that can effect the repairs in question and submit them to the insurer for approval and selection of which one to be used. An allowance of 30% per annum will be allowed by the insurer for loss of time until they decide and the vessel goes to the chosen yard under the tender. Of course, as said, tenders are used when the damage is not serious and the safety of crew, ship and cargo is not in question.

A few weeks after repairs are completed the surveyor will submit their detailed report, a copy of which will be passed to the ship operator. The report will usually include an opinion on the cause of the casualty. This report, together with copies of accounts covering repairs and other relevant expenses, will be sent by the ship operator to the average adjuster. Although appointed by the operator/assured, the average adjuster is strictly neutral and their job is to prepare a statement of claim in an impartial manner and in accordance with customary practice.

The average adjuster will probably request sight of logbooks, reports and any other relevant documents, which should be provided by the ship operator who has a duty to disclose all the pertinent facts.

It is important to note that some Scandinavian insurers do their own adjustments for PA claims and do not use independent firms.

The claim statement (or adjustment), when completed, will probably run to several, even hundreds, of pages. It will include a narrative, copies of reports, summaries of all expenditure showing average and other costs, details of policy conditions showing whether the casualty was the consequence of an insured peril or not and consequently, a calculation of the amount to be recovered from insurers less the owners' portion. This statement is sent to the brokers, who arrange collection from the underwriters. In the case of a large claim, to assist the owners, a payment on account may be arranged at the underwriters' discretion of, for example, 80% of the estimated total, since the finalisation of a major claim adjustment can take several months to complete. The London market does not allow interest payments on PA claims, although Scandinavian conditions do, but it does pay interest on GA payments.

4.8 PROTECTION AND INDEMNITY

Earlier it was explained how, in the middle of the 19th century, British steamship owners clubbed together to form mutual protection and indemnity associations principally to provide the one-quarter third-party collision liability cover which the London hull underwriters had refused to cover. These mutual associations, or clubs, soon started to assume wider liabilities on behalf of their members, including personal injury claims from crews and in particular, claims for loss of or damage to cargo. This was at a time when the laws relating to the carriage of goods by sea were gradually being codified and placed on a more equitable basis as between shipping companies and their customers. Over the years, the modern protection and indemnity insurance industries have built up and, alongside hull insurance, now constitute the two main areas of marine underwriting activity.

This part of the chapter describes the workings of the P&I Clubs from the ship operators', the owners' or the charterers' viewpoint and covers some of the other ancillary insurances which are frequently placed by operators.

It should be noted that while most P&I cover is provided by clubs on a mutual basis, there is an alternative on offer in some markets. Fixed premium P&I policies can be offered by commercial insurers offering the same degree of cover as the clubs but on a for-profit basis and not as a mutual. The attraction of these policies is that the full costs are known in advance and there are no supplementary or release calls payable. Due to there being a profit element in the premium payable, this alternative might be thought of as being more expensive than a mutual system as each member will pay the premium reflecting their own loss record and risk profile and not contribute to the losses of other members. However, that is not always true because, under the club system, other members' claims can have an adverse effect on the finances of a member making few or no claims. The overall view is that fixed premium clubs cover smaller tonnages than the international group clubs, which are all mutuals covering more than 90% of world shipping. Thereby fixed premium clubs insure 10% or less of world shipping, mostly being inland, coastal navigation vessels.

4.8.1 The principles of mutuality

In contrast with the sort of cover provided by Lloyd's underwriters and the commercial insurance companies (collectively referred to as the market), the P&I Clubs are invariably non-profit-making. If they do make a profit one year, this excess is then used to reduce or avoid any premium increases for the next policy year. They have no outside shareholders and are in effect owned by the shipowner-members themselves, who are in essence acting both as assureds and insurers. The clubs derive their income from the members by means of advance and supplementary cash calls, the equivalent to the premium under conventional insurance, and any revenue which is surplus to immediate requirements is carefully invested by the club managers. On the expenditure side, claims are paid, management costs are incurred and reinsurance is arranged through the market for the major catastrophe situations.

Each club is controlled by a board of directors, drawn from the senior management of the shipowner-members of that club. The club directors meet regularly to examine and approve members' claims, to monitor the investment programme and to consider how the scope of the cover being offered by the club can be improved for the benefit of all. Day-to-day management of the club's affairs is vested with a permanent staff or with a professional management company employing experienced claims handlers, the lawyers, underwriting specialists and so on. A further special feature of P&I Club cover is that, with the exception of pollution liabilities, there is a very high upper limit to the level of indemnity provided.

Another point to note about P&I Clubs is that their payments of claims are indemnity. That is to say that they reimburse or indemnify their members against claims paid by the members to third parties. They do not take over the claim, as do insurance companies. This has caused problems in the USA, which has laws permitting direct action by the claimant against the insurers if the defendant is considered financially weak or unable to be contacted. As P&I Clubs are not insurance companies, action against them in this context has hit obstacles.

At present, the international group of the world's largest P&I Clubs operates within a framework called the International Group Agreement (IGA). Under the IGA, each club is responsible for paying its own claims up to a maximum per claim of $10m, which is referred to as the club retention. Clubs are free to reinsure part of their own retention should they so wish. Any claim in excess of $10m is then pooled with the other members of the IGA, thus spreading the risk of such claims over a very large part of the international shipping industry. The group's reinsurance programme, otherwise called the pooling agreement, is the largest reinsurance programme in the world, offering the maximum cover, namely, the overspill, of $3.1bn for P&I claims and $1bn for oil pollution. The various layers of the programme can be seen on the reinsurance section of the group's website (www.igpandi.org).

By virtue of its size, the group has been able to place very favourable market reinsurance for the pooled claims. In the event of a claim exceeding the upper limit of market reinsurance, the cost would fall back on the clubs but, nevertheless, the unlimited liability principle remains in place.

4.8.2 Calls

The clubs assess their premium income requirements, or calls, using criteria broadly similar to those of hull insurers. They will consider the type and size of ship, the quality of the ownership and management, crew nationality, anticipated trading pattern and, in particular, the claims record over previous years. Since there is no limit to the liability based on value, the rating is more closely related to the type of risk envisaged. For example, a higher rate would apply if the ship intended to carry general cargo, with a higher risk of cargo claims, compared with operating in the bulk trades.

Again, like hull insurance, the owner will bear a deductible for each and every claim, and the size of deductible will be taken into consideration in fixing the call rate. The call rate is usually expressed as so many dollars or cents per gross registered tonnage (grt) for the ship in question. As claims settlements are frequently spread over a considerable period, there is no need for the clubs to be put fully in funds at the outset. Accordingly, most clubs endeavour to assist members' cash flow positions by levying an advance call for a limited proportion of the estimated total requirement for the year in question. Thereafter, supplementary calls relating to the year will be made at a later stage if the reserved funds to pay losses are exceeded and thus the club requires cash to pay the losses that exceeded their expectations. These include catastrophe losses or others that developed into a much bigger loss than initially thought. The size and timing of supplementary calls will be a matter for the club's directors to decide, as will the length of time in policy years they remain open, but three years is probably the norm.

If a vessel is sold, it is customary for the club to offer the owner a one-off release call relating to that ship so that they can tidy up their books without the risk of supplementary calls being made many years after the ship has been disposed of. Almost all P&I policy years start on 20 February, a curiosity which dates from the time that ice was supposed to have melted to allow trading into the Baltic Sea to recommence.

There is competition between the P&I Clubs for membership, as the larger the club, the greater the economies of scale in management and the bargaining position for reinsurance. This has led to periods when some clubs cut their rates to attract more business. Under the mutual system, this practice is only of short-term benefit to shipowners as the other mutual members will be obliged to make up any uncovered losses through supplementary calls for unclosed years. Clubs which are members of the IGA have developed a system to discourage a member from switching clubs to get an apparently better deal or to eliminate bad claims from its own fleet, sometimes called record dumping. It must always be remembered that under the mutual system each member is in effect both an insurer and an assured at the same time.

4.8.3 Club management

Under the mutual system, because the scope for price competition is necessarily restricted, clubs do compete effectively in the quality of service offered to their members. Many clubs are either managed directly or through managing agents in London, while northern England, Scandinavia, New York and the Far East are also major centres. All clubs have accredited correspondents at ports throughout the world staffed by experts in their field and can provide back-up practical and legal advice whenever a vessel is in trouble.

For instance, club guarantees, in the form of a letter of undertaking or a bank guarantee, with the former being more popular and accepted by claimants and free, while the latter, being a measure of last resort, incurs bank charges for the club and member. These can usually be arranged extremely quickly if a ship is threatened with arrest. Club management is also able to assist owners on a consultancy basis in drafting documentation such as bills of lading, passenger tickets, crew agreements and letters of indemnity. General advice to members is often contained in club circular letters, and most ship members arrange to distribute copies to ships in their fleet. Thus, in many ways, club managements can in effect become extensions of the shipowners' office.

Another way in which clubs can compete with each other is in the accuracy and reliability of their underwriting forecasts, avoiding unexpectedly heavy supplementary calls.

4.8.4 Club entry

When a shipowner wishes to be a member of a club, it is called the entry. In order for an owner or charterer to enter its vessels with a P&I Club they must first apply to the club. This can either be done through a broker or by direct contact. The club management will require the applicant to provide full details of the vessels in question and, in some cases, they will instruct an experienced surveyor to carry out a condition survey. This survey goes beyond a classification society survey since the P&I surveyors are specifically seeking to satisfy themselves with regard to the sorts of risks that the club will be asked to underwrite. They will, for example, be looking for proper qualification of crew and satisfactory condition of cargo spaces.

While retaining the right to inspect a member's vessel at any time, the club may carry out a full survey of a vessel, even though it has not changed hands, when it reaches an age of 10 years, and thereafter at regular intervals. The gaps between surveys will depend on the findings of the previous survey. When the vessel is accepted by the club, an entry certificate will be provided setting out the main details of the cover, call rate, deductibles and so on. In the same way as with hull insurance, the shipowner will appear as principal assured, with the ship operators (if they are a separate entity) appearing as a joint co-assured.

4.8.5 Risks covered

As clubs were introduced to offer protection and indemnity to their members, the rules delineate what these exactly cover, with additions to reflect the development of maritime law and the litigious environment of the industry today. These risks are listed below but briefly, they can be categorised as protection for liabilities relating to claims arising from collisions, passenger death or injury, crew injury, salvage and indemnity originally including liabilities relating to claims for cargo damage, breach of contract and costs such as fines.

Each club sets out details of the conditions of entry and risks covered in the form of a rulebook. Although club rules will vary in detail, they generally cover the same risks, and indeed, the IGA ensures exactly that, as well as ensuring that the co-operation between the member clubs of the international group allows smooth competition and observation of the pooling agreement. The clubs' rule wordings have to fall in line with the requirements of the pool agreement for the purpose of their reinsurance contract. The principal risks covered by the P&I Clubs are summarised below, with the main ones being discussed in more detail further below. The list is not exhaustive and readers can benefit from a careful study of at least one of the rulebooks to gain a better understanding of what is involved.

(a) Crew

Illness, injury or death of crew members, including costs associated with replacing crew members and deviation to obtain medical assistance.

(b) Passengers and others

Illness, injury or death of passengers and other persons connected with the ship such as stevedores. Passengers' baggage is also covered. In these days of high compensation awards following marine accidents, particularly by the courts in the USA, these first two sections of the cover are clearly of great importance. Costs associated with stowaways can also be covered.

(c) Collisions

Collision liabilities such as the one-quarter third-party liability arising out of the International Hull Clauses 2003. In addition to collision claims, the clubs also provide cover for claims of non-contact damage to other ships, such as wash damage. Some clubs offer $^4/_4$ collision instead of the typical ¼, which is supplemental to the ¾ obtained under the vessel's H&M cover.

(d) Fixed and floating objects

Liabilities incurred in respect of damage done to FFO such as buoys, jetties and pipelines. Cover is also offered in respect of removal of wreckage following a marine casualty.

(e) Pollution

Subject to an upper limit, costs and liabilities arising out of environmental pollution are recoverable from the club.

(f) Cargo

Liabilities in respect of cargo loss, shortage or damage, provided such cargo is carried under a bill of lading containing approved conditions. The clubs also lay down specific and detailed provisions relating to cargo liabilities and to the delivery of cargo against proper documentation.

(g) Freight demurrage and defence

This is an optional cover defending the member for liabilities arising under contract, such as charter party, bill of lading and crew disputes.

(h) Damage to hull

This is the heading covering the charterer's liabilities. Therefore, under this cover, a charterer will enter the vessel within a P&I Club for damages done to it while under charter and thus the charterer can indemnify the owner for any damages to the vessel while under charter.

(i) General average

The club will cover for general average contributions unrecoverable from cargo and other interests where failure to obtain contributions resulted from a breach of contract on the part of the carrier.

(j) Fines

Fines and other penalties imposed by authorities against the ship, including confiscation thereof, for technical offences can be recovered from the club subject to certain provisos.

(k) Deviation

Shipowners' liabilities for deviation from the projected route to pick up stores, bunkers or change of crew can be covered by the club provided notice is given and an additional premium, if required, is paid.

(l) 'Risks incidental to shipowning'

Clubs offer cover under an omnibus rule for any other expenditure which has not been specifically allowed for in any of the printed rules, strictly at the directors' discretion.

Some clubs have started offering war cover extension as currently, war P&I is excluded under the rules and is added as an extension under the hull war cover.

4.8.6 Claims handling

The handling of P&I claims calls for prompt notification to the club of claims or potential claims. Full co-operation with them and disclosure of all relevant facts by the member is essential. In contrast to hull claims (where in essence only two parties are concerned and the owners and underwriters are on opposite sides), P&I claims involve three or more parties, with members and clubs being on the same side. Consequently, the processing of P&I claims is characterised by close consultation between the member and their club where the merits of each claim are assessed and tactics agreed. Depending on individual circumstances, a settlement may be negotiated with the claimant either by the member or their operator, or by the club's claims-handling staff. Alternatively, the claim may be resisted, in which event litigation may follow. Provided the club agrees to support the member, the legal costs will be paid by the club.

Claims are dealt with by the claims-handling staff in the club management office, but the more important cases, particularly those where principles are at stake, are referred to the club directors for approval at one of their periodic meetings. Indeed, any claim can be referred to the directors if a member so wishes. Thus it is a group of fellow members, not insurance people, who, in the final analysis, decide on the nature of the mutual cover to be provided by the club.

4.8.7 Pollution

This is a major area of club activity and one which calls for special attention. It must be remembered in the first place that pollution does not only mean the major headline-grabbing incidents such as the *Exxon Valdez* or the *Erika,* but also the accidental spillage of bunker fuel, the discharge of sewage or the careless disposal of galley refuse. While all of these activities now rightly fall within the ambit of various national and international environmental protection laws and regulations, it is in the area of oil tankers where most attention is concentrated.

As already mentioned, pollution liability is the one area where the club's cover is not unlimited. Two international legal regimes were established: the International Convention on Civil Liability for Oil Pollution Damage (1969 Civil Liability Convention (CLC)) and the International Convention on the Establishment of an International Fund for Compensation for Oil Pollution Damage (1971 Fund Convention). These were subsequently updated to provide a satisfactory insurance framework for compensating victims of marine pollution by tankers. These conventions entered into force in 1975 and 1978, respectively, and both were amended in 1992.

From the clubs' position the main element that initially developed from this framework was the Tanker Owners' Voluntary Agreement concerning Liability for Oil Pollution (TOVALOP), first introduced in 1969. Tankers were entered in the TOVALOP scheme through their respective P&I Clubs, which assumed the responsibility for underwriting the compensation limit and for providing necessary documentary evidence of cover. There was a separate agreement between oil companies called a contract regarding a supplement to tanker liability for oil pollution (CRISTAL), designed to provide a further voluntary layer of compensation above that provided by TOVALOP.

TOVALOP and CRISTAL were discontinued on the introduction of the CLC and the Fund Convention. These were based on the premise that the costs resulting from a major oil spill should be shared between the shipowner and the cargo owner, that is, the oil company. It must be recognised that a significant portion of the world's tankers are still directly or indirectly owned by the oil companies and most of the balance, the independent fleets, only exist because the oil companies need them. Unlike dry cargo ships, tankers are locked into one commodity, not being able to switch to other cargoes in response to changes in the market.

The original regimes were enhanced in 1992 by the new conventions, the 1992 CLC and 1992 Fund Convention, as mentioned above. Under these conventions, an intergovernmental organisation was established to administer the compensation regime: the International Oil Pollution Compensation Funds (IOPC) 1992. These effectively comprise the current regime.

The conventions apply to persistent oil and exclude light oils such as gasoline, light diesel or kerosene. They apply only to tankers and not to bunkers carried on dry cargo ships. Under the CLC and Fund Convention, compensation is payable for expenses incurred in taking successful measures against 'a grave and imminent threat of pollution' as well as dealing with actual polluting incidents.

The conventions apply a strict liability regime against the tanker owner, who can avoid liability only if it can be proved that the pollution was directly due to the act or negligence of another party, such as war, sabotage, or the negligence of authorities in maintaining navigational aids.

There are maximum but very high limits of liability depending on ship size which are currently:

under 5,000gt	4.51m SDR
5,000 to 140,000gt	4.51m SDR plus 631 SDR per gross ton
over 140,000gt	89.77m SDR

There is a simplified procedure for increasing the limits under the 1992 CLC.

If the incident occurs as a result of the owner's actual recklessness or intent, the limitation of liability is forfeit.

All tankers carrying more than 2,000 tonnes of persistent oil as cargo must carry a certificate on board attesting that appropriate insurance cover is carried.

The USA is not a signatory to these conventions. Instead it relies on its own legislation, the Oil Pollution Act (OPA) 1990, which achieves the same ends, although with similar but potentially higher penalties under some circumstances. Vessels entering US waters must carry a certificate of financial responsibility (COFR) issued by their insurers.

The IMO International Convention for the Prevention of Pollution from Ships (MARPOL) 1973 and its protocol of 1978 cover regulations and liability relating to spillage of other pollutants, including garbage and sewage.

Under the pooling agreement, and to reflect the increasing oil pollution liabilities, the overspill allowed to be paid for an incident is US$3.2bn, as can be seen by the pooling agreement reinsurance structure.

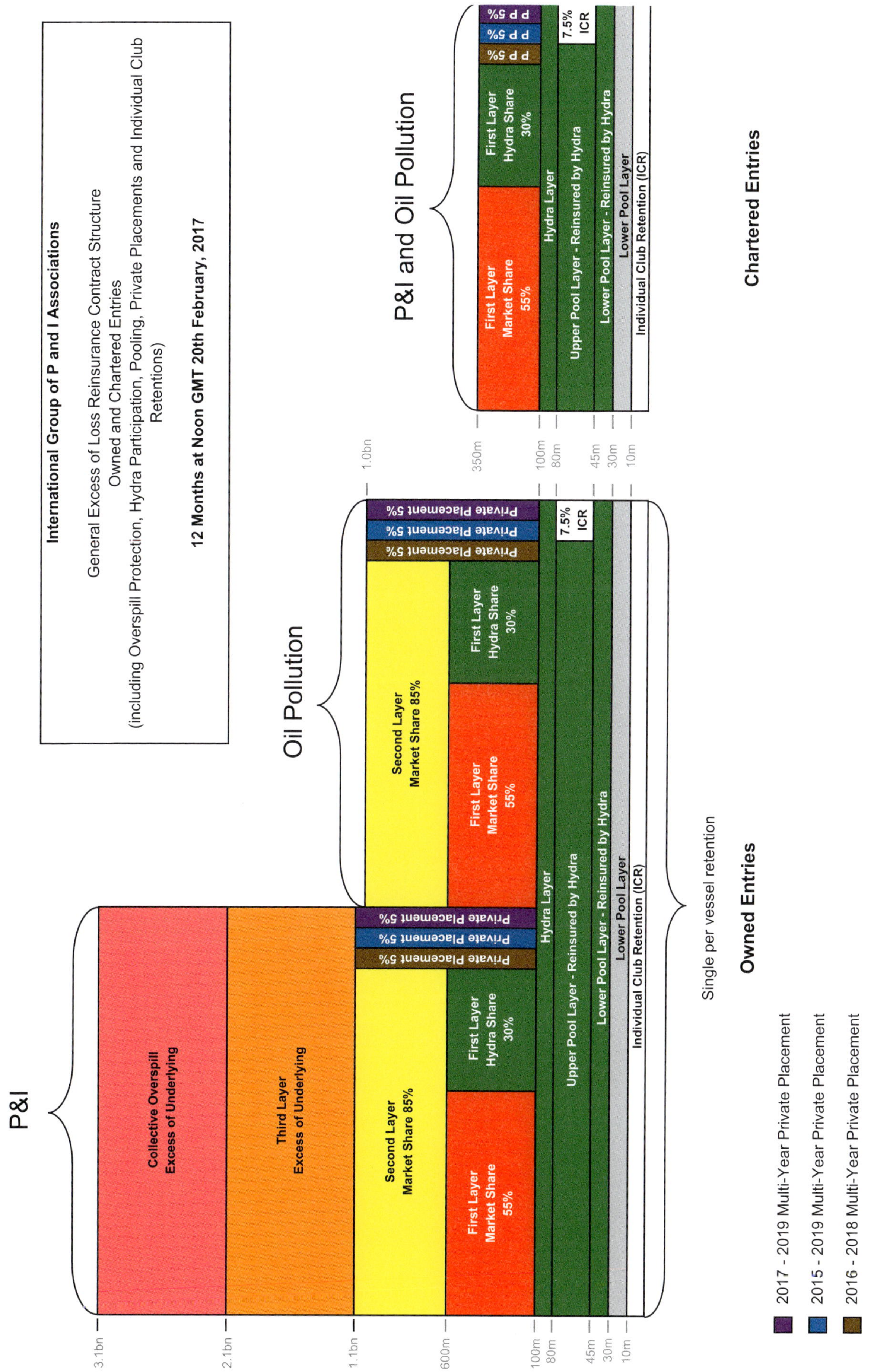

Source UK P&I Club

4.8.8 Cargo liabilities

Until the early part of this century, no generally recognised rules governed the distribution of liabilities between shipowners and shippers, the former being more or less free to set their own conditions of carriage. Then, in 1924, following an international convention in Brussels, a framework was agreed, called the Hague Rules, which subsequently received worldwide approval. These rules were subsequently incorporated into most national legal systems, such as in the UK and US Carriage of Goods by Sea Acts. An amended version, called the Hague-Visby Rules 1968, covered developments in the industry, particularly containerisation, rather than any change in fundamental principle. Most bills of lading used in international commerce incorporate either the Hague or Hague-Visby Rules.

The basic philosophy behind both Hague and Hague-Visby is that misfortune risks to cargo should be borne by the cargo owner, while misfortune risks to the ship should be borne by the shipowner. As far as human error risks are concerned, a compromise was reached in the rules whereby responsibility for the ship before commencement of the voyage lay with the shipowner since it had some direct control over the situation, while risks of events during the voyage would be borne by cargo. This somewhat dated concept is under some strain today because of the efficiency of modern communications whereby a ship can be in virtual constant touch with its owners.

Thus the Hague-Visby Rules as incorporated (for example, in the current (1971) UK Carriage of Goods by Sea Act) oblige the shipowner to exercise due diligence at the beginning of the voyage to make the ship seaworthy, properly to man, equip and supply the ship, and to make the cargo spaces fit for the carriage of the intended cargo. There is an absolute onus on the shipowner properly and carefully to load, handle, stow, carry, keep, care for and discharge the cargo. Provided that due diligence has been exercised, the burden of proof in this respect rests with the shipowner. However, establishing such proof is becoming increasingly difficult in today's legal climate given the wide range of defences available under the rules.

These include error in navigation or management of the ship, perils of the sea, fire, act of God, war, seizure, quarantine, strikes, riots, inherent vice, insufficiency of packing or marking of goods, latent defects not discoverable by due diligence and any other cause 'without the actual fault or privity of the carrier'.

A further part of the rules lays down a monetary limit of the carrier's liability per package or unit. Under the current protocol this is expressed in special drawing rights (SDRs) and the limit now stands at 666.67 SDRs per package or unit, or two SDRs per kg, whichever is greater. The value of SDRs fluctuates daily and is usually quoted in the rate of exchange section of the financial press.

The underlying principle in Hague and Hague-Visby allocates risks between cargo insurers and shipowners' liability insurers, the P&I Clubs. The system has stood the test of time and is supported by a wealth of case law in English and other jurisdictions.

What the shipowner is saying to the cargo interests through the rules is straightforward: 'Here is the point where my insurance underwriters' cover stops so your insurers should cover you from this same point onwards.' Furthermore, cargo owners' insurers know their clients' goods and can assess the risk well enough to charge competitive premiums, whereas if the shipowner had to carry insurance to cover all the different kinds of cargo that may be loaded, then the premium (which would have to be recovered via the freight rate) would be far higher than the shipper would otherwise have to pay. Therefore, from a risk management viewpoint the system is both fair and economic.

However, in 1978, a new liability convention regime was adopted by UNCTAD, called the Hamburg Rules. This provides for a shift of liability to the benefit of cargo interests. The traditional defences in the Hague and the Hague-Visby Rules, such as navigational error, are removed in favour of a provision to the effect that the carrier can only avoid liability if they can prove that they took all reasonable measures to avoid the occurrence. Among other provisions, higher limits of liability are included and the carrier becomes liable for delayed delivery.

The Hamburg Rules have been ratified by sufficient countries such that they have come into force in those countries that have enacted them into legislation. However, they impact on few major maritime routes and this presents a particular problem. Whereas Hague and Hague-Visby apply to cargo loaded in the ratifying country, the Hamburg Rules apply to cargo loaded or discharged. Thus an individual bill of lading might be subject to both conventions leading to jurisdiction-shopping by a claimant. Consider cargo loaded in the UK (Hague-Visby applies) but discharged in Morocco (a Hamburg signatory).

In 2009, the UN agreed the final draft of the latest convention on carriage of goods by sea. This new set of documents is known as the Rotterdam Rules and is at present open for ratification by countries. When sufficient ratifications have been achieved and the appropriate national legislation enacted, the new rules will have proper effect. The process of ratification can take months, or even years, but, because the Rotterdam Rules take more account of multi-modal transport than any previous conventions and are generally regarded as the most balanced set of rules to date, most industry observers believe they will eventually secure wide acceptance.

The Rotterdam Rules will come into force one year after ratification by the twentieth UN member state. At the time of going to print, Spain, Congo and Togo have done so.

Finally, mention should be made of the NYPE Inter-Club Agreement, whereby a clause is often inserted into time charter parties which states that liability for cargo claims is to be shared between the shipowner and the time charterer. The exact proportion to be borne by each party will depend on the circumstances giving rise to the claim.

The Rotterdam Rules take more account of multi-modal transport than any previous conventions

4.8.9 Narcotics

This is another area in which the clubs have been active on their members' behalf. In particular, the provisions of the US Anti-Drug Abuse Act placed onerous responsibilities onto shipowners trading to the United States of America and the clubs were quick to respond with advice and support for their members. Shipping companies were urged by their clubs to enter into a carrier initiative agreement with US customs, while club rules were quickly redrafted to ensure that adequate cover was available for all members. This is a good example of the flexibility inherent in the mutual system, where insured and insurer are one and the same and share a common interest.

4.8.10 Defence

Many P&I Clubs offer defence cover to owners as a separate class of insurance running parallel to P&I cover. Defence cover (called freight, demurrage and defence) is in respect of legal costs incurred by the member in defending claims or bringing actions against other parties. Again, the defence cover is arranged on a mutual basis.

Legal costs arising out of P&I claims, such as those covered by the rules, are paid by the club in any case, but defence cover as a separate entity comes into play in commercial situations where P&I rules do not apply. Nevertheless, there are sometimes areas of uncertainty in which club support is usually available.

Examples of areas where defence cover can be applied include charter party disputes, claims against contractors such as stevedores or ship repairers, and claims against ship builders for vessels failing to meet specifications. When handling defence claims, the clubs reserve the right to appoint (or, at any rate, approve) the appointment of lawyers and other experts acting on behalf of the member. As matters of principle are frequently involved, defence claims are almost invariably considered individually by the club's board of directors at each stage of the case as it progresses.

4.8.11 Through transport

Container ship operators can arrange insurance for through transport liabilities, again on a mutual basis. The leader in this field is the Through Transport Mutual Insurance Association, or TT Club, jointly operated by three of the major London-managed P&I Clubs.

Through transport cover will encompass risks arising out of the movement of cargo from inland depots by rail or road to the seaport, operations at the terminals, and likewise, inland haulage to final destination at the other end of the route. The cover extends to loss of or damage to the containers themselves or container shell cover, also to trailers and similar equipment and to personal injury risks at container freight stations during stuffing and unstuffing. This type of cover is available not only to container ship operators but also to non-vessel-operating common carriers (NVOCCs) which operate on a slot-chartering basis. Readers who are particularly involved in container operations are advised to examine the TT Club rulebook for further details of this specialised cover.

4.8.12 Strikes

There are certain mutual associations, some of which are linked to P&I Clubs, that provide shipowners with strike indemnity insurance. Strike cover can relate either to crew strikes or shore strikes, such as those involving stevedores. In either case, the shipowner declares a daily sum based on the ship's normal operating costs, which becomes the basis of the insurance indemnity and pays a premium calculated on that daily sum. If a strike takes place and the ship is delayed, it submits a claim and, if approved, receives payment in accordance with the daily entered sum. For the sake of good order, for shore strikes the club will obtain a report from their local correspondent at the port in question confirming that the strike really did take place.

4.8.13 Loss of hire

This type of cover is more closely akin to hull insurance and is in fact usually placed in the market. But, as with strike cover, a daily indemnity is agreed and a premium is calculated accordingly. There is an excess, or a deductible, and an agreed maximum number of days lost per claim and in all over the policy year. For example, the policy might read 15/90/180 meaning no claim for the first 15 days, then up to 90 days any one accident and 180 days in all during the year. Claims are only paid for time lost as a direct result of a marine accident as defined in the hull policy conditions, so a report from the insurer's surveyor is required to support the claim.

4.8.14 Summary

Mention has been made throughout this chapter of the relationship between the ship operator and its club. A prudent ship operator will cultivate this relationship, remembering that it is one of equals and should be a non-adversarial partnership. Club members will always bear in mind that in times of trouble they will want informed and expert advice immediately, not days or even, in some cases, hours later. They will also want to bear in mind that there will be occasions when their ship is in trouble and threatened with arrest. In such situations it does not matter if the reasons are real or imaginary, and they will want reputable local lawyers appointed to protect their interests and, if necessary, letters of guarantee issued, within minutes. In a large amount of P&I work, speed is of the essence.

Chapter 5

Costs and accounting

5.1 INTRODUCTION

This chapter aims to give a broad outline of a practical ship manager's approach to the subject of costs and accounting. It does not attempt to cover the issues in the detail required by the qualified and professional accountant. Nor does it venture into the realms of systems and computer software. It recognises that the technicalities of processing accounts are best left to the specialists and that different companies have their own methods and procedures for bookkeeping. The chapter does, however, address the way in which ship managers are accountable for their work and how the ship management function relates to the overall picture of shipping finance.

5.2 DEFINITIONS

The costs associated with running ships generally fall into three broad categories:

Capital or fixed costs

These are the fixed costs associated with the acquisition of a vessel and, for the purposes of this chapter, these are assumed to be fully within the control of the owner.

The costs could include pre-delivery expenses, loan repayments and interest, leasing charges, initial registration fees and, in certain cases, taxes. Where a vessel is taken on bareboat or demise charter, the charter hire is the equivalent of capital costs.

Where the owner has been able to purchase the vessel out of the company's own financial resources, the directors will have decided on an annual rate of depreciation together with an appropriate return on capital employed. Where the vessel has been purchased by means of a mortgage, loan repayment and interest will form the principal fixed cost.

Operating costs

These are the costs that are the fundamental responsibility of the ship manager. The costs could be considered to be semi-variable, some elements being more or less fixed over a fairly long period of time while others are variable and relate closely to the employment of the ship.

It is the primary task of the ship manager to arrange for operating costs to be accurately budgeted. They can be averaged on a daily basis and are usually referred to as the daily operating or running cost (DOC or DRC), and sometimes also as the cost per day or the daily cost items, so that the owner can easily estimate its voyage or charter profitability. Included in operating costs are the crewing, storing, maintenance, insurance and administration of the vessel.

Voyage costs

These are variable costs associated with the particular employment in which the ship is engaged from time to time. Specifically, voyage costs include bunkers, port and canal charges, pilotage, harbour tug hire, port agency fees and any loading and discharging expenses. Voyage costs fall within the control of the ship's commercial operator.

If the owner hires the vessel out on time charter, almost all the voyage costs become the responsibility of the time charterer.

5.3 SHIP MANAGEMENT COST FUNCTIONS

Ship managers may either work in-house as part of the shipowner's own organisation or as an independent entity contracted to the owning company under a management agreement. This chapter assumes that the ship manager is working as a separate entity on a full management package basis, which assists in making a clear distinction of the responsibilities falling upon the ship manager. Even in cases where the ship management department is in-house, the discipline imposed by operating as if the management is a separate entity is frequently beneficial. The accounting function forms the core of ship management. While the owners have control over capital costs, they must look to the ship manager to provide them with a safe, efficient and economical ship operation package which can be accurately costed to enable the owners to make the correct commercial decisions.

As far as accounting is concerned, the ship manager's job falls into three stages – budgeting, processing and reporting. The budget estimate will first be submitted to and discussed with the owner in detail so that agreement can be reached on the way the ship will be operated. The budget will normally cover a 12-month period and from it can be produced a cash flow forecast which will set out the anticipated expenditure on a monthly or quarterly basis. The second processing stage is reached as the ship is in service, expenditure is actually incurred and bills have to be paid. Finally, at regular intervals, the manager will prepare a detailed report analysing the costs incurred on behalf of the owner and compare these with the budget forecast.

This final stage is the acid test of the manager's efficiency and ability to forecast operating costs with accuracy. The budget versus actual cost analysis will also form the basis on which to prepare the budget estimate for the following year.

5.4 BUDGET PREPARATION

The preparation of operating budgets is one of the most important parts of the ship manager's job. For a vessel which is already part of the managed fleet, the preparation of the budget is normally fairly straightforward because the manager already knows the ship and its characteristics from experience. Things are different when trying to prepare a budget estimate for a new or a newly acquired ship. Clearly, the more information about a new ship due to come under management which is made available to the manager in advance, the more accurate will be the budget forecast.

Certain facts will need to be found out to enable accuracy as vessels can be very different in several ways. For example, the size of the vessel is important, bigger ships need larger spare parts, which cost more and attract higher delivery costs. Bigger ships also cost more to paint. Old ships generally will need more maintenance and are likely to be less efficient. The flag will be significant as some will allow more flexibility and probably cheaper crews as well as the benefits of certain registries. The type of ship will be important; tankers are more expensive to run than bulk carriers because they are scrutinised much more closely by port state and charterers. Where the vessel is planned to trade will be significant, both for storing costs and crew changes. The cargo equipment will be minimal on a Capesize bulker but on a handymax, the cranes and cargo-handling equipment may need extra skilled maintenance because of a heavy workload. The type of engine(s) and auxiliaries will determine the lubricant usage and maintenance requirements. Knowing all these would be essential before starting to make a budget.

Ideally, the manager will have had an opportunity to carry out a technical inspection of the ship and an examination of class records before preparing the budget. But this is not always possible if the owner requires a preliminary budget estimate on the basis of an unseen ship. As a minimum, the manager will want to know the size, type and age of a vessel, the type of main and auxiliary engines, intended registry, crew and, if possible, trading pattern. These main assumptions should be clearly explained in the budget estimate, not forgetting to state rates of exchange used when converting from one currency into another.

The following sections deal with the main cost headings which appear in a typical budget estimate.

5.4.1 Crew

The budget sets out the assumptions on which the crew costs have been estimated, in terms of numbers and nationalities of crew members. An experienced personnel department in a ship manager's office will be able to budget the main elements of the crew cost with accuracy. It must be remembered that the owner is not concerned about the individual pay of crew members but is rather looking for the total cost over a year of manning the ship. For instance, an officer may receive an annual salary of, say, $80,000, but if they are entitled to one month's leave for every two served, the manager must employ 1.5 officers to fill the post. Thus the total annual cost to the owner becomes $120,000.

Crew wage costs need to be enhanced to take into account not only leave entitlement but also any overlap time between individuals leaving and joining the ship. Some management companies refine this concept further by working on a unit cost basis. This means that they work out the average cost of filling each rank in their ships over a 12-month period and applying that cost factor across the board. Due allowance must also be made for any crew bonuses together with social costs, insurance contributions, pension funds and so on. Crew's overtime, if not consolidated, has also to be estimated based on the manager's experience of the trade in question.

In addition to direct crew costs, the managers should make provision in some way for crew establishment costs. These are the expenses involved in keeping properly qualified and trained crew available for the ships under their management. Such costs as recruiting expenses, training allowances, cadet training, study leave, standby and sick pay are all part of the cost of providing crews and have to be paid for in some way or other by the owners. In certain cases, some of these costs may be offset by various national government assistance schemes. The establishment costs may either be apportioned over the managed fleet as a direct charge or, in some cases, a fixed sum contribution from the owners is negotiated by the managers.

Crew travel and repatriation expenses are particularly difficult to budget accurately unless the ship is a liner engaged on a regular trading route. An element of educated guesswork is required here by the manager, based on the anticipated frequency of crew reliefs. A final element under crew costs covers sundry medical expenses, which are not otherwise recoverable under the terms of the P&I Club entry.

Crew travel and repatriation expenses are particularly difficult to budget accurately

5.4.2 Stores

Here, the manager's superintending staff need to call on the wealth of their experience of operating ships of the type in question. Stores first include victualling or provisioning the ship.

Nowadays this is quite frequently done on a contract catering basis as so much per person per day, which greatly simplifies the work of the manager's office.

The suppliers of ships' provisions (the ship chandlers) work in a very competitive market and, in some parts of the world, this has been known to cause problems. Managers must ensure that whichever system of provisioning is adopted it is properly supervised. Ship managers should be alert to the unscrupulous few in the ship chandlery trade who may succeed in putting irresistible temptation in the way of ships' officers or catering staff. Poor quality food, invoiced at full quality price, with the cash saved being shared, is a recipe for a discontented ship, which will inevitably become inefficient and even dangerous.

The second major area of storing is commonly referred to as 'rope, soap and dope'. There is sometimes difficulty in distinguishing between stores and spare parts, and the dividing line is frequently somewhat vague. However, if the concept of consumables is used then the distinction is drawn more easily. Under 'stores' one would normally include wires and ropes for mooring or cargo-handling gear, lashing material, packing material and gases or chemicals used for refrigerating-plant, boiler or tank-cleaning treatments and so forth. Paints are generally regarded as stores unless specifically ordered for drydocking purposes. Cabin stores, ship stationery, laundry and fresh water supplies also fall into this category.

A third major expenditure under stores would be lubricants and greases. The consumption of engine lubricating oil is a fairly simple matter of calculation depending on the size and type of engine and the number of running days per annum. For this purpose, knowledge of the anticipated trading pattern for the vessel is invaluable.

The accounting for stores can be on either a cash or consumption basis and the owners' wishes in this matter should be ascertained.

5.4.3 Maintenance

Under this heading are included costs of specific spare parts ordered as replacements for items which wear out or become damaged. The ship should always carry an accurate list of spare parts carried on board. Usually, an onboard inventory is undertaken every six months or every year and the results sent to head office. It is important that both the ship and the shore superintendents have copies of such lists so that these are available in cases of unplanned dockings. Many managers have planned maintenance systems with a subsystem on board each vessel to record stocks of spare parts on board and on order.

Maintenance budgets comprise the costs of maintenance, together with the cost of carrying out any repairs to deck or engine areas. The cost of shore labour used to carry out repairs in port is also included, together with the cost associated with any riding crews employed to carry out repairs to the ships at sea. The cost of maintaining automation, electronics and navigation aids in a modern, sophisticated vessel can be a major item of expense. Some of these items may be rented on a full maintenance basis rather than owned, in which case the rental charges will replace maintenance costs.

Survey and classification fees also fall into the maintenance category.

It is common practice for managers to estimate the cost of periodical drydockings and to spread the cost over a period of years on an accrual basis. Thus, if a vessel is expected to dock every second or third year, a half or a third of the estimated docking expenditure will be budgeted within each year leading up to the docking. This means that an allowance against the docking will have been built up or accrued in the owner accounts towards the eventual cost. On the other hand, some owners prefer to disregard docking expenditure from the budget, electing to accept the cost when incurred as a special item. Managers will have to establish from owners what their individual approach is in this regard at the budget agreement discussions. By the same token, consideration must be given as to whether drydocking remains within the budget or is shown separately.

Maintenance budgets comprise the costs of maintenance, together with the cost of carrying out any repairs to deck or engine areas

5.4.4 INSURANCE

The cost of insurance premiums and estimated P&I calls are based on quotations obtained or renewal negotiations. It is frequent practice for the P&I budget figure to be based on estimated total calls as applied for the year in question. This may, of course, be at slight variance with the actual cash position but it will allow the owner to accrue for the true cost of P&I insurance during the year in question.

The treatment of insurance deductibles is one for owners to decide. Sometimes, costs which are not recoverable by reason of the deductible are permitted to 'lie where they fall', probably as extra maintenance/repair items. Otherwise the budget can assume one or more insurance claims will arise in the year and so ensure that appropriate deductibles are allowed for.

5.4.5 Administration

Here one includes superintending expenses, renewable dues, subscriptions and fees (including agency costs where applicable for owners' items) and communication costs. Also shown under this section would be the management fee, assuming the vessel is operated under contract by an independent ship manager.

Where the ship management is an in-house department, a prudent owner will calculate the cost of running the management department and decide on an appropriate percentage to be apportioned to each ship in the fleet.

5.4.6 Accounts processing

Once the budget estimate has been discussed with and agreed by the owners, a cash flow forecast is prepared based on the budget. The cash flow forecast has been divided into monthly periods and the amounts expected to be called by the manager each month are estimated. The monthly amounts will vary depending on, for instance, when insurance premiums fall due or when drydockings are due to take place.

It is common practice in the case of independent managers for the cash flow forecast, having been agreed by the owners, to form the basis of a monthly funding requirement for the managers. This enables the managers to pay the crew and to settle bills received for supplies and services on the owners' behalf. There will also be an agreed process for the manager to apply to the owner for additional funds to cover unexpected or unbudgeted expenditure.

Different companies will each have their own procedures laid down for entering, checking, authorising and paying accounts but, however this is done, it leads on to the final all-important reporting stage of the manager's function.

5.5 REPORTING

The test of a ship manager's costing skill is contained in the budget versus actual analysis statement. This is prepared either monthly or quarterly as a record of management performance and uses the same cost headings as the budget estimate. The budget figures appear in one column, the actual costs incurred in a second column, and the difference, perhaps with a percentage variance calculation, in a third.

The frequency of these statements is a matter for discussion and agreement between owner and manager. While a monthly analysis is said to keep the manager alert, quite small differences in payment dates can lead to large and misleading fluctuations in costs. On the other hand, while a quarterly statement eliminates many of the fluctuations, if the analysis is being used as a sensible management tool, such a delay may result in problem areas not being identified promptly enough. Monthly statements, combined with a cumulative analysis as illustrated, probably provide the best compromise solution.

A list of figures, however, is not sufficient. Managers must support their analysis statements with a reasonably detailed commentary on all significant variances. They will be shown in a comments column. The ideal relationship between owner and manager should resemble a joint venture or partnership, featuring an honest, open approach. The manager should never try to conceal difficulties but be prepared to discuss them with the owner with a view to finding the best solution. Used properly, the analysis statement can frequently provide early warning of a ship's operating problems so that steps can be taken to avoid a deteriorating situation.

As stated above, the owners will look to the ship manager to provide them with essential information to enable the correct commercial decisions to be made. In the simplest terms, the sum of the owner's capital costs plus the ship manager's operating costs, averaged on a daily basis and compared with the current time charter market rate, will give a good measure of the ship's net profit potential. The situation becomes more complex when looking at voyage charters or liner operations, but these issues are dealt with elsewhere in other books published by the ICS.

5.6 THE LAY-UP DECISION

From time to time, the cyclical nature of international trade and the shipping market leads to periods of depression and this may become so severe that vessels are withdrawn from service to be laid up. This sort of situation calls for close co-operation and understanding between owners and managers, with a view to maintaining the asset value of the owner's investment and ensuring the prompt and problem-free reactivation of the ship when the market improves. The costs associated with the proper care and preservation of a large sophisticated vessel in lay-up are considerable.

It is certainly not just a case of paying off the crew, switching off the lights and locking up. Indeed, the vessel's insurers will normally require not only the classification society but also their own surveyor, such as the Salvage Association, to inspect and approve mooring arrangements, alarm systems and preservation procedures. The daily cost of a ship in lay-up may be less than a quarter of the normal operating cost after allowing for return of insurance premiums and other cost savings. But reactivation expenses are usually heavy, probably involving drydocking and extra survey work to ensure that the vessel is once more properly in class.

From a ship manager's viewpoint, the laying-up of tonnage causes particular problems relating to manpower requirements. Although some management agreements contain provisions whereby owners contribute towards lay-off or redundancy costs, generally these risks remain with the managers. The longer-term effects of a prolonged shipping recession can have far-reaching effects, especially in terms of a diminution of the worldwide pool of merchant navy manpower.

Laying-up a tanker causes problems of its own. Charterers need to see a continuous series of vessel inspections recorded in the SIRE reports. Ships need to have oil company approvals before they are employable. These are built up over a number of voyages and, if the vessel proceeds into lay-up, these lapse. Thus, when markets improve and the commercial climate exists for a vessel to trade at a profit again, the lack of oil company approvals may render the ship unemployable.

Large dry bulk charterers have also begun to rely on SIRE reports. A similar situation may increasingly arise in the bulk carrier sector.

Since 2008, an alternative strategy to laying-up vessels, particularly those operating in the liner trades, has been to practise slow-steaming. Quite clearly, a vessel that proceeds at a slower speed than usual will complete fewer voyages over time and potentially earn less freight. However, extending the time between calls at each port will allow for a greater build-up of cargo and the ship will perhaps sail more fully loaded than it might otherwise have done. In addition, slow-steaming reduces the overall capacity of the fleet and thus is a way to avoid laying vessels up.

The real dividend of slow steaming is that a relatively small reduction in speed for a modern container ship can produce a 10% or more saving in fuel use. Given the high cost of bunkers today, the financial savings achieved are significant.

An alternative strategy to laying-up vessels, particularly those operating in the liner trades, has been to practise slow steaming

5.7 CONCLUSION

This chapter has assumed that ship management costs are handled as a full package by a separate independent company, not part of the owner's own organisation. There are, however, many variations in the amount of responsibility delegated by the shipowner to the management company.

At one end of the scale, the contract could be simply for the supply of the crew, while at the other end, the contract could extend to include involvement in commercial operations and chartering. Indeed, in some management contracts, certain cost elements are fixed so that the ship manager accepts the direct risk of getting its sums wrong. However, this chapter has concentrated on those areas which are generally accepted as core ship management functions, assuming the conventional cost-plus method of working.

Ship management is a competitive business with, at one end, the large international operators or owner managers and, at the othe end the small companies with one or two ships trying to spread overheads. When owners are seeking management quotations they may receive a bewildering variety of responses. To accept the cheapest offer without carefully investigating the manager's background would be not only imprudent, but would imply a lack of due diligence on the owner's part.

Chapter 6

Operations

6.1 INTRODUCTION

The professional shipowner or manager will place great importance on having a knowledgeable, experienced and enthusiastic operations department. Once the employment of the vessel has been decided it is they who will act, not only as the link between the vessel and the shipowners, but also between the owning side and the vessel's charterers and other cargo interests.

The operations department has four primary tasks:

1. To ensure that the Masters know and understand exactly what is expected of them and their ship.
2. To monitor the voyage, with a view to minimising the expenses and maximising the income.
3. To be on the lookout for potential problems and disputes and to try to resolve them before they get out of hand.
4. To act as a clearing house for information within the ship manager's offices so that everyone knows all they need to know about what the ship is doing, thus enabling them to do their jobs effectively.

Once the nature of the employment has been decided, the full details should be passed to the operations department by the owners or by their chartering brokers.

These details should include:

- the cargo and its size;
- loading and discharging ports together with restrictions, if any;
- notices of readiness that are required to be given to the charterers and/or the shippers, and for the consignees and the agents;
- any special instructions and/or advice that needs to be given to the ship's command about the cargo.

This information must be relayed to the ship's Master without delay.

Here is a sample of voyage instructions that will be forwarded to the Master.

Voyage Instruction 1:

Re: Orient ship to be nominated

For good order's sake, please pass following voyage instructions to the owners/Master.

aa)

Load port: 1 SB Mobile

Disport: 1 SB Rotterdam

bb)

Cargo:

Load

Mobile

- 70,000MT +/- 10% MOLOO

Discharge

Rotterdam

- 70,000MT +/- 10% MOLOO

Laycan: Nov 01/Nov 10

ETA: Please advise

Kindly provide a provisional stowage plan for charterer's approval clearly stating arrival/departure draughts at loading/discharging ports.

Agents: Mobile

Agent's name and details

Rotterdam

Agent's name and details

cc)

Notices:

Master to inform charterers and each agent as follows: Charterer's email –

At load port

a) approximate ETA load port on fixing;

b) daily ETA notices for load port;

c) sailing from last port;

d) 10/5 days offloading port;

e) 72hrs offloading port – Application for cargo (Approximate quantity of cargo required) with proposed stow plan;

f) 48hrs offloading port;

g) 24/12/6hrs offloading port;

h) if vessel's ETA changes by more than 6hrs – inform charterers and load port agents;

i) immediately advise major deviations, if any.

At discharge port

Please provide at earliest opportunity the following information for passing to receivers:

a) sailing time;

b) daily ETA notices for disport;

c) arrival draught for disport;

d) cargo details including stowage plan;

e) bunkering en route to discharge port;

f) 10/5 days off discharge port with discharging sequence;

g) 72hrs off discharge port;

h) 48hrs off discharge port;

i) 24/12/6hrs off discharge port;

j) if vessel's ETA changes by more than 6hrs – inform charterers and discharge port agents;

k) immediately advise major deviation, if any.

dd)

Bilge pumping – Master to inform charterers and discharge port agents as follows:

On loaded voyages, vessel to pump out hold bilges at least twice every day. A daily record of bilge pumping is to be kept. Master to send a bilge report every three days indicating bilge water pumped out per hold and with it a grand/running total of the total bilge water pumped out per hold up to date. The running total to be shown on attached charterer's steel bilge pumping form.

Please acknowledge receipt of these instructions.

Regards

Voyage instructions 2:

Please find voyage instructions below.

Kindly revert with ship's ETA load port.

a) owners to consult CP for voyage orders to Master;

b) laycan: 30.03–05.04;

c) load port: Haypoint;

d) full and complete cargo and quantity: 153,000 metric tons 10% more or less in owners' option coal in bulk, 1–3 grades in charterers' option to be naturally segregated and shipped in accordance with IMO recommendations;

Intended cargo grade/split: – reverting;

e) Master to please give daily ETA notices since 15 days prior to load ports to:

1. load port agents;
2. loading port protective agents;
3. charterers.

f) load port agents;

g) disport: Chinese port tbn;

Local agents – reverting;

Please find below BHP Billiton's protective agent's details. Please request Master to include charterers on his daily notices to discharge port:

h) Master to give daily ETA disport notices to:

1. disport agents;

2. charterers and;
3. protective agents.

i) Bilge pumping report while en route:

Please send us a weekly report, every Sunday, on the bilge pumping performed during the laden passage to disports. At conclusion of the voyage please send us the complete water log summary for our records;

j) Governance

Pls relay below to Master:

During the course of your providing services to charterers, you MUST NOT give or offer to give to anyone (for example, pilots, surveyors, agents, port officials, customs officials or anyone else) anything of value, including cash, cash equivalents (for example, gift cards), hospitality (other than a modest meal), or gifts (for example, alcohol or cigarettes or other such items), directly or indirectly, for a service that may present an actual or perceived improper advantage or benefit to charterers, even if the thing of value is small, customary and/or would result in savings for charterers. Similarly, facilitation payments (small payments to speed up or expedite routine actions) and any other unofficial or undocumented payments must not be made when providing services to BHP Billiton.

Charterers are focused on ensuring its employees, contractors, consultants and other third parties engaged to conduct business on its behalf do not breach laws and our own internal policies regarding bribery and corruption. This standard aligns with the charterers' charter and its code of conduct, all of which can be viewed via our website or a copy passed to you on your request.

Incident reporting:

BHP Billiton requires ALL emergency incidents that seriously threaten the immediate or future safety of people, the environment, property or business to be reported. Emergency incidents include actual or probable, fatalities, serious injuries, marine pollution, collision, grounding, fire, explosion, and situations where the vessel is exposed to adverse reaction/publicity from authorities, the media, the general public or other credible source. In addition, the unplanned loss of any oil, chemical or gas from tanks, pipes and hoses to the deck/environment must be reported. Finally, any breach of vessel security where actual or probable loss of control over vessel operations, or harm to people, or damage to the environment did occur or could have occurred, shall be reported. This instruction is to be followed for BHP Billiton Emergency notification.

After address, preface message with 'Incident'

Name of ship

Nature of emergency/incident

Position of ship

Name, nationality and type of other ship(s) involved

Nature and extent of damage

Fatalities and/or personal injuries (if any)

State of sea and weather. Whether towage is required. Is the emergency/incident escalating or under control?

In the event of a bunker/oil spill, include – local time; date; location; type; approx volume; estimated rate of spill; and cause if known In the event of a bunker/oil spill please also advise whether a clean-up has been attempted or successfully achieved; and by whom. Name of terminal owner (if in port), and whether at a jetty, berth, anchorage, etc.

Any other comments. Time and origin of each report.

Best regards,

Voyage Instructions 3:

RE: MV CHINA VESSEL TO BE NOMINATED V3 CP dated 1 Aug/Voyage instructions

VOYAGE INSTRUCTION

===================

VESSEL:	MV CHINESE VESSEL TO BE NAMED
CARGO:	160,000MT +/– 10% MOLOO IRON IN BULK 'GRADE(S) TBA'
LOAD PORT:	1–2 SBS/1 SPS PORT HEDLAND, WESTERN AUSTRALIA
LOAD RATE:	80,000 MT PWWD SHINC/12 TT USC
DISCH PORT:	1–2 SBS/1–2 SPS SINGAPORE – JAPAN RANGE (INTENTION CHINA)
DISCH RATE:	30,000 MT PWWD SHINC/24 TT USC
NOR:	TENDER UPON ANCHOR DOWN AT ANCHORAGE
LAYCAN:	10–12 AUG 2014

AA) STOW PLAN:

PLEASE PROVIDE US WITH A PROPOSED STOW PLAN SOONEST BASIS A SINGLE GRADE OF IRON ORE (THE AGENTS WILL ADVISE THE CARGO GRADE(S) IN DUE COURSE AND THESE ARE SUBJECT TO CHANGE).

PLEASE CONFIRM THAT YOUR VESSEL WILL BE MAINTAINED WITHIN ACCEPTABLE LIMITS OF STRESS, TRIM, BENDING MOMENTS AND STABILITY.

THROUGH ALL STAGES OF LOADING AND DISCHARGING AND THROUGHOUT THE VOYAGE.

VESSEL'S TENTATIVE STOWAGE PLANS TO BE :

A) BASIS 17.5M

B) BASIS VESSEL'S MAX LIFT/DRAUGHT FOR PLANNING DUKC.

NB: AGENTS WILL ADVISE TIDE AND DRAUGHT RESTRICTIONS.

PRE-STOWAGE PLANS TO BE SENT TO THE FOLLOWING PARTIES LISTED BELOW:

1 CHARTERERS;

2 AGENTS;

3 TERMINAL;

- LOADING PLAN TO BE SENT TO LOAD PORT AT LEAST 7 DAYS PRIOR TO ARRIVAL MINIMISING HATCH CHANGES AND PRODUCT CHANGES.

BB) NOTICES:

(MASTER TO TENDER NOTICES AS MENTIONED IN ACCORDANCE WITH CP, FAILURE OF WHICH MAY RESULT IN NOR TO BE NULL & VOID).

- PLEASE ENSURE YOU PROVIDE US AND OUR AGENTS WITH DAILY PROSPECTS UPDATE NOTICE OF YOUR VSL EXPECTED ARRIVAL IN PORT HEDLAND ORDER TO MAINTAIN BERTHING LINE UP.

THIS INCLUDES YOUR LATEST ITINERARY.

- SAME WILL APPLY WITH DAILY PROSPECTS UPDATE NOTICE OF YOUR VSL EXPECTED ARRIVAL IN CHINESE DISCHARGE PORT.

- PLEASE ADVISE US IMMEDIATELY IF ANY ETA CHANGES BY MORE THAN 8 HOURS AT ONE TIME.

- ON THE VESSEL'S DEPARTURE PORT HEDLAND AND ON A DAILY BASIS PLEASE ADVISE THE VESSEL'S ETA BASIS PASSING SINGAPORE LATITUDE 01-18 N. ON PASSING THIS LATITUDE PLEASE ADVISE THE DATE AND TIME.

THE ABOVE IS IN CONJUNCTION WITH GIVING THE ETA'S BASIS THE BASE PORT OF QINGDAO OR THE DECLARED DISPORT(S).

CC) CLEANLINESS:

VESSEL TO ARRIVE AT LOAD PORT IN ALL RESPECTS READY TO LOAD THE A/M CARGO ENSURING FREE OF ANY PREVIOUS CARGO.

REMNANTS AND ALL HOLDS ARE CLEANED, SWEPT, FREE OF RESIDUE, DRY AND READY TO RECEIVE ANY GRADE OF IRON ORE.

IMPORTANT:

PLEASE ENSURE THAT THE DUTY OFFICER IS ON DECK AT ALL TIMES WHEN THE SHIP LOADER IS BEING MOVED BETWEEN HATCHES.

PRIOR TO COMMENCING A POUR, THE DUTY OFFICER MUST ENSURE THAT THE LOADER IS AT THE CORRECT HOLD, AS PER THE LOADING PLAN.

DD) FULL STYLES AND COMMUNICATION DETAILS:

1) PORT HEDLAND AGENTS:

+++

2) CHINA (GENERAL AGENTS) :

NB: NOMINATED DISCHARGE PORT AND LOCAL AGENT TO BE CONFIRMED AND WILL BE ADVISED ACCORDINGLY. PLEASE SEND ETA NOTICES.

BASIS QINGDAO PORT TO OUR PRINCIPAL AGENT.

+++

3) CHARTERER'S AGENTS

THE VESSEL WILL BE MONITORED WHILST ALONGSIDE LOAD PORT IN REGARDS TO SAFETY, OPERATIONS, CO-OPERATION OF THE OFFICERS & CREW WITH

THE LOADING OPERATIONS, AND SECURITY ON THE VESSEL. THE MASTER AND OFFICERS MUST BE MADE AWARE OF THESE REQUIREMENTS AND ARE TO PROVIDE MAXIMUM ASSISTANCE WITH THE SHORE LOADING PERSONNEL.

PLEASE DO NOT HESITATE TO CONTACT PIC ATDNSHINC.

KINDLY CONFIRM SAFE RECEIPT OF THIS VOYAGE INSTRUCTION AND KEEP US UPDATED DAILY WITH YOUR ETA TO SCHEDULE THE VESSEL AND FOR MAINTAINING THE BERTHING LINE UP.

HAVE A SAFE VOYAGE!

END

BEST REGARDS

The operations department should obtain a copy of the charter party as soon as possible so that complete details of what has been agreed can be studied. The relevant items should then all be discussed with the Masters so that they fully understand what is expected of them.

The next task for the operations department will be to contact the agents at the loading and discharge ports, and instruct them giving details of the voyage.

The first loading port agent should be asked for advice as to probable berthing and loading prospects. The port agents should each be asked to provide:

- a detailed proforma disbursement account;
- confirmation of any restrictions at the port or berth which may affect the vessel, bearing in mind that restrictions at the discharge port(s) may affect the volume of cargo which can be loaded or the port rotation;
- any other relevant information that they might consider useful.

In an ideal situation, the operations department should have the opportunity to contact the agents while the employment is under negotiation and before it is fixed – unfortunately, this is not always possible. At the same time, the operations departments should liaise with the appropriate departments within the ship management company to ensure that:

- the crew mail is despatched to the ship by the most expeditious means, always providing time permits;
- any spares ordered and awaiting despatch are sent to the ship, again, always provided time permits;
- any crew changes are organised well in advance;
- if required, all arrangements for classification surveys and renewal of certificates are made and appropriate;
- arrangements are made for stores and lubricants to be put on board, if needed;
- the Master advises how much cash the ship needs for advances to the crew. It is customary for members of the crew to draw part of the wages due to them in the currency of the country at which the ship is calling, or in US$, so that they have money to spend on shore leave.

Once the vessel has arrived at the loading port, the operations department will keep in close touch with the agents.

This is to ensure:

- that the pilot boards and the vessel berths promptly;
- that the notice of readiness has been tendered and accepted;
- that the loading operations are proceeding as fast as practical;
- that all the Master's requirements are being properly and expeditiously met and that any spares and so on, sent from elsewhere, have been collected and put on board the vessel;
- that an appropriate sum has been remitted to the agents to cover the disbursements for which the owner is responsible and the Master's cash advance requirements, if any;
- that the agents understand and will comply with any instructions which the shipowner/manager might have concerning bills of lading.

Once the ship has sailed, the operations department will repeat all these procedures for the discharging operations.

In the case of a time charter, the procedures will differ slightly from those for a voyage charter described above. The time charterers will be issuing voyage instructions to the vessel so that it is most important to ensure that the Master is advised who those charterers are, including the details of any manager or agent who is authorised to issue instructions on their behalf. The Master must also be advised of the length of the period and the intended trades as far as these are known. It is common for owners to prohibit certain dangerous or dirty cargoes and certain politically or geographically challenging areas. The Master will need to know about these so as to react promptly if they receive contrary orders from the time charterers.

The most urgent information will, of course, be the place of, and arrangements that have been agreed for, the delivery of the ship to the time charterers together with the name of the agents who will represent the owners at the time of that delivery.

An important area in a shipbroker's office is the operations or post-fixture department. In most shipbroking houses, the brokers conclude a fixture, with all subjects lifted. They pass all the paperwork to the post-fixture department. It is the latter's responsibility to obtain voyage instructions, to pass these to the Master via the shipowner. They should track the vessel's progress, spot any concerns and inform the relevant parties. They should check the freight invoice and pass it on. They are sometimes asked to draw up the charter party.

Increasingly, electronic storage of fixture details by a third party is used. The recap is sent to a central database. Both principals are asked to confirm that the recap is a full and fair representation of the concluded fixture. If they confirm that this is the case, the document is hallmarked and locked. Generally speaking, South Korean, Indian and Brazilian principals require a full paper copy of the charter party with all additional clauses signed by both principals or their agents.

As in so many things, communication is most important once the fixture has been concluded. Occasionally, a message may go astray, or the wrong email address is used, causing quite serious delays and service interruption. It has been recommended by the International Transport Intermediaries Club (ITIC) that all fixture terms include a post-fixture clause such as:

'It is essential that all messages in respect of operations be sent to the relevant email addresses, for example, (ops@broker.com). We can accept no responsibility for delay or other consequences if messages are sent to any other email address within the company. Please ensure that all important operational messages are followed up with a telephone call, especially after office hours.'

ITIC illustrates the reasoning behind the clause. In one case, a broker failed to pass on berthing instructions. The vessel remained at anchorage and a substantial demurrage claim was passed to the broker. In another case, a broker received instructions from the time charterer to notify the owner that the vessel should change direction. This message was not passed on for two days, during which time the ship had been steaming in the wrong direction. The broker received a claim for the costs incurred and the time lost.

6.2 VOYAGE PLANNING

Part of the role of the operations department is the planning of the movement of the vessel from the loading port to the discharging port. This can be divided into two, often interdependent sections, bunkering and routeing.

6.2.1 Bunkering

Fuel for the engine and other machinery in ships is still referred to as bunkers, an expression dating back to the earliest days of steamships when coal for the engine was stowed in compartments called bunkers. From that came bunker coal, which was shortened to bunkers, and the name continued to be used when ships changed from burning coal to burning oil in boilers, and that name has continued to this day. Although the oil is now consumed in an internal combustion engine, the name bunkers is still convenient and a generally understood piece of jargon. Old expressions in shipping die hard. For example, although steamships are now extremely rare, people still refer to a ship's progress at sea as steaming and the act of leaving port as sailing.

Most modern ships are equipped with diesel engines that burn one or more of several different grades of oil fuel. There are also some ships fitted with dual-fuel engines that can also burn liquefied natural gas (LNG) as well as oil. Regulations restricting the amount of harmful gases which are present in a ship's exhaust have concentrated industry minds. Emission control areas (ECAs) stipulate that, for example, the sulphur content (SOx) be limited to 0.1%. They currently include the Baltic, the North Sea, the English Channel, a 200-mile strip around the USA territory and Canada, Puerto Rico and the US Virgin Islands. In addition EU legislation mandates the use of 0.1% Sulphur fuel in **ALL** EU ports. But many areas have petitioned the IMO for their coasts to be included so, no doubt, the list will grow. Many of the major ports in China have implemented ECAs with a sulphur content limit of 0.5% and it is expected that the global limit will be limited to 0.5% sulphur from 2020.

Some ships are now having to use low sulphur marine diesel oil (LSMDO) or low sulphur marine gasoil (LSMGO) in their main engines and auxiliary machinery in these areas, or to fit exhaust gas scrubbers. These large and expensive scrubbers wash the engine exhaust gas to remove the SOx. The waste sulphides are then removed before the washwater is discharged into the sea but there are concerns over the disposal of the waste sulphides.

Another alternative is to burn natural gas. Most of the purpose-built LNG carriers, especially those constructed before 2006, use boil-off gas from the cargo to fuel a steam turbine which in turn supplies electric power to propulsion motors. Many ships also burn fuel oil (of one grade or another) to heat the ship's boiler, particularly when in port. The boiler provides hot water and steam for a variety of purposes and is essential in some tankers for providing cargo heating and to power the cargo pumps. There have been many studies into the use of LNG as fuel for non-LNG vessels. For many years, several small ferries in Scandinavia have burned LNG from a tanker truck loaded on deck. The short sailing distances involved enable the fuel trucks to be exchanged regularly. This has so far been impractical for deepsea vessels due to the large volume tanks which would be required; however, several of the latest deliveries of 20,000teu container ships are being constructed as 'LNG ready' with the capability of retrofitting to LNG-fueled vessels in future.

The most common fuel oil used on board ships in the main engine is generally intermediate fuel oil (IFO), although in recent times, as the price of fuel has increased, some owners have begun using cheaper heavy fuel oil (HFO). Smaller ships may run on much lighter fuels such as marine diesel oil (MDO) or marine gasoil (MGO). IFO and HFO are sometimes referred to as residual fuels and MDO and MGO as distillates. These terms refer to the refining process where crude oil is separated into different fuels. Lighter fuels are distilled out and the residue that remains consists of the thicker fuel types. IFO is often produced by blending some of the heavier fuels with MDO. Whereas in the past it was not viable for oil companies to produce ultra-low-sulphur fuel oil, such is the demand today that the likes of Exxon and Lukoil have been able to develop fuel oil with a sulphur content of 0.1%. The result is that ships only require to segregate two grades of fuel – 3.5% sulphur for ocean passages outside the SECA/ECA and 0.1% low sulphur fuel oil or low sulphur gasoil for coasting inside the SECA/ECA and EU ports.

Ships require power for more than just propulsion. There is also a need for electrical power to run the ship's instruments and machinery such as pumps and compressors, heating, ventilation and lighting systems among others. Some of the electrical requirements can be met using a device known as a shaft generator, which produces electricity from the excess power of the main engine. Most, however, will be provided by auxiliary alternators which are powered by dedicated diesel engines. In large ships, these auxiliary engines might also run on IFO or HFO but it is much more common for them to burn distillate fuel.

MDO may also be burnt in the main engine for short periods and this is usually done when regular changes in speed or direction are needed. This can be when starting the engine or manoeuvring in ports. Long-term burning of MDO can have a detrimental effect on the main engines unless special attention is given to operating parameters and choice of lubricants. In recent years it has become a requirement in many countries to burn low sulphur fuels during port stays and transits in territorial waters. These fuels can be very expensive and will require separate storage in the vessel. When planning voyages, due account must be taken of the regulations applying in areas where the ship will pass in the course of the voyage.

It is important to bear in mind that bunkering a ship is not like driving a car into a garage or petrol station, putting fuel into the tank and driving off again. Bunkering will always cause delay to the vessel and involve additional port expenses unless it is done concurrently with loading or discharging. If the ship has to deviate from its course to approach the bunkering port, it will inevitably incur charges for entering and using a pilot. If it is at anchorage, the bunker barge has to be awaited, and if it is at a jetty, the ship has to be securely moored before hoses can be connected. Further time has to be expended checking the quantity before and after bunkering by establishing exactly what is in the tanks (known as sounding or ullaging).

Even at an efficient bunkering port where the fuel itself can be pumped in at a rate of 250–300 tonnes an hour, a bunkering call seldom takes less than 12 hours. This means that there is no more evident a case of 'time is money' than when operating a ship.

Great care should therefore be paid to the question of bunkering as it is possible to make quite a difference to voyage costs with prudent bunker purchasing. The price of bunkers varies significantly throughout the world and a balance has to be made between the quantity of bunkers and the quantity of cargo lifted.

Bunker calculation, cargo uplift and resultant costings

This is an example of a vessel using both intermediate fuel oil (IFO) and marine diesel oil (MDO) with resultant costings, using a notional voyage with a range of bunkering options.

Employment Loading at A and discharging at C

Next likely employment loading at D

All costs are quoted in US$

Cargo 40,000MT 10% MOLOO Freight rate $18.5PMT

Vessel and port data

Vessel dwt 40,000dwt

Constants 350 tonnes

FW onboard 100 tonnes

Fuel consumption

24MT of IFO per day on passage ballast or loaded

2MT of MDO per day in port and at sea

At the commencement of the voyage, at arrival loading port A, the ship has bunkers remaining on board (ROB) of 550 tonnes of IFO and 90 tonnes of MDO. Bunker safety margin is calculated at six days at all times.

Bunkers are available at port A and D; however, no bunkers are available at port C.

On the voyage from A to C the vessel, without deviation, passes by port B (bunkering only) where bunkers are available at a lower price; however, calling costs (port charges) are $3,000 and delay to the vessel is worth $5,500. If vessel bunkers at B, it will use 2MT MDO for port call.

Bunker prices

Port A	IFO $750PMT, MDO $950PMT
Port B	IFO $720PMT, MDO $910PMT

Distances between ports have been established and the vessel speed applied to arrive at the number of voyage days used. Port time has been estimated based upon previous call times/ charter party load and discharge rates.

Days used therefore are as follows:

		FO	DO
Loading at port A	3 days		6
Steaming time from port A to port B	15 days	360	30
Time at port B if appropriate	1 day		2
Steaming time from port B to port C	10 days	240	20
Time estimated discharging at port C	20 days (using shore gear)		40
Steaming time from port C to port D	14 days	336	28
Safety margin	6 days	144	12

Bunkering option 1 – to bunker at the load port

A Consumption IFO

Steaming A to C	25 days (A to B to C)
Steaming C to D	14 days
Safety reserve	6 days
	45 days

Total steaming time 45 days x consumption IFO 24 MTPD =	1080MT
Less bunkers onboard	550MT
Uplift IFO at A	530MT

Consumption MDO

Total steaming time	39 days
Port time	23 days
Safety reserve	6 days
	68 days

Total time including safety reserve 68 days x 2 MTPD of MDO =	36MT
Remaining onboard at port A	90MT
Uplift MDO at port A	46MT

Costings for option 1 bunkering at port A	
Bunkering	
IFO	530MT x $750 = $397,500
MDO	46MT x $950 = $43,700
Cost of bunkers	$441,200
Cargo uplift at A	
Total cargo uplift (DWCC)	38,340 tonnes

Option 2 bunkering at port B Consumption IFO	
Steaming A to B	15 days
Steaming B to C	10 days
Steaming C to D	14 days
Safety reserve	6 days
	45 days
Total steaming time 45 days x consumption IFO 24 MTPD =	1080MT
Less bunkers onboard	550MT
Uplift IFO at B	530MT
IFO bunkers on departure port B	
ROB at port A	550MT
Consumption A to B (15 days x 24 MTPD)	360MT
Remaining onboard at port B	190MT Meets safety requirement
Uplift IFO at B	530MT
FO bunkers on departure B	720MT
MDO ROB at port A on departure	90MT
Used at Port A	6MT
Consumption A to B (15 days x 2 MTPD)	30MT
Used at Port B	2MT
Total used	38MT
Remaining onboard at port B	52MT
Required for remaining voyage	100MT
Uplift MDO at port B 48MT	
DO bunkers on departure	100MT

Costings option 2 bunkering at port B	
Bunkering	
IFO 530MT x $720 =	$381,600
MDO 48MT x $910 =	$43,680
Calling costs =	$3,000
Cost of delay =	$5,500
Cost of bunkers	$433,780

Cargo uplift	
Vessel's dwt	40,000MT
Less weights	
Constants	350MT
Freshwater	100MT
IFO	720MT
MDO	100MT
Total weights	1,270MT
Total cargo uplift (DWCC)	8,730MT

(Weights are taken as those on board at the time of sailing from port B because this will be the restriction where the maximum quantity of weights are on board. Assume that two tonnes of MDO have been burned during the port stay and bunkering at B.)

Costings	
Uplift when bunkering at port A =	38,340MT of cargo
Uplift when bunkering at port B =	38,730MT of cargo
Improved uplift =	390 tonnes
Freight gain at $18.50 per tonne	$7,215 (without brokerage commission)
Cost of bunkering at A	$441,200
Cost of bunkering at B	$433,780
Saving in bunker costs at B	$7,420
Overall gain bunkering at port B	$14,635

Bunkering comparison, cargo uplift and costs. 40,000 SDWT Constant 350MT 100MT FW

Safety margin is always six days for FO and DO. ROB 550MT FO and 90MT MDO.

Comparison of figures

	DAYS	Consumption A-C-D		Consumption A-B-C-D	
		FO	DO	FO	DO
Loading at A	3		6		6
Steaming A to B	15	360	30	360	30
Bunkering at B	1				2
Steaming to C	10	240	20	240	20
Discharge at C	20		40		40
Steaming to D	14	336	28	336	28
Reserve six days		144	12	144	12
Required for full voyage		1080	136	1080	138
Required for Voyage A-B		360	30	360	32
Required for voyage B-C-D		720	100	720	100
ROB		550	90	550	90
Bunkers to take at A		530	46		
Bunkers to take at B				530	48

Note A. 6MT less of DO will be on board at departure A.

Note B. 3MT less of DO will be on board at departure B.

Bunker at A	DWT
Vessel sdwt	40,000
Constant	350
FW	100
IFO	1,080
MDO 136-6 See Note A	130
Total	1,660
Max cargo to load	38,340

Bunker at B	
Vessel sdwt	40,000
Constant	350
FW	100
IFO	720
MDO 138-38 See Note B	100
Total	1,270
Max cargo to load	38,730

Bunker costs A	
530MT IFO x $750	$397,500
46MT DO x $950	$43,700
	$441,200

Bunker costs B	
530MT IFO x $720	$381,600
48MT DO x $910	$43,680
Calling cost	$3,000
Delay	$5,500
	$433,780
	$7,420

Cargo benefit	390MT
390 MT x $18.5	$7,215

Conclusion: Although the vessel takes a little longer on the voyage and uses an extra 2MT of DO, the voyage benefit is $7,215 in freight and $7,420 cheaper for the same amount of bunkers.

This calculation assumes that the entire voyage is outside the emission control areas. For voyages which include passage within those areas, a further calculation is required to consider the quantity of low sulphur gasoil required and the prices at each port.

However laborious these calculations might seem, they are the only way to establish the best bunkering policy. There are, of course, many voyages where they would be inappropriate, for example, when the vessel passes no main bunkering port or where substantial deviation is required to reach one. However, they are well worth doing if the vessel's voyage will take it past one of the main bunkering ports such as Rotterdam/Terneuzen, Las Palmas, Hong Kong, Shanghai, Cape Town/Durban, Jeddah, Singapore, New Orleans, Los Angeles, Gibraltar/Algeciras, Suez, Panama, Fujairah, Freeport, Bahamas, Malta, Houston, Busan, Genoa, Auckland, Guayaquil, Colombo, Los Angeles or Montevideo.

The bunker market is a very volatile one. Prices are constantly changing in response to the laws of supply and demand, as well as the crude oil price. Not only do prices vary from port to port but prices also differ among the suppliers within a port. A ship operator will have to keep a watchful eye on the worldwide bunker market, which comprises three elements – cost, availability and quality. A fourth consideration is time.

6.3 HIRES AND FREIGHT

Part of the duties of the operations department of the commercial division will be to ensure that all hires and freight are collected, that they are received in a timely manner and are correct in accordance with the terms of the charter party.

6.3.1 Hire

This is the income derived from a time charterer and it is usually paid every 15 days, in advance. The charterers may make various deductions from the hire, all of which must be specified in the charter party. These deductions will include:

- commissions due to the charterer;
- sums advanced by the charterers to cover the owners' items or expenses at the various ports of call.

It is customary that, with the first hire payment, the charterers add the value of the bunkers remaining on board at the time of delivery of the vessel. From the last hire payment, the charterers deduct the value of the bunkers that will probably remain on board the vessel upon its redelivery.

Unless it is a duty taken on by the technical department, it is for the operations department to ensure that the agents at the port of delivery arrange for a qualified person to make a precise check on the quantities of bunkers on board at that time. This is not the equivalent of a quick glance at a fuel gauge but a careful sounding of all the compartments in which oil bunkers (both IFO and MDO) may be stored, to establish the volume. The type of oil and the temperature at the time will then provide enough data to enable the weight to be calculated. The surveyor employed to do this must be approved by both parties otherwise there would have to be two surveyors (one representing each party) instructed to reach agreement on quantities. Exactly the same procedure has to be undertaken at the time of redelivery.

This is not the only duty to be undertaken by the appointed surveyors because all time charters, quite understandably, stipulate that the ship has to be redelivered in the same good order and condition, fair wear and tear excepted, as it was at the time of delivery. At delivery, and more importantly, at redelivery, the condition of those parts of their ship over which the time charterers have had control needs to be recorded. Such things as damage done by grabs are therefore of particular importance.

After redelivery final accounts will be drawn up and settlement made. The ship manager will want to ensure that any balance in an owner's favour, and there usually is one, is settled by charterers without too much delay.

When drawing up a management contract (in the case of an external ship management agreement) or at a meeting of the board of directors (when ship management is in-house), a clear understanding has to be reached as to whose job it is to vet time charterers.

It is a sad fact of life that there are rare occasions when a time charterer will concede a particularly attractive rate during negotiations, take the ship on, pay the first hires with impeccable promptness, load the ship with a full cargo and issue freight paid bills of lading, pocket the freights so collected (amounting to several months' hire) and disappear. No matter how unfair it may seem, the ship is obliged to carry such cargo to its proper destination without any recourse to the cargo owners and so the venture will be at a considerable loss to the owners.

There is no easy answer to this problem, hence the skill and experience of the market required from the chosen chartering broker to detect the warning signs and ensure that greed does not overcome prudence. The Baltic Exchange keeps a register of defaulting companies as a matter of routine.

After redelivery final accounts will be drawn up and settlement made

6.3.2 Freight

This is the income derived from a voyage charter or from liner operations. Whereas time charter hire is an agreed sum for the use of the entire ship and based upon the period of employment, freight is essentially paid for the carriage of a quantity of cargo from one place to another. Freight rates are almost invariably expressed as so many dollars or occasionally, another currency per tonne or cubic metre of actual cargo carried. The exception is in the case of a lump sum freight, where an agreed amount is paid in exchange for allowing the charterers to load as much or as little as they wish within the limits set by the cubic capacity of the holds and the ship's deadweight cargo-carrying capacity.

In ro-ro trades, freights are either charged per unit (vehicle) or per lane-metre, or for high/heavy cargo by weight/measure depending on whether the weight or volume is greater.

In the case of liner freights, the situation can be extremely complex because the vessel will carry many hundreds, or even thousands, of individual consignments during the course of the voyage. Freight is generally charged on each container carried and while there has been considerable simplification in liner tariffs in recent years, there will be many different rates according to the nature of the cargo carried, often linked with special contract arrangements with regular shippers. Container services add further complications in that the agreement with the shipper or consignee may include a door-to-door element, which can mean the line becoming involved in inland rail or road haulage.

It is, however, rare for ships involved in complex liner trading to be managed by independent management companies and an in-house management department will have a separate section devoted to monitoring the calculation and collection of freights. Greater detail of that aspect is beyond the scope of this book.

It is in the area of tramp freights where the operations department has a vital role to play. The importance of understanding when and where freight is to be paid and monitoring that charterers comply with the agreement cannot be overstated. The considerable sums of money are the very lifeblood of the ship's existence. It is worth looking carefully at any reports in the shipping press of chartering fixtures of vessels in the Panamax range and doing your own calculations. It will not be difficult to find instances where the loss of interest alone on a delayed freight payment could be running at the rate of over $10 an hour.

The freight will become payable in a manner that will be spelt out in the charter party. Typical examples are:

- fully prepaid on or within a specified number of days of signing bills of lading;
- proportionally prepaid (usually 90% or 95%) within a specified number of days of signing bills of lading;
- before breaking bulk, which is before the commencement of discharge;
- on right and true delivery, or completion of discharge;
- in tanker trades, freight is normally paid on completion of discharge at the final port of discharge.

Deadfreight arises when the charterer fails to load the full amount contracted under the charter party and is the agreed freight on the missing tonnage less any expenses which the owner would otherwise have had to pay on that quantity. Such expenses include stevedoring, if that is for the ship's account, or port costs, if they are levied on cargo quantity.

In tanker trade, single or consecutive voyage charterers, Worldscale is often used in the freight calculation. Here is how the Worldscale Association describes its roots:

'The concept of freight rate schedules is over 70 years old and originated during the 1939–1945 war.

Before the war, rates of freight for tanker voyage charters were expressed in dollars or shillings and pence per long ton (there were 20 shillings to a pound, 12 pence in a shilling) and this meant that when a charterer required wide-loading or discharging options it was necessary to agree many rates of freight.

During the war, first the British government and later, the US government, requisitioned shipping and owners received compensation on the basis of a daily hire rate.

However, from time to time, the government were able to make requisitioned tankers available on a voyage basis to the major oil companies for their private use, particularly during the period from the end of hostilities until control of shipping was relinquished. On such occasions, the oil companies paid freight to the government concerned and the rate of freight, which was dependent upon the voyage performed, was determined in accordance with a scale or schedule of rates laid down by that government.

The rates were calculated so that, after allowing for port costs, bunker costs and canal expenses, the net daily revenue was the same for all voyages.

Here then was the genesis of the principle for tanker rate schedules, namely, the owners should receive the same net daily revenue irrespective of the voyage performed.

The last schedule of tanker voyage rates to be issued by the British Ministry of Transport gave rates effective 1 January 1946 and this schedule became known simply as "MOT". Similarly, the last rates to be issued by the United States Maritime Commission, which took effect from 1 February 1946, became known as "USMC".

In fact, government control of shipping continued until 1948 and by that time the tanker trade had come to recognise the advantages of freight rate schedules and therefore, in the free market, the system evolved of negotiating in terms of MOT or USMC plus or minus a percentage as dictated by the demand/supply position in the market.

Between 1952 and 1962 a number of different schedules were issued as a service to the tanker trade by non-governmental bodies; Scales Nos 1, 2 and 3 and then Intascale in London, ATRS in New York.

Then in 1969, there came the joint London/New York production issued to replace both Intascale and ATRS called the "Worldwide Tanker Nominal Freight Scale", more usually known under its code name "Worldscale".

The full name is mentioned because it provides the opportunity to stress the word "nominal" and to emphasize that it was only during the period of government control that the schedule rates were intended to be used as actual rates. Subsequently, it has been freely negotiated percentage adjustments to the scale rates that have determined the actual rate used for the payment of freight.

Incidentally, with the introduction of Worldscale, it became the custom to express market levels of freight in terms of a direct percentage of the scale rates instead of a plus or minus percentage. This method is known as "Points of Scale" and thus Worldscale 100 means 100 points or 100 per cent of the published rate or, in other words, the published rate itself, sometimes referred to as Worldscale flat, while Worldscale 250 means 250 points or 250 per cent of the published rate and Worldscale 30 means 30 points or 30 per cent of the published rate. Under the older method these would have been referred to as plus 150 per cent and minus 70 per cent respectively.

During its life span, from September 1969 until the end of 1988, Worldscale was regularly revised for changes in bunker prices and port costs but the fixed daily hire element of $1,800 remained constant.

Finally, to bring the story up to date, New Worldscale was introduced with effect from 1 January 1989. However, in deference to the custom that emerged in the trade, the epithet "new" was soon dropped and now it is generally understood that Worldscale refers to the new scale, while the previous scale is called Old Worldscale.

Until the introduction of Old Worldscale, the various scales issued in London were all based on the old MOT rate of 32/6d (32 shillings and six pence) for the voyages Curaçao to London. Indeed, the daily hire element of $1,800 used for Old Worldscale was indirectly related to that rate insofar as this, at the rate of exchange of £1/$2.40 (as applied in 1969), was close to the sterling hire rate for its immediate predecessor, Intascale.

It was only when a replacement for Old Worldscale was being considered that a systematic attempt was made to establish, by a series of lengthy exercises, the size of standard vessel and the relevant daily hire element that would provide the best practicable basis for a scale. It was concluded, from the results of these exercises, that a standard vessel with a carrying capacity of 75,000 tonnes and a daily hire element of $12,000 was likely to provide such a basis for a scale to be used during the 1990s.

Both "Worldscales" are the joint endeavour of two non-profit-making organisations known as Worldscale Association (London) Limited and Worldscale Association (NYC) Inc. NYC standing of course for New York City. Each company is under the control of a management committee, the members of which are senior brokers from leading tanker broking firms in London and New York respectively.'

To calculate the freight, the flat rate for the voyage is searched for in the book or online, and the percentage amount agreed in the fixture is applied to the flat rate and will provide a dollars per tonne freight rate.

For example:	Flat rate	\$16.57
	Rate agreed	Worldscale (W)76 (This is 76% of the flat rate).
	Freight rate	\$16.57 x 0.76 = \$12.59 per tonne.

In tanker trade, single or consecutive voyage charterers, Worldscale is often used in the freight calculation

6.3.3 Demurrage/despatch

In voyage charters, the charterers are given a specific time, laytime, in which to effect the loading and discharging operations. This laytime, which, like the freight, is fully negotiable, can either be expressed as a certain number of days or an undertaking to load or discharge at the rate of so many tonnes per day. If the charterers take longer to effect the cargo operations then the shipowner receives liquidated damages in the form of demurrage at a negotiated sum per day. The owners will seek to have a daily rate of demurrage somewhat greater than the daily running cost of their ship to reflect the damages concept. When the opposite happens, and the charterers complete the cargo operations in a shorter time than allowed for by the laytime, then, in most dry cargo charters, they receive a reward in the form of despatch at an agreed sum, which is usually half the demurrage rate for every day saved or pro rata. Despatch is seldom, if ever, included in tanker charters.

Many disputes arise between owners and charterers in calculating the laytime used and thus the amount of demurrage or despatch payable. These disputes can start with the first arrival of the vessel (that is, the point when it is an arrived ship) but may continue throughout the cargo working because of delays from weather, holidays, breakdowns and so on.

The clauses in the charter party relating to laytime must be as unambiguous as possible, using straightforward terms that describe clearly what is meant.

The agents at loading and discharging ports must be clearly briefed about tendering notice of readiness (NOR) and be instructed to confirm to the managers as soon as they have done so in order that the ship manager can monitor this vital element in the time-counting scenario. The NOR must always be confirmed in writing.

The charter party will spell out what the vessel will have to do before it can be an arrived ship. There may be a requirement regarding the ship's geographic position within the port or at the berth and, where the latter is not available, that the ship is in the nearest place that it can reach safely. In some charters (such as for grain), a stringent level of cleanliness will be necessary before the ship can claim to be ready to load. Until these requirements are satisfied, the charterers will refuse to accept the NOR.

However, Masters and ships' agents should never delay presenting an NOR because of any argument about validity. The cardinal rule has to be 'when in doubt, present the NOR.' If it is not accepted or disputed, the NOR can continue to be represented. The legal experts can argue about whether the timing of the NOR was correct, but if presentation was delayed, much of the argument is lost before it starts.

It is important to bear in mind that the NOR determines at what point the time starts to count or, as one judge put it, 'when the laytime clock starts ticking.' The charter party may have various elements of excepted time such as turn-time, which states that time will not start to count until a period of some hours has elapsed after presentation of the NOR. This dates back to the days when the first intimation the charterers had of the arrival of the ship was when its signal flags became visible through a telescope and time was needed to arrange the berth and labour. Such turn-time may be considered to be an anachronism today when radio enables a vessel's time of arrival to be estimated within minutes, but old ideas die hard in shipping.

A charter party may be negotiated on the basis of Sundays and holidays excepted (SHEX) or Sundays and holidays included (SHINC), which is more usual at ultra-modern bulk terminals. A SHEX clause may be modified by the words 'unless used' and a time-counting clause may or may not agree to time counting sooner if work starts before the turn-time has expired. Most NOR clauses demand that notice be given in office hours but the charterers could well start work, for example, on Friday evening, work right through the weekend and have completed before notice of readiness can even be tendered. In Muslim countries, F for Friday will often replace the S for Sunday.

Added to this are the clauses which say what happens if the ship is ready but the charterer's berth is not available. It will be seen that the whole subject of demurrage and despatch is a potential minefield which has to be treated with caution. Time spent in studying charter party clauses relating to all aspects of time counting will never be time wasted.

There are many qualifications about time counting that are fought over during negotiations including WIPON (whether in port or not), WIBON (whether in berth or not) and WIFPON (whether in free pratique or not). Incidentally, it is worth recalling that the expression 'free pratique' dates back to the days when serious illnesses, even plagues, moved around the world in ships. Even until quite recently, a ship was, and in some places still is, obliged to fly a yellow signal flag on arrival and boarding a ship showing that flag was forbidden until the port health authorities had been on board and granted a clean bill of health, at which time it would be declared to be in free pratique. Nowadays, in most ports, the ship's Master is interrogated by radio about any apparent disease on board and, so long as there is none and it has not arrived from somewhere where some virulent illness is rife, the ship will be granted free pratique by radio. This is, however, not yet universal and the agent's advice can be valuable here.

It is usual for the port agent to be instructed to provide a statement of facts in which the date and time of every stage of the cargo operation is recorded. This covers such things as when the ship arrived, when the NOR was tendered, when loading or discharging actually commenced and which days were public holidays. It will also record such things as stoppages owing to bad weather, breakdown of machinery and industrial disputes.

It is, of course, important for the Master to record similar details in the ship's log as a cross-check. In an ideal world, the agent would get their statement of facts countersigned by the Master and the superintendent of the loading or discharging berth. Whether or not this is achieved, it is from the statement of facts that the ship manager produces the timesheet, the bottom line of which will be the amount of demurrage or despatch due to be paid.

There is no mystery in calculating a timesheet as it is simply a matter of painstakingly going through the statement of facts in conjunction with the charter party clauses. As each fact is set down, the time worked is shown in one column and the amount of time which will count as laytime used is put in a separate column. A running total of laytime used should be kept because the method of calculation changes when the time allowed is used up and the ship goes on demurrage.

The expression 'once on demurrage, always on demurrage' means that no matter what times are excepted from normal laytime, such as Sundays, holidays and stoppages due to bad weather, no time is excepted once the allowed time is used up. That will mean that the timesheet will show when the laytime expired. From that point on, every minute of every day until the job is finished counts for demurrage regardless of whether they are holidays, rainy days or even when labour in the port is on strike.

Calculating despatch is somewhat different depending on the wording of the charter party. In the majority of cases, the charter will read 'despatch on laytime' (or 'working time saved'), which means that all the excepted periods for calculating laytime will apply when calculating time saved. For example, if the ship finished work on Friday evening but the time allowed did not expire until midday Tuesday under an SHEX charter, then the owners would pay the charterers a day and a half 's despatch. Owners consider this fair and just on the basis that the calculation of time saved should be the same as for the time used.

Occasionally, however, the charterers will succeed in negotiating despatch on all time saved, arguing that the ship has been saved the time and what is good for demurrage is good for despatch. Regardless of the merits of the two arguments, if despatch is on all time then all the time from completion to when laytime expires will count for despatch.

It must be pointed out here that despatch is not something that is generally found in tanker charters. Normal laytime in tanker charters is 72 hours. In some charters, 48 hours is agreed and sometimes 84. This is for all purposes and is reversible so that unused time at the loading port will be given at discharge and vice versa. Tankers tend to work cargo in all weathers except, perhaps, electrical storms. Most tankers today can easily load a full cargo in 24 hours and discharge this in a further 24 hours.

6.4 COMMISSIONS

The chartering brokers involved in the negotiation of the charter will be rewarded by a commission or brokerage. Normally this is at the rate of 1.25% to each broker. You should remember there may well be more than one or two brokers, and quite a chain can become involved if the source of the business is very remote from the owner's base.

Commission is payable under a time charter on the total hire paid, and under a voyage charter on the gross freight. In several voyage charter parties, the commission clause will show it to be payable on freight, deadfreight and demurrage. Commissions are never payable on despatch.

In some trades, other deductions can be encountered, a common one being address commission. This is payable to the charterers themselves rather than to a broker and the precise reason for it may be obscure. Apart from lingering in a trade because of tradition, address commission is often a convenient way for a subsidiary company in an exporting group to receive its share of the income from the trade.

Another deduction one may encounter is an amount, usually 1%, in lieu of weighing. As the expression implies, the deduction is made because the charterers are willing to pay freight on the bill of lading quantity less 1% rather than weigh the cargo at the discharging port and pay freight on the outturn weight. The chances of the charterers ever opting to weigh the cargo out of the vessel are remote and this deduction is really another example of a tradition that continues without logical reason.

6.5 COMMERCIAL OPERATIONS

This chapter has described the ship manager's operations department as being a separate concern from those involved in working the ship on the market. There will always need to be close liaison between the chartering personnel and those managing the ship and, in the case of in-house management, those making the commercial decisions and authorising brokers to negotiate could well be part of the operations department. Quite how the various duties are allocated does not alter the content of the job functions described in this chapter.

Chapter 7

Crews and bunkers

7.1 INTRODUCTION

While this may seem an odd combination of apparently unrelated topics, crew's wages and the price of bunkers represent the two largest items in the cost of operating a vessel. It is therefore appropriate that, although both subjects have been touched on before in this book, they both deserve special consideration.

7.2 THE CREW

A ship without a crew is simply an expensive wasting asset. A ship with an incomplete or incompetent crew is, in the eyes of the law, unseaworthy. These somewhat self-evident points are made to highlight the fact that the crew is a vitally important element in a trading ship. Whether one is directly involved in crew matters or simply has to communicate with a ship from time to time, a knowledge of the human element in a working ship is essential.

The size of a ship's company of officers and ratings will, of course, vary in the first instance according to the size of the ship but other factors can also influence the numbers. The complexity of the ship and the degree of automation will have an effect as will the flag under which it operates. The latter impacts upon crewing. This is because different countries have different laws relating to manning. These have come about through a combination of views, including expectations for health and safety as well as agreements with trade unions.

Regardless of size, however, there is a basic pattern common to all ships in that there must first be a Master, the ship's captain and the person who is in overall charge. Assisting the Master will be the first officer, or chief officer, who has a traditional range of very important duties of their own as well as being the Master's deputy. Their most important duties lie with the correct stowage of cargo and their ship's stability calculations.

Beneath the first officer will be the second officer, whose primary role is that of plotting safe courses towards the vessel's next port of call. In port they keep a cargo watch and are duty officers along with the third officer. There is sometimes a fourth officer who is also a watchkeeper, thus relieving the first officer of watchkeeping duties. The number of watchkeeping officers is dictated by the ship's size. The minimum will always have to be enough to have at least one suitably qualified navigating officer on watchkeeping duties at all times. Large passenger ships such as cruise liners often have two or three watchkeeping officers on the bridge at one time.

Operating as a separate department are the engineers, presided over by the chief engineer. Again, this complement of officers will not only be dictated by size and national agreement but also by the sophistication of the engine room. Modern ships are so carefully monitored by electronic devices that the chief engineer can work normal office hours and lock up the engine room at night, leaving computerised sensors to set off alarms if an emergency occurs. Some ships carry an electrician in addition to the other engineering staff.

On some very small coasting ships it is possible for the role of Master and chief engineer to be combined and such ships may have a crew of only four or five people in total. Even large ships can have what would appear to be very few officers and crew. For example, the 15,300teu container ship *Emma Mærsk* famously had a total crew of just 13 when it was launched in 2006, although it does have accommodation for more than 30. In the 1960s and 1970s it would not have been unusual for the typical tweendeck liner vessel of the day to have a crew of 30 or more.

Both the deck and the engine room of a ship will have a number of ratings to carry out the routine work during the voyage and while loading or discharging. Some ships still carry a radio officer or, since the advent in the 1990s of the Global Maritime Distress and Safety System (GMDSS), an electronics engineer. The traditional work of a radio operator has been overtaken by technology, with satellites permitting email, internet access and voice-over internet protocol (VOIP) alongside the traditional communication forms of telex, fax and voice telephone. To meet the requirements of GMDSS, a certain number of crew, depending on the size of the vessel and the area of operation, must be certified to operate the GMDSS communication systems.

A few complex ships, such as refrigerated cargo carriers and certain specialist tankers whose cargo needs to be looked after throughout the voyage, will have a deck or cargo engineer's department quite separate from the propulsion engine room. A small group of catering staff completes the crew of an average merchant ship.

While crew members will have a primary role on board ship, all are expected to be able to perform additional duties as required, especially during emergencies. Some of those duties require special training and certification, details of which are contained in the Standards of Training, Certification and Watchkeeping for Seafarers (STCW) manuals.

Generally speaking, the ratings are no longer compartmentalised and work either on deck or on the machinery, whichever department needs them. They handle the mooring lines when berthing or sailing, under the supervision of the second mate or chief officer.

Also, there are generally catering staff on board, who cook for the officers and crew and serve the food.

7.3 THE MASTER AND MATES

Most of the contact between the manager's office and the ship will be via the Master. While modern communication enables immediate contact to be made at almost any time between the managers or owners and the Masters, they still have one of the loneliest responsibilities in the world. They have to fulfil three roles, sometimes all at the same time, and many of the decisions they have to make cannot be debated with shore-based colleagues. They are the Master's alone and they are all equally vital.

First of all, the Master is responsible for the safe navigation of the vessel, not just to preserve their employer's investment and that of the cargo, but the lives of all on board are in their hands.

That somewhat melodramatic statement is as true today as it was in the days of sail. It is true that the risks are few and far between, but even today's modern ships encounter problems with the weather and a wrong decision by the Master can still be fatal. So far as material damage is concerned, one only has to study the shipping casualty statistics to see that navigating a ship safely continues to be a heavy responsibility.

The Master's second task is that of administrator and disciplinarian, a more far-reaching responsibility than held by most of their shore-based counterparts. The days may be long gone when the Master could order a crew member to be flogged for insolence or even hanged for mutiny but the fact remains that, while the ship is at sea, there is no police force available to remove a crew member causing problems. The exception is passenger ships, which usually have a master-at-arms aboard. Also, except on passenger ships, there is not usually any medical help to call on and the Master, supported by the officers, often has to treat quite serious medical problems with only a telephone link to a doctor for help. Hence the Master is truly in charge of all those on board.

The third duty is that of being manager of a commercial enterprise. Again, this duty has changed enormously with the developments in telecommunications but there are still occasions where being the person on the spot means having to make decisions based on judgement.

For example, every country has different customs and immigration regulations. Some may appear overly bureaucratic and unnecessary. Time will be lost if the Master fails to anticipate what will be required in the way of documents, lists and suchlike.

Masters must also have a comprehensive knowledge of the major charter party clauses. No matter how conscientious the agents may be, it is for the Master to make certain that NORs are given in good time. To do this, Masters have to ensure that the ship complies with all the appropriate requirements so that it is indeed ready to load or discharge without delay.

While with ships engaged in liner trades it is normal for the agent to sign bills of lading (B/L) on behalf of the Master, under charter parties the Masters themselves will often have the B/Ls presented to them for signature. On occasions, they may be under pressure to do something unorthodox at a time when trying to discuss this with the managers at home could only cause serious delay. They have to be wise enough to assess the risk and either sign or wait for instructions.

In emergencies, there may be no time to consult anyone and major decisions have to be made hastily. Such responsibilities as signing Lloyd's Open Form of Salvage Agreement often still rest with the Master alone. It was argued a few years ago that an incident causing much of the catastrophic pollution of the Brittany coast might have been avoided if the Master of a grounded tanker had not wasted time discussing with the owner what to do instead of letting a tug commence salvage work straight away.

Considerable time has been spent describing some aspects of the Master's role because, as mentioned at the beginning, most contact between the manager's office and the ship will be via the Master. Quite often, there will be the paradox of instructions being sent to the Master, a highly qualified person, from someone with far less knowledge and experience. Nevertheless, one should never overlook the status that the Masters rightly have in the ships they command.

By the same token, it could well be the manager's job to recruit the Masters for the ships under their control. Hopefully, the insight provided here as to the Master's role gives readers an idea of the calibre of person needed to fill the post.

This need for care extends to all ranks even more today than before. The economic pressure to reduce the size of crews makes it imperative that every member of the ship's company is efficient.

Although the Master, as with everything else, is ultimately responsible for everything that happens on board, some duties are delegated to other officers. Typically, stowage of the cargo is the first officer's duty, although they may also be called the first mate or chief officer. Proper stowage, even of bulk cargoes, is of vital importance. Decisions have to be made about the amount to go into each compartment to ensure that the ship is properly trimmed fore and aft and athwartships. It is even important to calculate the order in which the holds are loaded and discharged so that undue strain is not placed on the structure of the ship during these procedures.

Mates on ships carrying general cargo have to develop considerable skill in all aspects of cargo stowage. Consider the factors which have to be taken into account. Heavy goods need to be near the bottom of the ship to ensure stability and could, if incorrectly positioned, crush more fragile pieces. Care must be taken to ensure one type of cargo does not contaminate another, as would be the case, for example, if a pungent-smelling commodity was stowed near foodstuffs. In the case of dangerous goods, some substances are quite benign on their own but become lethal in the presence of certain other materials.

On voyages with multiple load and discharge ports, the stowage has to be arranged so that goods to be discharged at the first port are accessible first and similarly for all discharges without disturbing the ship's stability, bearing in mind that the cargo may have been loaded at several different places. Finally, the possibility of an accident needs to be considered and stability assured as far as possible in the event that the ship's hull is damaged.

This same problem exists in modern container ships but, as the time taken to load such vessels is measured in hours and minutes rather than days, there is no time for the mate's skill to be utilised. Instead, a team of ship planners assists the ship's command by recording every container as it is booked and, using software programs, they calculate where each container must go to satisfy both the stability and accessibility considerations.

Most ships are equipped with a loading computer, which can make the necessary calculations much quicker and allow experimentation with different stowage configurations before the cargo is loaded. In addition to this use of computing on board, a new trend is developing for trim optimisation software that monitors the ship's attitude in real time and allows navigating officers the opportunity to make adjustments to ballast and bunker locations and to alter speed or course to ensure the vessel sails with the best trim possible given all circumstances. It has been estimated that this can reduce fuel consumption by as much as 5%, which represents a significant saving for any ship.

Regardless of their experience, mates are not at liberty to do as they wish with regard to cargo stowage. Each ship must carry documentation appropriate to its type that lays down some ground rules for stowing and securing cargoes. On a dry cargo ship this would include a cargo-securing manual and, most likely, a grain booklet, both of which are required to comply with SOLAS rules. All ships carrying solid bulk cargoes in general, and dangerous solid bulk cargoes in particular, are required to comply with the new International Maritime Solid Bulk Cargoes (IMSBC) Code. Owners must be aware that port state controls and the port authorities of a number of major trading countries require proof of compliance with the IMSBC Code. They require that a valid document of compliance for the carriage of dangerous solid bulk cargoes is available on board.

7.4 STANDARDS FOR TRAINING, CERTIFICATION AND WATCHKEEPING (STCW)

Ships' officers and ratings need proper training if they are to do their job safely and competently. Deck and engineering officers obviously have their own separate training routes. In the case of deck or navigating officers, there are three levels of certification, Class 3, Class 2 and Class 1, previously referred to as second mate, first mate and Master, each of which requires a combination of both study with examination and time spent serving at sea to qualify. Engineering qualifications are similarly structured. In all cases, the qualification achieved is recognised by a certificate of competence.

Ratings must also be properly trained, and, today, the traditional differences between those who work on deck and those who work in the engine room have all but disappeared. Most ratings today are trained as general purpose seamen, although some ship types (particularly tankers and gas carriers) do still carry specialist staff for certain duties.

Certificates of competence are issued by the flag administrations. There have been, and indeed still are, concerns about the quality of training required by some countries or indeed, the ability to obtain certificates without being competently examined. STCW establishes the minimum standards that should be achieved in each of the relevant areas. The Convention is amended from time to time with the current version being known as STCW 2011.

7.4.1 Recruitment

The previous paragraphs have emphasised the tremendous responsibility resting on the shoulders of a few officers in any one ship. It is also important to remember that many millions of dollars of capital is represented by the ship itself plus more millions for the cargo it is carrying. This combination can be seen as being a total contrast with the same investment made ashore, where decisions are usually taken by a board of directors assisted by several layers of management, each carrying its own share of responsibility. On board ship, the officer on the bridge may have only a few minutes in which to make decisions with no time to seek anyone else's advice.

It follows that there cannot be too much care taken in selecting Masters and officers for the ships under management. Ironically, many senior managers and directors in a shore-based enterprise have grown up with the company and have therefore had many years to show their qualities. Ships' officers, on the other hand, are often quite unknown to their employers before the time of making the appointment. There should never be any reluctance to check into the previous employment of such candidates.

Any inconsistencies in their career histories should be investigated and hints of problems should be double-checked. Most ship management companies ensure that shore-based former Masters and former chief engineers (in their roles as marine and engineer superintendents respectively) are closely involved in the recruitment process.

7.4.2 Offshore flags

One of the problems of shipping is its international character. If one goes back only a few decades, shipowning was mainly in the hands of a few traditional maritime countries whose costs and standards of living were largely similar. This meant that crew costs were roughly the same regardless of flag, and competition was at a very moderate level.

In more recent years, many different factors have combined to affect the financial position regarding crew costs and considerable effort has been taken to reduce such costs. The result has been the growth of open registries.

There was no single cause. Some say the Americans started the trend when their domestic wages began to outstrip those in other parts of the world, leading many shipowners to claim it was impossible to continue operating under the US flag without heavy subsidies. In consequence, such flags as Panama and Liberia were seen as increasingly attractive by even the most respectable shipowning companies in the USA.

Others hold the view that the biggest migration to non-national flags came in the 1950s when Greek shipowning expanded at a phenomenal rate but its government imposed such unsympathetic taxes that to this day, the Greek shipowning populations of London and New York are each probably far greater than that of Piraeus.

One cannot overlook the emergence of shipowning in countries not previously considered major users of maritime trade. Also to be noted are the massive fleets that were built up under the flags of the USSR and other communist countries, which over the past two decades have moved into private ownership.

Competition has now become fierce, with many national fleets being operated as a means of bringing in or saving foreign exchange and with crew costs being based on local wage scales far below those of the developed countries. Open registries permit citizens from any country to become members of ships' crews. Unfortunately, some of them are also somewhat lax in terms of the manning levels and competence they expect from their crews.

The latest response to this inequality of costs has been the emergence of offshore flags, which claim to be more respectable than full-blown open registries. While many of the safety regulations of the original country are retained, strict rules about the nationality of crew members are relaxed and national agreements regarding wage levels and the payment of social security contributions are circumvented.

The conditions under which seafarers work and rates of pay that they can earn have been made statutory under the Maritime Labour Convention 2006 (MLC), and amended in 2014.

The provisions can be summed up as follows:

- minimum requirements for seafarers to work on a ship;
- conditions of employment;
- accommodation, recreational facilities, food and catering;
- health protection, medical care, welfare and social security protection.

7.4.3 Crewing agencies

The growth of offshore and full-blown open registries has led to a similar burgeoning of crewing agencies. These companies are set up to specialise solely in that aspect of ship management and contract with shipowners to maintain suitable crews on board at all times. It is not unusual for ship managers to subcontract their crewing to one of these agencies.

The main advantage they provide is that the shipowner or manager could be based in, for example, the UK itself but as they are not the employers of the crew, they are not bound by the UK's employment laws. In addition, these agencies are able to offer economy of scale as many of them are supplying crews for far more ships than any one owner.

It is worth noting that although many more crewing agencies have emerged as a result of the growth of flagging out in recent times, they are by no means a novelty because many British ships in the first half of the 20th century employed eastern crews. These were provided by agencies who supplied men from the Indian Subcontinent or from China. This became such a well-established practice that successive agreements and legislation for UK merchant ships have continued to accommodate this source of relatively inexpensive crews.

Since those days, many countries have followed this example and have implemented a deliberate policy to train seafarers for export. The funds remitted home by such seamen to their families provide these countries with valuable contributions to their balance of payments. Probably the most well known of these countries is the Philippines but there are many other countries in Asia in a similar position.

Eastern Europe is another source of large numbers of seafarers, mostly as a consequence of the formerly state-owned fleets having been privatised. In these countries, where full employment was once guaranteed by the state, most ships were overmanned in comparison with those operated from western Europe. The training standards of the eastern European countries are generally considered to be very good, and with wage costs between those of the developed countries and Asia, seafarers from this region are a popular choice.

The types of crews supplied by agencies vary according to what the owner wants and the demands of the flag country. While most owners are quite happy with crews of quite different nationalities, this can bring its own problems. The first is one of finding a common language as it is essential for the safety of the vessel, crew and cargo that instructions and information given is properly understood. A command of English is required of all officers of any vessel carrying a flag and serving internationally.

Particular care must be taken with crews of mixed nationality. Many of these crews are recruited from countries across Asia with differing religions and customs. Apart from the possibility of any antipathy between different nationalities, cultural and ethnic differences often have a particular impact on the type and preparation of food, which must be catered for sympathetically.

Finding a common language is essential for the safety of the vessel, crew and cargo

7.4.4 Trade unions

All the traditional seafaring nations have well-established maritime trade unions which have negotiated with the employers, usually on a national basis. There are some who argue that the unions' very successes in improving wages and conditions have contributed in part to the moves towards flagging out. Whether or not that is true, one can appreciate the dismay of maritime unions as, progressively, more devices are found to enable shipowners and managers to avoid what have been hard-won improvements in conditions.

The problem inevitably lies with the wide variations in both the cost and the standard of living in the developed countries compared with the developing ones. For example, for people from the Philippines, a wage far below that of a Western seaman may well be regarded as a fortune in contrast to wages available ashore.

Furthermore, part of the struggle fought by the traditional maritime unions has been over manning levels but under many offshore flags, the shipowner decides on a crew size commensurate with their own assessment of the numbers needed for efficiency and safety. Of course, these decisions are influenced also by ideas of seaworthiness expressed by classification societies and insurers. Nevertheless, crew numbers as well as wage levels are inevitably lower on ships with so-called free flags.

It was in response to the loss of employment and to protect conditions for members of maritime unions in what were the traditional seafaring countries that the International Transport Workers' Federation (ITF) launched its anti-flag of convenience campaign.

Most practitioners in the shipping business are only too aware of the ITF, which was formed during the closing years of the 19th century as an international secretariat of transport unions all over the world. Around 700 unions representing over 4.5 million transport workers from some 150 countries are members of the ITF. It is one of several global union federation (GUF) unions allied with the International Trade Union Confederation (ITUC).

At the time of its formation there was no such thing as a flag of convenience but when that phenomenon emerged, the ITF saw it as an attempt to undermine trade unionism in general and the standards of seafarers' working and safety conditions in particular. In 1950, at its Stuttgart Congress, the ITF adopted a plan of action which, in principle, required all owners to adhere to certain defined minimum conditions. Failure would result in boycott action to bring such owners to the negotiating table. Much of that resolution remains in place to this day.

A more practical resolution was passed at the 1971 ITF congress in Vienna, when a standard agreement was drawn up for use by all ships whose crews were not covered by an agreement properly negotiated between union and employer. Such agreements also included provision for contributions to an ITF fund set up to sustain the campaign and to provide, in addition, a charity to support seamen's missions and other forms of welfare in port and on board. The strength of the ITF lies in the fact that almost all transport unions are affiliated to it. This means that immobilising a ship by arranging for services such as tugmen and lock-keepers to boycott the errant ship is quite easy. As many of the ITF's campaigns have support from affiliated unions, they are usually prepared to support any boycott. However, recent legislation in certain countries prevents the type of action that the ITF adopts and shipowners in Europe are less affected today than they have been in the past.

The ITF has its roots in the ports industry and port workers form a very large part of its membership. The dockworkers have tended to be more militant than the seafarers and are more likely to boycott vessels and owners targeted by the ITF. In 2006, the dockworkers' section began a ports of convenience (POC) campaign aimed at ports that its members suggested tried to gain a competitive advantage by compromising on areas such as safety, wage levels and employment contracts.

An important approach of the POC campaign is its focus on building union strength within the ports and terminals run by what it calls the global network terminal operators. These are terminals operated by global chains such as AP Møller-Mærsk, Hutchison, DP World and PSA. The terminals targeted are mostly container terminals and so are concerned more with liner trades than with dry bulk or liquid cargo trades.

Co-operation with other unions in the transport chain and building strength in landside operations such as warehousing, container freight stations, administration and planning are also important aspects of the campaign.

7.4.5 The personnel department

Administering ships' crews demands a well-disciplined organisation. Apart from the recruitment of the crew members, the task of ensuring they get the correct wages at the correct time is vital. Ships' crews are unable to simply call on the personnel department to clear up minor issues or mistakes and those left unattended can soon become sources of irritation and consequent poor morale. The department therefore has to be well founded so that data about basic pay, overtime, bonuses and so on feeds into the system smoothly. In many cases, the crew department takes on the task of passing some of the crew members' wages to their next of kin in compliance with allotment agreements. Such a payment may well be a family's only source of income so any mistakes can cause considerable hardship.

Apart from maintaining basic efficiency, a crew department can make a positive contribution to the company's profitability. Most contracts with crew members are for specific periods of time with appropriate leeway to allow time for a voyage to complete. Careful co-ordination with the timing of voyages can ensure that crew changes take place at the shortest travelling distance away. Precise timing can save accommodation costs for crew members arriving too early or, worse still, holding the ship up for a crew arriving too late. Even shopping around for the best deal from an airline or travel agent can make a worthwhile contribution to the crew department budget.

Precise record-keeping of seafarers' certificates and their validity periods is another essential, particularly as this is an aspect often targeted by port state control inspectors. A ship can be detained for the simple reason that one of the crew's competency or medical certificates has expired. To avoid such events, a crew department will need to ensure that the appropriate action to renew certificates is taken in good time.

As well as certificates required under STCW, crew members on ships visiting certain countries will need to obtain visas in advance of arrival if they wish to be permitted to go ashore during port stays. Similarly, some ports are situated in areas where diseases such as yellow fever are prevalent. Crew should be vaccinated against these diseases before visiting such ports and may be required to prove that they have been vaccinated by authorities at subsequent ports of call.

Apart from maintaining basic efficiency, a crew department can make a positive contribution to the company's profitability

7.5 BUNKERING

Arranging fuel for ships is not a task to be undertaken lightly because lack of skill and attention could have adverse effects ranging from mere loss of profit to severe damage to the machinery and even to major disaster.

There are three aspects of bunkering – quantity, quality and cost – but they are all interdependent. A fourth consideration is time.

7.5.1 Quantity

The operations department will explain the intended itinerary of the vessel's next programme. The quantity of fuel currently on board will be known and the voyage estimate will indicate the number of days steaming and time spent in port for the voyage concerned.

Quantities will then depend on how the geography of the voyage coincides with suitable bunkering ports. It may be necessary to adjust the route of the voyage to enable the optimum choice of bunkering port to be used.

It must be remembered that not all the refining of crude oil into a usable state takes place close to the areas of consumption rather than close to where the oil is produced.

Thus, as a general rule, one may expect the keenest prices and widest choice where the larger refineries are located. Such places as Rotterdam, New York, Cape Town and Rio de Janeiro are typical of refineries close to high-density population and thus high consumption. Places such as Singapore and Gibraltar tend to have been established as bunkering ports because of their strategic position relative to many different voyage routes.

Keeping track of where the keenest prices can be found is possible by reviewing the representative bunker prices published daily in trade journals or on the internet, www.bunkerworld.com, for example. Rates are generally published for a handful of major bunkering ports but, of course, fuel supplies are not limited solely to these locations.

Many ships today are specialised and so tend to keep to the same routes and thus their bunkering patterns become well established. Where, however, a modern bulk carrier or tanker is involved, first-time voyages may often occur and this is the stage that demands bunkering expertise.

So many factors have to be considered one against the other. For example, every tonne of bunkers carried means one tonne less cargo that can be loaded. Thus bunkering at the beginning of the trip for the round voyage may mean achieving the cheapest price, but this has to be balanced against the additional freight that could be earned if fewer bunkers are taken.

Another consideration is that while the voyage may take the vessel past a very cheap bunkering port, the saving on the bunker bill might not justify the cost of the time spent diverting into the bunkering port plus the port disbursements that have to be paid.

In planning, one always has to ensure that the ship never risks running short of bunkers. The chance of bad weather has to be borne in mind because a ship running out of fuel is at best a subject for a salvage job and at worst, a total loss of ship and crew. So a margin of safety appropriate to the ship and voyage always has to be factored into the bunker programme.

Normally, that safety factor will take into account the distance during that voyage sector from an alternative bunkering port. Shipowners often have a bunker safe margin policy of, say, five days.

7.5.2 Quality

It will help to recall the process of oil refining, which is a form of distillation. The crude oil is heated and the different fractions condense at different levels. At the top the gas is drawn off, next comes gasoline or petrol, then come the lighter grades of oils, which include kerosene or paraffin and jet fuel, gasoil and diesel oil. After these lighter grades come the heavier oils, which are grouped under the general title of residual oils.

Viscosity is an important element of the quality and can be described as the measure of an oil's reluctance to flow freely. At one time it was common to use the Redwood scale but today it is almost universal to classify bunker oils in centistokes. With all methods of referring to viscosity it is important to add the temperature on which the figure used is based and the viscosity temperature used when ordering bunkers is 50°C. Paradoxically, the ISO standard is based upon 100°C but this is an inconvenient temperature at which to work and testing is usually carried out at 80°C and extrapolated up to 100°C and down to 50°C respectively. Thus 180 centistokes (cSt) at 50°C equates to 25cSt at 100°C.

Bunker oil quality is based upon International Organization for Standardization (ISO) number 8217. Thus, when ordering bunkers, one would stipulate this as the standard ISO 8217, adding the viscosity required in cSt at 50°C. Other standards can also be used, including the British Standard (BSMA) and the International Council on Combustion Engines (CIMAC), but common residual fuels are ISO 8217 180cSt and 380cSt, both at 50°C.

These standards, as well as covering the viscosity, deal with the acceptable limits of various impurities such as ash, sulphur, vanadium, aluminium and silicon. To ensure that the fuel supplied does in fact comply with the standards specified it is always advisable to take a representative sample at the time of delivery.

Only the smallest ships now use marine diesel oil (MDO) for the propulsion machinery, and the very smallest use marine gasoil (MGO). The vast majority of motor ships today use intermediate fuel oil (IFO) of 180 or 380 cSt viscosity. Some ships can burn even heavier oils of up to 700 centistokes. It is, therefore, vital that the correct grade and quality of oil is purchased. The wrong grade will affect the vessel's speed and consumption performance and poor quality can create problems for the machinery and even result in permanent damage. Of course, vessels expecting to trade in any of the emission control areas may need to additionally load low sulphur fuel bunkers for the main and auxiliary engines, which must comply with strict quality standards.

IFO falls into the group referred to as residual oils, which suggests that many of the crude oil's residues may be present and these have to be dealt with or removed. Thus IFO has to undergo treatment on board the vessel to remove residues but some residues are inherent in the oil and if the percentage is too high, there is a risk of damage.

Where stating a standard for oil quality is particularly important is when placing a vessel on time charter. The time charterer will wish to economise as keenly as the owner or manager but the charterer does not have to worry about any long-term damage that the wrong fuel may cause. Thus a clear standard has to be set and the crew briefed to ensure that the standard is adhered to. Apart from the obvious risk of damage to the machinery, using a poor fuel will give poor speed and consumption figures. As those are one of the most frequently disputed areas under time charters, it is advisable to avoid adding the effect of poor fuel into such disputes.

7.5.3 Cost

As mentioned earlier, cost and quality are inextricably related and the key issue is always how to achieve the optimum quality at lowest cost. Choosing the right supplier is usually a key factor, but this is far from easy. In major ports, one finds the big names in the oil world but they are not necessarily the cheapest. As with so much in the business of shipping, knowing the market is of paramount importance.

One way to deal with the issue is to employ a bunker broker. There are several of these around the world, many of whom have an established reputation for market skill and fair dealing as well as the knowledge to give appropriate advice when a ship is venturing into unknown territories.

Another aspect of bunkering to consider is pollution. When talking of oil pollution, the tendency is to think in terms of tankers grounding or careless ballast dumping but careless bunkering is often cited as causing oil spills. Such events may not be on the scale of the catastrophes such as the *Erika* or *Prestige* but can be just as damaging. Under the headings of MARPOL or the ISM Code, most owners will have procedures for the crew to follow. These are vital so that simple mistakes, such as failing to tighten hose connections fully or directing oil into a bunker tank that is already full or failing to seal deck scuppers, do not happen.

7.5.4 Time

Time may seem an odd choice in a bunkering strategy but time is money, particularly in shipping. Stopping to take bunkers on a ballast passage may not waste any time if the ship is due to arrive at the load port well in advance of the laycan. But if this is not the case, then any delay will impact on tendering NOR at the load port with the consequent loss of time. If the vessel is going to bunker on the loaded passage then any time lost doing this will delay the vessel finishing the voyage and being available for its next employment. In addition, the charterer may have to give agreement for the vessel to take bunkers as it is normal that vessels are fixed on the basis that they are fully bunkered for the intended voyage. Bunkering on tankers is rarely, if ever, allowed to be carried out concurrent with cargo operations so it takes place before or after, which may lead to some further lost time.

7.5.5 A more detailed and comprehensive description of bunkers

Bunkers

1. What are bunkers and how did the name arise?
2. What are the main considerations to take into account when planning to take bunkers?
3. What are the regulations about bunkers that will affect your vessel?
4. What information do you need about the arrangement of bunker tanks on a vessel?
5. How should you calculate the cost of the bunkers used on a voyage?
6. Should you use a bunker-testing programme such as DNVPS or FOBAS?
7. What is the MARPOL sample and why is it significant?
8. What are the rules for commingling?
9. Where are the major bunker ports located and why are they there?
10. What specification should be used to purchase bunkers?
11. What are the significant quality parameters when considering a fuel oil?

1. What are bunkers and how did the name arise?

Bunkers are the fuel that ships use for propulsion and for power generation. In the past, the fuel was coal, burned in boilers to produce steam. It was stored on board the vessel in special spaces for coal and as storage places for coal on land were called bunkers, the name became synonymous not only for the store but for its contents.

Coal was plentiful but suitable coal for making steam (steaming coal) was more limited and stocks of this were set up around the world at coaling or bunker stations. Yet coal had some disadvantages as a shipboard fuel. One was that it was a hard, dirty, unpopular job loading coal into ships' bunkers and one that was carried out by the whole crew with few exceptions. Coal also needed to be easily accessible to the boiler room to allow access for the stokers and this meant that storage had to be arranged in the vicinity. Finally, ships needed a lot of coal to increase their effective range and coal took up a considerable amount of space, valuable space that could be used for cargo or other purposes. An alternative fuel was needed.

The discovery of oil in the late 19th century and its refining to make kerosene produced a lot of residual oil. Here was a fuel that could be burned in a boiler to produce steam and its increasing availability meant that it was a viable alternative. It had many advantages: it could be loaded and handled easily, it could be stored anywhere on board and pumped to where it was needed, and the tanks to hold it could be fitted into any awkward spaces on board. It also helped the ship's stability. The weight of bunkers stored at the bottom of the ship allowed increased weight higher in the vessel, a particular advantage with warships. Then along came the diesel engine, which used the fuel in an internal combustion process. Its adoption over the past 70 years in all vessels has consigned the steam engine to the museum.

Yet the revolution in the development of the marine diesel engine has marched in step with radical changes to the make-up and quality of the fuel that is today being used as bunkers. Fuel has led the way, and the rapid growth in demand for gasoline and diesel has meant that more needs to be produced from each barrel than would have been dreamed possible 70 years ago. What has been left for the residual fuel market has changed radically and not for the better. With the need for engines to burn a wide range of fuels from residual to low sulphur to MDO for manoeuvring, this range of fuels used today for propulsion, and increasingly for auxiliary purposes, has made demands on engine makers. They have risen to the challenge but there is little margin for error. As you will see, bunkers are a vital part of an efficient marine operation.

2. What are the main considerations to take into account when planning to take bunkers?

The main considerations are availability, quality, price, quantity and time as has already been discussed above and in chapter 6.

3. What are the regulations about bunkers that will affect your vessel?

There are several areas of the world where emissions are controlled either by ECA/SECAs or other regulations and where it is required to comply with regulations on air quality which entails the burning of higher quality bunkers. Currently, these areas are in Europe, North America and parts of the Caribbean and China. They are described in detail later.

4. What information do you need about the arrangement of bunker tanks on a vessel?

In the days before ECAs were introduced, the number of fuel oil tanks on a vessel was generally the minimum needed to provide flexibility for the intended voyages of the vessel. One large and one smaller storage tank might be the minimum, with a vessel bunkering whenever the large tank became empty and transferring to the smaller tank during the voyage. In addition, a settling and a service tank would be provided, the former to allow fuel to settle out impurities and the latter to hold fuel after purification for supply to the engine. In addition, the vessel would probably have a diesel or gasoil storage tank and a small day tank for ready use. Today, this will be insufficient for any vessel which is likely to engage in worldwide trading where this will take the ship into a controlled area. Such vessels will need sufficient fuel oil storage tanks for low sulphur and high sulphur fuels, a settling tank and two or more sets of service tanks. In addition, they may also need storage for distillate fuel.

5. How should you calculate the cost of the bunkers used on a voyage?

In most cases, the cost of bunkers used during a voyage is done on a first in, first out (FIFO) basis, where the fuel on board at the start of the voyage is assumed to be used in the order that it came on board the vessel. In this way, only the fuels actually used on the voyage are part of the voyage cost; the bunkers taken on the voyage are only included in the cost if some is actually used.

6. Should you use a bunker-testing programme such as DNVPS or FOBAS?

Yes. As an owner, it is vital to protect the value of your asset. Putting poor quality fuel into your ship could lead to catastrophic consequences. As a charterer, you are duty-bound to supply fuel meeting an agreed specification. Failing to do so leaves you liable for any damage caused, which could be substantial.

7. What is the MARPOL sample and why is it significant?

The bunker delivery note (BDN) must record any fuel oil delivered on board for combustion purposes. The sulphur content (%m/m) must be specified to verify that the fuel oil quality is in accordance with regulation 18 of MARPOL VI. A declaration should be signed and certified by the fuel supplier's representative, to the effect that the fuel is in conformity with regulations 14 and 18. Each BDN must be accompanied by a MARPOL Annex VI fuel sample, and Resolution MEPC 96 (47) recommends that the seal number is included in the BDN for cross-reference purposes.

The MARPOL Annex VI fuel sample is not primarily to be used for commercial purposes. For vessels participating in a fuel oil quality testing scheme, for example, DNV Petroleum Services, the MARPOL sample should be considered as the fourth sample (in addition to the sample sent to the laboratory for testing, the supplier's sample and the retained-onboard sample). Keeping a MARPOL sample on board in case of port state control inspections is good practice.

8. What are the rules for commingling?

Rule 1. Do not. Commingling fuels can lead to stability problems in the mixture owing to incompatibility of the components of each fuel used in the blend. Any problems that arise or damage that is done will be the responsibility of the person who took the decision and ordered the commingling. Fuel suppliers take responsibility for the fuel they deliver, but they cannot be held responsible for its compatibility with other fuel.

Rule 2. Still do not. If it is unavoidable, check the compatibility of the two fuels in advance and make the final decision based on the test result. Your fuel-testing provider has the ability to do this.

Rule 3. If it is not possible to make a compatibility check because one of the fuels is not available at the decision time, then you should consider reducing the amount in the tank to be used for commingling as much as possible so that, when adding the new fuel, the proportion is less than a ratio of 20/80, 10/90.

As a general rule, fuels of the same viscosity and similar densities have a better chance of being compatible.

9. Where are the major bunker ports located and why are they there?

Successful bunker ports normally rely on three elements for their success.

The first is a refinery close at hand to provide a ready supply of fuel oil and other heavy residual products and blendstocks. Where there are a number of refineries then bunkering will probably succeed. Examples would be Rotterdam, Hamburg, Antwerp, Genoa, Piraeus, Jeddah, Kuwait, Novorossiysk, Singapore, Shanghai, Yokohama, Kobe, Nagoya, Kaohsiung, Busan, Houston, New Orleans, Los Angeles, Philadelphia, St Eustatius and Curaçao.

The second is a large number of vessels calling at the port or close by so that there are a large number of customers. Most of the above will also meet this requirement and at busy ports where there is no refining, then a supplier might well set up with storage and supply at a slightly higher price to cover the transport costs. All of the above would count plus New York, Norfolk, Seattle, Tacoma, Portland, Boston, Recife, Bremerhaven, Gioia Tauro and Hong Kong.

The third would be for a port that is located at a choke point of the world's trade routes. If you look at a map of the world, it is easy to list the choke points and there is a bunker port at most of them. Skaw, Falmouth, Gibraltar, Algeciras, Ceuta, Suez, Istanbul, Aden, Fujairah, Cape Town, Las Palmas, Colombo, Singapore, Panama and St Eustatius are all located at places where shipping is forced to pass close by.

The most successful ports meet more than just one of the criteria. Singapore meets all three, which is why it is the largest in the world.

10. What specification should be used to purchase bunkers?

The worldwide standard for bunkers is ISO 8217 2010, although some ports are still using 2005. Within these standards are a number of specifications for fuel oils and gasoils, although changes in legislation have brought about a lot of revisions. When purchasing bunkers you should specify what you want, that is, ISO 8217 2010 RMG 380 max 3.5% sulphur, not 380cSt.

11. What are the significant quality parameters when considering a fuel oil?

Given that fuel oils are often designated by their viscosity, for example, 380cSt, it might be thought that this is the most important parameter but, like much in the bunker world, this is historical. In the days when the fuels burned originated from conventional atmospheric refineries this was important but today, most heavy fuels are the result of much more complex refining processes and the spotlight is now on different specifications for these fuels.

The following are in the specification:

Kinematic viscosity at 50°C	RMG spec max 380 mm^2/s
Density at 15°C	RMG spec max 0.991 at 15°C

The maximum density limit is important as purification of the fuel is necessary before use and purifiers must be able to handle this. The density is also important to ensure satisfactory fuel ignition for the lower viscosity grades.

CCAI	RMG spec max 870

Calculated carbon aromaticity index (CCAI) is a measure of the ignition and combustion characteristics of the fuel. It is a calculation based on the density and viscosity and provides an indication of the ignition delay.

Sulphur	As per statutory requirements
Flash point	RMG spec min 60°C

Only an indication as stored fuel can create a hazardous atmosphere in the tank space.

Hydrogen sulphide	RMG spec max 2ppm

This is a measure of the liquid phase content. Hydrogen sulphide (H_2S) is a highly toxic gas; at low concentrations it smells of rotten eggs, but at higher levels it causes loss of smell and can be fatal.

Acid number	RMG spec max 2.5

The presence of high levels of acidic compounds in fuel can lead to damage to engines, in particular in the fuel injection equipment.

Total sediment aged	RMG spec max 0.10% mass
Carbon residue (micro)	RMG spec max 18% mass
Upper pour point	RMG spec max 30°C
Water	RMG spec max 0.5% volume

Water is an issue with some suppliers. High water can be accepted but a commercial settlement should be looked for.

Ash	RMG spec max 0.100%

High ash level can cause choking up of components as the ash fails to melt and adheres to surfaces.

Vanadium	RMG spec max 350ppm

A natural component of fuel oil which cannot be removed and depends mainly on the level of ash.

Sodium	RMG spec max 100ppm

Normally indicates the presence of sea water.

Al + Si (aluminium and silicon)	RMG spec max 60mg/kg

One blending component of a fuel oil is heavy cycle oil, which retains some damaged aluminium silicate catalyst particles when it comes out of the catalytic cracker. These cat fines can abrade and damage the fuel system and must be limited.

Used lubricating oil (ULO)	Free from ULO

Normally, used motor crankcase oils, which can contain both detergents and additives.

7.5.6 Air emissions and control areas

Pollution does not only arise from fuel oil or cargo being spilled into the sea. Annex VI of MARPOL recognises the effect of ships' exhausts on atmospheric pollution. Three gases in particular have come in for special attention, nitrous oxide (NO_x), sulphur oxide (SO_x) and carbon dioxide (CO_2).

MARPOL lays down limits for the amount of NO_x and SO_x that can be produced by ships in the open oceans and in special areas closer to land. So far, no limit on CO_2 has been set but this is an issue that is currently under discussion at the IMO. With effect from January 2013, all ships have been obliged to have on board a ship energy efficiency management plan (SEEMP), which is designed to reduce fuel use and hence lower emissions.

New vessels contracted after January 2013 have also been required to comply with the Energy Efficiency Design Index, which involves a complex calculation around the carrying capacity of a ship and its energy use. The result of the calculation, which takes account of energy-saving devices installed on the vessel, gives a figure which must be equal to or less than a benchmark for that particular ship type. The intention is that ships which do not reach the figure will not be permitted to trade.

However, the regulations do not apply equally to all countries and those which are considered developing nations according to UN criteria can waive or suspend the regulation for a considerable length of time. Even though the rules have been agreed, there is still considerable debate as to how they will be universally applied. As things stand, there are considerable loopholes available to owners wishing to circumvent them, not least by registering vessels in open registers of developing countries, which would include Liberia and Panama.

Under MARPOL there is a rolling programme for the further reduction of NO_x and SO_x. In addition to the international measures being carried out under MARPOL, some national and local governments, particularly in Europe, where EU regulations apply, and China, have introduced their own regulations, all of which apply to the operation of ships.

Not all of these local measures add to operating costs. In Norway, for example, there is a charge called the NO_x tax made on ships operating in its waters but there is also a special NO_x fund that can be used to give grants to ships for equipment and technologies aimed at reducing the amount of NO_x emitted.

While NO_x can be reduced using in-engine modifications, the other two gases cannot be so easily reduced. CO_2 emissions can only be reduced by burning less fuel, so ship operators will either have to rely on engine builders and naval architects to produce more efficient ships or adapt their methods of operation. The latter choice could involve slower steaming for fast ships such as container vessels, while for bulk carriers and tankers, joining some form of carbon trading scheme may be the only option. Of all the gases mentioned, SO_x has attracted most attention and poses the most problems.

Alternative technologies to burning low sulphur fuels include:

- the use of scrubber technology. Some vessels are already fitted with scrubbers to remove SO_x emissions but these will not at present remove NO_x emissions, so may need to be modified or supplemented to meet the upcoming regulations. They work by cleaning the exhaust gas, usually using water in a washing system and are effective but require the retrofitting of expensive equipment, the space to do this, training for staff and also produce a residue that needs to be removed;
- the adoption and modification of the vessels' systems to use LNG. This may not be practical for all vessels, as the storage of LNG presents a challenge in space and equipment as well as expertise unless the vessel is an LNG tanker. However this may be gaining some headway with the positioning of some vessels to provide bunkering of LNG;
- the use of shore connection facilities where this is available, cold ironing as it is called. Here, the power supply for the ship in port is provided at a cost by the port using a shore power connection as often used in a drydock. This of course has its limits but while alongside in port may be the best solution.

The special areas established under MARPOL are called emission control areas (ECAs).

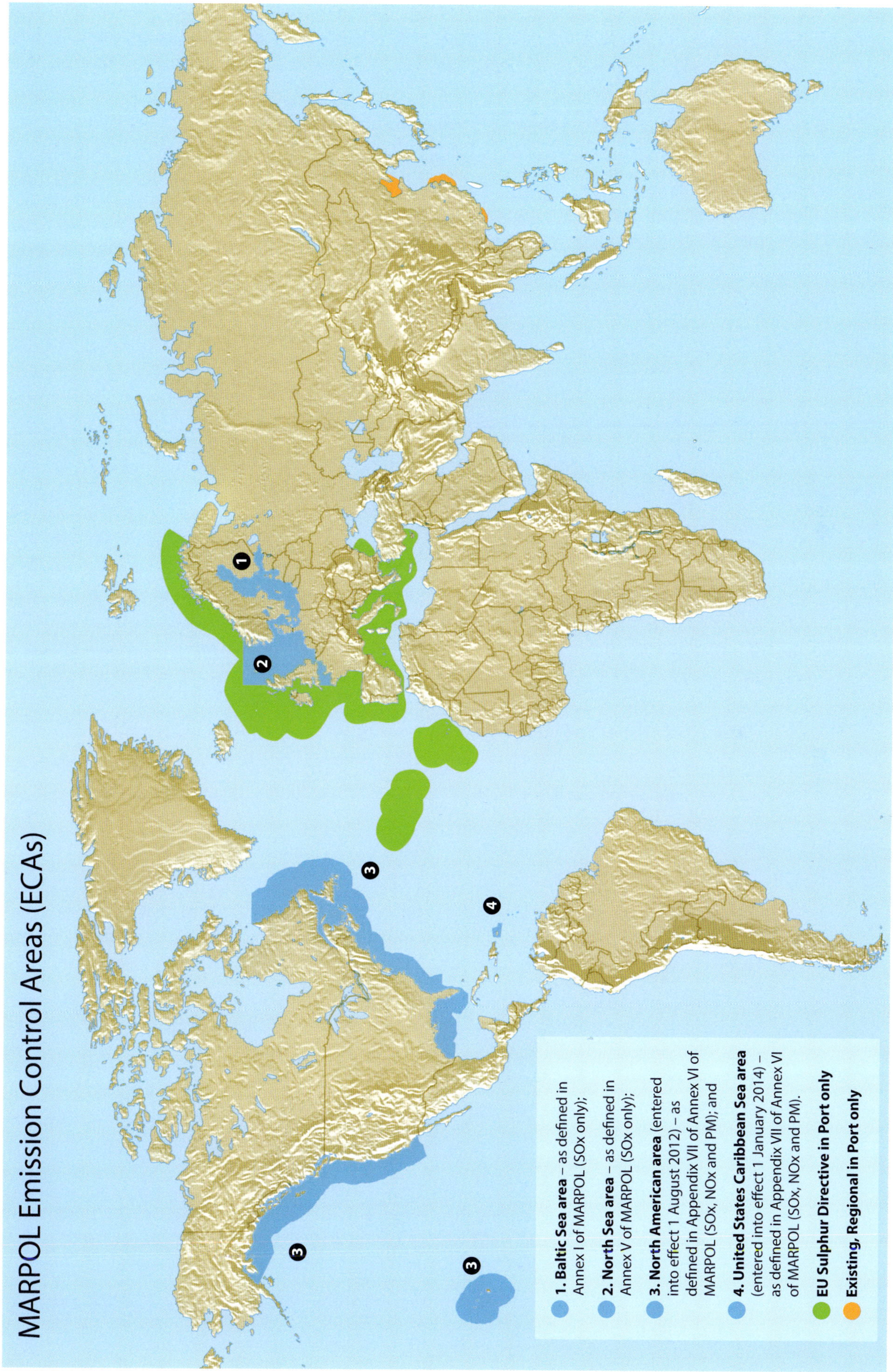
MARPOL Emission Control Areas (ECAs)
1
2
3
3
3
3
4
1. Baltic Sea area – as defined in Annex I of MARPOL (SOx only);
2. North Sea area – as defined in Annex V of MARPOL (SOx only);
3. North American area (entered into effect 1 August 2012) – as defined in Appendix VII of Annex VI of MARPOL (SOx, NOx and PM); and
4. United States Caribbean Sea area (entered into effect 1 January 2014) – as defined in Appendix VII of Annex VI of MARPOL (SOx, NOx and PM).
EU Sulphur Directive in Port only
Existing, Regional in Port only

In addition to the MARPOL regulations, the European Union and the Chinese government have also established ECAs. As they are primarily concerned with sulphur reduction, they are also referred to as sulphur emission control areas (or SECAs). The current areas are as follows:

1. The SECA around north-west Europe and the Baltic

This covers all ports and sea areas within the English Channel, the North Sea and the Baltic. Within the boundary of a line from Falmouth to Ushant and from the north of Scotland on the longitude of 4° west due north to the 62° parallel of latitude to the Norwegian coast, the use of very low sulphur fuels is now mandatory.

By very low sulphur fuel we mean a distillate or residual fuel oil with a sulphur content not more than 0.1%.

2. The EU regulations

These are stringent and more complicated. Marine gasoil used within the territorial waters and ports of the EU but with some exceptions (the Canary Islands, the Azores, Madeira and the French overseas departments and territories) must have a maximum sulphur content of no more than 0.1%. As marine gasoil is currently defined by viscosity and density into two grades, DMX and DMA, these products must comply. However, marine diesel oil meeting the specification DMB and DMC can still be sold and used with a maximum sulphur content of 1.5%. So, if the vessel is using distillate then any such product used will need to meet one specification or the other and will have to be clearly labelled as such on the bunker delivery receipt. For the avoidance of doubt, where a vessel uses gasoil in an EU port this gasoil must have a maximum sulphur content of no more than 0.10%. In addition, all fuel used in the port must be gasoil, except for the main engine, which can use fuel oil for berthing and unberthing unless the vessel is also in a SECA.

3. The North America ECA

From 1 January 2015 all vessels within 200 nautical miles of the North American coastline (USA, Canada and some Caribbean countries) have to use fuel of a maximum 0.1% sulphur for all purposes.

4. The China ECAs

The Hong Kong government established a regulation as from 1 July 2015 that all non-exempt vessels alongside are required to burn low sulphur fuel with a limit of 0.5% sulphur. The change over to low sulphur fuel is required one hour after berthing until one hour before departure.

Since 2016, the Chinese government have been bringing progressively more stringent regulations into force and have established three ECAs in the Pearl River Delta, Yangtze River Delta and Bohai Sea. Currently, as of 1 January 2017, all vessels alongside at key ports in these ECAs are required to burn low sulphur fuel with a limit of 0.5% sulphur. The change over to low sulphur fuel is required one hour after berthing until one hour before departure or, alternatively, use shore power or other measures such as exhaust gas scrubbers. The key ports are Shenzen, Guangzhou, Zhuhai, Shanghai, Ningbo, Zhoushan, Suzhou, Nantong, Taijin, Qinhuangdao, Tangshan and Huanghua.

From 1 January 2018, vessels alongside ALL ports in the Pearl River Delta, Yangtze River Delta and Bohai Sea ECAs must comply with the 0.5% limit and the change over to low sulphur fuel must take place prior to vessel berthing.

From 1 January 2019, all vessels must comply with the 0.5% limit anywhere within the Pearl River Delta, Yangtze River Delta and Bohai Sea ECAs and the change over to low sulphur fuel must take place prior to entering any of the ECAs.

As already mentioned, sulphur is present in most heavy fuels and excess quantities of it are a quality issue because of its corrosive nature. However, some corrosion in engines is highly desirable because it allows the lubricating oils to perform better and prevents a condition known as lacquering, which can cause sticking of fuel injection pumps, scuffing of cylinder liners and increased lubricating oil consumption. Sulphur oxide also causes acid rain and so politicians and environmentalists are anxious to see it eliminated.

As sulphur is only found in residual fuels, some believe that a wholesale switch to distillate fuels would be the best action to take. While this might seem an attractive proposition, distillate fuels are considerably more expensive than residual fuels and the refining companies do not have sufficient capacity to produce them in the quantities that would be needed. Refining companies are now producing 'hybrid' residual fuels with the sulphur removed. The process increases the cost to that of low sulphur gasoil, but it is more compatible with marine engines designed to burn residual fuels.

From the operator's point of view, the location of all of the ECAs in force needs to be taken into account when routeing ships or fixing employment. If a ship is to load or discharge in an ECA or even pass through one, then it must carry sufficient supplies of the low sulphur fuel needed. This means that one of the ship's bunker tanks must be dedicated to low sulphur fuel or a call will need to be made at a bunkering port to take on supplies of the fuel away from the start of the ECA. To further complicate matters, ships' engines may not be able to make rapid changes to the fuel in use and there may be a change-over procedure that will need to be followed, which can take several hours to complete, before entering an ECA.

Under MARPOL Annex VI, the global limit of sulphur content of all fuel is expected to be limited to 0.5% from 1 January 2020.

7.5.7 LNG as a fuel

Liquefied natural gas (LNG) has been carried by ships since the 1960s but is only transported in specialised LNG carriers. To liquefy the gas it has to be refrigerated to very low temperatures and stored in insulated tanks. During the voyage a small amount of the gas boils off as the cargo warms slightly and this would ordinarily be vented to the atmosphere.

This was clearly wasteful and consequently ways were devised to use the boil-off gas, or BOG, as a fuel for the ship. Until the last 10 years or so, most gas carriers used the gas in a boiler to power a steam turbine which produced electricity for the propulsion motors. Such ships were not therefore fitted with diesel engines for propulsion.

In the early days of the 21st century, when LNG was valuable and fuel oil was cheap, engine makers decided that it would be a good idea to develop a dual-fuel engine which would be similar to a normal diesel engine but which could run on either LNG or fuel oil. The first of these were installed in LNG carriers and by May 2012, at least 100 LNG carriers were fitted with dual-fuel engines.

As well as the dual-fuel engines available from the main engine makers Wärtsilä and MAN Diesel, Rolls-Royce produces a pure natural gas-burning engine range which has been installed in a number of vessels, mostly small ferries and shortsea vessels operating in Scandinavian waters. These vessels are able to bunker frequently by way of LNG tanker trucks loaded on deck.

By 2009, fuel oil costs were beginning to rise sharply and LNG costs were dropping globally. As a result, the idea of using dual-fuel engines in other ship types was first actively pursued. The concept was also considered to be in line with the new environmental regulations that were being imposed because LNG does not contain sulphur and has very little NO_x in its exhaust.

Although the number of ships currently able to use natural gas is small and represents less than 0.5% of the world fleet, there is an impetus for gas to be more widely used. Some new vessels such as 20,000teu container ships are being designed as 'LNG ready' for conversion to LNG fuel in future. There are many issues to be overcome, such as the large volume tanks required and the infrastructure on board to cope with this ultra-low-temperature fuel. Whether this comes about remains to be seen.

7.5.8 Bunker contract terms and conditions

In 1995 the Baltic & International Maritime Council (BIMCO) produced a standard form of contract for bunker supplies which was entitled 'Fuelcon'. This form was not widely used because it was considered far too biased towards the buyer, the shipowner.

The form was revised and in 2001, BIMCO produced the standard bunker contract, which is in two parts. The confirmation note confirms the bunker nomination and the general terms and conditions set out the agreement.

The confirmation note is in the traditional BIMCO box style, the headings of each box being self-explanatory. In the general terms and conditions, it will be seen that several of the points mentioned in this chapter have been formalised. The main clauses cover:

quality – clause 2;

quantities – clause 3;

sampling – clause 4;

delivery and title – clauses 5 and 10;

price and payment – clauses 7 and 8.

It is interesting to note that a significant part of the form deals with environmental issues (clause 14) and dispute resolution (clause 15). These terms and conditions should be thoroughly studied. Not all, or even the majority of bunker supplies are carried out under BIMCO contracts, although this 2001 version is rather more popular than its predecessor. However, the BIMCO form provides a clear and logical compilation of the essential points to be considered when contracting for a supply of bunkers.

7.6 ECDIS

An electronic chart display and information system (ECDIS) will eventually replace paper navigation charts. But some shipping companies prefer the officers to continue to use paper charts, with ECDIS as an aid used for checking, and better still, for training. Formally, they are described as follows:

'ECDIS, as defined by IHO Publications S-52 and S-57, is an approved marine navigational chart and information system, which is accepted as complying with the conventional paper charts required by Regulation V/19 of the 1974 IMO SOLAS Convention, as amended. The performance requirements for ECDIS are defined by the IMO and the consequent test standards have been developed by the International Electrotechnical Commission (IEC) in International Standard IEC 61174.'

The regulations provide implementation dates where ECDIS may replace paper charts. These vary between 1 July 2013 and 1 July 2018, depending on the ship type. So, although a vessel is fitted with two separate ECDIS set-ups, the owner or the Master may still require paper charts to be used. And these must be updated regularly. The second officer is usually in charge of chart corrections. Admiralty notices to mariners are printed and circulated weekly in booklet form. They can also be downloaded from the Admiralty website or corrections for individual charts can be located using a web search.

Here is what the UK P&I Club says about ECDIS and its implementation:

'The adoption by MSC 86 of the amendments to SOLAS and the introduction of ECDIS must be understood from two viewpoints.

The first is that the mandated use of ECDIS springs from the promotion of safety of life at sea. As such, it is not optional nor should it be considered as an extra. It is a fundamental – though sometimes misunderstood – safety tool that demands real commitment to play its role correctly.

Skimp on that commitment, fail to provide training and monitoring and the results can be ECDIS-assisted groundings and collisions and a lingering suspicion that ECDIS is another technology foisted on already over-worked navigators and superintendents.

From the opposite perspective, ECDIS is a tool that repays the user with time and efficiency savings that translate into bottom-line savings. Regular users commonly report a steady flow of benefits from real-time navigation using chart data that can be updated quickly and automatically.

ECDIS optimises navigation tasks and lessens bridge workload, creates better situational awareness and reduces stress when navigating in congested waters where most accidents occur. Better voyage planning has been shown to deliver tangible fuel savings on single voyages.

Unsurprisingly given these contradictions, research by the UK Hydrographic Office has found confusion among shipowners and managers about what a carriage requirement for ECDIS will mean for them. Many in the industry are unsure of their responsibilities under the revised SOLAS regulations. Others lack information about the benefits that ECDIS can bring the mariner of the 21st century.'

Ship managers should take notice of both the benefits and drawbacks of ECDIS

Chapter 8

Cargoes and geographic factors

8.1 INTRODUCTION

Before any type of cargo can be loaded, the vessel must be in a proper and fit condition to carry that cargo. The ship manager must be aware of the needs and requirements of each cargo, as well as the port facilities and restrictions, and properly instruct the Master so that the cargo is safely loaded, carried and discharged.

8.2 DRY CARGOES

The first requirement for any cargo is that the vessel's holds have to be clean and dry. The degree of cleanliness will depend on the cargo to be loaded. A vessel about to load mineral sand or bulk grains will have to be very much cleaner than a vessel about to load iron ore or coal. However, the degree of cleanliness even for these cargoes will vary widely depending on the type of cargo involved. For example, a high quality coal for which the sulphur content would be critical could not be safely loaded if residues from high-sulphur ores remained in the holds. Conversely, crude sugar, which will be highly refined and processed before sale to the public, can tolerate a surprising amount of extraneous dust.

In any event, the vessel will have to pass a hold cleanliness survey before the loading can commence so, at the very least, all the residue of the previous cargo will have had to be removed prior to the vessel's arrival at the loading port. It is unlikely that discharging stevedores will always sweep clean the holds as well as they could, which usually leaves a certain amount of cleaning work to be done by the vessel's crew.

The vessel will have to have any specialised equipment required available and ready for use. The Master will have to work out exactly where to stow the cargo and the loading sequence. The vessel must always stay in safe trim, not only for the ocean voyage but also during the course of the actual loading so as to avoid undue strain on the structure of the vessel.

The vessel will have to pass a hold cleanliness survey before the loading can commence

IMSBC

8.2.1 Bulk cargoes

The carriage of bulk cargoes is a relatively simple operation but care needs to be taken to ensure that the requirements of the IMSBC Code are taken into account. As mentioned, the holds will have to be clean and dry to the charterer's satisfaction before loading starts. In the case of sensitive cargoes, it is usual to employ an independent surveyor. In modern bulk terminals, cargoes are now loaded by chute or grabs in such a way that no actual trimming of the cargo is necessary in order for the cargo to be in seaworthy trim. Many charterers make it clear in their conditions that the cargo will be loaded and spout-trimmed free of expense to the vessel.

In less sophisticated ports, manual trimming may be necessary to spread the cargo across the holds. This obviates the risk of the cargo shifting dangerously during the voyage, which might happen if it were simply left to take up its natural angle of repose leading to a peaked pyramid shape in the centre of the hold.

Some common problem cargoes include:

Bulk grain – before loading can commence, the vessel's holds will have to be cleaned to a high standard, dry and free from loose rust scale. In other words, 'grain clean', and a surveyor is normally appointed to certify this. In addition, because bulk grain is free-flowing, there is a risk of the cargo shifting when the vessel rolls in bad weather. This could cause a list from which recovery is difficult and capsizing becomes a real possibility.

The Master will, therefore, have to present to the surveyor stability calculations for checking and approval based on the data in the vessel's grain book, which will have been approved by the government of the country whose flag the vessel flies. Among other things, the vessel's grain book will state how many holds can be part loaded or slack. As this number is usually limited to only one hold, great care has to be taken in calculating exactly how much cargo the vessel can take and remain in a stable, safe condition.

Not all loose bulk cargoes flow and vessels loading a non-shifting cargo such as iron ore can load with all holds slack.

Ores and concentrates – these are usually fairly innocuous cargoes, but some grades of ores that have a tendency to liquefaction can present a danger of capsizing the ship. Some methods of treating ores before shipment can leave the cargo prone to oxidation and, as a result of the chemical reaction that takes place, large amounts of heat can be produced which may cause fires.

There is a wide range of mineral cargoes that may liquefy, and they vary in their appearance and physical properties. One subgroup of cargoes has a particularly dangerous combination of risk factors, and accounts for a large proportion of recent casualties, near misses and contentious load port disputes during carriage of cargoes that may liquefy. The Gard P&I Club tells us of the problems:

'The cargoes in question are unprocessed ores, the most widely encountered of which are iron ore fines, mainly exported from India, and nickel ore, mainly exported from Indonesia, the Philippines and New Caledonia. Unlike concentrates, these are simply dug out of the ground in open-cast mines in mineral-rich, and often remote, locations and are presented for ocean transport with little or no processing. Thus, whereas concentrates have a highly uniform particle size and physical consistency, unprocessed ores are heterogeneous, consisting of a mixture of fine-grained ore, clay-like material, pebble-sized stones and the occasional larger lump.

For shipowners contemplating carriage of these cargoes, and for Masters instructed to load them, a major difficulty is that neither iron ore fines nor nickel ore have a specific listing in the IMSBC code and thus it is not immediately obvious from consulting the code that these are indeed cargoes that may liquefy. Unless they are already aware of the potential hazards from other sources, the Master is dependent on shippers correctly declaring the cargo as a liquefaction hazard. Although most shippers do indeed acknowledge that the cargo is a liquefaction hazard by supplying a declaration of moisture and the transportable moisture limit (TML) certificate, albeit frequently flawed, some shippers do not. Without expert knowledge it is difficult for the Master to know that they should insist on a declaration of moisture and TML certificate before allowing loading to commence.'

Concentrates liable to similar problems include zinc, bauxite, copper and nickel concentrates. Similar precautions should be taken with these cargoes as with unprocessed ores.

Coal – some coal is subject to spontaneous heating and combustion; markedly so if the coal is extracted from a methane-rich seam. However, there are sufficiently adequate supplies of coal throughout the world that consumers are generally able to avoid purchasing such grades. Nevertheless, shipowners and managers contemplating the coal trade should ensure they know which coals may cause problems.

Whatever the grade, almost all coal cargoes give off flammable gas and so ventilation of the holds is important although natural ventilation is usually sufficient. Some grades of coal have a high moisture content. Masters are asked to empty the ship's bilges before loading is commenced. Upon loading, they should pump the bilges at set intervals and measure the amount of water discharged, reporting to the owners or charterers.

Scrap – by its very nature, metal scrap can include heavy or jagged pieces which, loaded carelessly, can cause damage to the vessel's frames. Some scrap will be steel turnings, the residue from drilling and turning steel. Such material is drenched in cutting oil which is generally of vegetable origin. It does, therefore, decompose and, in doing so, generates so much heat that spontaneous combustion can result. Indeed, steel can burn in such circumstances.

By its very nature, metal scrap can include heavy or jagged pieces which, if loaded carelessly, can cause damage to the vessel's frames

Motor blocks, secondhand engines and machinery – however well drained, motor blocks particularly will still drip some oil during the voyage, which is very difficult to remove from the vessel's holds.

Sulphur – this can damage a vessel's steelwork unless it is coated with limewash before loading commences.

Fishmeal – this is liable to spontaneous combustion and infestation by insects and rodents.

The total quantity of bulk cargo is usually established by shore weighing. The Master should double-check the figure by means of a draught survey.

8.2.2 The IMSBC Code and its content

Up to January 2011, SOLAS also required bulk cargoes to be carried in accordance with guidelines laid out in the Code of Safe Practice for Solid Bulk Cargoes referred to generally as the BC Code. From January 2011, this code was replaced by a new set of rules laid out in the International Maritime Solid Bulk Cargoes (IMSBC) Code. All ships carrying solid bulk cargoes in general, and dangerous solid bulk cargoes in particular, are required to comply with the new IMSBC Code. Owners must be aware that port state controls and the port authorities of a number of major trading countries require proof of compliance with the IMSBC Code. They require that a valid document of compliance for the carriage of dangerous solid bulk cargoes is available on board.

The format of the IMSBC Code categorises cargoes into three groups:

- group A consists of the cargoes that may liquefy if shipped with moisture content in excess of their transportable moisture limit;
- group B consists of cargoes that possess a chemical hazard which could give rise to a dangerous situation on a ship;
- group C consists of cargoes that are not liable to liquefy as group A does and do not possess chemical hazards as in group B.

Detailed requirements relating to each type of cargo are stated in the code's individual schedules.

8.2.3 Non-bulk dry cargoes

The loading of non-bulk cargoes is a much more complex, labour-intensive and slower operation. The range of cargoes is much wider and so are the problems which can be met. They cannot just be poured into the vessel's holds like bulk cargo. They have to be carefully stowed and, if necessary, lashed and secured.

The quantity of non-bulk cargoes is usually established by a shore tally but the accuracy of such tallies is often poor and, in some ports, the tally is virtually non-existent. The Master should arrange for the ship to spot-check the tally to ensure its accuracy.

Bagged cargoes – in addition to the holds being clean, cargo battens have to be in place. These are horizontal battens placed at regular intervals up to the vessel frames in the holds, designed to keep the bagged cargo away from the vessel's sides thus reducing the risk of condensation damage and tearing on the frames. All bagged cargo is liable to problems caused from the bags being torn during loading/discharging operations. This has been partly offset by the use of very large bags fitted with lifting bands and moved around, not by hand, but with the use of a forklift truck. These are less likely to be damaged and speed up loading and discharging.

But the problems associated with the most common bagged cargoes are found with:

Bagged rice – not only does the vessel have to be fully cargo-batten-fitted but also ventilation channels have to be built into the stow of the cargo.

Bagged ammonium nitrate – is subject to spontaneous combustion, especially if the nitrogen content of the cargo is above 27%.

Bagged fishmeal – like bulk fishmeal, it is subject to spontaneous combustion and infestation by insects and rodents.

Unit loads – these cargoes will all have to be carefully loaded and lashed to prevent movement during the voyage.

Steel – the weight of each piece will have to be watched to ensure that the maximum loadings permissible on the vessel's tank tops are not exceeded. This problem particularly applies when steel coils are being loaded. The major problem with steel cargoes is when they are unprotected, about which more will be said later in this book.

Logs – can be loaded on deck. The vessel will have to erect stanchions on deck and provide chains. Both these items will keep the deck cargo from shifting during the voyage. Care will also have to be taken when loading logs are floated out to the ship and loaded direct from the water as opposed to being loaded from a jetty or wharf. These floaters will be loaded wet and drying out the hold after stowing can be difficult. Logs can also, because of their weight and size, cause impact damage to the vessel if not loaded and discharged with very great care. Wood cargoes also give off CO2, which cannot support life and can kill in confined spaces.

8.3 STOWAGE FACTOR

A very important piece of information about any cargo is its density in the vessel's hold or stowage factor (SF). A vessel has only a limited volume in its holds, called its cubic capacity, and it might well be that with a light cargo the vessel's holds are full before all the vessel's deadweight cargo capacity is utilised. Conversely, with a heavy cargo, the full deadweight can be used with space still available (but unusable) in the holds. While metric ratios of one cubic metre to one tonne are now commonly used, the imperial measurement equivalents of 40 cubic feet to one ton are still frequently seen. Both units are given in the examples below, conveniently rounded where appropriate.

To give two examples, consider the following:

> Your vessel has a DWCC of 25,000t and a grain cubic of 34,000m^3 (1,200,000ft^3)
>
> How much bulk phosphate can the vessel load with an SF of 0.90m^3/t (31.8ft^3/t)
>
> 34,000m3/0.90 = 37,780t. But maximum DWCC on your vessel is 25,000t so the vessel cannot load more than this as it has reached its max dwt.
>
> The max volume the vessel can load is 25,000t × 0.90 = 22,500m^3
>
> How much bulk grain can the vessel load with a SF of 1.47m3/t (51.9ft^3/t)
>
> 34,000m3/1.47 = 23,130t. While the vessel has spare deadweight capacity available the ship is cubically full, it has cubed out, and no further cargo can be loaded.
>
> The max cargo weight the vessel can load is 23,130t × 1.47 = 34,000m^3.

The stowage factor of the cargo is of crucial importance to those arranging the employment of the ship. To obtain the same income, a higher freight rate per tonne will have to be negotiated for a lighter cargo than for a heavy cargo. It is also important to the Master, who will have to have the information so that he can arrange the loading sequence to keep the vessel in a safe trim. The Master will also need this information if the cargo consists of two or more different commodities, each with a different stowage factor, so that the stowage can be arranged in such a way as to keep the vessel in trim.

A higher freight rate per tonne will have to be negotiated for a lighter cargo than for a heavy cargo

8.4 DANGEROUS CARGO

One of the most sensitive issues in shipping today is the carriage of dangerous cargoes and potentially polluting cargoes. For many years, the major maritime nations have required specific action by all those concerned with the movement of dangerous goods both on land and afloat. The International Maritime Organization (IMO) is the part of the United Nations responsible for formulating international maritime law, especially in the areas of safety, pollution, environmental protection and exploitation. Its headquarters is in London.

The international carriage of dangerous and maritime polluting goods is governed by the IMO International Maritime Dangerous Goods Code (IMDG Code). These rules supplement any local rules that apply within countries, to the extent that they represent the minimum standards that must be adopted. In some countries, there are national regulations (or local port rules) that have more stringent requirements and the ship manager must be fully aware of any variations applying to cargoes in transit as well as being loaded or discharged at ports in the vessel's itinerary.

Most countries also apply similar laws on shore to the producer, who is required to label anything containing dangerous goods and to complete documentation which specifies the nature and hazards of the goods when they are on the move by any form of transport. The stowage of these dangerous goods requires special consideration, as will be explained below.

8.5 THE IMO INTERNATIONAL MARITIME DANGEROUS GOODS CODE (IMDG CODE)

This code was traditionally published in five loose-leaf volumes, but is now available from the IMO in a wide variety of software formats and is updated when required. This is usually when a hazard occurs which has not happened before, or a new substance comes on to the market. Local additions or modifications to the maritime rules are often made by individual governments and published as notices to mariners.

8.5.1 Dangerous goods declaration

Every known dangerous commodity is listed and is allocated a class and a UN number. The listing describes in detail the nature of the hazard and the type and amount of packing that is required for that particular dangerous commodity. The person actually packing the goods is required to sign a declaration included in the dangerous goods shipping note (or declaration) (DGN) confirming that the goods have been packed in accordance with the code. The declaration must include the proper technical name of the substance as well as any trade name, the class and the UN number. The external packing and the container or vehicle in which the goods are transported must also have the appropriate diamond-shaped warning label displayed on them.

8.5.2 Cargo segregation

The other essential feature of the UN requirements is to segregate the cargoes on board ship – recognising that some, when mixed together, can produce catastrophic results – and to instruct ships' crews on dealing with leakage and fires.

To this end, the cargoes are divided into the following classes:

Class 1	Explosives (military and commercial)
Class 2	Gases
Class 3	Flammable liquids
Class 4	Flammable solids
Class 5	Oxidising agents
Class 6	Poisonous (toxic) substances
Class 7	Radioactive substances
Class 8	Corrosives
Class 9	Miscellaneous dangerous substances

The purpose of the different classes is to ensure that:

- the goods are packaged safely and properly labelled by the manufacturer;
- they receive the correct stowage requirements during land transportation and on board ship;
- personnel involved with the transportation of these goods know how to deal with spillage and what action to take if fire breaks out in the same compartment;
- personnel know whom to contact for advice.

The essential feature of the separation of classes on board ship is the distance and level of separation between incompatible cargoes such that it may be necessary for stowage in different holds separated by steel bulkheads. In the most extreme cases, it may even be too dangerous to stow cargo in adjacent holds. This gives some indication of the serious consequences of allowing two different classes to combine.

The diagrams below are examples from the IMDG Code showing the sort of separation required for incompatible dangerous substances.

Container ships and conventional vessels usually have enough decks and bulkheads as well as the separation of steel containers themselves to be able to carry most of the dangerous cargo offered on any one voyage. However, even this may be a problem for cargo that must be carried on deck.

IMDG separation requirements

(1) Reference *package* ....

(2) *Package* ....

(3) Deck resistant to fire and liquid ....

Note: Full vertical lines represent transverse bulkheads between cargo spaces (compartment holds) resistant to fire and liquid

Away from:

Effectively segregated so that the incompatible goods cannot interact dangerously in the event of an accident but may be carried in the same compartment or hold or on deck provided a minimum horizontal separation of 3 metres projected vertically is obtained.

Separated from:

In different compartments or holds when stowed under deck. Provided the intervening deck is resistant to fire and liquid, a vertical separation, that is, in different compartments, may be accepted as equivalent to this segregation. For on-deck stowage, this segregation means a separation by a distance of at least 6 metres horizontally.

Separated by a complete compartment or hold from:

Means either a vertical or a horizontal separation. If the intervening decks are not resistant to fire and liquid, then only a longitudinal separation, that is, by an intervening compartment or hold, is acceptable. For on-deck stowage, this segregation means a separation by a distance of at least 12 metres horizontally. The same distance has to be applied if one package is stowed on-deck, and the other one in an upper compartment.

Separated longitudinally by an intervening complete compartment or hold from:

Vertical separation alone does not meet this requirement. Between a package 'under deck' and one 'on-deck' a minimum distance of 24metres including a complete compartment must be maintained longitudinally. For 'on-deck' stowage, this segregation means a separation by a distance of at least 24metres longitudinally.

Segregation in cargo transport units.

The carriage of dangerous cargo on ro-ro ferries is especially critical. A ferry may not have sufficient decks or bulkheads to achieve a proper segregation of trucks which may be carrying incompatible categories. Great care must therefore be taken when dangerous cargoes are booked to ensure that proper separation is possible. Usually, ships carrying Class 5 goods do not carry any other classes, and the ferry operators try to arrange that no more than one class is carried on one ship.

Explosives – Class 1

Special rules apply to the carriage of Class 1 cargo. Without examining the detailed requirements, it should be noted that many ports do not permit any Class 1 cargoes within port limits. Others do permit the IMDG Code exceptions (such as fireworks and safety ammunition) in limited quantity and on the basis of direct removal from the port area. Most ports also have very strict restrictions on Class 1 cargoes remaining on board in transit.

Most countries have one or more special berths or anchorages where explosives may be handled.

8.5.3 Dangerous goods manifest and cargo plan

Vessels carrying dangerous goods must have on board a dangerous goods manifest and a copy of the dangerous goods declaration for each item of cargo. Throughout the EU, in the USA and in many other parts of the world, there are very stringent rules relating to the ability of the carrier through its nominated local ship's agent to provide details of dangerous cargoes carried to the authorities on demand.

Before accepting dangerous cargo, the ship manager must check:

- if the ship can meet with the onboard stowage conditions;
- if either the vessel's hull underwriters or P&I Club have to be advised. It is in fact wise to consult with the P&I Club, which should have useful additional information and guidance for the owners in respect of the loading, stowing and discharge of the dangerous cargo;
- if the vessel's articles call for additional payment to the crew if dangerous cargo is carried.

8.6 BILLS OF LADING

As each consignment is loaded the mate's receipt is issued. This notes the nature of the consignment, its weight, marks and condition. From these receipts the bill of lading is drawn up. A bill of lading is:

- the Master's formal receipt for the goods and, when released to the shipper, becomes the document of title to the goods;
- evidence of the contract of carriage.

A ship manager will frequently come upon requests that the bill of lading be endorsed:

1. Freight prepaid or freight paid. In this case it also becomes a receipt for the freight. Some shippers ask that the bills of lading be so endorsed against a promise to pay the freight later. It must be recognised that once the bill of lading has been marked 'freight paid', the consignee is entitled to demand delivery of the goods at destination. In the event that the shipper's promise to pay has not been fulfilled, the shipowner has lost the security of their lien on the cargo for that freight. The ship manager will therefore come to their own commercial decision about giving a receipt for what can be a substantial sum without actually having received it.
2. Clean on board. This is a statement that the cargo is in perfect condition. Unfortunately, some shippers ask for such an endorsement even though the cargo is not in perfect condition. Not only is this practice fraudulent, but it also makes the chances of defending a cargo claim virtually non-existent. There may be a particular problem where cargo is sold under a letter of credit. That documentary credit calls for clean on board bills of lading and the banks will not negotiate the credit if it is claused in respect of cargo condition even though the cargo has already been loaded.

Although all bills of lading are marked 'weight, quality and quantity unknown', the Master should only sign a bill of lading for a quantity of cargo they genuinely believe to be on board using, if needs be, a draught survey for checking the shore weight. A bill of lading is a negotiable document, and whoever owns the bill of lading owns the cargo mentioned on it. At the end of the voyage, the Master must only deliver the cargo to its proper owner, who should surrender the bill of lading in return for the goods. If no bill of lading is available, Masters should take very good care that they do not release the cargo to the wrong person. If they do, they become liable for the full value of the goods to their owner. To safeguard themselves, the Master must insist, in the event of the non-availability of the bill of lading, that the receiver signs a letter of indemnity, which must be countersigned by a bank.

Following the completion of loading, the following will be drawn up and issued in addition to the bill of lading:

- cargo manifest for each port of loading/port of discharge combination – a list of all the cargo on board, giving bill of lading number, the description of the cargo and the name of the shipper. For containerised cargo, the container number and seal number is also listed;
- stowage plan – a plan of the ship showing where all the cargo is stowed.

8.7 CARGO CLAIMS

The Master is obliged to deliver the cargo in the same good order that they received it. This is why it is important for any defects found during the loading to be noted on the bill of lading, failing which the Master will be responsible for these defects even though they were present before shipment.

While there is no defence against a genuine cargo claim, ship managers must be fully aware of the steps they can take to minimise the risk of being subjected to an opportunistic cargo claim. It is always worth remembering that some countries demand a cash deposit against cargo claims before the ship is allowed to sail and that subsequently, by the merest chance, the cargo claim is found to be of the same size as the cash deposit. To protect the owner's interest, the ship manager should ensure that:

- in the event of bad weather on the voyage, the Master should always lodge a note of protest on arrival. That is, they should appear before a notary public or the appropriate local official of the country to declare that the vessel encountered adverse weather during the voyage;
- for steel cargoes, the P&I Club's requirement of a pre-shipment survey of the cargo be strictly followed and an independent survey at the discharge port be effected;
- in the event of a homogenous cargo (either bagged or bulk) to a country with a reputation for a flexible approach to cargo claims, the Master should arrange for the customs to seal the hatches at the loading port. The Master should also arrange, in conjunction with the P&I Club representatives, to carry out a draught survey before the discharge starts and upon completion of discharge. In addition, in the case of a non-bulk cargo, they should also arrange a check tally;
- in the event of any doubt, they should consult with the P&I Club and follow its recommendations.

8.8 LIQUID CARGOES

Predominantly oil or petroleum products, but can be any liquid cargo including beer, wine or chemicals, carried in a tanker or tank container on a container ship. The general terms 'oil' and 'petroleum products' cover a very wide variety of cargoes, normally termed either 'dirty' or 'clean'. These include black oils, which would be solid at ambient temperature, and gases only made liquid under pressure or at a very low temperature, spiked crudes (crudes to which light fractions such as butane have been added), topped crudes, feedstocks and petroleum chemicals as well as the more commonly known gasoline, kerosene and gasoil or diesel. Chemicals are generally divided into 'easy chems' and the rest, with the easy chems capable of being carried on a conventional clean products tanker and the rest requiring a chemical tanker and its specialised construction.

8.8.1 Crude oil

This is the single largest commodity transported by sea, accounting for some 30% in deadweight terms. The different crude oils vary widely in appearance, consistency and characteristics, not just from country to country but from oilfield to oilfield. They range from pale brown liquids, which flow like water far below zero degrees Celsius, to viscous semi-solids; from crudes with very few light fractions not far removed from fuel oils to crudes which are highly gaseous; and from crudes with a specific gravity of 0.99 to crudes with a specific gravity of less than 0.80. They can be broadly divided into two main classes: the paraffin-based crudes (which contain varying quantities of paraffin wax and little asphaltic material) and the naphthenic crudes (which contain little or no wax but have a high proportion of asphaltic material).

All crude oils are volatile, depending on temperature, and therefore are a potential source of flammable vapours. The flashpoint of any oil is the lowest temperature at which enough vapour will be given off to form a flammable mixture with air. Below that concentration of vapour the mixture is too weak and should not ignite. With a very high concentration (for example, in an over-rich situation) there should be insufficient oxygen to support ignition. Between the two levels, if there is a source of ignition, an explosion will be the result.

Familiarity with handling petroleum in its various forms should never be allowed to lead to over-confidence and to cutting corners with safety procedures. All regulations and precautions must be strictly observed.

Most crude oils are, in varying degrees, acidic, with sulphur compounds occurring in widely varying amounts, sometimes even in crudes from different fields in the same production area. In general, the Middle East crudes have a high sulphur content, some over 6%, while some of the Far East, North African and North Sea crudes may have less than 0.2%. An obnoxious smell may indicate a high hydrogen sulphide content in a crude oil. Exposure to this may dull the sense of smell so that there is the danger of that usual olfactory warning being ignored.

The appropriate handling of each crude type will depend on its characteristics. The majority of Middle East crude oils, for example, require no special preparation of tanks before loading and, unless very low ambient or sea temperatures will be encountered on the voyage, will not require any heating.

The tank cleaning between such cargoes will only be that necessary for good housekeeping to prevent the build-up of sediments in the tanks. Some solids, semi-solids, waxy and oily deposits will be left in the cargo tanks after every voyage. An accumulation of these deposits might affect discharging by hindering the flow of oil across the tank bottoms, so the need for routine cleaning is obvious, even when questions of cleanliness for cargo quality reasons, or to drydock for repairs, do not arise.

Provided the tanks have been well drained after discharging, most crudes (whether heavy, medium or light) may be loaded without any further tank preparation. There are exceptions and before loading wax-free naphthenic crudes (such as Tia Juana Pesado, Cabimas or Lagunillas) the tanks should be hot washed and all wax deposits lifted unless the previous cargo was a wax-free crude or a naphthenic distillate. These particular crudes are not moved in very large parcels. They require a fairly high degree of heating and also, with the very large crude carriers, the lifting of deposits is not really a practical proposition.

Often, charterers are unable to arrange for full homogenous cargoes for the larger VLCCs and, therefore, these classes, which tend to be thought of as homogenous cargo carriers, may nevertheless be required to carry more than one type or quality of crude oil. The segregation requirements are likely to be such that single valve separation and pipeline admixture will be perfectly acceptable, although most vessels will be able to segregate at least three different parcels with double-valve segregation. With the advent of crude oil washing (COW) and double-hull vessels, the water washing of cargo tanks has become less common but is still required for occasional maintenance in the tank or following particular types of crude with certain quality issues such as high wax or H_2S. Load on top of residues is the practice with most crude cargoes but not all crude oils are compatible with each other and after some cargoes, tank washings may have to be segregated or put ashore in accordance with the charterer's instructions. However, this is unusual provided the tanks have been crude oil washed and well drained.

Information about all crude oils suitable for COW and a wealth of other information about the carriage and the significant parameters of crude, pour pt, wax content, H_2S, etc is available from the Institute of Petroleum's *Hydrocarbon Management Guidelines* (HM 40).

8.8.2 Heating

Few of the present generation of VLCCs are in fact equipped to heat cargo and those that are have a fairly low heating capability. Those crude oils which require heating will most often be carried in vessels under 100,000 tonnes. But with the advent of double-hull vessels, unheated VLCCs are often used for fuel oil cargoes from the Atlantic region to Singapore without serious problems arising.

When cargo heating is required it must be carried out correctly, with neither overheating nor underheating taking place. Either could result in cargo loss or damage. Overheating can damage the cargo and boil off valuable light fractions, while underheating will increase the precipitation of some of the heavier components and increase the viscosity of the cargo, causing discharge difficulties and thus probably cause outturn losses. When waxy crudes cool too far, the wax starts to precipitate and falls to the tank bottom. On the cold tank bottoms, it will harden, and because the deposits are then below the heating coils, these can have little effect on such deposits. For the same reason, when discharging any high heat cargo it is important to quickly strip the tank bottoms while the cargo is still liquid and pumpable.

If the temperature of any cargo is permitted to fall below its pour point it will start to solidify. Some of the crude oils which are shipped as so-called 'no heat crudes' can solidify if the voyage becomes protracted. For example, an intended short voyage can unexpectedly increase in duration because of a sudden port strike. The minimum temperature at which cargo is to be maintained is usually 10°C above its pour point, and consideration should be given to the wax appearance temperature of the crude in question. It is essential to adhere as closely as possible to the charterer's instructions on when heating should start and the temperature at which the cargo should be maintained and delivered, having regard to the conditions that are likely to be encountered on the voyage.

When discharging in low ambient temperatures it may be necessary to keep the cargo circulating through the deck lines to prevent solidifying and a blockage of the lines. On most existing tankers, the suction lines pass through the tanks and the cargo in the tanks keeps these lines heated. Where these lines are not located in the tanks, it is important to strip the suction lines after loading to ensure that the cargo remaining in them does not solidify on passage. This is particularly important with some very waxy cargoes. Problems with wax vary greatly depending on sea and air temperatures. For example, a cargo which presents no particular problems in a tropical area may rapidly solidify in the deck lines during a stoppage in discharging in winter conditions.

An owner's contractual obligation may be that the vessel should maintain the temperature of the cargo or it may be to raise the temperature if required by the charterer. If the obligation is to maintain the temperature and the cargo is loaded at a lower temperature, this fact should be logged in writing. Raising the cargo temperature may be difficult to achieve on a short voyage or in adverse weather conditions and can be costly in terms of bunkers. Waiting in a river port where the water temperature as well as the air temperature may be very low may use a large amount of bunkers and this needs to be taken into account in the reserve bunkers carried.

8.8.3 Inert gas

In most countries in the world, crude carriers over 20,000dwt, and most product carriers over 20,000dwt, are not permitted to load or discharge unless their inert gas systems are in operation. The quality of the inert gas being produced by the inert gas generator and the oxygen content of the gas in the tanks must be regularly monitored. The inert gas in the tanks must be kept topped up during the voyage but the biggest demands on the inert gas plant are when discharging, when air could be sucked into the tanks, and after cleaning/gas freeing. Cargo surveyors and inspectors may require the inert gas pressure in the tanks to be reduced to ullage, dip or inspect tanks. This should be done in accordance with the owner's recommended procedures. Visual inspection of the inerted tanks of large ships is difficult and not always satisfactory because the inert gas reduces visibility in the tanks. If further cleaning is required after a vessel's arrival at the loading port, then, in addition to the time lost de-inerting and cleaning, up to 48 hours may be needed for re-inerting.

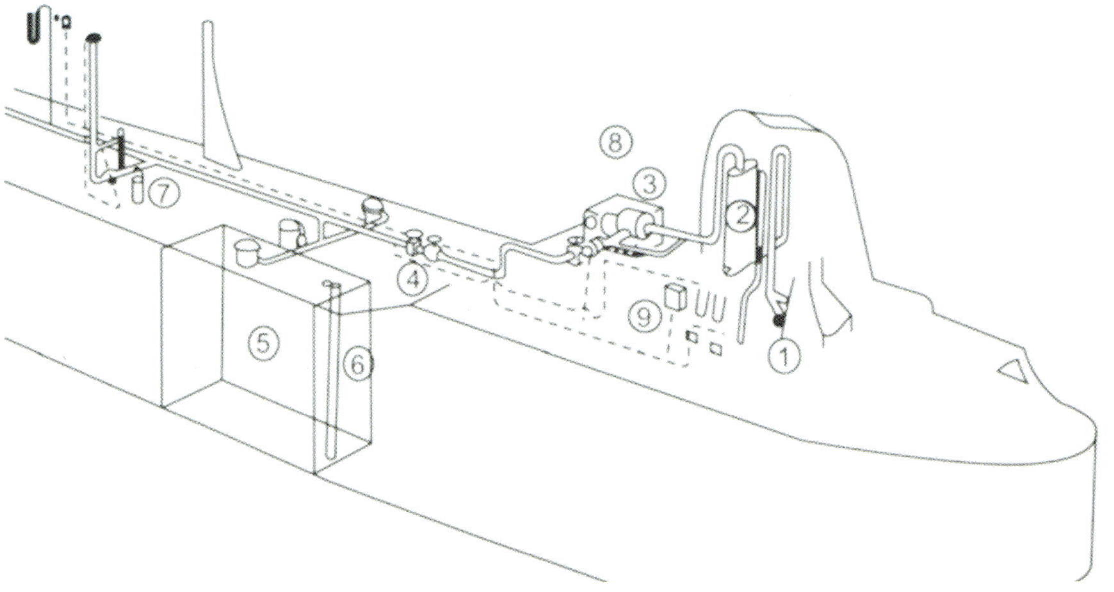

The inert flue gas system

This diagram shows the basic layout of an inert gas system. Combustion gases are drawn from the furnace uptakes in the funnel at (1) and pass upwards through a waterfall scrubbing tower (2), drawn by a high-capacity electronically driven fan (3), which blows the washed, cooled gas along a main header through a system of check, control and safety valves (4). The gas from the main header is delivered by way of the ordinary vapour branch lines into the tank coamings and then on to the cargo compartments as at (5). Each compartment has a pipe, known as the 'purge pipe' extending from the crown of the tank to within about a foot of the bottom. This is shown at (6). When the top of the purge pipe is uncovered it permits a complete circulation of the inert gas within the tank and when the oxygen level has been sufficiently reduced (ideally to about 5% instead of the 21% of oxygen normally in air) the purge pipe is closed. Thereafter, the system maintains a slight pressure. If this, for any reason, becomes excessive there is an oil seal safety arrangement in the line at (7) which will blow and release to atmosphere. A number of gauges and alarms are provided on the bridge as at (8) and in the engine room as at (9). The layout illustrated utilises the inside of the funnel casing in the forward part of which the scrubbing tower is located. In other designs, this tower is smaller and is built into the top of the engine room. The installation above has only one fan, while other installations may have two.

Although the inert gas is passed through a scrubber to remove solid particles, sooty deposits in the tanks can cause discolouration of clean cargoes and a common inert gas venting system presents some risks of contamination by transmission of vapours between different parcels of cargo. In the event of a collision or any other incident breaching the hull, the inert gas will be rapidly lost and the atmosphere in the tank will become potentially explosive.

8.9 TANK CLEANING

8.9.1 Washing

Until the introduction of crude oil washing, tanks had to be washed with water. The water method used employs sea water delivered under high pressure to the tanks via rotating nozzles, which can best be likened to gigantic lawn sprinklers. These are positioned in such a way that the high pressure jets reach every part of the tank. The manufacturer most often associated with this system is Butterworth, although there are several other types. The water used is usually at ambient temperature although, before a drydock, the water may be heated. This is because it is vital to ensure all residues are completely removed to avoid the risk of asphyxiation or flammable fumes being present.

8.9.2 Crude oil washing

Washing a tank with cargo does not seem an obvious method of cleaning, and if a tank was left for perhaps 24 hours to drain after discharge, much of the clingage (on the tank sides, stiffeners and other surfaces in the tank) would drain to the tank bottoms without any assistance. Pumping crude oil through the tank- washing machines as each tank is discharged shifts much of the clingage from the tank sides and the residues and oily deposits from the horizontals and tank bottoms. Although carried out concurrent with discharge of other tanks, it reduces the overall rate of discharge because a pump has to be used to feed the washing machines but it is quicker and much more effective than just natural drainage. It also shifts the solids and semi-solids which would otherwise remain where they have settled on the horizontals and tank bottoms. After each tank is washed, the tank bottoms are stripped to a collecting tank from where the collected oil will be pumped ashore. The advent of double-hull vessels has greatly assisted this drainage and reduced the requirement for washing because tank sides and bottoms are largely free of frames, stiffeners and longitudinals, which are now in the double-bottom and side ballast tanks, and most cargo tanks have a drainage well for the pump suctions.

In the process of crude oil washing, gas is generated which will be vented from the tank, so there is an increase in the loss of valuable light fractions. However, because the washing moves the clingage and deposits to the tank bottoms from where they can be stripped ashore, it increases the overall cargo outturned. It leaves the tanks much cleaner, so easing the problems of cleaning and reduces the consumption for the boilers for subsequent tank washing. This is the primary advantage to the shipowner, who might otherwise face a claim for short delivery but for the extra oil recovered and put ashore as a result of crude oil washing. Except on the last discharge before drydocking (when it is to the owner's advantage to have all the tanks cleaned), the number of tanks that the shipowner will generally wish to crude oil wash is about one-third. By this means, all the tanks are washed over a cycle of three voyages and this is sufficient to prevent the undue build-up of residues in the tank bottoms.

Crude oil washing increases the overall discharge time, for which the charterer may or may not have to pay depending on the type and terms of the charter, although any increase in the outturn quantity is to the cargo receiver's advantage. This is because it is better for them to receive the maximum cargo delivery, rather than have a potential claim for short delivery.

Many charterers therefore request that all tanks containing their cargo should be crude oil washed, which unfortunately increases the chance of a claim for short delivery on the subsequent voyage. Not all crude oils are suitable for crude oil washing. Some very heavy or waxy crudes, because of their viscous or waxy nature, could increase rather than reduce the clingage. For a crude oil to be suitable for crude oil washing its viscosity should be less than 600cSt at discharge temperature and this temperature should exceed its pour point by at least 10°C.

8.10 PETROLEUM PRODUCTS

The division between crude oils and products, and between clean and dirty products, is not as clear-cut as perhaps might be expected. Crude oils may not always be shipped in the same state as they are extracted at the wellhead. They may be treated by the addition or the removal of some components. A cargo described as a feedstock may be a product (such as dirty naphtha) or a topped crude oil. The dividing line between a dirty and a clean product is blurred. Gasoil falls on the dividing line. A light-coloured gasoil will almost certainly be a clean cargo whereas a darker gasoil may be regarded as a dirty product and shipped on a crude carrier. A product carrier with good segregation can carry both clean and dirty products, but this is very rare.

Bitumen is a product which is solid at ambient temperature but not a lot is now shipped in bulk as most bitumens require a specially designed ship with very high heating capacity. Bitumen cutbacks (bitumen to which a solvent has been added) need less heating. Bitumen will foam if any water is left in the tanks and special precautions are necessary. Other dirty products include the very heavy fuel oils, a few of which may have a specific gravity as high as 1.00, carbon black feedstock, which may have a specific gravity of more than 1.00, waxy distillates; diesel oils and dirty gasoils. Clean products include clear gasoils, lubricating oils, kerosene, aviation turbine fuel, motor gasoline and aviation gasoline.

For dirty products, heating can be a major consideration. Heavy fuel oils may have to be kept at 57°C or even more, otherwise their very high viscosity will cause protracted pumping time and increased outturn losses. With clean products, the requirements for the degree of cleanliness of the tanks, pumps and lines are likely to be much more critical and exacting. For all clean products, the charterer will wish to know the previous three cargoes carried to ensure that the tanks can be made suitable for the cargo to be loaded. If heated cargo is carried in tanks adjacent to light clean products or gaseous crudes, there will be increased vapour losses, and possibly vapour pressure problems when discharging, particularly if there is a high ambient temperature.

The most common size of clean product carrier is about 45,000 tonnes deadweight while the average size dirty product carrier is larger, in the region of 112,000 tonnes. Size of cargo tanks is also a consideration in this respect insofar as cargo receivers can only take their product parcels in quantities consistent with the size of their shore tanks. Unless there is a big saving in shipping supplies in larger parcels, the cargo receiver is not going to invest in larger shore tanks.

Most of the large product carriers are designed to carry crude and/or other dirty products so that they can be programmed more economically. Their tank coatings, mainly zinc or epoxy-based, enable them to be cleaned more quickly between cargoes, from crude oils to dirty products or even to clean products, with either a cold or hot wash depending on the cargo to be loaded. But charterers take careful notice of previous cargo history. For some products, including all clean products, it may also be necessary to flush the tank bottoms, gas-free, lift scale and mop up. For colour-critical grades, flushing the tanks and lines with suitable wash oil may be needed. Because of the steel wastage in unprotected tanks in the clean oil trade, any ship without coatings is likely to carry only dirty cargoes, except perhaps if it was employed clean on its initial voyages after delivery from the builder's yard.

Cleaning requirements between one grade and another must be strictly observed and all major charterer shave their cleaning tables and special requirements. Various products have their own critical properties. Products may be colour critical or their flashpoint or sulphur content may be changed owing to contamination. Other factors to be considered include viscosity, octane number, wax and asphaltenes.

Information about all petroleum products and other information about cleaning is available from the Institute of Petroleum's *Hydrocarbon Management Guidelines* (HM 50). These include guidelines for the cleaning of tanks and lines for marine tank vessels carrying petroleum and refined products.

8.11 CHEMICALS

Chemical carriers operate in a very specialised trade carrying a wide range of chemicals and a variety of other petroleum products such as aromatics and unleaded gasoline.

If any cargo, whether chemicals or otherwise, has specialised requirements which would not be within the knowledge of the owner of the normal type of vessel carrying such cargoes, the charterer has a duty to advise the owner of these special requirements. With chemicals, because of the range of types, and because different manufacturers and chemical traders often have different names for the same chemical product, an owner needs to know exactly what the product is and not just its brand name. This is essential for all aspects of cargo care and handling, and for the safety of the ship and its personnel. However, liquid chemicals in bulk tend to be the province of a relatively small number of chemical producers and an even more limited number of ship operators operating vessels with the sophisticated hardware for carrying such chemicals with both sides having expert knowledge in their own fields. The terminals at which such cargoes are handled are similarly staffed with experts and well equipped.

There are chemical carriers over 40,000 tonnes deadweight but the majority of chemicals shipped in bulk are carried in small quantities. This means the average size of chemical carrier is small, with suitable size tanks and good segregation capability. The nature and high unit value of such products justifies the cost of stainless steel tanks or expensive coatings, separate pumps and lines, and extra safety features. The hazardous nature of many of these chemicals, which may be toxic to breathe or if in contact with the bare skin, necessitates strict adherence to safe handling procedures. Appropriate protective equipment must be worn.

Chemical carriers operate in a very specialised trade

8.11.1 Tank coatings

Coating manufacturers furnish lists of the products and temperatures for which their coatings are suitable. If the cargo and coatings are not compatible, the cargo may damage the coatings or the coatings contaminate or discolour the cargo. Not all charterers have the same criteria regarding suitability of certain coatings for specific cargoes. If a coating starts to fail, the tank surface is no longer fully protected and also, cleaning problems increase. The merest trace of some substances can cause the deterioration of a cargo and a single blister in a coating may conceal potentially contaminating quantities of the previous cargo.

8.12 LIQUID GAS CARRIERS

These vessels fall into two classes, liquefied natural gas (LNG) carriers and liquified petroleum gas (LPG) carriers. There are three designs of LNG carriers in general use. The most widely used have the Moss Rosenberg spherical tank system and the other two best-known systems are the Technigas and Gaz Transport integral tank systems. The LNG is carried at minus 162° C and the boil-off gas is either used as fuel in the main propulsion or put through a cryogenic plant on board and returned to the tanks. LNG has a specific gravity in the area of 0.50 depending on the composition of the gas, so LNG carriers need to have a large cubic capacity in relation to their deadweight. Most of the existing LNG schemes use dedicated ships of a common design. The shipping fleet for a gas project always has spare capacity to take into account drydocking and repairing time. However, if there should be an unexpected loss of part of such a dedicated fleet, it could be difficult and expensive to obtain replacement tonnage which would be suitable (or could be made suitable) for the project terminals which have been designed for one class and size of ship.

For large quantities of gas to be carried over long distances, refrigeration tends to be the most economical method of transportation because of the saving of weight and cost by the reduction in steel needed for the tanks. The larger LPG carriers are usually fully refrigerated but the smaller ones are usually fully refrigerated, or part refrigerated and part pressurised.

LPG liquefies at a much higher temperature than LNG. Butane liquefies at -14.5°C and propane at -48.4°C. They have a refrigeration plant on board to reliquify the boil-off gas and return it to the cargo tanks. There is less tendency for LPG carriers to be dedicated ships and there is a much more general market for LPG carriers which may carry other cargoes besides butane and propane.

The gas used for inerting the tanks of both LNG and LPG carriers is nitrogen, not flue gas which would not be pure enough for these cargoes. The shore may supply the initial nitrogen blanket for the cargo and this is topped up on the voyage by the vessel.

The most widely used LNG carriers have the Moss Rosenberg spherical tank system

8.13 ULLAGE, DEADFREIGHT AND SLACK TANKS

With any form of cargo, the owner has a claim for deadfreight if the charterer does not supply the full agreed quantity. All gas carriers have sophisticated instrumentation for measuring the tank contents because there can be no question of opening the tanks to measure the contents. Indeed, any gas in the tanks prior to loading or after discharge has to be taken into account.

The measurement of cargo on a few older oil tankers is less automated and not all tankers are equipped so that the ullages can be read in a central control room. This means that the deck officer in charge of loading will ensure all tanks are ullaged, that is, the free space above the cargo is measured. Ullaging is usually carried out using a steel tape on the end of which is a heavy calibrated brass bob. A full tank will only be loaded to 98% of its capacity to allow room for cargo expansion on the voyage. The tanks will be ullaged through the ullage openings in the deckhead.

The accuracy of such measurements, electronic or manual, may be affected by any movement of the ship and, of course, any rounding off of the measurements. A small inaccuracy in ullaging a large tank can represent a significant quantity of the cargo.

The content of the tanks must also be measured and recorded before discharge and again after discharge. Ullaging the tanks after discharge, to find any quantities remaining in the tanks, is usually referred to as 'dipping the tanks', although on all modern tankers this is done electronically with gauges and back-up systems in the cargo control room.

Apart from the question of deadfreight when a full cargo is not supplied, there may be considerations of seaworthiness if the vessel has slack tanks. This applies to all tankers but is particularly important with gas carriers, where the surface movement of cargo in the tanks could damage their structure. With LNG carriers, the spherical tanks (because of their shape) allow a greater range of quantities in the part-filled tank than the box-shaped integral tanks, where the surface movement can be greater.

If a vessel cannot load to its full deadweight because, owing to the low specific gravity of the cargo, it is full to capacity but not down to its marks, the right to recover deadfreight, or not, will depend on the contract. Many charters are fixed on a minimum basis, for example, 'Min 80,000MT (NDFFCA PMQS)' (no deadfreight for charterer's account provided minimum quantity supplied). The economics of the voyage are done using this figure. If the vessel can actually take more cargo with this density (known as the overage) then this is a bonus for the vessel owners and the charterers, and this overage may well be negotiated at the chartering stage for a different rate per tonne. Whenever the vessel could load more cargo but the shore stops the loading, the ship should protest in writing to the shore, inform the charterer and await their authority before sailing. Shortloading or overloading contrary to the charterer's wishes could result in a claim for damages.

8.14 GEOGRAPHY AND METEOROLOGY

8.14.1 Ports and terminals

Most ship managers will find that ships under their management tend to prefer certain trades and will become familiar with the pros and cons of different loading and discharging terminals. There is, however, one piece of advice which is always worth taking – that it is better to remember where to find the facts than to try to remember lots of facts.

Having said that, any source of facts must be up to date. There are many excellent but costly volumes available which list details of almost every berth in the world, many of them printed in new editions each year. The reality is that there is constant change in the world of ports, docks, berths and terminals. Usually, the change is for the better but shortage of money or even topographical changes can result in some facilities deteriorating.

An inevitable problem with any port directory is its sheer size. This results in possibly several months passing between the input of the information and the actual publication date. There is usually no substitute for local knowledge, which means that if any dimension or restriction is critical, it is always advisable to contact and use a reputable agent at the port concerned. When contacting any agent, always remember to ensure that the question is very clear, so that the answer is equally so.

Quite often, the charter party will stipulate a safe berth when referring to the loading or discharging port, which places the onus on the charterer to ensure that the nominated berth is safe for the ship concerned.

It should not be overlooked that although the ship manager will be relieved of many tasks when a ship is on a time charter rather than voyage charter, monitoring the safety of where the ship is ordered still has to be done.

There is no substitute for experience in knowing about berths and no obvious short cuts to gaining that knowledge. One can, however, speed up one's learning process by studying fixture lists in the shipping press and looking up details of the ports to which other owners' ships similar to your own are trading.

8.14.2 Tides

Tides may have an impact on the safety of a berth. There is, for example, nothing unsafe about a berth to which the access is restricted (such as by a sandbar at certain states of the tide) so long as the berth itself allows the ship to be afloat at all times. Some shortsea charters even allow for a 'not always afloat but safely aground' (NAABSA) situation but, unless the charter is negotiated in such a way to ensure time counts while waiting for the tide, then the owner incurs the cost of that delay. Theoretically, this could be several days because, during neap tides when there is the smallest variation, the depth may not increase sufficiently to allow access and the ship will have to wait for spring tides, which could be as much as a week or more. Conversely, where a berth is of a restricted depth, the under-keel clearance (UKC) of the vessel may well be a critical issue and a period of neap tides may be better as the overall depth at the berth will not change as greatly between high and low water.

Where ships are engaged in short voyages, knowledge of tides can be even more important. There is no point in ordering overtime to discharge more quickly or rushing at full speed to the loading port if the ship has to wait several hours for the tide to rise before it can enter the berth.

8.14.3 Ice

Several areas in the world which are important to shipping can have navigation impeded or even made quite impossible during winter months.

For example, by looking at a map of North America, it appears far more economical for the farmers in the Canadian prairies to deliver their grain for export to Churchill in the Hudson Bay. However, navigation is only possible there for the four months from July to October.

The St Lawrence Seaway linking the Atlantic to the Great Lakes allows oceangoing ships to reach deep into the heart of the North American continent but ice closes this route from about the middle of December to the beginning of May. Fortunately, weather forecasting is fairly reliable and, so far, there have not been any cases of large numbers of ships being trapped in the lakes by an unexpected early freeze-up.

In northern Europe, parts of the Baltic Sea and the different gulfs leading off it become ice-bound from November to March and, despite the sophistication of the ice-breakers, including a few that are nuclear-powered, some of the ports are closed during the depths of winter.

On some occasions, there are very attractive rates to be obtained for late season cargoes in ice- affected areas but the risks have to be very carefully calculated.

Marine insurance policies may be void if trading outside the Institute Navigating Limits (discussed below), that is, in the areas prone to icing. Insurers may allow such trading after prior authorisation and payment of additional premiums.

8.14.4 Storms

Some areas of the world are notorious for difficult weather conditions, including the North Atlantic in winter, Cape Horn at almost any time and the southern tip of Africa on occasions. Even ordinary bad weather can lengthen a voyage enough to erode the profits of all parties involved and this will be discussed later.

There are seasonal bouts of extremes of weather which can be damaging, occasionally fatal, even to today's modern ships. In different parts of the world they go by different names but in essence they are similar in meteorological terms. They are areas of extreme low atmospheric pressure which produce violent revolving storms (anticlockwise in the northern hemisphere, clockwise south of the equator) which develop over the sea and produce wind speeds averaging around 75 knots and gusts reaching twice that speed at times. As well as damaging high winds, these tropical revolving storms bring exceptionally heavy rain and occasionally, the wind and low pressure will cause a tidal surge to build up which can cause tremendous flooding damage ashore.

The Intertropical Convergence Zone (ITCZ), known by sailors as the doldrums, is the area encircling the earth near the equator where the north-east and south-east trade winds converge and tropical revolving storms are formed. The worst of these storms occur along the Tropics of Cancer and Capricorn (23.5 degrees north and south of the equator). Not only do they present a direct hazard to any shipping in the affected areas but, when they hit land, they can damage port installations such that they are put out of action and can devastate crops which would otherwise be available for export.

Among the areas where such storms are prevalent is the southern Indian Ocean, where they are simply known by the meteorological name of cyclones, and may be encountered from November to May.

Although these storms can occasionally reach as far north as the Indian Subcontinent they should not be confused with monsoons. These bring, between June and August, occasional gales and heavy rains which are vital to agriculture in parts of India and Pakistan. The gales are not of the same severity as cyclones but are violent enough to delay shipping and, of course, the rains will interrupt loading and discharging.

In the Gulf of Mexico and the West Indies area the storms are called hurricanes. These often take a heavy toll on crops, property and human lives because their paths can take them along the line of the Caribbean Islands then on to the mainland, where they do further damage before being slowed down by passage over the land mass. The hurricane season is between June and November, with maximum frequency between August and October.

In the Far East, the Chinese name for big wind is '*tai fung*' from which the Europeans have derived the label 'typhoon'. Again, there are many islands in the area which often suffer severe economic loss when whole crops of sugar, rice and palm oil are wiped out. Typhoons can occur at any time between May and December, with maximum frequency between July and October.

Between January and April some areas around Australia experience similar conditions. The winds are known as 'willy-willies' when they blow on land over dry regions, and port work in places such as Darwin and Port Hedland often bear the brunt.

Obviously, no ship manager deliberately routes their ships through such storms, and equally, no prudent ship's Master would follow such a routeing. It is, therefore, essential for the risk of seasonal storms occurring to be borne in mind when planning voyages through such areas during the critical times.

8.14.5 Fog

A sea fog is different from fogs experienced inland because the latter is invariably associated with calm conditions while at sea, quite fresh winds may be involved. The essential ingredient for a sea fog is warm, moist air blowing over a cold sea.

The situation may occur anywhere but, in some parts of the world, fogs are particularly prevalent, such as:

Area	Maximum likelihood
Off Newfoundland	May to September
Off California	June to September
Bering Sea	June to August
Baltic Sea	November to January
Turkish Straits	November to February
Hudson Bay	June to September

8.14.6 Icebergs

The same cold Labrador Current which is responsible for the Newfoundland fogs also brings down icebergs, large pieces of ice which have broken off the Polar ice cap. They are every bit as dangerous today as they were to the ill-fated *Titanic*, although modern detection methods make it far easier to avoid these hazards.

8.15 ROUTEING SERVICES

The concept of weather routeing is not new and when it started there was considerable scepticism about the benefits but, in recent years, there have been significant improvements in both forecasting technology and communications between ship and shore. In addition, the changing climate means that an owner or charterer need no longer rely solely on the Master's experience, extensive though that may be.

In particular, the enhanced accuracy and use of latest near-real-time current data, gathered from satellite and other observations, means that service providers are able to considerably improve route choice by ensuring that the routed vessel takes the fullest advantage of favourable weather and sea conditions while avoiding those that are unfavourable. The benefit of this in terms of crew comfort, improved safety and the minimising of cargo damage is of real importance to the vessel.

More tangibly for the owner or charterer, while time saved may be small, the high cost of bunkers (and hire) means that even a modest saving in steaming time can result in a significant cost reduction. Fuel savings in the region of 2–4% are claimed, which, on most voyages, would repay the costs of the service many times over. In addition, time saved in a rising market means having the vessel ready earlier to take advantage of that rise.

Using a big-weather routeing provider brings a wealth of observations from other vessels to add to the satellite data which may be instrumental in convincing Masters of the value. While it can only ever be a recommendation, it is intended to act as a support to allow the Master to choose a safe and efficient passage.

It can, of course, be used by a charterer or an owner to check on the performance of the vessel as charterers have long been sceptical of owners' weather reports being used as a basis for refuting speed and performance claims. Modern data is far better today and recent court cases have attested to the accuracy of the information.

Benefits of using weather routeing

The safety of the vessel, its crew and its cargo is always compromised by bad weather. By avoiding this or reducing the effect on the vessel, safety is greatly improved. In addition, bad weather does not just create what could be called mechanical injuries such as falls and injuries from moving items, it also has an effect on judgement as it brings tiredness and fatigue as well as seasickness.

Bad weather can also bring damage to the vessel and its cargo. By avoiding the worst aspects of bad weather, these are reduced, in turn reducing costs of repair, insurance claims and so on.

Weather routeing can improve scheduling and can assist in voyage planning as bad weather has a dramatic effect on a ship's timings. Scheduling can be more precise, avoiding missed tides and other restrictions.

Increased bunker consumption during bad weather is an extra burden on the owner and charterer, whereas reduced fuel consumption results in fewer emissions. Proper planning using good weather routeing is claimed to make significant savings.

Weather routeing can also be used to avoid or minimise transit in fog and avoid ice. Both can seriously impact the vessel's schedule and speed, and can, in addition, be an extra hazard to mariners. Fewer weather delays mean shorter passage times, which improves earnings for the vessel.

Apart from such specific attention to the weather through the use of experts, all ship managers should ensure they have a good background knowledge of elementary climatology.

For example, ice closes the Great Lakes and the St Lawrence Seaway during winter and a close watch has to be kept on a ship's position if it is venturing into such areas late in the season. Legal arguments as to whether a ship is off-hire or on-hire while trapped for several months are futile if the time charterers have gone bankrupt in the meantime.

Ice also closes many ports in the Baltic Sea and other places around that north-west corner of the European continent as well as parts of Alaska, while the Hudson Bay is closed for a longer time than it is open. Winter weather generally can be troublesome, especially in the North Atlantic, where storms can cause severe delays, even structural damage.

At the other end of the climatic scale there is a variety of storms in tropical areas. Monsoon gales and torrential rains around the Indian Subcontinent in June, July and August can seriously disrupt cargo working.

Even more violent are the cyclonic storms (known as hurricanes in the Caribbean area) from July to October and, in the South Pacific, from December to March. Typhoons are seen in the Far East any time between May and January but more likely July to October. In the southern Indian Ocean, such storms are called cyclones, which are at their worst between November and May. Some catastrophic wave formations occasionally result from cyclones off the coast of southern Africa, where ships have been known to break in two. Off the east, north and west coasts of Australia the cyclones are at their most violent between January and March. It is worth remembering that cyclones in the northern hemisphere rotate anticlockwise while south of the equator they spin clockwise.

While routeing services have proven their worth over time, a new development is taking place which may threaten their future.

An increasing number of ships are now fitted with an electronic chart display and information system (ECDIS) and these are growing in sophistication. It is possible for them to integrate tidal currents and weather information obtained from satellite subscription services with interactive electronic charts. This can give Masters much more information than a commercial weather routeing service and thus permit them to make an informed judgement of the best route themselves. Furthermore, in the event of a possible dispute, all the information used by the Master in coming to a decision would be recorded on computer or the ship's voyage data recorder.

8.16 LOADLINES

A ship's loadline, which indicates the minimum freeboard, and therefore the greatest depth, to which it may be loaded, varies depending upon the density of the water, the time of the year and the part of the world in which the ship is trading.

The question of density of water is simply that if the ship is loading in fresh water it can load to a greater depth because when it reaches the sea, the greater density of salt water will lift it up to its saltwater loadline.

The impact of the time of the year, however, is that the ship will have a greater freeboard, thus being higher out of the water for safety's sake in winter when rougher weather may be encountered. For this reason, the greatest freeboard is demanded for Winter (W), or more rarely now, Winter North Atlantic (WNA) (only applicable to vessels under 100m in length), whilst the least freeboard in salt water is the line marked 'T' for Tropical.

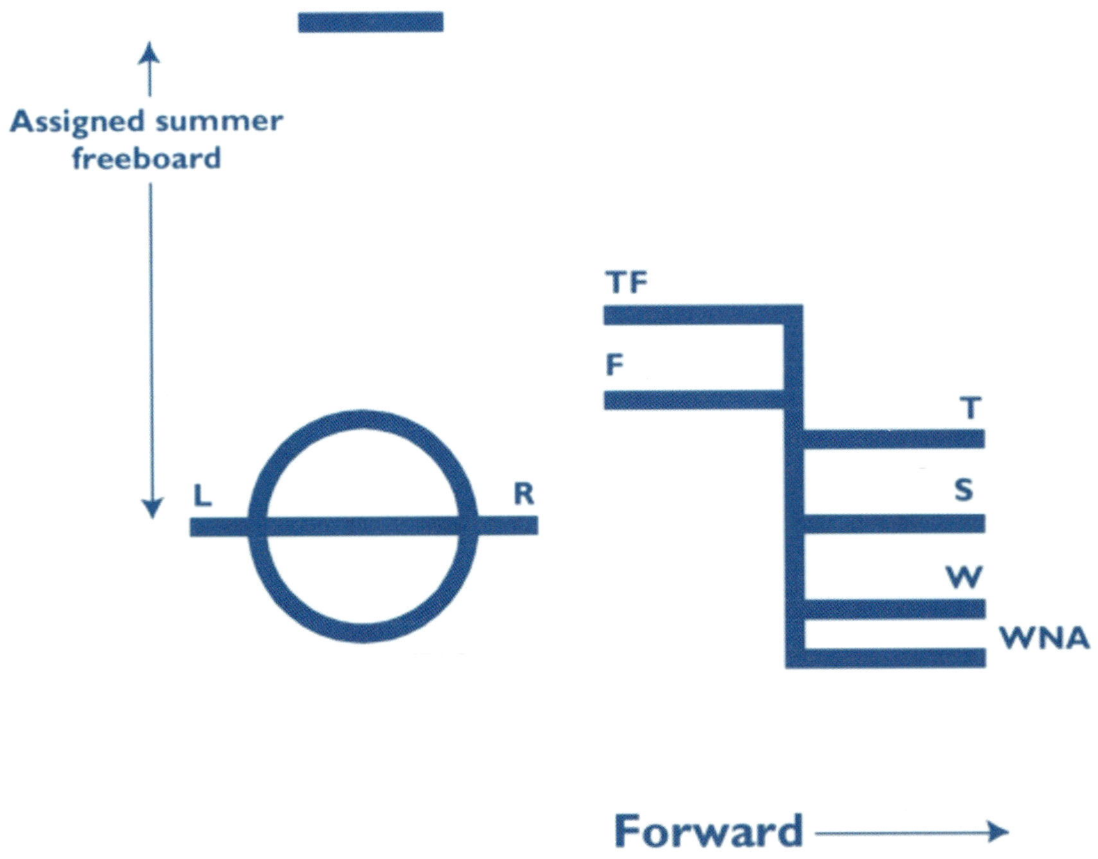

Plimsoll mark which is painted on each side of the ship

Universal marking of all ships with a Plimsoll line dates from an international convention concluded in 1930. That was 40 years after the philanthropist and campaigner, Samuel Plimsoll, persuaded the British government to take action to safeguard the lives of seafarers by adopting the statutory marking of all British ships in this way. It seems that reaching international agreement on shipping matters took even longer in those days than it does now!

At the same time as the measurement and marking of ships was agreed, the International Loadline Convention devised a method of dividing the world into zones to correspond to the lines on the Plimsoll mark. Readers are recommended to study a maritime atlas to appreciate the full extent of the different zones with the dates when seasons change between summer and winter. There is a wide band around the world extending several degrees either side of the equator, marked 'T' for tropical zone, which permits the deepest draught in sea water. Obviously, if one can trade one's ships within that area, the additional depth means more cargo and therefore more income. Conversely, trading between northern Europe and North America in winter will mean loading to the lightest mark (W or WNA) and care will always have to be exercised so as to avoid an area in that zone where winter restrictions are imposed from October to April.

Most voyages, however, are likely to involve more than one zone, which is why ship managers need to have a picture of the loadline zones clearly in their minds or, better still, on their computer or hung on the office wall. The main impact of these zones is usually on bunker planning.

Many factors of availability, price, time and cargo affect bunkering decisions and the loadline zones present yet another element to add into the equation. There is nothing new in planning one's bunkering to take full advantage of the zones. There is to this day an important oil bunkering station at St Vincent in the Cape Verde Islands which dates back to the days of coal burners. An active market at the time was coal out to Argentina and grain home to the UK, and owners found that they could maximise their cargo liftings by taking just enough bunkers to get them from Cardiff to St Vincent, which is in the tropical zone. There they would bunker right down to their tropical marks, which was generally enough to last them down to the River Plate and back to Cardiff again.

Today's voyages may be more complex but the principle is the same. One should remember also that there is a converse to this where care would have to be taken if a ship were to load right down to its tropical marks at a port on the edge of the tropical zones and then steam due north into a winter zone without having burnt off enough bunkers to bring it up to the winter marks.

Even arriving with the winter marks clear may not be enough. Surveyors on port state control duties are always vigilant and they can easily work out from the ship's deadweight scale whether or not the ship has nevertheless been sailing through winter zones with the appropriate mark well submerged. This can be a very serious matter indeed and is likely to result in serious action being taken. Not only can Masters find themselves facing heavy fines but an overloaded ship is technically unseaworthy and therefore its insurance cover could be in jeopardy.

8.16.1 International Navigating Limits (INL)

Mention has been made of these limits, which, as a result of general agreement among marine underwriters, are incorporated into hull and machinery insurance policies.

In 2000, the Institute of Chartered Underwriters in London revised the Institute Warranty Limits (IWL). Since 1 November 2003, the limits have been referred to as the International Navigating Limits (INL). The INL define the geographical limits within which ships are able to operate without incurring additional insurance premiums from hull and machinery and other relevant underwriters. Operating outside the INL, in areas which can include significant hazards such as ice, could lead to damage to the ship and delay necessitated by repair.

The International Hull Clauses impose an undertaking upon the ship not to trade into icy regions during cold weather. Although these conditions can be broken if an application is made to the underwriters and the appropriate additional premium is paid, this is another weather problem which the ship manager must take into consideration.

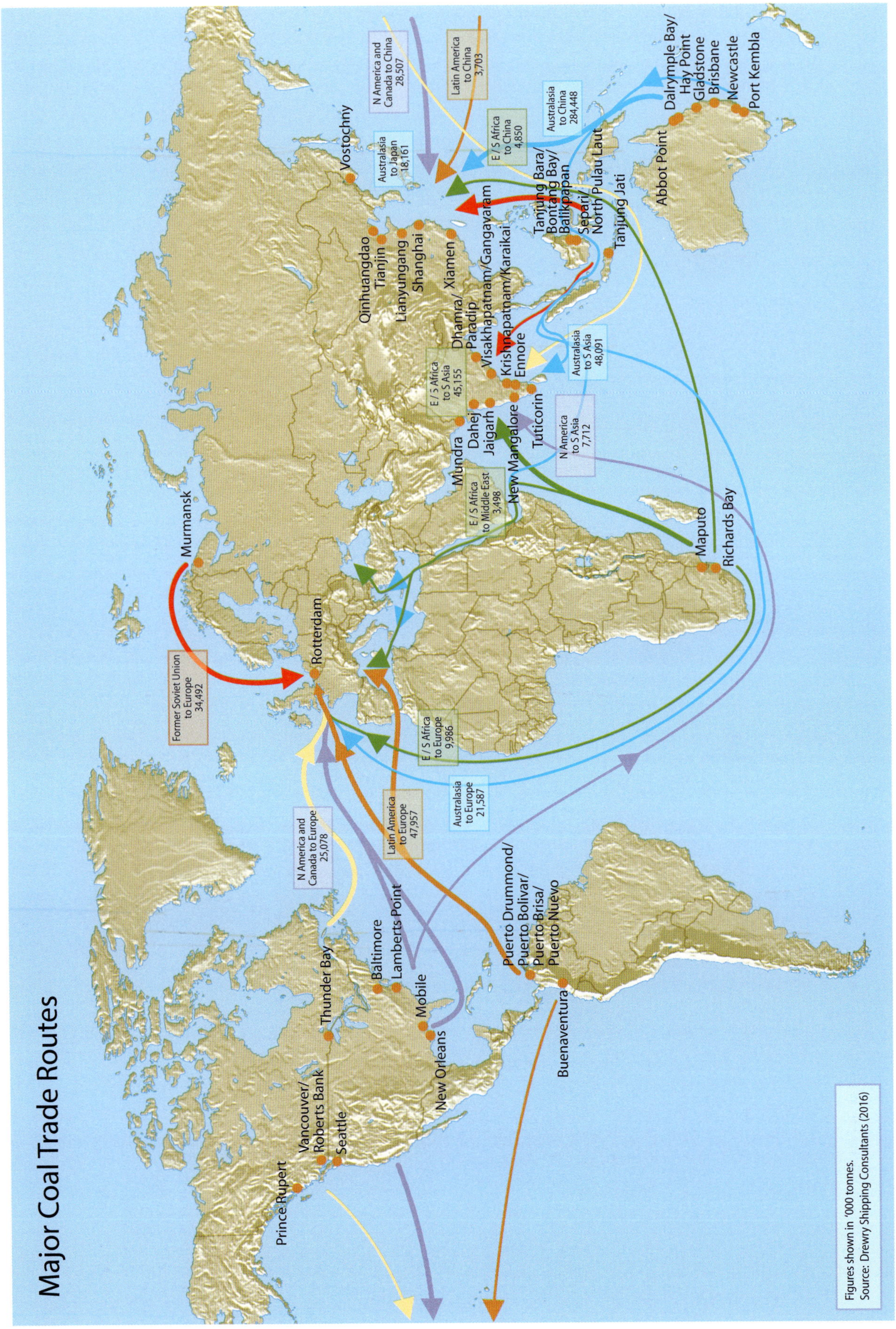
Major Coal Trade Routes
Prince Rupert
Vancouver/
Roberts Bank
Seattle
Thunder Bay
Baltimore
Lamberts Point
Mobile
New Orleans
Puerto Drummond/
Puerto Bolivar/
Puerto Brisa/
Puerto Nuevo
Buenaventura
N America and
Canada to Europe
25,078
Latin America
to Europe
47,957
Australasia
to Europe
21,587
E / S Africa
to Europe
9,986
Former Soviet Union
to Europe
34,492
Murmansk
Rotterdam
E / S Africa
to Middle East
3,498
Maputo
Richards Bay
Mundra
Dahej
Jaigarh
New Mangalore
Tuticorin
N America
to S Asia
7,712
E / S Africa
to S Asia
45,155
Dhamra/
Paradip
Visakhapatnam/Gangavaram
Krishnapatnam/Karaikal
Ennore
Australasia
to S Asia
48,091
Qinhuangdao
Tianjin
Lianyungang
Shanghai
Xiamen
Vostochny
Tanjung Bara/
Bontang Bay/
Balikpapan
Sepati/
North Pulau Laut
Tanjung Jati
Australasia
to Japan
18,161
N America and
Canada to China
28,507
Latin America
to China
3,703
E / S Africa
to China
4,850
Australasia
to China
284,448
Abbot Point
Dalrymple Bay/
Hay Point
Gladstone
Brisbane
Newcastle
Port Kembla
Figures shown in '000 tonnes.
Source: Drewry Shipping Consultants (2016)

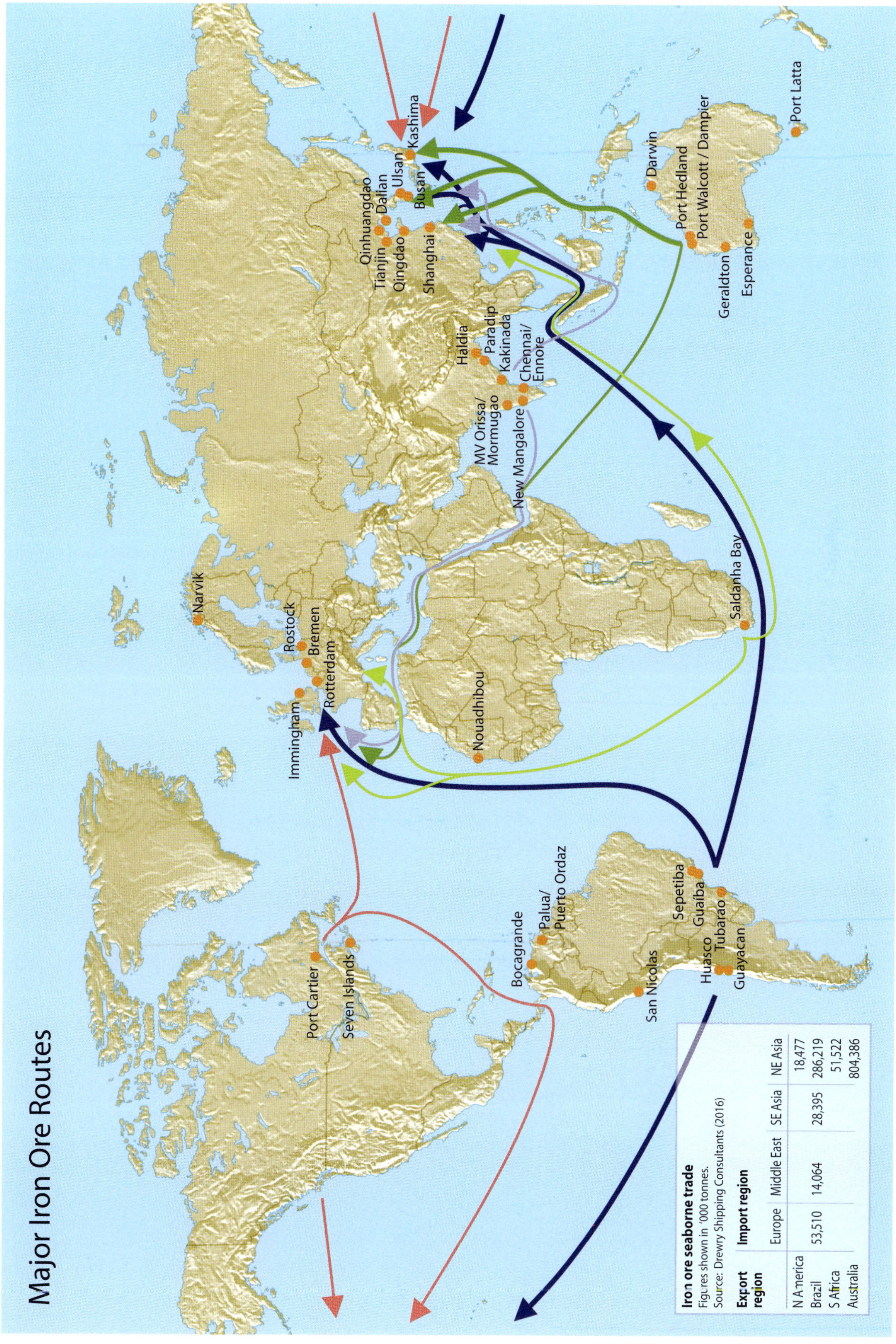

Iron ore seaborne trade
Figures shown in '000 tonnes.
Source: Drewry Shipping Consultants (2016)

Export region	Import region			
	Europe	Middle East	SE Asia	NE Asia
N America				18,477
Brazil	53,510	14,064	28,395	286,219
S Africa				51,522
Australia				804,386

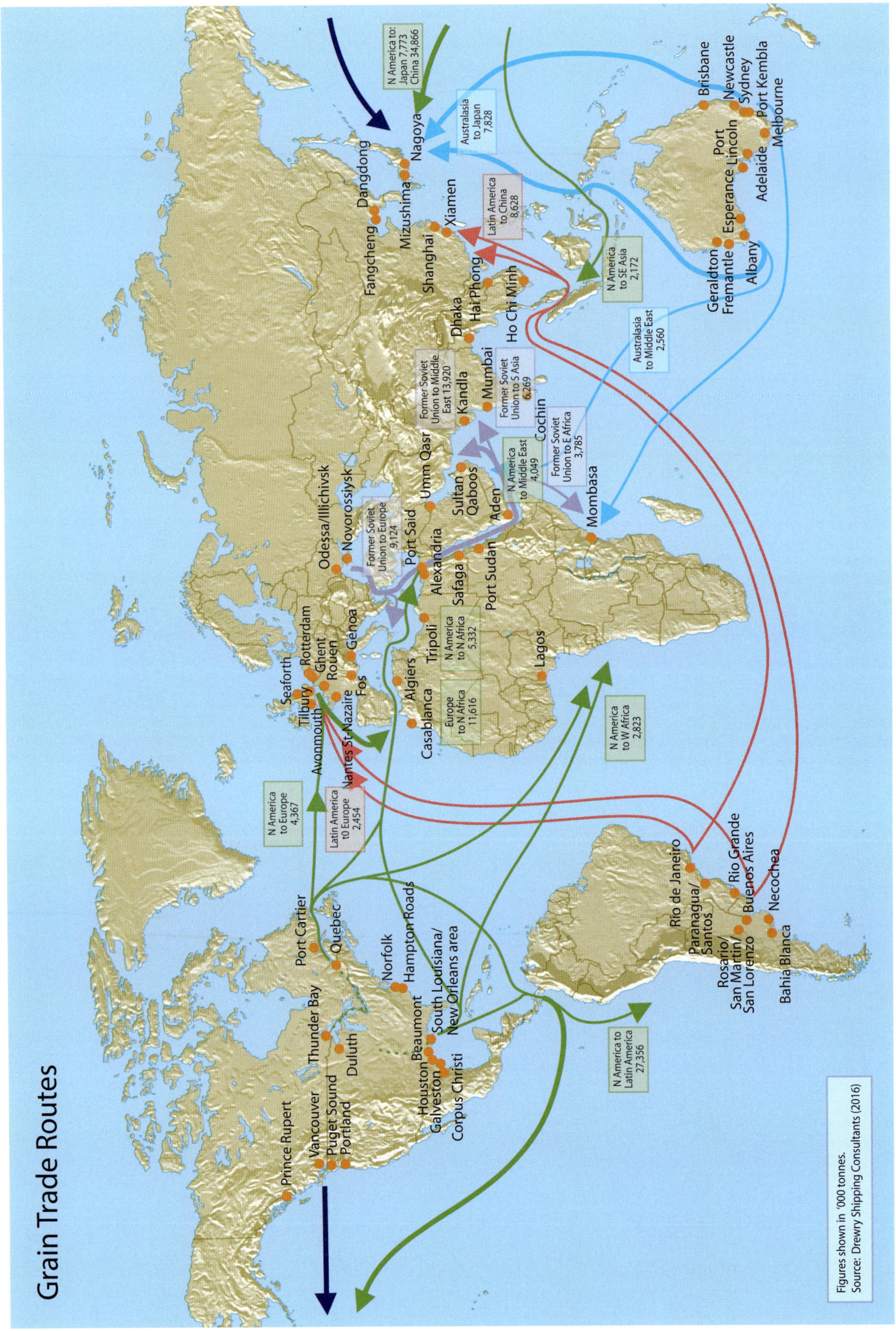
Grain Trade Routes
N America to: Japan 7,773 China 34,866
Australasia to Japan 7,828
Latin America to China 8,628
N America to SE Asia 2,172
Australasia to Middle East 2,560
Former Soviet Union to Middle East 13,920
Former Soviet Union to S Asia 6,269
Former Soviet Union to E Africa 3,785
N America to Middle East 4,049
Former Soviet Union to Europe 9,124
N America to N Africa 5,332
Europe to N Africa 11,616
N America to W Africa 2,823
N America to Europe 4,367
Latin America t0 Europe 2,454
N America to Latin America 27,356
Prince Rupert
Vancouver
Puget Sound
Portland
Thunder Bay
Duluth
Port Cartier
Quebec
Norfolk
Hampton Roads
Houston
Galveston
Corpus Christi
Beaumont
South Louisiana/ New Orleans area
Rio de Janeiro
Paranagua/ Santos
Rio Grande
Rosario/ San Martin/ San Lorenzo
Buenos Aires
Necochea
Bahia Blanca
Seaforth
Tilbury
Rotterdam
Ghent
Rouen
Avonmouth
Nantes St-Nazaire
Fos
Genoa
Odessa/Illichivsk
Novorossiysk
Casablanca
Algiers
Tripoli
Lagos
Alexandria
Port Said
Safaga
Port Sudan
Umm Qasr
Sultan Qaboos
Aden
Mombasa
Kandla
Mumbai
Cochin
Dhaka
Hai Phong
Ho Chi Minh
Fangcheng
Shanghai
Xiamen
Dangdong
Mizushima
Nagoya
Geraldton
Fremantle
Albany
Esperance
Port Lincoln
Adelaide
Melbourne
Port Kembla
Sydney
Newcastle
Brisbane
Figures shown in '000 tonnes.
Source: Drewry Shipping Consultants (2016)

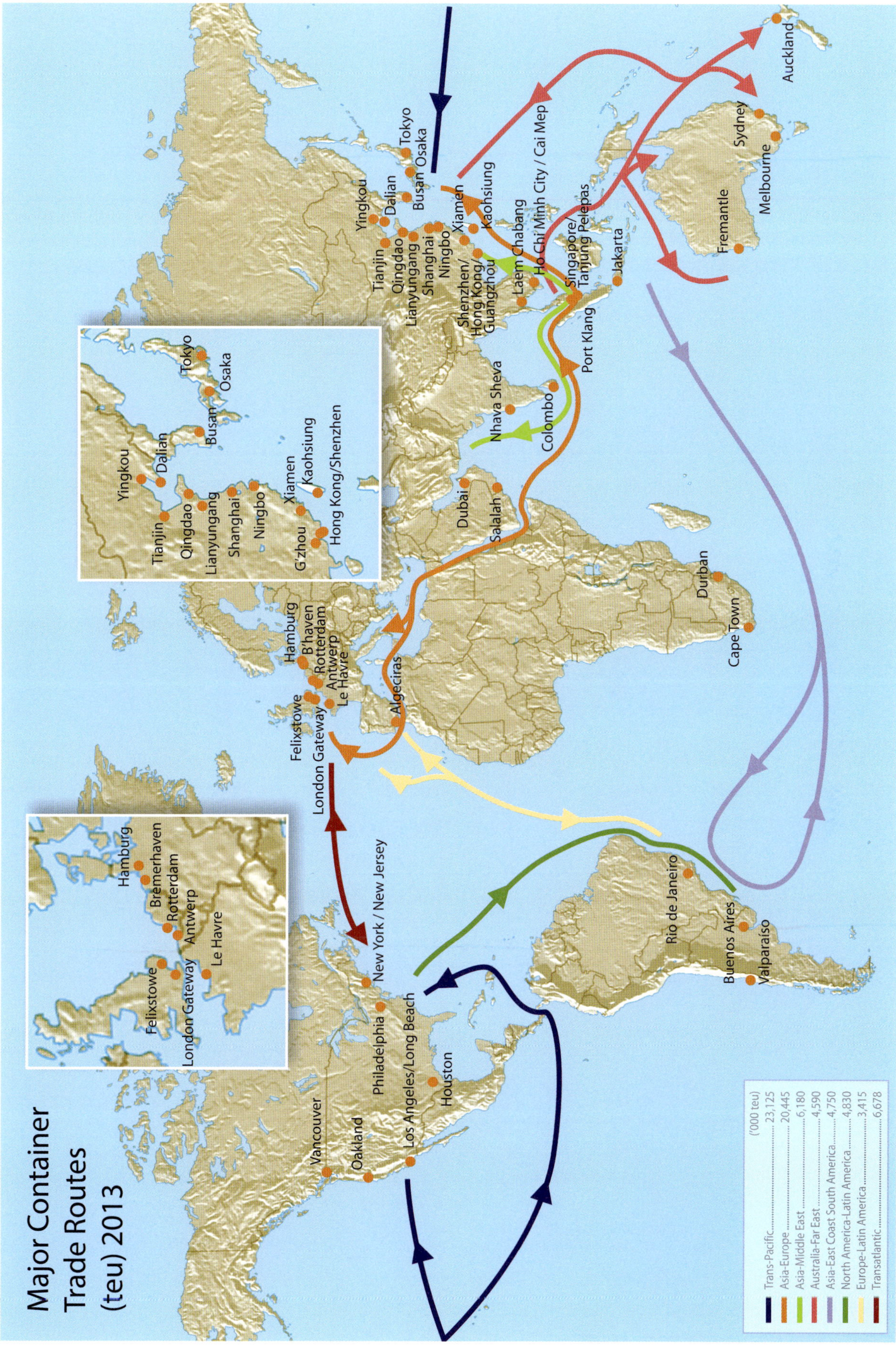
Major Container Trade Routes (teu) 2013
Vancouver
Oakland
Los Angeles/Long Beach
Houston
Philadelphia
New York / New Jersey
Felixstowe
London Gateway
Le Havre
Antwerp
Rotterdam
Bremerhaven
Hamburg
B'haven
Algeciras
Dubai
Salalah
Nhava Sheva
Colombo
Port Klang
Singapore/ Tanjung Pelepas
Jakarta
Laem Chabang
Ho Chi Minh City / Cai Mep
Shenzhen/ Hong Kong/ Guangzhou
G'zhou
Hong Kong/Shenzhen
Kaohsiung
Xiamen
Ningbo
Shanghai
Lianyungang
Qingdao
Tianjin
Yingkou
Dalian
Busan
Osaka
Tokyo
Fremantle
Melbourne
Sydney
Auckland
Durban
Cape Town
Rio de Janeiro
Buenos Aires
Valparaiso
('000 teu)
Trans-Pacific 23,125
Asia-Europe 20,445
Asia-Middle East 6,180
Australia-Far East 4,590
Asia-East Coast South America 4,750
North America-Latin America 4,830
Europe-Latin America 3,415
Transatlantic 6,678

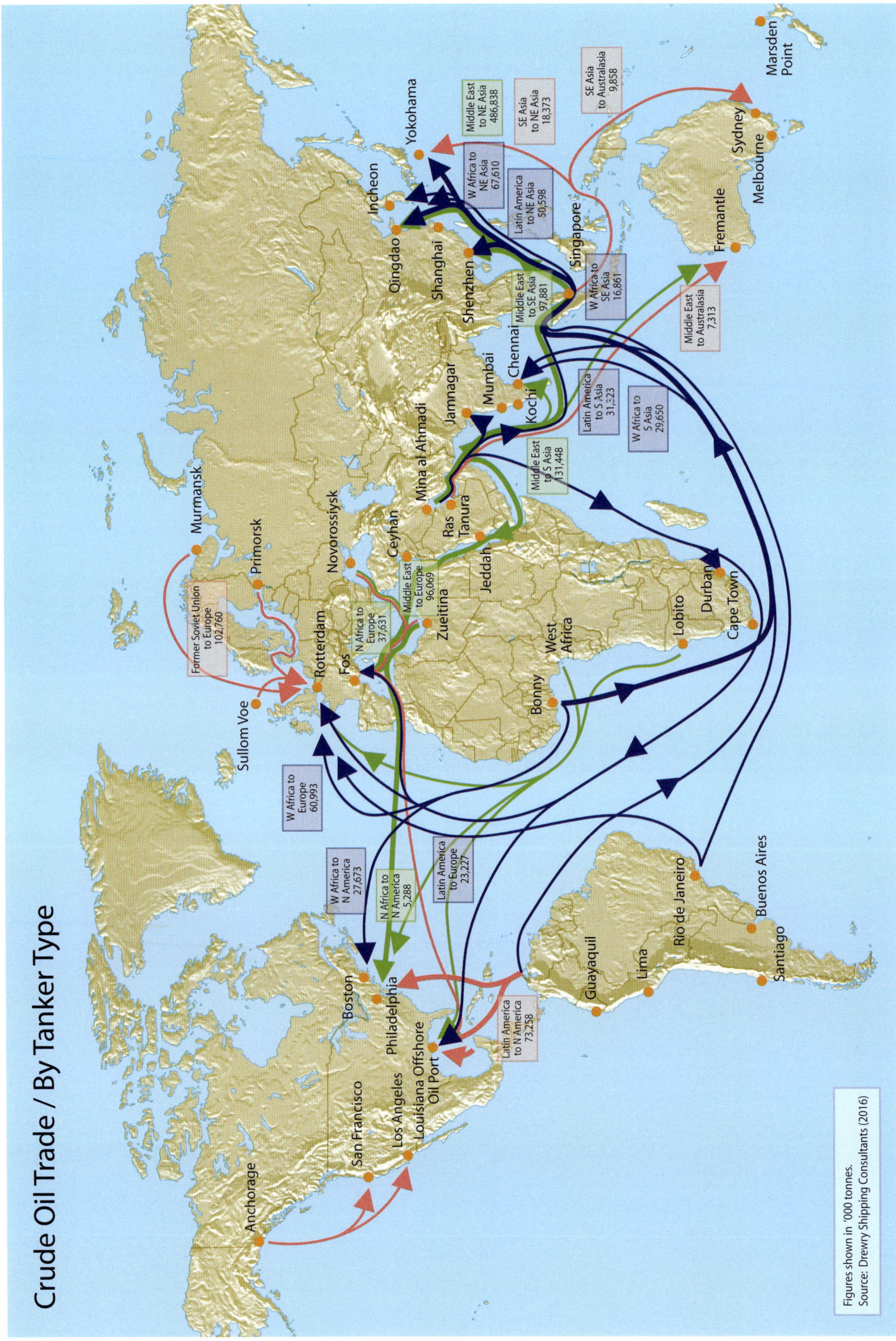
Crude Oil Trade / By Tanker Type
Anchorage
San Francisco
Los Angeles
Louisiana Offshore Oil Port
Philadelphia
Boston
Latin America to N America 73,258
W Africa to N America 27,673
N Africa to N America 5,288
Latin America to Europe 23,227
W Africa to Europe 60,993
Guayaquil
Lima
Santiago
Rio de Janeiro
Buenos Aires
Sullom Voe
Rotterdam
Fos
Former Soviet Union to Europe 102,760
Murmansk
Primorsk
Novorossiysk
N Africa to Europe 37,631
Middle East to Europe 96,069
Zueitina
Ceyhan
Jeddah
Ras Tanura
Mina al Ahmadi
Bonny
West Africa
Lobito
Durban
Cape Town
Jamnagar
Mumbai
Kochi
Chennai
Middle East to S Asia 131,448
Latin America to S Asia 31,523
W Africa to S Asia 29,650
Middle East to Australasia 7,313
Middle East to SE Asia 97,881
W Africa to SE Asia 16,861
Singapore
Shenzhen
Shanghai
Qingdao
Incheon
Yokohama
Latin America to NE Asia 50,598
W Africa to NE Asia 67,610
Middle East to NE Asia 486,838
SE Asia to NE Asia 18,373
SE Asia to Australasia 9,858
Fremantle
Melbourne
Sydney
Marsden Point
Figures shown in '000 tonnes.
Source: Drewry Shipping Consultants (2016)

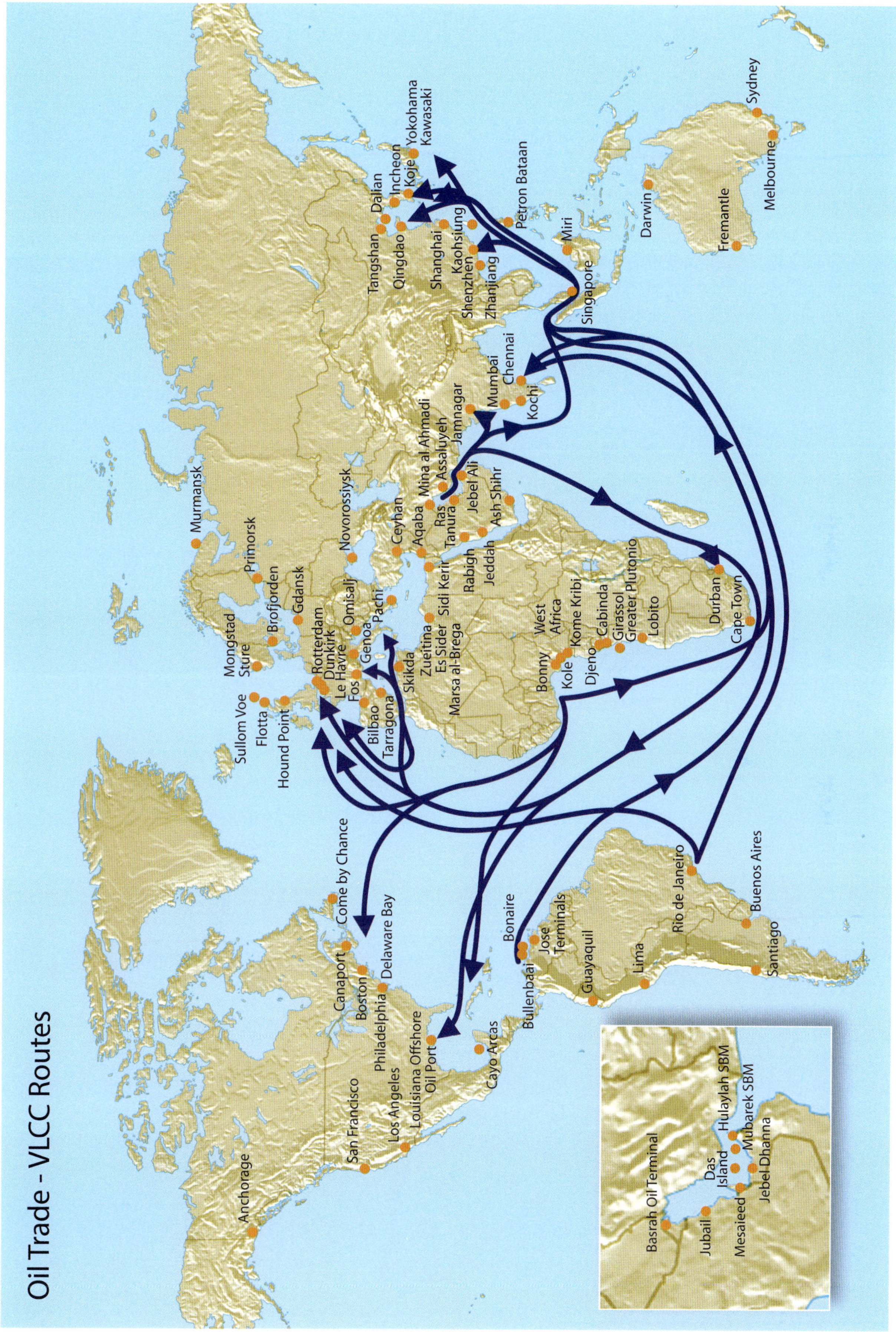
Oil Trade - VLCC Routes
Anchorage
San Francisco
Los Angeles
Louisiana Offshore Oil Port
Philadelphia
Delaware Bay
Boston
Canaport
Come by Chance
Cayo Arcas
Bullenbaai
Bonaire
Jose Terminals
Guayaquil
Lima
Rio de Janeiro
Buenos Aires
Santiago
Hound Point
Flotta
Sullom Voe
Sture
Mongstad
Brofjorden
Primorsk
Murmansk
Gdansk
Rotterdam
Dunkirk
Le Havre
Fos
Bilbao
Tarragona
Genoa
Omisalj
Pachi
Novorossiysk
Skikda
Zueitina
Es Sider
Marsa al-Brega
Sidi Kerir
Ceyhan
Aqaba
Rabigh
Jeddah
Ras Tanura
Mina al Ahmadi
Assaluyeh
Jebel Ali
Ash Shihr
Jamnagar
Mumbai
Kochi
Chennai
Bonny
West Africa
Kole
Kome Kribi
Djeno
Cabinda
Girassol
Greater Plutonio
Lobito
Durban
Cape Town
Singapore
Miri
Petron Bataan
Zhanjiang
Shenzhen
Kaohsiung
Shanghai
Qingdao
Tangshan
Dalian
Incheon
Koje
Yokohama
Kawasaki
Darwin
Fremantle
Melbourne
Sydney
Basrah Oil Terminal
Jubail
Das Island
Mesaieed
Hulaylah SBM
Mubarek SBM
Jebel Dhanna

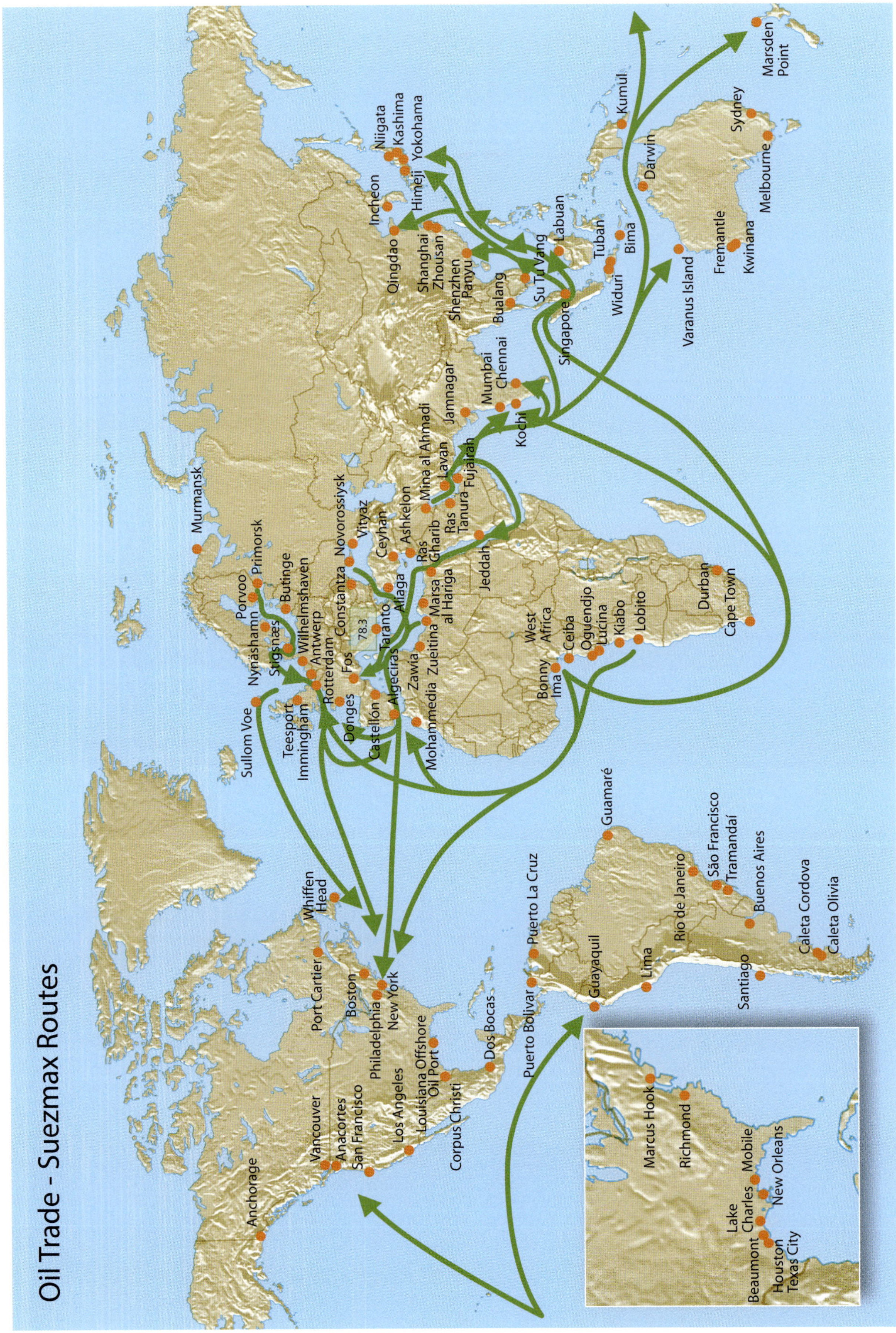
Oil Trade - Suezmax Routes
Anchorage
Vancouver
Anacortes
San Francisco
Los Angeles
Louisiana Offshore Oil Port
Corpus Christi
Philadelphia
New York
Boston
Port Cartier
Whiffen Head
Dos Bocas
Puerto Bolivar
Puerto La Cruz
Guayaquil
Lima
Santiago
Rio de Janeiro
São Francisco
Tramandaí
Buenos Aires
Caleta Cordova
Caleta Olivia
Guamaré
Marcus Hook
Richmond
Mobile
New Orleans
Lake Charles
Beaumont
Houston
Texas City
Sullom Voe
Teesport
Immingham
Nynäshamn
Stigsnæs
Porvoo
Primorsk
Butinge
Wilhelmshaven
Antwerp
Rotterdam
Donges
Fos
Castellón
Algeciras
Mohammedia
Zawia
Zueitina
Taranto
Constantza
Novorossiysk
Vityaz
Ceyhan
Aliaga
Ashkelon
Marsa al Hariga
Ras Gharib
Jeddah
Murmansk
78.3
Mina al Ahmadi
Lavan
Ras Tanura
Fujairah
Jamnagar
Mumbai
Chennai
Kochi
West Africa
Bonny
Ima
Ceiba
Oguendjo
Lucina
Kiabo
Lobito
Durban
Cape Town
Qingdao
Incheon
Shanghai
Zhousan
Shenzhen
Panyu
Bualang
Himeji
Niigata
Kashima
Yokohama
Su Tu Vang
Labuan
Singapore
Tuban
Widuri
Bima
Kumul
Darwin
Varanus Island
Fremantle
Kwinana
Melbourne
Sydney
Marsden Point

Oil Trade - Aframax Routes
Anchorage
Prince Rupert
Anacortes
San Francisco
Los Angeles
Louisiana Offshore Oil Port
Corpus Christi
Philadelphia
Boston
New York
Cartagena
Punta de Palmas
La Salina
Pointe-à-Pierre
Guayaquil
Lima
Madre de Deus
Rio de Janeiro
Santos
Buenos Aires
Santiago
Marcus Hook
Richmond
Mobile
New Orleans
Lake Charles
Beaumont
Houston
Texas City
Murmansk
Sullom Voe
Dundee
Whitehead
Coryton
Sture
Kalundborg
Naantali
Primorsk
Ventspils
Klaipeda
Hamburg
Amsterdam
Rotterdam
La Pallice
La Coruna
Fos
Huelva
Bejaia
Arzew
Ravenna
Gela
Midia
Odessa
Novorossiysk
Batumi
Kulevi
Ceyhan
Banias
Haifa
Malta
Zueitina
Zaafarana
Ras Tanura
Jebel Ali
Mina al Ahmadi
Jeddah
Aden
Jamnagar
Mumbai
Kochi
Chennai
Vietsovpetro
Benchamas
Wenchang
Shenzhen
Chiwan
Fuzhou
Shanghai
Qingdao
Incheon
Sakaide
Yokohama
Shimonoseki
Taichung
Subic Bay
Tatawan
Singapore
Camar
De-Kastri
West Africa
Ima
Bonny
Okwori
Oguendjo
Lucina
Yombo
Kiabo
Lobito
Mombasa
Dar es Salaam
Durban
Cape Town
Barrow island
Airlie island
Fremantle
Melbourne
Sydney
Botany Bay
Brisbane
Marsden Point
Gijon
Venice
Bourgas
Thessaloniki
La Skhirra

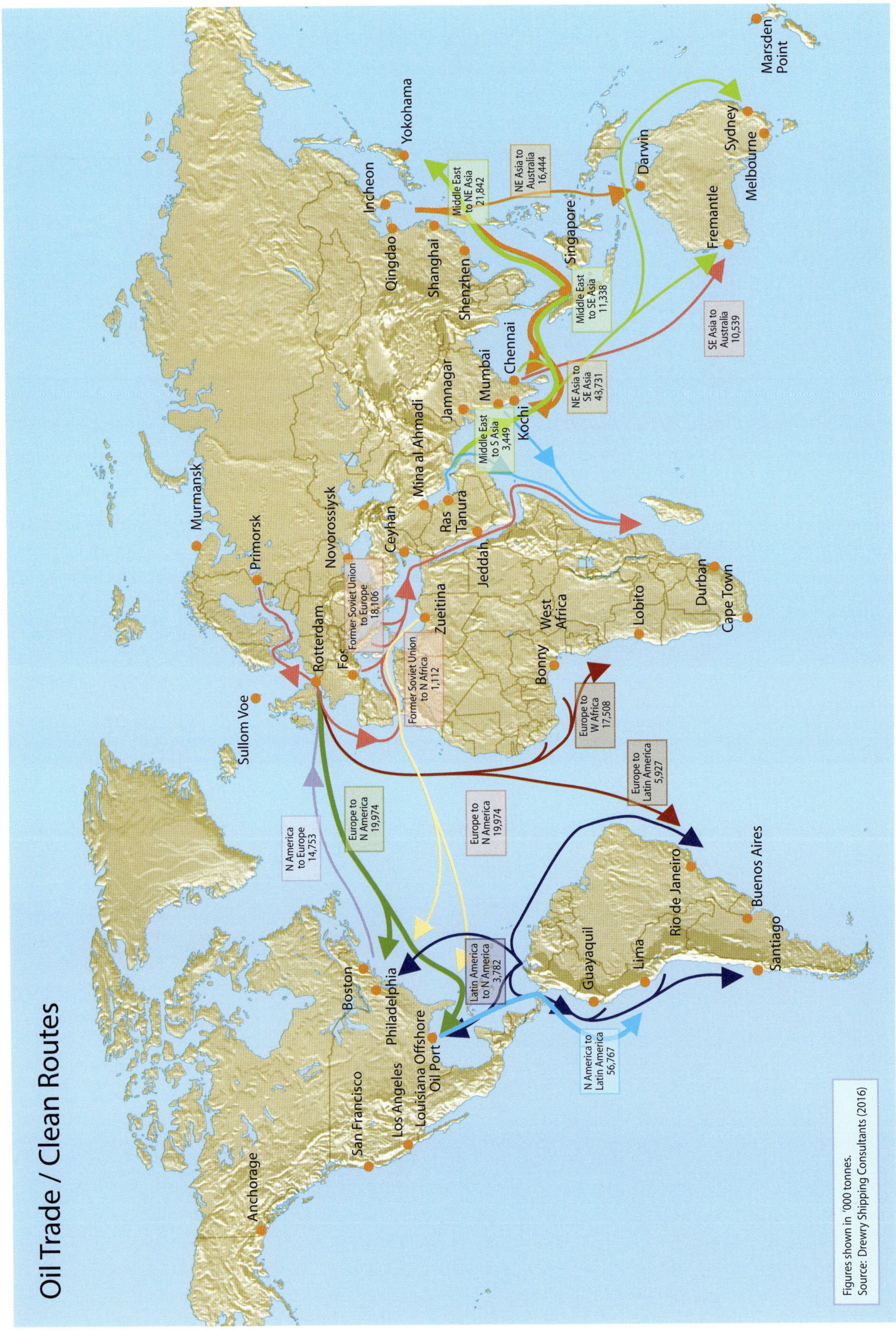

Oil Trade / Clean Routes
Anchorage
San Francisco
Los Angeles
Louisiana Offshore Oil Port
Philadelphia
Boston
Sullom Voe
Murmansk
Primorsk
Rotterdam
Fos
Novorossiysk
Ceyhan
Zueitina
Jeddah
Ras Tanura
Mina al Ahmadi
Jamnagar
Mumbai
Kochi
Chennai
Shenzhen
Shanghai
Qingdao
Incheon
Yokohama
Singapore
Darwin
Fremantle
Sydney
Melbourne
Marsden Point
West Africa
Bonny
Lobito
Durban
Cape Town
Guayaquil
Lima
Rio de Janeiro
Buenos Aires
Santiago
N America to Europe 14,753
Europe to N America 19,974
Europe to N America 19,974
Former Soviet Union to Europe 18,106
Former Soviet Union to N Africa 1,112
Europe to W Africa 17,508
Europe to Latin America 5,927
Latin America to N America 3,782
N America to Latin America 56,767
Middle East to S Asia 3,449
NE Asia to SE Asia 43,731
Middle East to SE Asia 11,338
Middle East to NE Asia 21,842
NE Asia to Australia 16,444
SE Asia to Australia 10,539
Figures shown in '000 tonnes.
Source: Drewry Shipping Consultants (2016)

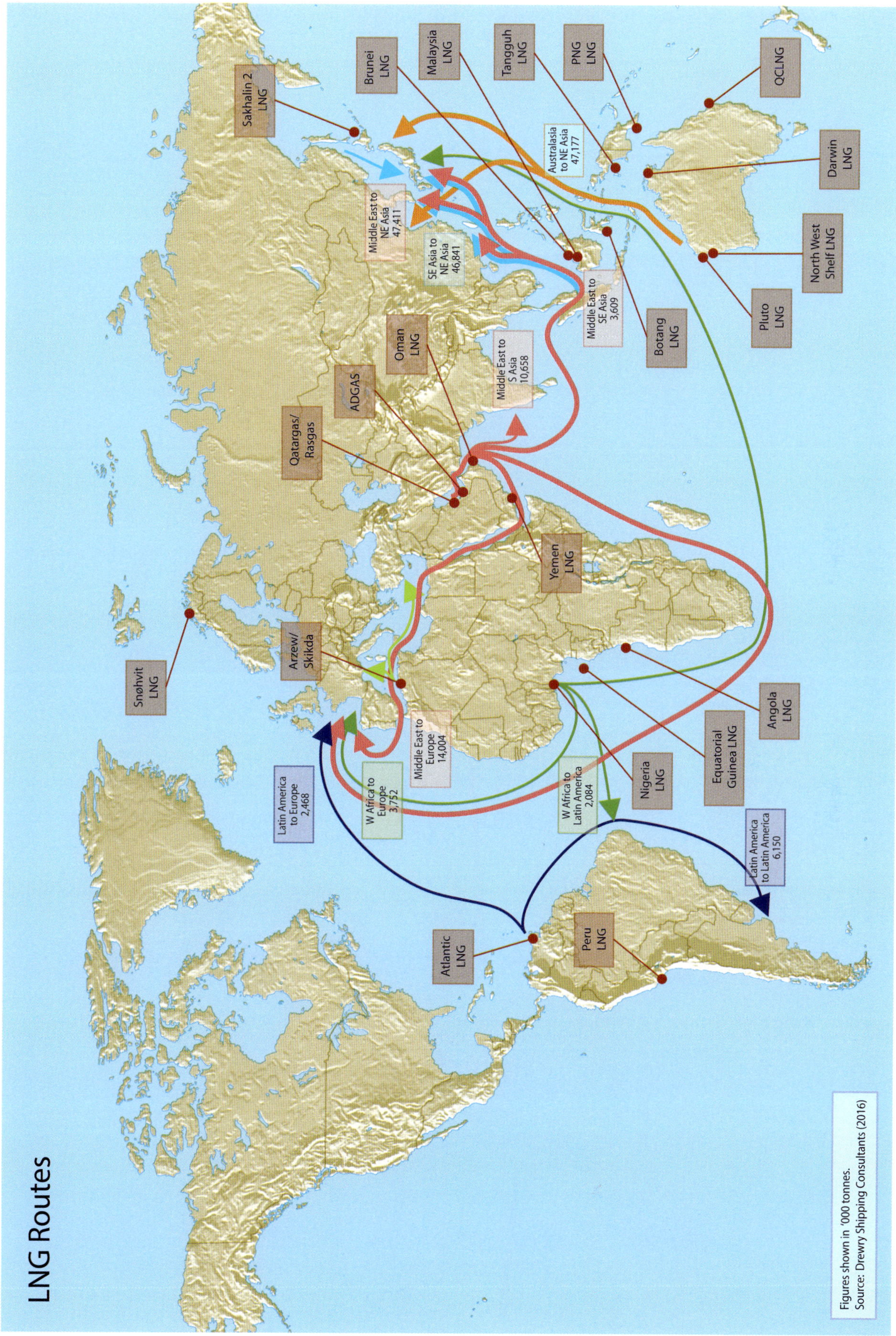
LNG Routes
Sakhalin 2 LNG
Brunei LNG
Malaysia LNG
Tangguh LNG
PNG LNG
QCLNG
Darwin LNG
North West Shelf LNG
Pluto LNG
Botang LNG
Australasia to NE Asia 47,177
Middle East to NE Asia 47,411
SE Asia to NE Asia 46,841
Middle East to SE Asia 3,609
Middle East to S Asia 10,658
Oman LNG
ADGAS
Qatargas/ Rasgas
Yemen LNG
Snøhvit LNG
Arzew/ Skikda
Middle East to Europe 14,004
Latin America to Europe 2,468
W Africa to Europe 3,752
W Africa to Latin America 2,084
Nigeria LNG
Equatorial Guinea LNG
Angola LNG
Latin America to Latin America 6,150
Atlantic LNG
Peru LNG
Figures shown in '000 tonnes.
Source: Drewry Shipping Consultants (2016)

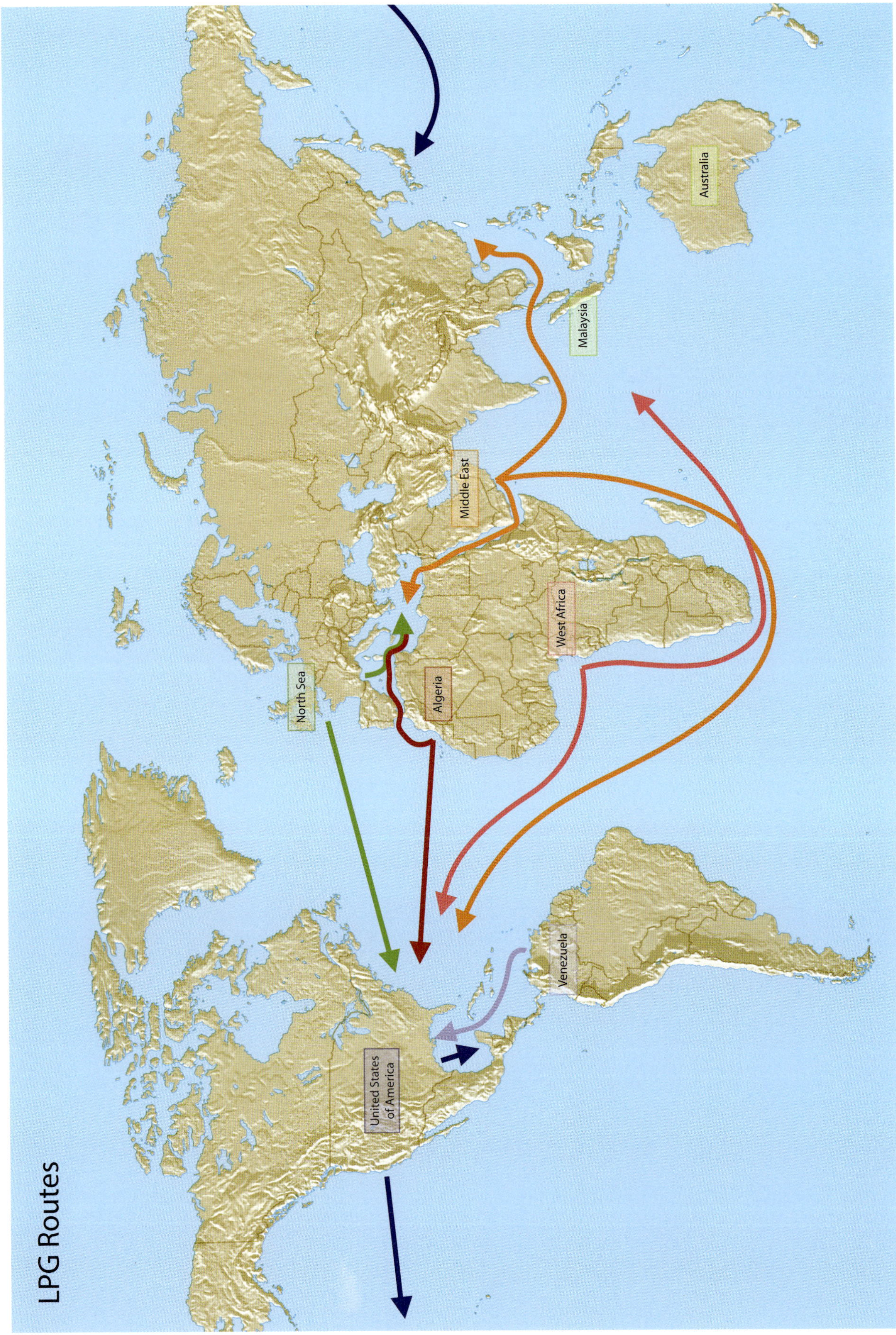
LPG Routes
Australia
Malaysia
Middle East
West Africa
Algeria
North Sea
Venezuela
United States of America

Chapter 9

Voyage estimating

9.1 INTRODUCTION

We now discuss the importance of accurate forecasting of outgoings or costs, which is every bit as vital as forecasting income. Inevitably, this will involve comparing one course of action with another to see which produces the best yield.

Whether the management department or company becomes closely involved in such calculations or whether this problem is left entirely to the shipowner's chartering department, it is important that the ship manager is fully aware of the process of voyage estimating. If for no other reason, it is vital to understand how various pieces of data, supplied by the ship manager, fit into the process of evaluating the profitability of a proposed voyage.

In this day and age, most voyage estimates will be done on computer using either an off-the-shelf software package or an in-house or personally devised system. However, it is imperative that a user has an understanding of the essential elements involved in voyage estimating, both as a way of checking the computerised result and as a back-up in case of circumstances where the IT-based systems are unavailable.

It is also good practice to compare estimates with actual results once the voyage has been completed. This will not only add to experience by way of highlighting port-related factors but can also show up incorrect information used in the original calculations. It is not unknown for sources of information to be wrong (as a comparison of some of the distances quoted in commercially available distance tables can testify), particularly for less commonly used ports, where the variations can be considerable.

The first essential is to examine the subject heading itself. Voyage estimating includes both voyage and time charter trips. The latter are rarely as straightforward as they seem and the pitfalls will be explained in due course. The word 'estimate' speaks for itself, and it is necessary to point out that ships do not run like clockwork and it is impossible to calculate to perfection. That is not to suggest that the aim should be less than total accuracy and it is essential to seek to achieve this and to test the accuracy of the estimates against the final voyage results.

For voyage estimating it is also essential to have knowledge of maritime geography, with particular regard to distances and loadline zones. There are several sets of distance tables commercially available which can be used but, to avoid obvious mistakes, one should have a fairly accurate idea of the distances between key locations worldwide. A useful method is to divide the world into areas, which naturally may mean according to the different oceans, and then to learn a number of strategic mileages across each.

Alternatively, instead of the actual distances involved, it is possible to think in terms of days steamed. As a useful guide, a speed of 14 knots works out at almost exactly three days per 1,000 nautical miles. On this basis, it is easy to remember that a transatlantic voyage from the US Gulf to Rotterdam is 15 days while that from Hampton Roads to the same destination lasts 11 days. Using this straightforward approach, representative voyages can be calculated and memorised. Provided corrections are made to the time for vessels of differing speeds, this should make the task considerably easier.

Having worked out the length of the sea voyage, an outline can be produced onto which can be added the details of the estimate and the basic requirements that should be considered.

9.2 THE LENGTH OF THE VOYAGE

Perhaps the first essential is to define the word 'voyage' since this can mean different things to different people. The main point is to ensure consistency and it is recommended that the commencement of the voyage is usually from the time and the place where the ship drops the outward pilot or completes discharge of the previous cargo. In this manner, the first part of the voyage will be a ballast leg unless the manager is lucky enough to find a cargo out of the last discharge port.

Some people follow the Worldscale model and commence the voyage at the loading port and follow the laden passage with a theoretical ballast back to the loading port again. While this might at times be realistic for tankers, dry cargo tramp vessels rarely proceed on the same voyage twice so this may not prove to be a practical solution.

With distances to hand, it is not difficult to estimate the length of the sea passage including the ballast leg. Working out the time spent in port can be a greater problem. For tankers, this may be relatively simple as most tanker charters include a standard requirement of 72 hours all purposes laytime plus six hours each end for NOR. However, dry cargo voyages vary enormously in the port time they require.

The major obstacle to calculating the port time is that it requires knowledge of the cargo quantity, which in turn often needs the required bunker quantity, which in itself will partially depend on time spent in port. Fortunately, dry cargo vessels do not consume much fuel in port and so this can safely be ignored for the purposes of initial cargo calculations.

Care must be exercised over the route selected. Sometimes there are alternatives and only a marginal difference will make one appear more attractive than the other. Factors such as bad weather at certain times of the year, high canal tolls on one route, cheaper bunkers on another all have to be considered.

Speed is another important factor. In some cases, it might be better to proceed more slowly and economise on bunkers. This is particularly the case in coastal estimating, where voyages are often dependent on tides. There may be little point in steaming full speed only to await a suitable tide for some hours following arrival off a port. When fuel costs were low, slow steaming was almost never practised but, as has already been mentioned, it is an important consideration for the modern operator.

Whenever a slow-steaming strategy is planned it is as well to agree this during the preliminary negotiations. Most charter parties require a ship to sail between the load and discharge ports at the fastest safe speed of the ship. Failure to do this could result in an action by the cargo interests against the owner if the former believes that they have suffered financially as a result of the delayed arrival of the ship.

With distances to hand, it is not difficult to estimate the length of the sea passage, including the ballast leg

9.2.1 Cargo quantity

Initially, one needs to know the vessel's total deadweight, based on the assumption that there are no draught limitations anywhere on the voyage. From this figure must first be deducted the constants (consisting of stores, lubricants, spares and even the weight of the crew). This tonnage is rarely critical, and is usually in the region of 400 to 500 tons for most deepsea vessels of 30,000dwt and above.

The other deductible, before arriving at the true cargo capacity, is the weight of bunkers on board. This can be a complex calculation and is best explained by examples (see section 6.2 in chapter 6). At this point, we should assume that a suitable figure for deadweight cargo capacity is established, although this is not the end of the problem. The vessel may be able to lift a particular tonnage of cargo but the issue to resolve is whether the vessel has the space to carry it. This is where the importance of the stowage factor (SF) enters into consideration and, although there are fewer very light cargoes around than there used to be, the SF is still a relevant factor.

In theory, the vessel's volume capacity is reached by dividing the grain or bale cubic (whichever is most appropriate to the type of cargo under consideration) by the stowage factor. However, if there are several types or grades of cargo to be separated, it may be impossible even to fill the vessel, while trim and stability must also be considered.

Knowledge of loadline zones is essential. All zones transited between loading and discharging ports must be considered as a vessel cannot enter a winter zone, for example, when loaded to summer marks. The restricting loadline must be considered and the cargo calculated accordingly.

9.2.2 Time in port

Once the cargo quantity and the loading and discharging rates per day being offered by the charterers are known, the port time can be estimated with some accuracy. As always, there are pitfalls because it is rare for weekends and holidays to count in dry cargo fixtures and these, coupled with notice time and weather delays, extend the port time before demurrage is likely to start. The following example illustrates this point.

> A vessel is to load 35,000 tonnes of cargo and the charter loading rate is 2,500 tonnes per weather working day of 24 consecutive hours, Sundays and Holidays excepted.
>
> By dividing 35,000 by 2,500 it will be seen that the loading time allowed to the charterers is 14 days. This, however, excludes weekends and if the working week is only five days, the time permitted approaches three weeks. If allowances are also made for notice time and some weather delays, it will become realistic to allow 20 days in port for loading. If loading is to take place over a period of extensive public holidays such as Christmas and New Year or Ramadan, even more port time should be allowed. Needless to say, if the time allowed includes Sundays and holidays (SHINC), fewer allowances will be needed; perhaps 15 days. Even with SHINC, there are inevitable delays in arrival, shifting, notice time and waiting for tides and so on.

This approach is quite adequate for most charters and, in general, the full-time allowance should be put in the estimate, and demurrage and despatch ignored. Unfortunately, nothing in shipping is ever straightforward and different criteria have to be used for what are commonly called 'despatch charters'. In certain trades, it is well known that vessels habitually load and discharge well within their laytime and, indeed, shippers and receivers expect to earn considerable despatch. It is likely, therefore, that comparing two voyages, where one is a charter of this nature, will show a significant disparity. Regrettably, there is no substitute for knowledge in a case such as this and a voyage estimator must be aware of the trades where fast turnarounds are to be found. Only in such cases is it correct to estimate a lesser port time than allowed but, in that event, a suitable addition to the expenses must be made to cover the inevitable despatch bill.

If more than one port of loading and/or discharging is used, extra hours must be allocated for the time involved in the actual process of entering and leaving, particularly if a river passage to and from the berth is required.

9.2.3 Other delays

Under this heading can be calls for bunkering, which may, on occasion, be lengthy. For estimating purposes, however, it is sufficient to allocate one day for each call.

Canal transit inevitably lengthens the voyage and it is safer to allow two days each for passage through Suez and Panama because time can be lost waiting, as well as during the transit itself.

It is not normal to allow additional steaming time for possible bad weather, unless it is certain from the nature of the voyage that delay will be experienced.

9.3 COMMENCING THE VOYAGE ESTIMATE

Once the main essentials are available, the calculations can begin and these broadly consist of comparing income against expenditure. The form and procedure used is a matter of personal preference but they can all be classified under one heading, that of method. Most companies will have their own layout depending, to some extent, on the type of ship they work or the computer program they have purchased but the example method below is as good as any for manual calculations.

It is very easy to reduce an estimate to a very brief outline and indeed, there are times when speed of negotiating will make this imperative. However, before that stage is reached, considerable experience will have to be gained at a more leisurely pace and this is where familiarity with a set format is essential. If all the various items of income and expenditure are set out, it is far more difficult to forget the odd item, which can make the difference between profit and loss. Consequently, if you are likely to be involved in regular voyage estimating, it is worthwhile drafting a suitable form or spreadsheet and using it regularly. There are, of course, computer programs for voyage estimating but mastering the manual method is vital to avoid mistakes when using software programs.

The estimate can, of course, be produced adequately on paper. The crucial point is to acquire and use a method to arrive at the estimate. The following method is suggested and the later examples are based on it:

1. Plan out the voyage, duration and bunker consumption. This will enable instant oversight of just what is intended. This is called the itinerary.
2. Next, calculate what cargo can be loaded. Sometimes this section needs to be completed in conjunction with the itinerary, for example, when port time is assessed against a daily loading or discharging rate.
3. Tabulate all expenses – of which bunkers, port and canal costs, stevedoring, despatch (if anticipated) and extra insurance premiums are prominent examples.
4. Assess the income and profit and loss.

In each of these four stages there are important points that need to be considered but the expense of fuel consumption is probably the hardest to calculate.

Estimating the cost of bunkering a vessel is always a balancing act and no two voyages are likely to be exactly the same, owing to seasonal changes, price fluctuations and the need to balance fuel prices against freight income. Passing through emission control areas requires the burning of low sulphur fuel, which is more expensive, so this must be factored in too.

When transiting a canal or a narrow waterway, a ship may run on diesel oil in the main engine although this is becoming less common with modern engine designs. This fuel is of a higher quality than other fuel and, although more expensive, will result in more immediate engine response to navigation movements and a tonne of diesel oil will take the vessel further than a tonne of fuel oil. Accordingly, ordinary daily speeds and consumptions will not apply. The vessel will be proceeding slowly and will burn fuel or diesel more economically. Thus it may be necessary to estimate normal speed and consumption to and from either end of the canal, adjusting time and consumption appropriately.

Port charges cannot easily be assessed without experience and most companies will keep records of previous calls by their ships at the ports to assist them. Organisations such as BIMCO and INTERTANKO provide valuable information on many ports. However, probably the most accurate method, if time permits, is to contact an agent at the port in question with basic details of the vessel, asking them to give you a proforma disbursement account.

Of course, ethics demand that the same agent should be appointed if the ship is fixed for the voyage in question. In the same vein, canal dues are usually fixed on the basis of the vessel's canal tonnage as the canal authorities in question tend to add in more cubic-earning spaces when they grant the vessel its canal certificate. Mere calculation of the canal dues payable will not be enough, as extras will mount up for such items as agency and towage, either actual or for escort purposes.

As already mentioned, there is the possible expense of despatch payable if the trade is such that the ship is turned round much faster than the laytime allows. If in any doubt, it is better to allow full time in the estimate because a calculation thus arranged will show the most pessimistic result and it is better to underestimate if there is any uncertainty.

Other incidental costs which must be thought of may include cargo-handling expenses and extra insurance premiums, such as those for breaching Institute Navigating Limits or for trading to a war-risk area. The cost of anti-piracy measures was also a factor in the recent past.

The method of calculating the cargo intake has been explained earlier and it is, therefore, only necessary to multiply this quantity by the rate of freight thought to be obtainable. The amount thus achieved is known as the gross freight, from which has to be deducted any commissions due. In addition, it is usual to deduct any freight tax at this stage, both these items being almost invariably a percentage of the freight. This also applies to such charges as 1% in lieu of weighing. The resultant figure after these items have been removed is the net freight.

Now that all the relevant figures are available, the estimate result required can be produced by deducting expenses from income and dividing the result by the number of days taken for the voyage. The result is the gross daily profit and this will give you an easily comparable figure for any selection of different voyages. To calculate the net daily profit it will be necessary to incorporate the daily running costs. The estimator will not be concerned as to how that daily figure is made up but will simply want a figure per day. It is a decision of the shipowner whether or not the capital costs are included in this figure but, whether included or not, it is vital to be consistent.

Estimating the cost of bunkering a vessel is always a balancing act

9.4 TANKERS

There are only a few differences between voyage estimates for dry cargo ships and tankers. For those charters based on Worldscale, the laytime calculation is easier as the scale allows for 72 running hours in aggregate for loading and discharging all purposes and 96 hours total in port.

An expense in tankers which does not occur in dry cargo involves the consumption of bunkers for ancillary purposes such as cargo heating, pumping cargo and tank cleaning.

It is extremely difficult to assess bunker consumption for heating cargo, depending as it does on the temperature at which the cargo is loaded and on the ambient temperature of the sea and air during the voyage. Only the technical department can give an accurate assessment for this purpose because, without access to its statistics, any estimate is likely to be sheer guesswork. Pumping and tank cleaning are easier to cost, although again, the technicians must be asked for an average consumption based on past experience. Depending on the size of the ship, it may consume as much as 100 tonnes of fuel or low sulphur gasoil to discharge a full cargo.

9.5 TIME CHARTER

As the practice of charterers taking vessels on time charter for trips has become widespread, there is clearly a need to estimate the daily profit on this type of fixture in the same way as a voyage charter to compare the two results. Merchants often prefer to take a vessel on time charter, either for a trip or period, as it gives them flexibility and also the possibility of reducing their costs. Fortunately, this is a much simpler exercise if the ship is taken on delivery at the previous discharge port and redelivered on completion of the voyage in question, as it is only necessary to deduct the daily running cost from the hire earned per day to achieve the daily profit. Of course, commission must be allowed for and, should there be any difference between the charter price of bunkers paid by charterers on delivery and the actual price paid by owners, this must similarly be taken into account in the calculations.

Problems arise on time charters when the vessel is not taken on hire immediately after the previous employment and allowance has then to be made, not only for the time lost to owners while the vessel is unemployed, but also for the bunkers consumed during that period. Even here, the resultant calculation is not difficult if the income and expenditure and the number of days for the entire voyage is considered. By grossing up the daily hire receivable for every day the ship is likely to be on charter and deducting the daily running cost, the profit for the entire exercise is obtained. The daily running cost must be charged not only for the trip period but also for the ballast or waiting time before hire commences plus any bunkers, port charges, canal dues and so on, which are incurred by the owners prior to coming on hire. To obtain the daily profit it is then necessary to divide by the number of days involved, which will include those days ballasting or waiting prior to delivery, not just the days the vessel is on hire. In that way, a comparable figure is achieved to be set against other voyage estimates.

Frequently, a time charterer can be persuaded to contribute to the positioning of a vessel from its last discharging port to arrival at the point where the time charter is to commence. This may be because the charterer has been unable to find a suitable vessel closer to where the time charter is to begin and is anxious to fix, or because the hire rate being asked is particularly attractive but the owners are not willing to undertake the ballast run for their own account. The amount that a charterer is prepared to pay is known as a 'ballast bonus' and if one is paid, then this would be added to the income side of the estimating.

In conclusion, it is important to point out that should several estimates show similar results, it is up to the principal to decide whether they prefer a short or long voyage. This may depend on the view of the future rise or fall of the market and also depend on which area the owner prefers to finish the voyage for the purposes of future trading. Owners may sometimes prefer a voyage with a lower return if it positions the ship ideally for a following commitment, such as a contract voyage or drydocking.

9.6 PRACTICAL CALCULATIONS

We will now look closely at a voyage estimate question. This concerns a choice of voyages for owners of two vessels named *Steel Dream* and *India Venture*. It involves two voyage estimates. The questions are set out in detail below giving all the information required to do the calculations. This is, of course, simplifying the problem that would normally arise in practice, where one would have to look up all the information including the calculation of distances and also search for the cheapest bunkers available. It is suggested that you use a blank voyage estimate form (which is not available in the examination) and complete the details as they are worked out in the examples. Put the information regarding the ship and the voyage at the top of the form in order that the details of the voyage can easily be checked at a later stage and that they will not get mixed up.

The following calculations are based on voyages, one carrying grain, the other phosphates. Some of the bunker prices and freight rates may seem outdated now but it is worth noting that although bunker costs have reduced recently, oil prices can always go back up again.

Operators often find themselves in a position where the only cargoes available may produce very low, breakeven or even negative profitability. It is not a good strategy to allow this to happen too frequently but sometimes it is unavoidable or even foreseen. If, for example, an operator has made a voyage to an unpopular destination it is likely that they would have been able to charge a fairly high freight rate and are prepared to accept a poorer result on the next leg because overall a good average is achieved. Sometimes, a long ballast leg without any intermediate port costs or lengthy port stays that add to running costs may prove a better option.

9.7 VOYAGE ESTIMATE

The examples are in the form of typical exam questions.

9.7.1 Example one

READ THE QUESTION. What does it ask for? Normally, this is the cargo to load, the bunkers to take and the daily earnings. Occasionally, you may be asked a simple supplementary question.

So now let us look at the question. This is actually quite complicated but, by reading the question and laying out an answer, it can be simplified. A lot of candidates do not do this and will not identify the key points of the question or show any familiarity with the terms used.

Question

Using the factors below:

a) What cargo quantity can be loaded? (Show calculation.)

b) Where would you take bunkers and what quantity would you stem? (Give your reasons.)

c) What voyage result do you estimate?

The vessel: MV *Steel Dream*, Liberian flag discharging at Rotterdam.

Bunkers remaining on board (ROB) on completion at Rotterdam 125 MT IFO 380cSt low-sulphur at $470 PMT and 200MT IFO 380cSt standard fuel at $440.

Summer DWAT	74,756MT on 14.02M
Winter DWAT	71,789MT on 13.728M
Grain Cubic	86,763.5m^3
LOA 225M	
Constant incl FW	750MT
Loaded speed/cons	14KTS on 32MT IFO 380cSt
Ballast speed/cons	14KTS on 28MT IFO 380cSt
Port consumption	3MT IFO 380cSt pd

The cargo: 60,000MT grains (SF 1.42) 10% MOLOO. Santos, Brazil to Koahsiung, Taiwan Max DWAT at load port 61,400MT no draught restriction at load/discharge/bunkering ports

10,000 SHINC load/6,000 SHEX discharge Demurrage/half despatch $35,000/d

Freight USD60 FIOS per metric tonne

Commission 5%

Distances: Rotterdam to Santos = 5,430nm

Rotterdam to SW edge of North Sea Sulphur Emission Control Area = 400nm
(Vessel then switches to standard fuel)

Santos to Kaohsiung = 10,384nm

Santos to Singapore = 8,943nm

Singapore to Kaohsiung = 1,601nm

Bunker prices: Rotterdam IFO 380cSt – $450PMT
(can be taken concurrent with cargo discharge)

Santos IFO 380cSt – $495PMT

Singapore IFO 380cSt – $425PMT – calling cost $7,500

Kaohsiung IFO 380cSt – $545PMT

Let us look at answering this question.

You have been given all the information you need. You may know from experience that loading at Santos always takes much longer/shorter because the load rate is actually much less/greater than shown and in real life you would plan accordingly but the examiner wants you to show you have read the question and understand what to do. You may know that bunkering at Rotterdam, Santos, Singapore or Kaohsiung is often/seldom delayed, and in real life you would find this out and allow for this, but you are told clearly the conditions to take into account so answer the question that is set. In real life, you will happily round up days so that 12.31 days becomes 13 because you would rather estimate a little less expected income than you actually earn than the other way round. However, for the exam 12.31 days is 12.31 days, not 12.3 or 13. Remember that rounding up days will also affect the amount of bunkers you calculated would be used. If you are a chief engineer you will always overestimate usage so you have a little in reserve but this is an exam. Work to two decimal points in days. Work to one decimal point in bunkers until you get a total and then round it up to a whole number. Do not add your own safety margins. You should be told what safety margin you need to have and it will only be for the bunkers but, if you are not told anything, as in this case, then you should probably allow about three days' supply. In real life, you may well add a few extra days as well because of your knowledge of the weather or the currents or other factors, and that will make you a better operator, but you must not do this in an exam as you are trying to answer a set question.

A. First, find out the distance the vessel will go per day at load and ballast speed and also put down the amount of bunkers used per day. Also do this for the port consumption and also what amount, if any, of MDO/LSGasoil is used. Read the question carefully to make sure you get this right.

B. Put details of the voyage in a box below this showing the voyage and the cargo and charter party (CP) requirements. What does MOLOO mean? You must know. It is a commercial tolerance in the CP quantity and means that in this case the CP quantity is 60,000MT but 10% of this is More Or Less in Owner's Option. Obviously, an owner will want to load as much as possible but they may be limited by their deadweight or by the cubic capacity of their ship so anything between 54,000 and 66,000MT will be within the CP.

   Using the stowage factor, determine whether the cargo is limited by the deadweight or the grain cubic capacity. If this is a cubic cargo, determine the maximum quantity that the vessel can load. If it is a deadweight cargo, note here that this is a cargo limited by deadweight. As a general rule, it is probable that cargoes with a stowage factor less than about 1.2 will be deadweight cargoes but check it out. If your vessel is loading a deadweight cargo, then you will have to work out what items constitute the deadweight on the vessel at the point of sailing from the load port. This is the deadweight all told (DWAT), which is a variable amount at any particular point of a voyage. Deadweight is the weights that are on the vessel but do not include the lightweight of the ship. So a ship sailing from a load port with 5,000MT cargo, constant of 500MT, bunkers of 700MT and 100MT of fresh water will have a DWAT of 6,300MT on departure. On its arrival at the disport, the DWAT might be different as it will have burned bunkers but might have made more water or taken some ballast to stay even keel so its DWAT could be the total of 5,000MT cargo, constant of 500MT, bunkers of 350MT, 120MT of fresh water and 250MT of ballast, a total of 6,220MT DWAT.

C. Now work out the voyage legs and the fuel consumption. To do this you need to look at the voyage and the likely sequence of port calls on the voyage. List all of these. They should be:

Rotterdam – SW edge of SECA	400 nautical miles (nm)
SW edge of SECA to Santos	(5430nm – 400nm) = 5,030nm
Santos to Kaohsiung	10,384nm
Santos to Singapore	8,943nm
Singapore to Kaohsiung	1,601nm

Remember to divide the distances between the ports by the daily distance steamed and remember to apply the correct fuel usage for ballast, loaded or in port.

Also list the fuel usage and time at the ports of the voyage

Load

Discharge

Bunkering

Other

At this stage you will be able to determine most of the times and consumptions accurately. As already mentioned, do not round up days. 15.56 days might be rounded up to 15.6 days or to 16 in real life but not in an exam because, although small, it has a magnified effect on the bunker consumption and on the daily earnings. Do not add extra days as a safety margin in the exam unless told to do so.

15.55 x 26MT is 404.3MT 15.6 x 26MT is 405.6MT 16 x 26MT is 416MT

Bunkers can be rounded up as shown in the example but only when you have a total.

You will not be able to accurately determine the time in port because this will depend on the amount of cargo but you can have a quick look at a simple calculation. You already know that the vessel must sail with a max DWAT at the load port Santos of 61,400MT. So first you need to determine what bunkers to have on board for the voyage so go to section E.

D. So now look at the cargo.

Cargo quantity.

Grains with a stowage factor of 1.42 means that this is a cubic cargo so will be limited by the cubic capacity of the vessel and then any other restriction. The vessel will always be in the summer loadline area, so its winter DWAT is immaterial for this question. So, first look at what maximum cargo the vessel can cubically take. Cubic grain is 86,763.5, SF is 1.42. Therefore, 86,763.5/1.42 = 61,101MT. This is the maximum the vessel can take.

Rough calculation.

If the vessel loads 61,100, how long will it take to discharge and what quantity of bunkers will be consumed? Remember that SHEX is Sundays excluded and that you will need to multiply the days by 1.2 to take account of this.

61,100/6,000 SHEX = 10.18 × 1.2 SHEX = 12.22 days × 3MT = 36.7MT bunkers for discharge.

So now it is necessary to determine what the different components of the DWAT will be and where the ship will have the maximum deadweight on board.

The max DWAT will be that on board on departure Santos. It is after all the load port. So how much of this DWAT will be cargo and how much will be other weights?

The vessel must have sufficient bunkers on board for this loaded leg of the voyage from Santos to Kaohsiung plus the port call at Kaohsiung as well as the constant, and must have 92MT LSFO, which we will call a safety margin on completion (calculated in section E). So, using the voyage legs table, you should work out the bunkers needed on sailing from Santos.

This should be 989MT + amount for discharge (approx 36.7MT) + 92MT LSFO reserve. This is a total of 1,026MT IFO and 92MT LSFO. What other weights are on board? The constant which is 750MT and this includes fresh water. So this is a total of 1,868MT.

What is the max DWAT at Santos? It is 61,400MT. You will now be able to calculate accurately the time in port and the amount of bunkers used.

So cargo is 61,400 – 1,868 = 59,532MT CARGO TO LOAD   ANSWER A

E. Common sense and the voyage legs calculation should show that the bunkers you have on board are not sufficient to reach Santos without bunkering at Rotterdam. So should you take some at Rotterdam and some at Santos? No, Rotterdam is much cheaper and whatever happens, the bunkers for the loaded voyage, or perhaps most of it, will have to be on board when you sail from Santos.

How about bunkering at Rotterdam sufficient to get to Singapore, then top up and sail on to Kaohsiung, thereby enabling you to load more cargo at Santos? Possibly, but what is the benefit?

Well, you will have seen that you use 33.4MT of LSFO from Rotterdam until you leave the SECA. This will leave you with 91.6MT of LSFO, which you could call a safety margin as it is approximately three days' supply. You have not been told what will happen at Kaohsiung so that is the entire safety margin you need for this calculation.

The distance Santos–Kaohsiung is	10,384nm
The distance Santos–Singapore–Kaohsiung is (8,943 + 1,601)	10,544nm

There is therefore a deviation of 160nm. There will be an extra 15.3MT of fuel used. This is an extra 0.476 days' steaming at loaded speed.

There will be some time taken to bunker at Singapore but this is not stated. There are calling costs of $7,500.

Fuel used 15.3MT × $450 = $6,857.

Cost is at least $14,300 plus extra time on the voyage and some extra fuel in port cost.

What is the benefit?

Bunkering at Singapore for the voyage to Kaohsiung means you could sail with reduced bunkers for sailing the reduced distance to Singapore, which is 1,441nm shorter.

1,441/336 = 4.29 days = 137MT.

You could also not take the fuel for discharge at Kaohsiung, which would be about 31MT. In theory, you would gain 168MT × ($60 × 0.95) = $9,576 in additional freight.

It is not worth bunkering at Singapore as the deviation cost would be more than the additional freight.

It is seldom worth deviating to take bunkers from a financial point of view. Always carefully check first.

So you will bunker at Rotterdam.

How much will you take? Look at the voyage legs.

You start with 200MT HSFO and 125MT LSFO. You use 33.4MT of LSFO and this leaves you with 91.6MT as a safety reserve.

Now for the HSFO. You use 1,463MT on the voyage. If you take 1,263MT at Rotterdam you will max the cargo and have a small reserve of LSFO for use at Kaohsiung and a safety margin.

Bunker at Rotterdam and take 1,263MT of bunkers   ANSWER C

Now go back to D.

F. The calculation of the earnings for the voyage should be straightforward. Using the form, list the voyage expenses, which are the bunkers used on the voyage and port costs. Remember that fuel should be used on a FIFO basis, which means 'first in, first out'.

The vessel has 200MT of fuel ROB at Rotterdam at a cost of $440PMT. Total usage of bunkers on the voyage was 1,463MT, so you have used 1,263MT of the new fuel from Rotterdam, costing $450 PMT. List the port costs, which were $65,000 and $83,000, and do not forget to add in the costs of the use of the LSFO in the SECA of $15,698.

This comes to a total of $820,048, which are the expenses of the voyage, the voyage costs.

G. Now to the freight earned.

Cargo was 59,532MT and freight rate was $60PMT. This is $3,571,920 total freight. Now apply the commission, which is 5%.

An easy way is to multiply the total freight by 0.95 so ($3,571,920 × 0.95) = $3,339,324. Now deduct the voyage costs of $820,048.

You have the earnings for the voyage of $813,044 – $327,600 = $2,573,276.

Now divide this by the voyage length, which, from the total in the voyage leg section, is 65 days.

$2,573,276/65 = $39,407 per day. If you are asked for the net daily profit you must now deduct the DOC/DRC or daily operating costs, which are given as a rate per day.

EARNINGS PER DAY $39,407 PER DAY OR TOTAL PROFIT $2,573,276 ANSWER C

	STEEL DREAM		SPEED	DIST PD	BUNKERS	FO	DO	PORT
A		L	14	336		32		3
		B	14	336		28		
B	VOYAGE	SANTOS-KAOHSIUNG GRAIN 60,000 +/- 10% MOLOO 54,000-66,000MT						
	DETAIL	86763.5/1.42= 61,101MT				(MAX 66KT)		
	VOYAGE LEGS		MILES	DAYS	LSFO	FO	DO	
	ROTTERDAM-SECA		400	1.19	33.4			
C	SECA-SANTOS		5030	15		419.2		
	SANTOS-KAOHSIUNG		10384	30.9		989		
	LOAD 59532/10,000 SHINC			6		18		
	DISC 59532/6000 SHEX			12.22		36.7		
	SAN-SING-KAOH		**10544**	**31.38**		**1004.2**		

	TOTALS			65.31	33.4	**1462.9**		
				MT				
	CARGO CALC	Max 61,101MT					61400	dwat
	RESTRICTION?	**Yes DWAT 61,400MT at Santos**				less	750	cons
D	BUNKER CONSTRAINT						989	S-K
	COST OF BUNKERS						37	Disc
	cu cap 86,763.5/1.42 =	61,101 max dwt cubically			**CARGO TO LOAD**		92	LSFO
							59532	**Max-**
								Cargo
	No safety margin is mentioned but 92MT LSFO is available.							
					E	BUNKER QUICK CALC		
	VOY EXPENSES				Option Bunker Rdam and/or Singapore.			
	FO ROB 200 * $440	88,000			Not at Santos. Singapore?? No.			
	FO ROB 1263*$450	568,350						
F	LOAD PORT	65,000			If Bunker at Rotterdam to get to Sing then			
	DISC PORT	83,000			benefit is only 168*$57 =$9576 in extra			
	OTHER				freight. Deviation is 160 NM + 0.5 days			
	LSFO 33.4 *$470	15,698			plus bunker time + call cost $7500 + $6857			
					extra usage of bunkers. Take all at RDAM.			
	TOTAL EXP	820,048						
	CARGO	RATE	COMM	NET				
	59532	60	5%	3,393,324	FREIGHT			
G				820,048	EXPENSES			
	TOT EXPENSES			2,573,276	EARNINGS			
				65	VOY LENGTH*DRC			
					PROFIT			
				39406.9831546708	**EARNING PER DAY**			
	ANSWER A	CARGO TO LOAD		59,532MT				
	ANSWER B	BUNKER		Bunker Rotterdam take 1263MT				
	ANSWER C	DAILY NET PROFIT		$39,407	Total Earnings for Voyage		$2,573,276	

9.7.2 Example two

You should now have a good general idea about doing a voyage estimate that will enable you to do one in your daily work life but, in fact, the SOM exam calculation is actually simpler than that shown in the worked example. Shown in the following pages is the sequence of working to enable a candidate to make a good attempt at getting the right answer.

You must have some idea of how to lay out a calculation, so practise doing so using a blank form. For those who have taken other Institute exams you should be familiar with the exam booklet layout but for those who have not, the booklet is made up of several sheets of A3 paper folded to make a series of double-page spreads of two sheets of A4. You might choose a clear double page and show the calculation on the right-hand page and the working on the left, which allows you to clearly show that you know what you are doing.

READ THE QUESTION. What does it ask for? Normally, this is the cargo to load, the bunkers to take and the daily earnings. Occasionally, you may be asked a simple supplementary question.

Question

One of your managed vessels described below has been fixed for a voyage from Jorf Lasfar in Morocco to Santos in Brazil with phosphate rock. Vessel is assumed in summer zone throughout. Using the information below, calculate:

a) what cargo quantity can be loaded; (Show calculation.)

b) where you would take bunkers, how much you would order, and your reasons for this choice;

c) what daily net profit you anticipate earning for this voyage.

The vessel: MV *India Venture*, Panama flag, currently completing discharge at Barcelona in Spain.

Bunker ROB on completion 300MT. IFO 380 at US$600 PMT, and 50MT LSGasoil.

Vessel will not use any further LSGasoil after departure Barcelona. Intention is to place vessel on spot market on completion Santos with same quantity of bunkers as on completion Barcelona. Vessel must have five-day safety margin on board at all times. At load or discharge port bunkering is concurrent with cargo operations.

SDWT 45,255MT on 11.5M SW.

Grain Cubic 61,150m^3, 5 HO/HA Constant including FW 650MT

Loaded speed/cons 13KTS on 26MT IFO 380 PD

Ballast speed/cons 14KTS on 25MT IFO 380 PD Port consumption 4MT/day

Daily running cost $9,600/day

The cargo:	40,000MT bulk phosphate (SF 0.95) 10% MOLOO. Jorf Lasfar to Santos.	
	Max draught load and disport 11.6M SW.	
	11,000 SSHEX load/9,000 SSHINC disch.	
	Freight US$19.5PMT FIOS Commission 5%.	
Distances:	Barcelona to Gibraltar	= 523nm
	Barcelona to Jorf Lasfar	= 769nm
	Gibraltar to Jorf Lasfar	= 254nm
	Jorf Lasfar to Santos	= 4,154nm
Bunker prices:	Barcelona – $590PMT IFO 380	
	Gibraltar – $575PMT IFO 380 (calling cost $500 and six hours to take bunkers)	
	Jorf Lasfar – $650PMT IFO 180 only available	
	Santos – $600PMT IFO 380	
Port costs:	Load port	US$27,000
	Discharge port	US$35,000

Let us look at answering this question.

You have been given all the information you need. You may know from experience that loading at Jorf Lasfar always takes much longer/shorter because the load rate is actually much less/

greater than shown, and in real life you would plan accordingly, but the examiner wants you to show you have read the question and understand what to do. You may know that bunkering at Barcelona or Gibraltar or Jorf Lasfar is often/seldom delayed, and in real life you would find this out and allow for this, but you are told clearly the conditions to take into account, so answer the question that is set based only on the information given. In real life, you will happily round up days so that 12.31 days becomes 13 because you would rather estimate a little less expected income than you actually earn than the other way round. You are doing an exam! Therefore 12.31 days is 12.31 days, not 12.3, not 13. Remember that rounding up days will also affect the amount of bunkers you calculated will be used. If you are a chief engineer you will always overestimate usage so you have a little in reserve but this is an exam. Work to two decimal points in days. Work to one decimal point in bunkers until you get a total and then round it up to a whole number. Do not add your own safety margins. You will be told what safety margin you need to have and it will only be for the bunkers. In real life you may well add a few extra days because of your knowledge of the weather or the currents or other factors, and that will make you a better operator, but you must not do this in an exam.

A. First, find out the distance the vessel will go per day at load and ballast speed and also put down the amount of bunkers used per day. Also do this for the port consumption and what amount, if any, of MDO/LSGasoil is used. Read the question carefully to make sure you get this right.

B. Put details of the voyage in a box below this showing the voyage and the cargo and CP requirements. What does MOLOO mean? You must know. It is a commercial tolerance in the CP quantity and means that in this case the CP quantity is 40,000MT but 10% of this is More Or Less in Owner's Option. Obviously an owner will want to load as much as possible but they may be limited by their deadweight or by the cubic capacity of their ship so anything between 36,000 and 44,000MT will be within the CP.

   Using the stowage factor, determine whether the cargo is limited by the deadweight or the grain cubic capacity. If this is a cubic cargo, determine the maximum quantity that the vessel can load. If it is a deadweight cargo, note here that this is a cargo limited by deadweight. As a general rule it is probable that cargoes with a stowage factor less than about 1.2 will be deadweight cargoes but check it out. If your vessel is loading a dwt cargo then you will have to work out what items constitute the dwt on the vessel at the point of sailing from the load port. This is the DWAT, which is a variable amount at any particular point of a voyage. Deadweight is the weights that are on the vessel but do not include the lightweight of the ship. So a ship sailing from a load port with 5,000MT cargo, constant of 500MT, bunkers of 700MT and 100MT of fresh water will have a DWAT of 6,300MT on departure. On its arrival at the disport the DWAT might be different as it will have burned bunkers but might have made more water or taken some ballast to stay even keel so its DWAT could be the total of 5,000MT cargo, constant of 500MT, bunkers of 350MT, 120MT of fresh water and 250MT of ballast, a total of 6,220MT DWAT.

C. Now work out the voyage legs and the fuel consumption. To do this you need to look at the voyage and the likely sequence of port calls on the voyage. List all of these. They should be:

   Barcelona–Jorf Lasfar

   Or

   Barcelona–Gibraltar Gibraltar–Jorf Lasfar

   Jorf Lasfar–Santos

   Remember to divide the distances between the ports by the daily distance steamed and remember to apply the correct fuel usage for ballast, loaded or in port.

Also list the fuel usage and time at the ports of the voyage.

Load

Discharge

Bunkering

Other

At this stage you will be able to determine most of the times and consumptions accurately. Do not round up days. 15.56 days might be rounded up to 15.6 days or to 16 in real life but not in an exam because, although small, it has a magnified effect on the bunker consumption and on the daily earnings. Do not add extra days as a safety margin in the exam unless told to do so.

15.55 × 26MT is 404.3MT   15.6 × 26MT is 405.6MT 16 × 25MT is 416MT

Bunkers can be rounded up as shown in the example but only when you have a total.

You will not be able to accurately determine the time in port because this will depend on the amount of cargo but you can have a quick look at a simple calculation.

You already know that the vessel must sail with:

650MT constant + 300MT ROB reserve + 50MT gasoil + 346MT for voyage to Santos = 1,346MT

Vessel loads 45,255 – 1,346 = 43,909MT/SHINC 9,000 = 4.878 days × 4MT = 19.5MT = 20MT

This 20MT must be on board as well for the discharge.

D. So now look at the cargo.

Cargo quantity.

Phosphate rock with a stowage factor of 0.95 means that this is a deadweight cargo so will be limited by the SDWT. The vessel will be in summer zone throughout the voyage so now it is necessary to determine what the different components of the DWAT will be and where the ship will have the maximum deadweight on board.

The max DWAT will be that on board on departure Jorf Lasfar. It is, after all, the load port. So how much of this DWAT will be cargo and how much will be other weights?

The vessel must have sufficient bunkers on board for this loaded leg of the voyage from Jorf Lasfar to Santos plus the port stay at Santos, and must have 300MT IFO and 50MT gasoil on completion. So, using the voyage legs table, you should work out the bunkers needed on sailing Jorf Lasfar.

This should be 346MT + amount for discharge (approx 20MT) + 300MT reserve + 50MT gasoil. This is a total of 666MT IFO and 50MT gasoil. What other weights are on board? The constant, which is 650MT, and this includes fresh water. So this is a total of 1,366MT.

What is the summer deadweight? It is 45,255MT. You will now be able to calculate accurately the time in port and the amount of bunkers used. Remember that SSHEX is Saturday/Sundays excluded and that you will need to multiply the days by 1.4 to take account of this.

So cargo is 45,255 – 1,366 = 43,889MT CARGO TO LOAD   ANSWER A

E. Where are you going to bunker and how much are you going to take? From the voyage legs and the port consumptions you will be able to see that you will need about 450MT for the voyage. You start with 300MT FO and need to put vessel on the spot market at Santos with the same amount. This is 300MT and this easily covers your safety margin of five days. So the amount of fuel to take is the amount that you use for the voyage, approximately 450MT.

Let us compare bunker ports:

Barcelona – $590PMT IFO 380

Gibraltar – $575PMT IFO 380 (calling cost $500 and six hours to take bunkers)

Jorf Lasfar – $650PMT IFO 180 only available

Santos – $600PMT IFO 380

Barcelona will cost $15 more than Gibraltar × 450MT = $6,750 more than Gibraltar

Gibraltar will cost six hours' delay × the DRC $9,600 pdpr (per day pro rata)	= $2,400
Calling cost is $500	= $500
Six hrs × 4MT pdpr bunker usage = 1MT current fuel	= $600
Consumption for extra steaming distance (523 + 254) – 569 = 8NM/(336 × 25) 0.6MT	= $360

Extra steaming time is only about 30 minutes, so negligible.

Extra cost at Gibraltar is $3,860.

Jorf Lasfar is much more expensive and the wrong viscosity.

Santos. You do not have enough to get to Santos so you must bunker somewhere. Is there a benefit to increase the cargo by minimising the bunkers taken at Gibraltar, always keeping a safety margin of 130MT on board at all times? You would arrive at Santos with 130MT and take 190MT of bunkers there to make up for the use at Santos and the amount planned for placing on the market of 300MT but what would it cost you? The bunkers cost $25 more per tonne at Santos and the freight you earn on a tonne of cargo is ($19.5 x 0.95) = $18.53 per tonne so the answer is no.

Gibraltar is the only choice, so now this is decided you can complete the voyage legs appropriately and you find that the fuel consumed on the voyage is 448MT of IFO.

BUNKER AT GIBRALTAR AND TAKE 448MT ANSWER B

F. The calculation of the earnings for the voyage should be straightforward. Using the form, list the voyage expenses, which are the bunkers used on the voyage and port costs. Remember that fuel should be used on a FIFO basis.

The vessel has 300MT of fuel ROB at Barcelona at a cost of $600PMT. Total usage of bunkers on the voyage was 448MT so you have used 148MT of the new fuel from Gibraltar costing $575PMT. List the port costs, which were $27,000 and $35,000, and do not forget to add in the calling costs at Gibraltar of $500.

This comes to a total of $327,600, which are the expenses of the voyage, the voyage costs.

There is an argument that the calling cost and additional one tonne of bunkers used for calling at Gibraltar should be added to the total cost of the fuel. This is perfectly valid but it takes extra time and you will not gain or lose extra marks for doing this.

If you do, then the fuel cost 448MT × $575 = $257,600 + $3860 = $261,460/448 = $583.62PMT, but then you run into a problem apportioning the extra time and cost to this voyage and the next so you should avoid doing this.

G. Now to the freight earned.

Cargo was 43,889MT and freight rate was $19.5PMT. This is $855,835.5 total freight. Now apply the commission, which is 5%, multiply the total freight by 0.95, so ($885,835.5 × 0.95) = $813,043.73 net freight.

Now deduct the voyage costs of $327,600.

You have the earnings for the voyage of $813,044 – $327,600 = $485,444.

Now divide this by the voyage length, which, from the total in the voyage leg section, is 26.4 days.

$485,444/26.4 = $18,388 per day to give the gross daily profit. As you are asked for the net daily profit you must now deduct the DOC/DRC or daily operating costs, which are given as $9,600 per day.

$18,388 – $9,600 = $8,788 earnings per day

NET EARNINGS PER DAY $8,788 ANSWER C

	INDIA VENTURE		SPEED	DIST PD	BUNKERS	FO	DO	PORT
A		L	13	312		26		4
		B	14	336		25		4
B	VOYAGE	BARC-GIB-JORF LAS-SANT			PHOSPHATE SF 0.95			
	DETAIL	40,000MT PHOSPHATE 10% MOLOO				(MIN 36KT-MAX 44KT)		
	CuCap = 61,150 /0.95 = 64368MT This is way above the deadweight. This is a dwt cargo.							
			MILES	DAYS		FO	DO	
C	VOYAGE LEGS							
	BARC-GIB	B	523	1.56		39		
	GIB - JOR LAS	B	254	0.76		19		
	JOR LAS - SANT	L	4154	13.31		346		
	LOAD (SSHEX 43889/11,000*1.4)			5.6		23		
	DISC (SSHINC 43889/9,000)			4.9		20		
	BUNKERING			0.25		1		
E	TOTALS			**26.4**		**448**		
	CARGO CALC			MT				
	RESTRICTION?	YES SDWT		45255			43889	
D	BUNKER CONSTRAINT		CONS	650			11000	9000
	COST OF BUNKERS			44605			1.4	
			BUNK	716				
				43889	**CARGO TO LOAD**		5.59	4.88
	BUNKER CONSUMPTION 448MT . SO BUNKERS TO TAKE = 448MT							

	VOY EXPENSES				E.	BUNKER QUICK CALC		
F	FO (300 * $600) ROB	$180,000			SANTOS	300	50	
	FO (148 * $575) ROB	$85,100			PORT	20	0	
	LOAD PORT	$27,000			JL-SA	346		
	DISC PORT	$35,000			TOT	666	50	
	OTHER GIB	$500						
							716	
	TOTAL EXP	$327,600						
	CARGO	RATE	COMM%	NET				
	43889	19.5	5	$813,044	NET FREIGHT			
G	TOT EXPENSES			$327,600	EXPENSES			
				$485,444	TOTAL EARNINGS			
	26.4 DAYS			$18,388	TOT EARNING/VOY LENGTH			
	drc = $9,600 PD			$9,600	DRC			
				$8,788	**EARNING PER DAY FOR 26.4 DAYS**			
			ANSWER A	CARGO TO LOAD 43,889MT				
			ANSWER B	BUNKER AT GIBRALTAR 448MT				
			ANSWER C	EARNINGS PD $8788				

to nominate someone to fulfil that role. This creates an anomaly whereby the managers are agents but have placed themselves in the position of a principal in the eyes of the law with all the potential responsibilities that involves.

This problem is addressed in the contract, which seeks to ensure that the owners are no better but no worse off than if they managed the ship themselves. Having obtained such indemnification from the owners as is appropriate, it is vital that the managers then insure against claims resulting from their own negligent acts or omissions as well as those of subcontractors that the managers may have properly employed in the fulfilment of their obligations under the contract. This protection and indemnity insurance in favour of the manager covers any liabilities to the owner or other parties.

Although management companies may be granted very wide discretion in the ordering of supplies and services, and enjoy comforting reassurances in their contracts with their principals, they are still only agents. What comfort, therefore, is there for those supplying goods or services to the managers? It is, after all, open to agents to disclaim liability for a debt incurred on behalf of their principal if the latter cannot or will not pay up. This very situation has, from time to time, caused great difficulties for port agents who have taken instructions in good faith from a manager whose principal has subsequently become insolvent. There have, of course, been some interesting results in situations such as this where it has been proved that the managers never made their role clear and allowed the agent to believe they were, in fact, the principals. So managers should take care never to conceal their agency status unless they are prepared to risk the consequences.

The same ability to walk away from a debt affects the manager *vis-à-vis* the owner's P&I association. If, as is usual, the managers will not be liable for P&I calls, then the club will limit the extent to which they include the manager in the P&I cover. It is, of course, important for the managers to be co-insured in all other insurances relating to a vessel whether the insurance is arranged by the managers or the owners themselves.

While there is no certainty that the agreement between the owners and the managers will be on the BIMCO form, the latter was compiled after worldwide research and it provides an excellent way of appreciating the duties and responsibilities of both parties to a ship management contract.

10.3 LEGAL PROBLEMS

The BIMCO contract obliges the manager to deal with any legal problems which may arise. Many of these will eventually be handled by the P&I association but inattention or, worse still, the wrong initial response to a legal problem by the manager can make a difficult situation worse and can result in losses against which there is no insurance.

A typical case could be a cargo claim for shortage or damage. Such claims occur more frequently in the general cargo trades than with bulk cargoes but, wherever they occur, the principle is the same. Someone's insurance company will have a claim to pay and the procedure is to establish which party it will be. As with all claims by third parties, a hasty admission of liability can result in the other party having a valid claim against you without you in turn having the ability to be reimbursed by your insurance.

However, the opposite of haste is not inertia in such cases because the shipper knows their claim will be time-barred within a year under the Hague or Hague-Visby Rules. Their recourse in the absence of a satisfactory reaction to a claim is to bring suit which, in most jurisdictions, means obtaining a writ which can be used to arrest the ship if necessary.

10.4 ARREST *IN REM*

Freely translated from the Latin term '*in rem*', it simply means against a thing which differentiates it from in person, or against a person. The big advantage of proceeding against the ship is that it is not necessary to locate the owners and then discover that they live in a country where taking legal action against them would be expensive and difficult. By taking action against the ship it is not necessary even to name the owners. However, the circumstances which permit action *in rem* are limited and the best way to envisage these is to see it restricted to debts owned by the ship. It is by no means a new procedure and the way it operates varies from country to country, although steps continue to be taken in an endeavour to produce a fully recognised international convention.

The procedure for arrest is similar in most countries, although the courts and officials concerned may vary. There are certain countries where the procedures for arresting a vessel are particularly straightforward, including the Netherlands and South Africa.

In the UK there is a special section of the judicial system dealing with maritime affairs and the act of arresting a ship is controlled by the Admiralty Marshal. The days are gone when the Admiralty Marshal actually nailed a writ to the ship's mast. Today's equivalents are more procedural but the effect is just the same. An officer of the customs, who acts as agent for the Admiralty Marshal, will board the ship and attach a notice with adhesive tape to a prominent place inside the bridge. Once that is done no one may move the ship at all without risking a charge of contempt of court for which the penalties still include imprisonment. It is even very difficult simply to move the ship off the berth to allow the terminal operator to use the jetty for other ships. Incidentally, the arresting officer has the right to remove some vital part of the ship's machinery to ensure its immobility if there is any risk, in their judgement, of the ship departing despite the threat of penalties.

The watchword under these circumstances has to be speed because the writ can only be removed on the order of the Admiralty Marshal and whatever a manager does to get the writ removed has to be done while the marshal is contactable, namely, in normal office hours. The procedure to obtain release is quite simple, in that the owner's P&I Club will provide a guarantee or letter of undertaking to pay whatever is found to be legally due under the claim in question. This will satisfy the plaintiff, who is obliged then to instruct the marshal to release the ship from arrest.

In more civilised situations, the claimant will advise the manager that they have the writ and threaten the arrest unless the guarantee is forthcoming but managers still have to move promptly to avoid the threat of arrest being turned into action.

10.5 FREEZING ORDERS, ALSO KNOWN AS MAREVA INJUNCTIONS

This is another legal device which may be encountered but should prove a rare occurrence if a management operation is reasonably efficient. It gets its title from the name of one of the litigants, Mareva Compania Naviera SA, which was involved when the procedure was first invoked by Lord Denning in England in 1975. In essence, the procedure stops the defendant in a legal dispute from moving their assets out of the court's jurisdiction. A situation where this might occur could be where the defendant is not a UK resident but has funds in this country. The plaintiff may fear that, while action is proceeding, the defendant will transfer those funds to another country so that, even if the plaintiff wins their case, there will be no money to satisfy the judgement. The way to avoid such an injunction paralysing the defendant's operations is for an arrangement to be made to deposit sufficient funds in some form of joint account or to provide a bank guarantee or some such irrevocable undertaking. This enables the injunction to be lifted and the remainder of the defendant's funds can be freed, and they may let money come into the country without the risk of that too being frozen.

Although one generally thinks of immobilising of assets involving money, any portable asset can also be the subject of such an injunction. One case some years ago assisted a port agent with a disbursement outstanding against a time charterer. It was impossible to arrest the ship as the debts were not due by the shipowner but, because it was still on hire to the same charterers and some of the bunkers in it were the charterer's property, it was that oil which became the subject of a Mareva injunction.

This effectively immobilised the ship as there was no way for it to move away without taking the oil outside the jurisdiction. Judges will always be very careful in cases like this, however, because they will have to be convinced that there is no risk of an innocent third party being adversely affected. In this case, it could have been the shipowner had the judge not been reassured that the time charter still had some time to run.

10.6 FREIGHT AND HIRE PAYMENTS

The manager may have to invoke the law when freight or hire payments are late. All voyage charters will say exactly when freights have to be paid and if, for example, the charter states that freight is payable before breaking bulk, there is a difficult decision to be made if the ship is at the discharging port but there is no sign of the cash. If discharging is allowed to proceed, the ability to enforce payment could be lost since there is no obligation to deliver the cargo until freight is paid.

While the cargo is in the ship there is no need to resort to any complex legal proceedings, but merely to refuse to allow it to be taken off. Left simply sitting idle, however, it is not earning income for the owner and help via the local agent or from a local lawyer appointed by the P&I Club may be needed. One device could be letting the cargo go ashore but to place a lien on it so that the importer cannot take possession of it until they have paid. Such situations are rarely as straightforward as that in many parts of the world, particularly if the receiver of the cargo is a state-owned entity, a powerful organisation locally or, as may well be the case, the owner of the berth or warehouse. This is where skill and foresight are the ship manager's most vital assets. Every time a fixture is concluded, the ship manager or shipowner is taking a calculated risk. They are using their judgement as to whether the charterer will comply with their side of the agreement and, if they do not, whether recourse to legal action will be effective. This is never more important than in the case of a time charter. It is vital to be sure that the charterer is able and willing to fulfil their side of the agreement.

The immediate recourse if a hire payment is late, and any time allowed for technical delay has expired, is to withdraw the ship from the service of the time charterer. That is by no means as easy as it sounds because the ship may be full of cargo which almost certainly belongs to an innocent third party. If the owner of the cargo has not yet paid the freight then it should be possible to ensure that they pay the freight direct to the owner. In the event of this being more than is necessary to settle what is due then the balance can be handed over to the charterer.

The reality is, however, that when a time charterer defaults, one generally finds that the cargo in the ship is the subject of freight prepaid bills of lading (B/Ls). In such a case, the law is very clear and it states that the ship has to deliver that cargo to the consignees named in the bills of lading without in any way being able to demand any payment from them. Without going into the details of this apparently iniquitous situation, suffice it to say that a freight prepaid B/L gives the holder of that B/L a clear title to the goods, and failure to hand these over to them would be an offence under any legal system.

So the solution, when legally binding clauses seem at times to be worthless, comes down in the end to sound judgement. It is vital to know the background of a time charterer. The fraud of taking a ship on time charter, paying the first hire with commendable promptness, filling it with cargo, issuing freight prepaid B/Ls to shippers, pocketing the money and disappearing is by no means an unknown scenario.

10.7 DEALING WITH PORT AGENTS

A ship needs an agent at every port of call. Ideally, the appointment should be in the owner's hands but it is by no means unusual for the charterers to secure the right to nominate the agent as a clause in the charter party. There are many reasons why a charterer may demand this right. In the case of some major charterers (such as oil companies), they have highly sophisticated terminals which need reliable information from, and communication with, agents to operate efficiently. By insisting on one company with suitably expert skills, they can be more confident of a consistent service.

Another reason is the fear a charterer may have of their cargo being handled by, and their secrets being disclosed to, a local competitor and this can be avoided by insisting on their own nomination. Other far less important reasons may underlie the charterer's agents clause, such as ensuring they are kept fully in the picture regarding the ship's progress in the port without having to pay for it. At the bottom end of the scale, some charterers try to insist on the clause to enable them to sell the agency to whichever agent will offer them the highest share of the agency fee.

It is for the chartering experts to decide whether or not the clause can be deleted from the negotiations but, if the clause remains, then the problem has to be overcome. One thing about which it is important to be clear, is that no matter who nominates them, the agent is legally the servant of the owner. The charterer's agent clause gives the charterer the right to nominate the agent who will act on behalf of, and be paid by, the owner. In many cases, where responsible charterers are involved, the agent will give just as good a service to the owner as if it has been an owner's appointment. There are, of course, exceptions to every rule and sometimes the agent nominated by the charterer is simply not providing a good enough service.

Theoretically, as the contract is with the owner, proper performance can be demanded but to set down in writing the difference between a first class service and one that is legally correct but not good enough is not easy. Although that difference is difficult to describe, it can be vitally important. The only thing left to do in such situations is for the owner to appoint a supervisory agent to keep an eye on things with only the owner's interests in mind. The owner may appoint his own agent anyway if there are owner's items such as a crew change or repair to be carried out at that port.

Regardless of how the agent is nominated, adequate instructions have to be given and the sooner contact is made the better. The first thing needed is an estimate of how much the call at that port will cost. This is usually provided as a proforma disbursement account. Before the agent can provide this it will need details of the ship, including net and gross tonnages, to calculate dues. Additionally, the agent will need to know what the ship is going to be doing in that port. With details of the shipper or consignee, the agent can obtain some idea of the length of time the ship will be there. Naturally, vital information, such as who pays for the stevedoring and whether the ship will be bunkering, must also be advised to the agent.

The agent's proforma will probably be divided into three main sections – port charges, cargo charges and ship's items.

a) Port charges will include such items as:

conservancy dues – the charge made by the authority that controls the river or total port area and will probably be based on the ship's gross or net tonnage;

dock dues – these are the charges made by the operator of the actual berth being used and may be based on the length of the ship, the tonnage, the time likely to be alongside or some permutation of these factors;

towage – the tug company may have a direct contract with the owners so the agent needs to be advised if this is so;

pilotage – this is compulsory in many places but, if the ship is a regular caller at that port, the Master may have an exemption certificate. Pilotage is often levied on the ship's draught;

boatmen – principally, these people are used for handling the lines for mooring and unmooring of the ship but boatmen will be used more extensively if the ship is not alongside a jetty all the time it is in port.

b) Cargo charges. Here, the agent should give an estimate of the stevedoring costs if these are for the ship's account. If the ship has to discharge part of the cargo into barges to reduce its draught sufficiently to come alongside, these costs should also be detailed. The agent must know what has been agreed at the chartering stage regarding the use of shore cranes and who pays for them. Alternatively, if the ship is to use its own loading/discharging gear, the agent will need to explain whether the labour regulations in the port allow these to be operated by the ship's crew or whether shore labour has to be employed. Some commodities (such as bagged cargoes) require tallying and, in many ports, the labour regulations insist that this is done by shore personnel, which once again may be an item for the agent to include in the proforma.

c) Ship's items. These will comprise all those charges which relate to the domestic needs of the ship. The first will be cash to the Master. If the ship has been at sea for some time and is due at a port where shore leave is attractive to the crew, the likelihood is there will be a demand for some of their wages to be paid in local currency or in US$.

It is important that the amount which the agent is authorised to advance to the Master is clearly understood by all concerned because it can be a substantial figure.

The other items under this heading can range from supplies of fresh water, stores and provisions to medical and dental treatment for the crew. Minor repairs and servicing of ship's equipment may also be included here but it is rare for the agent to become involved in major repairs as this is a subject for the marine and/or engineering superintendents.

The proforma should also clearly show the fee the agent proposes to charge for their services. If the agent is one that is regularly used, this will probably have been agreed well in advance. Most agency associations publish a scale of agency charges for their members and the ship manager should be familiar with those countries where the scale provides a convenient basis for negotiations and those where the scale is mandatory and is supported by the government. In some countries, the publication of agency fee scales is illegal under antitrust or fair competition regulations. Whatever the position, it is important to have the fee agreed before the event rather than it be disputed afterwards.

There is, incidentally, no reason not to drive an extremely hard bargain with a port agent. The old adage that 'you get what you pay for' applies equally to port agency and the difference between an enthusiastic service and something barely acceptable may be difficult to define but makes a great deal of difference. An enthusiastic agent may well work tenaciously to get the ship finished and away tonight, whereas a disgruntled one may assure their client they have done all possible but the ship has still lost 12 hours or has incurred unnecessary overtime. Such differences can cost far more than was saved in hard bargaining when negotiating the agency agreement.

On receiving the proforma by email, you will be asked for funds in advance. This is accepted as customary practice by both agents' and shipowners' associations because it would be quite impossible for any agent to finance all the ships calling to their agency. Many of the items (especially the large amounts under the port charges heading) have to be paid in advance otherwise the authorities will not let the vessel sail. This means that seeking advance funding is not just a scheme by agents to earn interest on their principal's money but a practical necessity.

All ship managers should be conscious of cash flow and interest incurred, which creates the temptation to delay sending funds to agents until the last possible moment. However, time must be allowed for the money to pass through the banking systems. In many countries, the exchange control regulations are strict or there are simply laws to protect port authorities from bad debts, which can mean that, if your funds have not reached the agent, the ship is held by the port authority until they do. The port authorities do not have to obtain a writ or effect an arrest to have the power to immobilise the ship until the money is paid.

When the ship has sailed, the agent's duty is to assemble all the accounts which they have paid on behalf of the ship and present them with a disbursement account. This may take some weeks because some suppliers of goods or services can be surprisingly slow to submit their bills. The agent's disbursement account should clearly relate all the individual suppliers' invoices to the heading of the different activities in the account itself.

The owner should expect that every item is explained, and this especially applies to those amounts expended by the agent on sundries such as car mileage, telephone charges and crew mail. Equally, any credit balance should be repaid promptly as indeed the agent will expect the owner to settle any debit balance. Ship managers who decline to release significant sums of money that are due to an agent while they query some very minor item may consider it a normal business practice but, by doing so, they may find themselves welcomed by only the least reputable agents in the port.

10.8 DEALING WITH CHARTERING BROKERS

The manager's contact with those responsible for negotiating employment for the ships will depend entirely upon the extent of the management contract. If the agreement covers everything, including arranging employment, then it is possible that this will take place within the same office. It may either be the brokers themselves or those who grant authority to remote brokers to give and receive firm offers from the charterers.

Even if the commercial matters are dealt with by the owners with their brokers or broking department, the ship manager will still become involved. Every time a piece of business is proposed there will be questions for the management departments and, if the ship is in the process of hard negotiations, the answers will be required instantly. Firm offers in these days of rapid communication are valid for very short periods of time and the negotiators will wish to go back firm without feelings of uncertainty and without undue delay.

Once the fixture is confirmed, even if this is only by a telephone conversation, there can be no going back on either side.

Appendices

Appendices Contents

BIMCO

SHIPMAN 2009

STANDARD SHIP MANAGEMENT AGREEMENT

PART I

1. Place and date of Agreement **Click here to enter text.** **Click here to enter text.**	2. Date of commencement of Agreement (Cls. 2, 12, 21 and 25) **Click here to enter text.**
3. Owners (name, place of registered office and law of registry) (Cl. 1) (i) Name: **Choose an item.** (ii) Place of registered office: **Click here to enter text.** (iii) Law of registry: **Click here to enter text.**	4. Managers (name, place of registered office and law of registry) (Cl. 1) (i) Name: **Choose an item.** (ii) Place of registered office: **Click here to enter text.** (iii) Law of registry: **Click here to enter text.**
5. The Company (with reference to the ISM/ISPS Codes) (state name and IMO Unique Company Identification number. If the Company is a third party then also state registered office and principal place of business) (Cls. 1 and 9(c)(i)) (i) Name: **Click here to enter text.** (ii) IMO Unique Company Identification number: **Click here to enter text.** (iii) Place of registered office: **Click here to enter text.** (iv) Principal place of business: **Click here to enter text.**	6. Technical Management (state "yes" or "no" as agreed) (Cl. 4) **Click here to enter text.** 7. Crew Management (state "yes" or "no" as agreed) (Cl. 5(a)) **Click here to enter text.** 8. Commercial Management (state "yes" or "no" as agreed) (Cl. 6) **Click here to enter text.**
9. Chartering Services period (only to be filled in if "yes" stated in Box 8) (Cl.6(a)) **Click here to enter text.**	10. Crew Insurance arrangements (state "yes" or "no" as agreed) (i) Crew Insurances* (Cl. 5(b)): **Click here to enter text.** (ii) Insurance for persons proceeding to sea onboard (Cl. 5(b)(i)): **Click here to enter text.** *only to apply if Crew Management (Cl. 5(a)) agreed (see Box 7)
11. Insurance arrangements (state "yes" or "no" as agreed) (Cl. 7) **Click here to enter text.**	12. Optional insurances (state optional insurance(s) as agreed, such as piracy, kidnap and ransom, loss of hire and FD & D) (Cl. 10(a)(iv)) **Click here to enter text.**
13. Interest (state rate of interest to apply after due date to outstanding sums) (Cl. 9(a)) **Click here to enter text.**	14. Annual management fee (state annual amount) (Cl. 12(a)) **Click here to enter text.**
15. Manager's nominated account (Cl.12(a)) **Click here to enter text.**	16. Daily rate (state rate for days in excess of those agreed in budget) (Cl. 12(c)) **Click here to enter text.** 17. Lay-up period / number of months (Cl.12(d)) **Click here to enter text.**
18. Minimum contract period (state number of months) (Cl. 21(a)) **Click here to enter text.**	19. Management fee on termination (state number of months to apply) (Cl. 22(g)) **Click here to enter text.**
20. Severance Costs (state maximum amount) (Cl. 22(h)(ii)) **Click here to enter text.**	21. Dispute Resolution (state alternative Cl. 23(a), 23(b) or 23(c); if Cl. 23(c) place of arbitration must be stated) (Cl. 23) **Choose an item. Click here to enter text.**
22. Notices (state full style contact details for serving notice and communication to the Owners) (Cl. 24) **Click here to enter text.**	23. Notices (state full style contact details for serving notice and communication to the Managers) (Cl. 24) **Click here to enter text.**

It is mutually agreed between the party stated in Box 3 and the party stated in Box 4 that this Agreement consisting of PART I and PART II as well as Annexes "A" (Details of Vessel or Vessels), "B" (Details of Crew), "C" (Budget), "D" (Associated Vessels) and "E" (Fee Schedule) attached hereto, shall be performed subject to the conditions contained herein. In the event of a conflict of conditions, the provisions of PART I and Annexes "A", "B", "C", "D" and "E" shall prevail over those of PART II to the extent of such conflict but no further.

Signature(s) (Owners) **Click here to enter text.**	Signature(s) (Managers) **Click here to enter text.**

Continued

Printed by BIMCO's *idea*

InterManager

ANNEX "A" (DETAILS OF VESSEL OR VESSELS)
TO THE BIMCO STANDARD SHIP MANAGEMENT AGREEMENT
CODE NAME: SHIPMAN 2009

Date of Agreement: **Click here to enter text.**

Name of Vessel(s): **Choose an item.**

Particulars of Vessel(s): **Click here to enter text.**

Continued

Printed by BIMCO's *idea*

ANNEX "B" (DETAILS OF CREW)
TO THE BIMCO STANDARD SHIP MANAGEMENT AGREEMENT
CODE NAME: SHIPMAN 2009

Date of Agreement: **Click here to enter text.**

Details of Crew: **Click here to enter text.**

Numbers **Click here to enter text.** Rank **Click here to enter text.** Nationality **Click here to enter text.**

Continued

Printed by BIMCO's *idea*

InterManager

ANNEX "C" (BUDGET)
TO THE BIMCO STANDARD SHIP MANAGEMENT AGREEMENT
CODE NAME: SHIPMAN 2009

Date of Agreement: **Click here to enter text.**

Managers' initial budget with effect from the commencement date of this Agreement (see **Box 2**): **Click here to enter text.**

Continued

Printed by BIMCO's *idea*

InterManager

ANNEX "D" (ASSOCIATED VESSELS)
TO THE BIMCO STANDARD SHIP MANAGEMENT AGREEMENT
CODE NAME: SHIPMAN 2009

NOTE: PARTIES SHOULD BE AWARE THAT BY COMPLETING THIS ANNEX "D" THEY WILL BE SUBJECT TO THE PROVISIONS OF SUB-CLAUSE 22(b)(i) OF THIS AGREEMENT.

Date of Agreement: **Click here to enter text.**

Details of Associated Vessels: **Click here to enter text.**

Continued

Printed by BIMCO's *idea*

InterManager

ANNEX "E" (FEE SCHEDULE)
TO THE BIMCO STANDARD SHIP MANAGEMENT AGREEMENT
CODE NAME: SHIPMAN 2009

Click here to enter text.

Continued

PART II
SHIPMAN 2009
Standard ship management agreement

SECTION 1 – Basis of the Agreement

1. Definitions

In this Agreement save where the context otherwise requires, the following words and expressions shall have the meanings hereby assigned to them:

"Company" (with reference to the ISM Code and the ISPS Code) means the organization identified in Box 5 or any replacement organization appointed by the Owners from time to time (see Sub-clauses 9(b)(i) or 9(c)(ii), whichever is applicable).

"Crew" means the personnel of the numbers, rank and nationality specified in Annex "B" hereto.

"Crew Insurances" means insurance of liabilities in respect of crew risks which shall include but not be limited to death, permanent disability, sickness, injury, repatriation, shipwreck unemployment indemnity and loss of personal effects (see Sub-clause 5(b) (Crew Insurances) and Clause 7 (Insurance Arrangements) and Clause 10 (Insurance Policies) and Boxes 10 and 11).

"Crew Support Costs" means all expenses of a general nature which are not particularly referable to any individual vessel for the time being managed by the Managers and which are incurred by the Managers for the purpose of providing an efficient and economic management service and, without prejudice to the generality of the foregoing, shall include the cost of crew standby pay, training schemes for officers and ratings, cadet training schemes, sick pay, study pay, recruitment and interviews.

"Flag State" means the State whose flag the Vessel is flying.

"ISM Code" means the International Management Code for the Safe Operation of Ships and for Pollution Prevention and any amendment thereto or substitution therefor.

"ISPS Code" means the International Code for the Security of Ships and Port Facilities and the relevant amendments to Chapter XI of SOLAS and any amendment thereto or substitution therefor.

"Managers" means the party identified in Box 4.

"Management Services" means the services specified in SECTION 2 - Services (Clauses 4 through 7) as indicated affirmatively in Boxes 6 through 8, 10 and 11, and all other functions performed by the Managers under the terms of this Agreement.

"Owners" means the party identified in Box 3.

"Severance Costs" means the costs which are legally required to be paid to the Crew as a result of the early termination of any contracts for service on the Vessel.

"SMS" means the Safety Management System (as defined by the ISM Code).

"STCW 95" means the International Convention on Standards of Training, Certification and Watchkeeping for Seafarers, 1978, as amended in 1995 and any amendment thereto or substitution therefor.

"Vessel" means the vessel or vessels details of which are set out in Annex "A" attached hereto.

2. Commencement and Appointment

With effect from the date stated in Box 2 for the commencement of the Management Services and continuing unless and until terminated as provided herein, the Owners hereby appoint the Managers and the Managers hereby agree to act as the Managers of the Vessel in respect of the Management Services.

3. Authority of the Managers

Subject to the terms and conditions herein provided, during the period of this Agreement the Managers shall carry out the Management Services in respect of the Vessel as agents for and on behalf of the Owners. The Managers shall have authority to take such actions as they may from time to time in their absolute discretion consider to be necessary to enable them to perform the Management Services in accordance with sound ship management practice, including but not limited to compliance with all relevant rules and regulations.

PART II
SHIPMAN 2009
Standard ship management agreement

SECTION 2 – Services

4. Technical Management

(only applicable if agreed according to Box 6).

The Managers shall provide technical management which includes, but is not limited to, the following services:

(a) ensuring that the Vessel complies with the requirements of the law of the Flag State;

(b) ensuring compliance with the ISM Code;

(c) ensuring compliance with the ISPS Code;

(d) providing competent personnel to supervise the maintenance and general efficiency of the Vessel;

(e) arranging and supervising dry dockings, repairs, alterations and the maintenance of the Vessel to the standards agreed with the Owners provided that the Managers shall be entitled to incur the necessary expenditure to ensure that the Vessel will comply with all requirements and recommendations of the classification society, and with the law of the Flag State and of the places where the Vessel is required to trade;

(f) arranging the supply of necessary stores, spares and lubricating oil;

(g) appointing surveyors and technical consultants as the Managers may consider from time to time to be necessary;

(h) in accordance with the Owners' instructions, supervising the sale and physical delivery of the Vessel under the sale agreement. However services under this Sub-clause 4(h) shall not include negotiation of the sale agreement or transfer of ownership of the Vessel;

(i) arranging for the supply of provisions unless provided by the Owners; and

(j) arranging for the sampling and testing of bunkers.

5. Crew Management and Crew Insurances

(a) *Crew Management*

(only applicable if agreed according to Box 7)

The Managers shall provide suitably qualified Crew who shall comply with the requirements of STCW 95. The provision of such crew management services includes, but is not limited to, the following services:

(i) selecting, engaging and providing for the administration of the Crew, including, as applicable, payroll arrangements, pension arrangements, tax, social security contributions and other mandatory dues related to their employment payable in each Crew member's country of domicile;

(ii) ensuring that the applicable requirements of the law of the Flag State in respect of rank, qualification and certification of the Crew and employment regulations, such as Crew's tax and social insurance, are satisfied;

(iii) ensuring that all Crew have passed a medical examination with a qualified doctor certifying that they are fit for the duties for which they are engaged and are in possession of valid medical certificates issued in accordance with appropriate Flag State requirements or such higher standard of medical examination as may be agreed with the Owners. In the absence of applicable Flag State requirements the medical certificate shall be valid at the time when the respective Crew member arrives on board the Vessel and shall be maintained for the duration of the service on board the Vessel;

(iv) ensuring that the Crew shall have a common working language and a command of the English language of a sufficient standard to enable them to perform their duties safely;

(v) arranging transportation of the Crew, including repatriation;

(vi) training of the Crew;

PART II
SHIPMAN 2009
Standard ship management agreement

(vii) conducting union negotiations; and

(viii) if the Managers are the Company, ensuring that the Crew, on joining the Vessel, are given proper familiarisation with their duties in relation to the Vessel's SMS and that instructions which are essential to the SMS are identified, documented and given to the Crew prior to sailing.

(ix) if the Managers are **not** the Company:

(1) ensuring that the Crew, before joining the Vessel, are given proper familiarisation with their duties in relation to the ISM Code; and

(2) instructing the Crew to obey all reasonable orders of the Company in connection with the operation of the SMS.

(x) Where Managers are **not** providing technical management services in accordance with Clause 4 (Technical Management):

(1) ensuring that no person connected to the provision and the performance of the crew management services shall proceed to sea on board the Vessel without the prior consent of the Owners (such consent not to be unreasonably withheld); and

(2) ensuring that in the event that the Owners' drug and alcohol policy requires measures to be taken prior to the Crew joining the Vessel, implementing such measures;

(b) Crew Insurances
(only applicable if Sub-clause 5(a) applies ***and*** *if agreed according to Box 10)*
The Managers shall throughout the period of this Agreement provide the following services:

(i) arranging Crew Insurances in accordance with the best practice of prudent managers of vessels of a similar type to the Vessel, with sound and reputable insurance companies, underwriters or associations. Insurances for any other persons proceeding to sea onboard the Vessel may be separately agreed by the Owners and the Managers (see Box 10);

(ii) ensuring that the Owners are aware of the terms, conditions, exceptions and limits of liability of the insurances in Sub-clause 5(b)(i);

(iii) ensuring that all premiums or calls in respect of the insurances in Sub-clause 5(b)(i) are paid by their due date;

(iv) if obtainable at no additional cost, ensuring that insurances in Sub-clause 5(b)(i) name the Owners as a joint assured with full cover and, unless otherwise agreed, on terms such that Owners shall be under no liability in respect of premiums or calls arising in connection with such insurances.

(v) providing written evidence, to the reasonable satisfaction of the Owners, of the Managers' compliance with their obligations under Sub-clauses 5(b)(ii), and 5(b)(iii) within a reasonable time of the commencement of this Agreement, and of each renewal date and, if specifically requested, of each payment date of the insurances in Sub-clause 5(b)(i).

6. Commercial Management
(only applicable if agreed according to Box 8).
The Managers shall provide the following services for the Vessel in accordance with the Owners' instructions, which shall include but not be limited to:

(a) seeking and negotiating employment for the Vessel and the conclusion (including the execution thereof) of charter parties or other contracts relating to the employment of the Vessel. If such a contract exceeds the period stated in Box 9, consent thereto in writing shall first be obtained from the Owners;

(b) arranging for the provision of bunker fuels of the quality specified by the Owners as required for the Vessel's trade;

(c) voyage estimating and accounting and calculation of hire, freights, demurrage and/or despatch monies due from or due to the charterers of the Vessel; assisting in the collection of any sums due to the Owners related to the commercial operation of the Vessel in accordance with Clause 11 (Income Collected and

PART II
SHIPMAN 2009
Standard ship management agreement

Expenses Paid on Behalf of Owners);

If any of the services under Sub-clauses 6(a), 6(b) and 6(c) are to be excluded from the Management Fee, remuneration for these services must be stated in Annex E (Fee Schedule). See Sub-clause 12(e).

(d) issuing voyage instructions;

(e) appointing agents;

(f) appointing stevedores; and

(g) arranging surveys associated with the commercial operation of the Vessel.

7. Insurance Arrangements

(only applicable if agreed according to Box 11).

The Managers shall arrange insurances in accordance with Clause 10 (Insurance Policies), on such terms as the Owners shall have instructed or agreed, in particular regarding conditions, insured values, deductibles, franchises and limits of liability.

PART II
SHIPMAN 2009
Standard ship management agreement

SECTION 3 – Obligations

8. Managers' Obligations

(a) The Managers undertake to use their best endeavours to provide the Management Services as agents for and on behalf of the Owners in accordance with sound ship management practice and to protect and promote the interests of the Owners in all matters relating to the provision of services hereunder.

Provided however, that in the performance of their management responsibilities under this Agreement, the Managers shall be entitled to have regard to their overall responsibility in relation to all vessels as may from time to time be entrusted to their management and in particular, but without prejudice to the generality of the foregoing, the Managers shall be entitled to allocate available supplies, manpower and services in such manner as in the prevailing circumstances the Managers in their absolute discretion consider to be fair and reasonable.

(b) Where the Managers are providing technical management services in accordance with Clause 4 (Technical Management), they shall procure that the requirements of the Flag State are satisfied and they shall agree to be appointed as the Company, assuming the responsibility for the operation of the Vessel and taking over the duties and responsibilities imposed by the ISM Code and the ISPS Code, if applicable.

9. Owners' Obligations

(a) The Owners shall pay all sums due to the Managers punctually in accordance with the terms of this Agreement. In the event of payment after the due date of any outstanding sums the Manager shall be entitled to charge interest at the rate stated in Box 13.

(b) Where the Managers are providing technical management services in accordance with Clause 4 (Technical Management), the Owners shall:

(i) report (or where the Owners are not the registered owners of the Vessel procure that the registered owners report) to the Flag State administration the details of the Managers as the Company as required to comply with the ISM and ISPS Codes;

(ii) procure that any officers and ratings supplied by them or on their behalf comply with the requirements of STCW 95; and

(iii) instruct such officers and ratings to obey all reasonable orders of the Managers (in their capacity as the Company) in connection with the operation of the Managers' safety management system.

(c) Where the Managers are **not** providing technical management services in accordance with Clause 4 (Technical Management), the Owners shall:

(i) procure that the requirements of the Flag State are satisfied and notify the Managers upon execution of this Agreement of the name and contact details of the organization that will be the Company by completing Box 5;

(ii) if the Company changes at any time during this Agreement, notify the Managers in a timely manner of the name and contact details of the new organization;

(iii) procure that the details of the Company, including any change thereof, are reported to the Flag State administration as required to comply with the ISM and ISPS Codes. The Owners shall advise the Managers in a timely manner when the Flag State administration has approved the Company; and

(iv) unless otherwise agreed, arrange for the supply of provisions at their own expense.

(d) Where the Managers are providing crew management services in accordance with Sub-clause 5(a) the Owners shall:

(i) inform the Managers prior to ordering the Vessel to any excluded or additional premium area under any of the Owners' Insurances by reason of war risks and/or piracy or like perils and pay whatever additional costs may properly be incurred by the Managers as a consequence of such orders including, if necessary, the costs of replacing any member of the Crew. Any delays resulting from negotiation with or replacement of any member of the Crew as a result of the Vessel being ordered to such an area

PART II
SHIPMAN 2009
Standard ship management agreement

shall be for the Owners' account. Should the Vessel be within an area which becomes an excluded or additional premium area the above provisions relating to cost and delay shall apply;

(ii) agree with the Managers prior to any change of flag of the Vessel and pay whatever additional costs may properly be incurred by the Managers as a consequence of such change. If agreement cannot be reached then either party may terminate this Agreement in accordance with Sub-clause 22(e); and

(iii) provide, at no cost to the Managers, in accordance with the requirements of the law of the Flag State, or higher standard, as mutually agreed, adequate Crew accommodation and living standards.

(e) Where the Managers are **not** the Company, the Owners shall ensure that Crew are properly familiarised with their duties in accordance with the Vessel's SMS and that instructions which are essential to the SMS are identified, documented and given to the Crew prior to sailing.

PART II
SHIPMAN 2009
Standard ship management agreement

SECTION 4 – Insurance, Budgets, Income, Expenses and Fees

10. Insurance Policies

The Owners shall procure, whether by instructing the Managers under Clause 7 (Insurance Arrangements) or otherwise, that throughout the period of this Agreement:

(a) at the Owners' expense, the Vessel is insured for not less than its sound market value or entered for its full gross tonnage, as the case may be for:

(i) hull and machinery marine risks (including but not limited to crew negligence) and excess liabilities;

(ii) protection and indemnity risks (including but not limited to pollution risks, diversion expenses and, except to the extent insured separately by the Managers in accordance with Sub-clause 5(b)(i), Crew Insurances;

NOTE: If the Managers are not providing crew management services under Sub-clause 5(a) (Crew Management) or have agreed not to provide Crew Insurances separately in accordance with Sub-clause 5(b)(i), then such insurances must be included in the protection and indemnity risks cover for the Vessel (see Sub-clause 10(a)(ii) above).

(iii) war risks (including but not limited to blocking and trapping, protection and indemnity, terrorism and crew risks); and

(iv) such optional insurances as may be agreed (such as piracy, kidnap and ransom, loss of hire and FD & D) (see Box 12)

Sub-clauses 10(a)(i) through 10(a)(iv) all in accordance with the best practice of prudent owners of vessels of a similar type to the Vessel, with sound and reputable insurance companies, underwriters or associations ("the Owners' Insurances");

(b) all premiums and calls on the Owners' Insurances are paid by their due date;

(c) the Owners' Insurances name the Managers and, subject to underwriters' agreement, any third party designated by the Managers as a joint assured, with full cover. It is understood that in some cases, such as protection and indemnity, the normal terms for such cover may impose on the Managers and any such third party a liability in respect of premiums or calls arising in connection with the Owners' Insurances.

If obtainable at no additional cost, however, the Owners shall procure such insurances on terms such that neither the Managers nor any such third party shall be under any liability in respect of premiums or calls arising in connection with the Owners' Insurances. In any event, on termination of this Agreement in accordance with Clause 21 (Duration of the Agreement) and Clause 22 (Termination), the Owners shall procure that the Managers and any third party designated by the Managers as joint assured shall cease to be joint assured and, if reasonably achievable, that they shall be released from any and all liability for premiums and calls that may arise in relation to the period of this Agreement; and

(d) written evidence is provided, to the reasonable satisfaction of the Managers, of the Owners' compliance with their obligations under this Clause 10 within a reasonable time of the commencement of the Agreement, and of each renewal date and, if specifically requested, of each payment date of the Owners' Insurances.

11. Income Collected and Expenses Paid on Behalf of Owners

(a) Except as provided in Sub-clause 11(c) all monies collected by the Managers under the terms of this Agreement (other than monies payable by the Owners to the Managers) and any interest thereon shall be held to the credit of the Owners in a separate bank account.

(b) All expenses incurred by the Managers under the terms of this Agreement on behalf of the Owners (including expenses as provided in Clause 12(c)) may be debited against the Owners in the account referred to under Sub-clause 11(a) but shall in any event remain payable by the Owners to the Managers on demand.

(c) All monies collected by the Managers under Clause 6 (Commercial Management) shall be paid into a bank account in the name of the Owners or as may be otherwise advised by the Owners in writing.

12. Management Fee and Expenses

PART II
SHIPMAN 2009
Standard ship management agreement

(a) The Owners shall pay to the Managers an annual management fee as stated in Box 14 for their services as Managers under this Agreement, which shall be payable in equal monthly instalments in advance, the first instalment (pro rata if appropriate) being payable on the commencement of this Agreement (see Clause 2 (Commencement and Appointment) and Box 2) and subsequent instalments being payable at the beginning of every calendar month. The management fee shall be payable to the Managers' nominated account stated in Box 15.

(b) The management fee shall be subject to an annual review and the proposed fee shall be presented in the annual budget in accordance with Sub-clause 13(a).

(c) The Managers shall, at no extra cost to the Owners, provide their own office accommodation, office staff, facilities and stationery. Without limiting the generality of this Clause 12 (Management Fee and Expenses) the Owners shall reimburse the Managers for postage and communication expenses, travelling expenses, and other out of pocket expenses properly incurred by the Managers in pursuance of the Management Services. Any days used by the Managers' personnel travelling to or from or attending on the Vessel or otherwise used in connection with the Management Services in excess of those agreed in the budget shall be charged at the daily rate stated in Box 16.

(d) If the Owners decide to layup the Vessel and such layup lasts for more than the number of months stated in Box 17, an appropriate reduction of the Management Fee for the period exceeding such period until one month before the Vessel is again put into service shall be mutually agreed between the parties. If the Managers are providing crew management services in accordance with Sub-clause 5(a), consequential costs of reduction and reinstatement of the Crew shall be for the Owners' account. If agreement cannot be reached then either party may terminate this Agreement in accordance with Sub-clause 22(e).

(e) Save as otherwise provided in this Agreement, all discounts and commissions obtained by the Managers in the course of the performance of the Management Services shall be credited to the Owners.

13. Budgets and Management of Funds

(a) The Managers' initial budget is set out in Annex "C" hereto. Subsequent budgets shall be for twelve month periods and shall be prepared by the Managers and presented to the Owners not less than three months before the end of the budget year.

(b) The Owners shall state to the Managers in a timely manner, but in any event within one month of presentation, whether or not they agree to each proposed annual budget. The parties shall negotiate in good faith and if they fail to agree on the annual budget, including the management fee, either party may terminate this Agreement in accordance with Sub-clause 22(e).

(c) Following the agreement of the budget, the Managers shall prepare and present to the Owners their estimate of the working capital requirement for the Vessel and shall each month request the Owners in writing to pay the funds required to run the Vessel for the ensuing month, including the payment of any occasional or extraordinary item of expenditure, such as emergency repair costs, additional insurance premiums, bunkers or provisions. Such funds shall be received by the Managers within ten running days after the receipt by the Owners of the Managers' written request and shall be held to the credit of the Owners in a separate bank account.

(d) The Managers shall at all times maintain and keep true and correct accounts in respect of the Management Services in accordance with the relevant International Financial Reporting Standards or such other standard as the parties may agree, including records of all costs and expenditure incurred, and produce a comparison between budgeted and actual income and expenditure of the Vessel in such form and at such intervals as shall be mutually agreed.

The Managers shall make such accounts available for inspection and auditing by the Owners and/or their representatives in the Managers' offices or by electronic means, provided reasonable notice is given by the Owners.

(e) Notwithstanding anything contained herein, the Managers shall in no circumstances be required to use or commit their own funds to finance the provision of the Management Services.

PART II
SHIPMAN 2009
Standard ship management agreement

SECTION 5 – Legal, General and Duration of Agreement

14. Trading Restrictions

If the Managers are providing crew management services in accordance with Sub-clause 5(a) (Crew Management), the Owners and the Managers will, prior to the commencement of this Agreement, agree on any trading restrictions to the Vessel that may result from the terms and conditions of the Crew's employment.

15. Replacement

If the Managers are providing crew management services in accordance with Sub-clause 5(a) (Crew Management), the Owners may require the replacement, at their own expense, at the next reasonable opportunity, of any member of the Crew found on reasonable grounds to be unsuitable for service. If the Managers have failed to fulfil their obligations in providing suitable qualified Crew within the meaning of Sub-clause 5(a) (Crew Management), then such replacement shall be at the Managers' expense.

16. Managers' Right to Sub-Contract

The Managers shall not subcontract any of their obligations hereunder without the prior written consent of the Owners which shall not be unreasonably withheld. In the event of such a sub-contract the Managers shall remain fully liable for the due performance of their obligations under this Agreement.

17. Responsibilities

(a) *Force Majeure*

Neither party shall be liable for any loss, damage or delay due to any of the following force majeure events and/or conditions to the extent that the party invoking force majeure is prevented or hindered from performing any or all of their obligations under this Agreement, provided they have made all reasonable efforts to avoid, minimize or prevent the effect of such events and/or conditions:

(i) acts of God;

(ii) any Government requisition, control, intervention, requirement or interference;

(iii) any circumstances arising out of war, threatened act of war or warlike operations, acts of terrorism, sabotage or piracy, or the consequences thereof;

(iv) riots, civil commotion, blockades or embargoes;

(v) epidemics;

(vi) earthquakes, landslides, floods or other extraordinary weather conditions;

(vii) strikes, lockouts or other industrial action, unless limited to the employees (which shall not include the Crew) of the party seeking to invoke force majeure;

(viii) fire, accident, explosion except where caused by negligence of the party seeking to invoke force majeure; and

(ix) any other similar cause beyond the reasonable control of either party.

(b) *Liability to Owners*

(i) Without prejudice to Sub-clause 17(a), the Managers shall be under no liability whatsoever to the Owners for any loss, damage, delay or expense of whatsoever nature, whether direct or indirect, (including but not limited to loss of profit arising out of or in connection with detention of or delay to the Vessel) and howsoever arising in the course of performance of the Management Services UNLESS same is proved to have resulted solely from the negligence, gross negligence or wilful default of the Managers or their employees or agents, or sub-contractors employed by them in connection with the Vessel, in which case (save where loss, damage, delay or expense has resulted from the Managers' personal act or omission committed with the intent to cause same or recklessly and with knowledge that such loss, damage, delay or expense would probably result) the Managers' liability for each incident or series of incidents giving rise to a claim or claims shall never exceed a total of ten (10) times the annual management fee payable hereunder.

(ii) *Acts or omissions of the Crew* - Notwithstanding anything that may appear to the contrary in this

Agreement, the Managers shall not be liable for any acts or omissions of the Crew, even if such acts or omissions are negligent, grossly negligent or wilful, except only to the extent that they are shown to have resulted from a failure by the Managers to discharge their obligations under Clause 5(a) (Crew Management), in which case their liability shall be limited in accordance with the terms of this Clause 17 (Responsibilities).

(c) *Indemnity*
Except to the extent and solely for the amount therein set out that the Managers would be liable under Sub-clause 17(b), the Owners hereby undertake to keep the Managers and their employees, agents and sub-contractors indemnified and to hold them harmless against all actions, proceedings, claims, demands or liabilities whatsoever or howsoever arising which may be brought against them or incurred or suffered by them arising out of or in connection with the performance of this Agreement, and against and in respect of all costs, loss, damages and expenses (including legal costs and expenses on a full indemnity basis) which the Managers may suffer or incur (either directly or indirectly) in the course of the performance of this Agreement.

(d) *"Himalaya"*
It is hereby expressly agreed that no employee or agent of the Managers (including every sub-contractor from time to time employed by the Managers) shall in any circumstances whatsoever be under any liability whatsoever to the Owners for any loss, damage or delay of whatsoever kind arising or resulting directly or indirectly from any act, neglect or default on his part while acting in the course of or in connection with his employment and, without prejudice to the generality of the foregoing provisions in this Clause 17 (Responsibilities), every exemption, limitation, condition and liberty herein contained and every right, exemption from liability, defence and immunity of whatsoever nature applicable to the Managers or to which the Managers are entitled hereunder shall also be available and shall extend to protect every such employee or agent of the Managers acting as aforesaid and for the purpose of all the foregoing provisions of this Clause 17 (Responsibilities) the Managers are or shall be deemed to be acting as agent or trustee on behalf of and for the benefit of all persons who are or might be their servants or agents from time to time (including sub-contractors as aforesaid) and all such persons shall to this extent be or be deemed to be parties to this Agreement.

18. General Administration

(a) The Managers shall keep the Owners and, if appropriate, the Company informed in a timely manner of any incident of which the Managers become aware which gives or may give rise to delay to the Vessel or claims or disputes involving third parties.

(b) The Managers shall handle and settle all claims and disputes arising out of the Management Services hereunder, unless the Owners instruct the Managers otherwise. The Managers shall keep the Owners appropriately informed in a timely manner throughout the handling of such claims and disputes.

(c) The Owners may request the Managers to bring or defend other actions, suits or proceedings related to the Management Services, on terms to be agreed.

(d) The Managers shall have power to obtain appropriate legal or technical or other outside expert advice in relation to the handling and settlement of claims in relation to Sub-clauses 18(a) and 18(b) and disputes and any other matters affecting the interests of the Owners in respect of the Vessel, unless the Owners instruct the Managers otherwise.

(e) On giving reasonable notice, the Owners may request, and the Managers shall in a timely manner make available, all documentation, information and records in respect of the matters covered by this Agreement either related to mandatory rules or regulations or other obligations applying to the Owners in respect of the Vessel (including but not limited to STCW 95, the ISM Code and ISPS Code) to the extent permitted by relevant legislation.

On giving reasonable notice, the Managers may request, and the Owners shall in a timely manner make available, all documentation, information and records reasonably required by the Managers to enable them to perform the Management Services.

(f) The Owners shall arrange for the provision of any necessary guarantee bond or other security.

PART II
SHIPMAN 2009
Standard ship management agreement

(g) Any costs incurred by the Managers in carrying out their obligations according to this Clause 18 (General Administration) shall be reimbursed by the Owners.

19. Inspection of Vessel
The Owners may at any time after giving reasonable notice to the Managers inspect the Vessel for any reason they consider necessary.

20. Compliance with Laws and Regulations
The parties will not do or permit to be done anything which might cause any breach or infringement of the laws and regulations of the Flag State, or of the places where the Vessel trades.

21. Duration of the Agreement
(a) This Agreement shall come into effect at the date stated in Box 2 and shall continue until terminated by either party by giving notice to the other; in which event this Agreement shall terminate upon the expiration of the later of the number of months stated in Box 18 or a period of two (2) months from the date on which such notice is received, unless terminated earlier in accordance with Clause 22 (Termination).

(b) Where the Vessel is not at a mutually convenient port or place on the expiry of such period, this Agreement shall terminate on the subsequent arrival of the Vessel at the next mutually convenient port or place.

22. Termination
(a) *Owners' or Managers' default*
If either party fails to meet their obligations under this Agreement, the other party may give notice to the party in default requiring them to remedy it. In the event that the party in default fails to remedy it within a reasonable time to the reasonable satisfaction of the other party, that party shall be entitled to terminate this Agreement with immediate effect by giving notice to the party in default.

(b) *Notwithstanding Sub-clause 22(a):*

(i) The Managers shall be entitled to terminate the Agreement with immediate effect by giving notice to the Owners if any monies payable by the Owners and/or the owners of any associated vessel, details of which are listed in Annex "D", shall not have been received in the Managers' nominated account within ten days (10) of receipt by the Owners of the Managers' written request, or if the Vessel is repossessed by the Mortgagee(s).

(ii) If the Owners proceed with the employment of or continue to employ the Vessel in the carriage of contraband, blockade running, or in an unlawful trade, or on a voyage which in the reasonable opinion of the Managers is unduly hazardous or improper, the Managers may give notice of the default to the Owners, requiring them to remedy it as soon as practically possible. In the event that the Owners fail to remedy it within a reasonable time to the satisfaction of the Managers, the Managers shall be entitled to terminate the Agreement with immediate effect by notice.

(iii) If either party fails to meet their respective obligations under Sub-clause 5(b) (Crew Insurances) and Clause 10 (Insurance Policies), the other party may give notice to the party in default requiring them to remedy it within ten (10) days, failing which the other party may terminate this Agreement with immediate effect by giving notice to the party in default.

(c) *Extraordinary Termination*
This Agreement shall be deemed to be terminated in the case of the sale of the Vessel or, if the Vessel becomes a total loss or is declared as a constructive or compromised or arranged total loss or is requisitioned or has been declared missing or, if bareboat chartered, unless otherwise agreed, when the bareboat charter comes to an end.

(d) *For the purpose of Sub-clause 22(c) hereof:*

(i) the date upon which the Vessel is to be treated as having been sold or otherwise disposed of shall be the date on which the Vessel's owners cease to be the registered owners of the Vessel;

(ii) the Vessel shall be deemed to be lost either when it has become an actual total loss or agreement has been reached with the Vessel's underwriters in respect of its constructive total loss or if such agreement with the Vessel's underwriters is not reached it is adjudged by a competent tribunal that a constructive

PART II
SHIPMAN 2009
Standard ship management agreement

loss of the Vessel has occurred; and

(iii) the date upon which the Vessel is to be treated as declared missing shall be ten (10) days after the Vessel was last reported or when the Vessel is recorded as missing by the Vessel's underwriters, whichever occurs first. A missing vessel shall be deemed lost in accordance with the provisions of Sub-clause 22(d)(ii).

(e) In the event the parties fail to agree the annual budget in accordance with Sub-clause 13(b), or to agree a change of flag in accordance with Sub-clause 9(d)(ii), or to agree to a reduction in the Mangement Fee in accordance with Sub-clause 12(d), either party may terminate this Agreement by giving the other party not less than one month's notice, the result of which will be the expiry of the Agreement at the end of the current budget period or on expiry of the notice period, whichever is the later.

(f) This Agreement shall terminate forthwith in the event of an order being made or resolution passed for the winding up, dissolution, liquidation or bankruptcy of either party (otherwise than for the purpose of reconstruction or amalgamation) or if a receiver or administrator is appointed, or if it suspends payment, ceases to carry on business or makes any special arrangement or composition with its creditors.

(g) In the event of the termination of this Agreement for any reason other than default by the Managers the management fee payable to the Managers according to the provisions of Clause 12 (Management Fee and Expenses), shall continue to be payable for a further period of the number of months stated in Box 19 as from the effective date of termination. If Box 19 is left blank then ninety (90) days shall apply.

(h) In addition, where the Managers provide Crew for the Vessel in accordance with Clause 5(a) (Crew Management):

(i) the Owners shall continue to pay Crew Support Costs during the said further period of the number of months stated in Box 19; and

(ii) the Owners shall pay an equitable proportion of any Severance Costs which may be incurred, not exceeding the amount stated in Box 20. The Managers shall use their reasonable endeavours to minimise such Severance Costs.

(i) On the termination, for whatever reason, of this Agreement, the Managers shall release to the Owners, if so requested, the originals where possible, or otherwise certified copies, of all accounts and all documents specifically relating to the Vessel and its operation.

(j) The termination of this Agreement shall be without prejudice to all rights accrued due between the parties prior to the date of termination.

23. BIMCO Dispute Resolution Clause

(a) This Agreement shall be governed by and construed in accordance with English law and any dispute arising out of or in connection with this Agreement shall be referred to arbitration in London in accordance with the Arbitration Act 1996 or any statutory modification or re-enactment thereof save to the extent necessary to give effect to the provisions of this Clause.

The arbitration shall be conducted in accordance with the London Maritime Arbitrators Association (LMAA) Terms current at the time when the arbitration proceedings are commenced.

The reference shall be to three arbitrators. A party wishing to refer a dispute to arbitration shall appoint its arbitrator and send notice of such appointment in writing to the other party requiring the other party to appoint its own arbitrator within 14 calendar days of that notice and stating that it will appoint its arbitrator as sole arbitrator unless the other party appoints its own arbitrator and gives notice that it has done so within the 14 days specified. If the other party does not appoint its own arbitrator and give notice that it has done so within the 14 days specified, the party referring a dispute to arbitration may, without the requirement of any further prior notice to the other party, appoint its arbitrator as sole arbitrator and shall advise the other party accordingly. The award of a sole arbitrator shall be binding on both parties as if he had been appointed by agreement.

Nothing herein shall prevent the parties agreeing in writing to vary these provisions to provide for the appointment of a sole arbitrator.

PART II
SHIPMAN 2009
Standard ship management agreement

In cases where neither the claim nor any counterclaim exceeds the sum of USD50,000 (or such other sum as the parties may agree) the arbitration shall be conducted in accordance with the LMAA Small Claims Procedure current at the time when the arbitration proceedings are commenced.

(b) This Agreement shall be governed by and construed in accordance with Title 9 of the United States Code and the Maritime Law of the United States and any dispute arising out of or in connection with this Agreement shall be referred to three persons at New York, one to be appointed by each of the parties hereto, and the third by the two so chosen; their decision or that of any two of them shall be final, and for the purposes of enforcing any award, judgment may be entered on an award by any court of competent jurisdiction. The proceedings shall be conducted in accordance with the rules of the Society of Maritime Arbitrators, Inc.

In cases where neither the claim nor any counterclaim exceeds the sum of USD50,000 (or such other sum as the parties may agree) the arbitration shall be conducted in accordance with the Shortened Arbitration Procedure of the Society of Maritime Arbitrators, Inc. current at the time when the arbitration proceedings are commenced.

(c) This Agreement shall be governed by and construed in accordance with the laws of the place mutually agreed by the parties and any dispute arising out of or in connection with this Agreement shall be referred to arbitration at a mutually agreed place, subject to the procedures applicable there.

(d) Notwithstanding Sub-clauses 23(a), 23(b) or 23(c) above, the parties may agree at any time to refer to mediation any difference and/or dispute arising out of or in connection with this Agreement.

(i) In the case of a dispute in respect of which arbitration has been commenced under Sub-clauses 23(a), 23(b) or 23(c) above, the following shall apply:

(ii) Either party may at any time and from time to time elect to refer the dispute or part of the dispute to mediation by service on the other party of a written notice (the "Mediation Notice") calling on the other party to agree to mediation.

(iii) The other party shall thereupon within 14 calendar days of receipt of the Mediation Notice confirm that they agree to mediation, in which case the parties shall thereafter agree a mediator within a further 14 calendar days, failing which on the application of either party a mediator will be appointed promptly by the Arbitration Tribunal ("the Tribunal") or such person as the Tribunal may designate for that purpose. The mediation shall be conducted in such place and in accordance with such procedure and on such terms as the parties may agree or, in the event of disagreement, as may be set by the mediator.

(iv) If the other party does not agree to mediate, that fact may be brought to the attention of the Tribunal and may be taken into account by the Tribunal when allocating the costs of the arbitration as between the parties.

(v) The mediation shall not affect the right of either party to seek such relief or take such steps as it considers necessary to protect its interest.

(vi) Either party may advise the Tribunal that they have agreed to mediation. The arbitration procedure shall continue during the conduct of the mediation but the Tribunal may take the mediation timetable into account when setting the timetable for steps in the arbitration.

(vii) Unless otherwise agreed or specified in the mediation terms, each party shall bear its own costs incurred in the mediation and the parties shall share equally the mediator's costs and expenses.

(viii) The mediation process shall be without prejudice and confidential and no information or documents disclosed during it shall be revealed to the Tribunal except to the extent that they are disclosable under the law and procedure governing the arbitration.

(Note: The parties should be aware that the mediation process may not necessarily interrupt time limits.)

(e) If Box 21 in Part I is not appropriately filled in, Sub-clause 23(a) of this Clause shall apply.

Note: Sub-clauses 23(a), 23(b) and 23(c) are alternatives; indicate alternative agreed in Box 21. Sub-clause 23(d) shall apply in all cases.

24. Notices

PART II
SHIPMAN 2009
Standard ship management agreement

(a) All notices given by either party or their agents to the other party or their agents in accordance with the provisions of this Agreement shall be in writing and shall, unless specifically provided in this Agreement to the contrary, be sent to the address for that other party as set out in Boxes 22 and 23 or as appropriate or to such other address as the other party may designate in writing.

A notice may be sent by registered or recorded mail, facsimile, electronically or delivered by hand in accordance with this Sub-clause 24(a).

(b) Any notice given under this Agreement shall take effect on receipt by the other party and shall be deemed to have been received:

(i) if posted, on the seventh (7th) day after posting;

(ii) if sent by facsimile or electronically, on the day of transmission; and

(iii) if delivered by hand, on the day of delivery.

And in each case proof of posting, handing in or transmission shall be proof that notice has been given, unless proven to the contrary.

25. Entire Agreement

This Agreement constitutes the entire agreement between the parties and no promise, undertaking, representation, warranty or statement by either party prior to the date stated in Box 2 shall affect this Agreement. Any modification of this Agreement shall not be of any effect unless in writing signed by or on behalf of the parties.

26. Third Party Rights

Except to the extent provided in Sub-clauses 17(c) (Indemnity) and 17(d) (Himalaya), no third parties may enforce any term of this Agreement.

27. Partial Validity

If any provision of this Agreement is or becomes or is held by any arbitrator or other competent body to be illegal, invalid or unenforceable in any respect under any law or jurisdiction, the provision shall be deemed to be amended to the extent necessary to avoid such illegality, invalidity or unenforceability, or, if such amendment is not possible, the provision shall be deemed to be deleted from this Agreement to the extent of such illegality, invalidity or unenforceability, and the remaining provisions shall continue in full force and effect and shall not in any way be affected or impaired thereby.

28. Interpretation

In this Agreement:

(a) *Singular/Plural*
The singular includes the plural and vice versa as the context admits or requires.

(b) *Headings*
The index and headings to the clauses and appendices to this Agreement are for convenience only and shall not affect its construction or interpretation.

(c) *Day*
"Day" means a calendar day unless expressly stated to the contrary.

CERTIFICATE OF MALTA REGISTRY

Issued in terms of section 19 of the Merchant Shipping Act

Expiring on or before the

Official No.	Call Sign	IMO No.	Name of Ship	No., Year and Home Port

Previous Registry	Propulsion

When Built	Where Built	Builders

Number of Decks Number of Masts Rigged Stem Stern Build Framework & Description of vessel Number of Bulkheads		Metres	C'mtrs
	Length Article 2(8)		
	Moulded breadth Reg 2(3)		
	Moulded depth amidships to upper deck Reg 2(2)		
	Moulded draught Reg 4(2)		
	Length of engine room		

Number and Description of Engines	When Made	Name and Address of Makers	Reciprocating Engines
	Engines	Engines	No. and diameter of cylinder in each set Length of stroke
			Rotary Engines
Particulars of Boilers	Boilers	Boilers	No. of cylinders in each set
Description Number Loaded Pressure			Combined KW Estimated speed of ship

GROSS TONNAGE

NET TONNAGE

A detailed summary of the tonnage for this ship is shown on the International Tonnage Certificate

The number of seamen and apprentices for whom accommodation is certified:

I, the undersigned, Registrar of Ships at Valletta Malta, hereby certify that: the Ship, the description of which is prefixed to this my Certificate has been surveyed; the above description is in accordance with the Register; and the Name/s, Residence and Description of the Owners and their interest in the ship are as follows:-

Dated at Valletta, Malta this day of

Registrar of Maltese Ships

Notice – A Certificate of Registry is not a document of title. It does not necessarily contain notice of all changes of ownership, and in no case does it contain an official record of any mortgages affecting the ship. In case of any change of ownership it is important for the protection of the interest of all parties that the change should be registered according to law. Changes of ownership, address, or otherwise registered particulars should be notified to the Registrar of Maltese Ships at Valletta, Malta. Should the vessel be lost, taken by the enemy, burnt or broken up, or ceasing, whether by reason of a transfer to persons not qualified to own a Maltese ship, or for any reason, to be a Maltese ship, notice thereof, together with the Certificate of Registry, if in existence, should immediately be given to the Registrar or Maltese Ships at Valletta, Malta, under the penalties prescribed by law, for default.

Merchant Shipping Directorate, Malta Maritime Authority, Maritime House, Lascaris Wharf, Valletta VLT 01, Malta. Tel: +356 21250360, 99494317 Fax: +356 21241460 Tlx:1362 REGSHP MW

MS(R) 7ITC.

INTERNATIONAL TONNAGE CERTIFICATE
(1969)

No...............

RINA No. ____________

Issued under the provisions of the
INTERNATIONAL CONVENTION ON TONNAGE MEASUREMENTS OF SHIPS, 1969
under the authority of the Government of

____

for which the Convention came into force on ____________________

by the

RINA • REGISTRO ITALIANO NAVALE

IMO Number[1] ....

Name of ship	Distinctive number or letters	Port of registry (Regulation 2(3))	Date[2]

MAIN DIMENSIONS

Length (Article 2(8))	Breadth (Regulation 2(3))	Moulded depth amidships to upper deck (Regulation 2(2))

THE TONNAGES OF THE SHIP ARE:

GROSS TONNAGE ____________________

NET TONNAGE ____________________

This is to certify that the tonnages of this ship have been determined in accordance with the provisions of the International Convention on Tonnage Measurement of Ships, 1969.

The undersigned declares that he is duly authorized by the said Government to issued this Certificate.

Issued at: ____________________ on ______________

____

RINA • REGISTRO ITALIANO NAVALE

1 In accordance with the IMO Ship Identification Number Scheme, adopted by the Organization by resolution A.600 (15).

2 Date on which the keel was laid or the ship was at a similar stage of construction (Article 2 (6)), or date on which the ship underwent alterations or modifications of a major character (Article 3 (2) (b)), as appropriate.

Form STAITC – 02/2000

This certificate consists of 2 pages

IMO No.	Name of ship	Certificate No.	Page 2 /2

SPACES INCLUDED IN TONNAGE					
GROSS TONNAGE			NET TONNAGE		
Name of space	Location	Length	Name of space	Location	Length

EXCLUDED SPACES (Regulation 2 (5))	NUMBER OF PASSENGERS (Regulation 4 (1)) Number of passengers in cabins with not more than 8 berths ……………...... Number of other passengers ……………......
An asterisk (*) should be added to those spaces listed above which comprise both enclosed and excluded spaces.	MOULDED DRAUGHT (Regulation 4 (2))
Date and place of original measurement	………………………………………………………………
Date and place of last previous remeasurement	……………………………………………..........……………
REMARKS	

FORM GIVING PARTICULARS OF UNIFORM TONNAGE CALCULATION

RINA No.______________

ENCLOSE TO INTERNATIONAL TONNAGE CERTIFICATE No. ________________ RELEVANT TO

____

GROSS TONNAGE

Item No.	Name of Space	Location	Length	Moulded Volume
	Underdeck			
	Poop			
	Bridge			
	Forecastle			
	Deckhouses			
	Hatches, etc.			
		Total Volume		

NET TONNAGE

Item No.	Name of Space	Location	Length	Moulded Volume
	No. 1 Hold			
	No. 2 Hold, etc.			
	No.1 Tween Decks			
	No. 2 Tween Decks, etc.			
	Hatches, etc.			
		Total Volume		

Lloyd's Register

Certificate No:

Page 1 of 3

Certificate of Class

This certificate is issued to the
LR Number
Date of Build
Port of Registry
Gross tons

to confirm that having been surveyed by and having been found in compliance with the Rules and Regulation for the Classification of Ships, the aforesaid ship has been assigned the class

Date Special Survey Assigned
This Certificate is valid until*

* Unless extended after completion of a Special Survey (see page 3) or in accordance with Part 1, Chapter 2, Section 3.5.9 of the Rules and Regulations (see page 3) and is subject to surveys as prescribed (see page 2) being satisfactorily completed. (See notes 1 to 4, page 3)

Issued at on

Surveyor to

A member of the Lloyd's Register Group

Note: 1. To establish the classification status of this ship, the ClassDirect Live web site and the Interim Certificates issued on Completion of classification surveys should be consulted in addition to this certificate. Access to ClassDirect Live is available via http://www.cdlive.lr.org.

Form 1717 (2004.01)

Lloyd's Register

Certificate No:

Page 2 of 3

Ships Name

LR number

Annual/Intermediate survey endorsements

1st Annual Survey endorsement

Signed: ______________________

Place of Survey

Date

2nd Annual Survey/Intermediate Survey* endorsement

Signed: ______________________

Place of Survey

Date

3rd Annual Survey/Intermediate Survey* endorsement

Signed: ______________________

Place of Survey

Date

4th Annual Survey endorsement

Signed: ______________________

Place of Survey

Date

* Delete as appropriate

Form 1717 (2004.01)

Lloyd's Register

Certificate No:

Page 3 of 3

Ships Name

LR number

Extension of special survey completion date

In accordance with the Rules and Regulations for the Classification of ships this certificate is extended until (see note 2).

Place of survey

Signed: ______________________________

Date

Special survey completion

This Special Survey having been completed, this certificate is extended until.

Place of survey

Signed: ______________________________

Date

Notes:

1 In accordance with the Rules and Ragulation for the Classification of Ship's, class will be automatically suspended and this certificate becomes invalid if not endorsed annually within three months of the due date of the Annual or Intermediate Surveys.

2 This certificate expires on the due date of the Special Survey. Consideration can be given at the discretion of the Committee to any exceptional circumstances justifying an extension to the Special Survey completion date for a maximum period of three months beyond the validity of this certificate.

3 Prior to the endorsement of this certificate all overdue hull and machinery surveys should be dealt with or postponed by agreement.

4 In normal circumstances the Annual or Intermediate Survey is to be held in conjunction with the Periodical Load Line Inspection and the Safety Construction Annual Survey.

Form 1717 (2004.01)

OMB APPROVAL 1625-0017

CARGO SHIP SAFETY EQUIPMENT CERTIFICATE

This Certificate shall be supplemented by a Record of Equipment (Form E)

Issued under the provisions of the International Convention for the Safety of Life at Sea, 1974 as modified by the Protocol of 1988 relating thereto under the authority of the Government of:

THE UNITED STATES OF AMERICA

by the

UNITED STATES COAST GUARD

Particulars of Ship

Name of Ship	Distinctive Numbers or Letters	Port of Registry	Gross Tonnage
RYLAN T	1128385	NVDC	871

Deadweight of Ship *(metric tons) (Note 1)*	Length of Ship *(regulation III/3.12)*	IMO Number *(Note 2)*	Date on which keel was laid *(Note 3)*
	154.8		31Jul2002

Type of Ship

- ☐ Bulk Carrier
- ☐ Oil Tanker
- ☐ Chemical Tanker
- ☐ Gas Carrier
- ☒ Cargo ship other than any of the above.

Notes:

1. For Oil Tankers, Chemical Tankers and Gas Carriers only.
2. In accordance with resolution A.600(15):IMO Ship Identification Number Scheme, this information may be included voluntarily.
3. Date on which keel was laid or ship was at a similar stage of construction or, where applicable, date on which work for a conversion or an alteration or modification of a major character was commenced.

An agency may not conduct or sponsor, and a person is not required to respond to, a collection of information unless it displays a valid OMB control number.

The Coast Guard estimates that the average burden for this report is 5 minutes. You may submit any comments concerning the accuracy of this burden estimate or any suggestions for reducing the burden to: Commandant (G-MOC), U.S. Coast Guard, Washington, DC 20593-0001 or Office of Management and Budget, Paperwork Reduction Project (2115-0056), Washington DC 20503.

U.S. DEPT. OF HOMELAND SECURITY, USCG, CG-3347 (Rev. 04-09)
PREVIOUS EDITIONS ARE OBSOLETE

Page 1 of 5

SR(GMDSS)check

ClassNK

CHECK LIST FOR **INITIAL/ RENEWAL SURVEY OF PASSENGER / CARGO SHIP SAFETY RADIO EQUIPMENT (GMDSS)**
Under the provision of the SOLAS 1974 as amended and the Rules for Radio Installations for GMDSS ships

Tests and measurements are to be done in accordance with the applicable provisions of the Guidance for Radio Installations. The provision numbers quoted in the round brackets correspond to those of the Guidance unless otherwise indicated particularly.

Ship's Name		Ship's Flag	
Ship's Owner			
Class No.		IMO No.	
Distinctive No.		Gross Tonnage	

Inspection Place : ....   Inspection Date : ....

Tested and measured by :

Radio Inspector : ....   Radio Firm : ....

Signature : ....

1. Station License (2.1.5)

Validity of radio station license	☐ Valid (until)		
Call Sign		MMSI	
Selcall No. for NBDP *		ID for DSC(VHF) *	
1st ID for INMARSAT-B/F		ID for DSC(MF/HF) *	
2nd ID for INMARSAT- B/F		ID for DSC(MF)*	
ID for Satellite EPIRB		ID for Satellite EPIRB	
ID for 1st INMARSAT-C		ID for 2nd INMARSAT-C	
ID for LRIT		ID for AIS-SART**	
Type of ship			
Sea area in which the ship is certified to operate ☐ A1 ☐ A1+A2 ☐ A1+A2+A3 ☐ A1+A2+A3+A4			
Maintenance requirements			
☐ Duplication of equipment:	VHF and		
☐ Shore-based maintenance:	Maintenance agreement	☐ Yes	☐ No
☐ At-sea electronic maintenance:	Measuring instruments	☐ Yes	☐ No
	Technical document	☐ Yes	☐ No
	Special spare parts & tools	☐ Yes	☐ No

* If assigned separately from the MMSI. ** If fitted.

2 Radio Personnel (2.1.5-1(3))

2.1 Radio operator

☆	Name and Nationality	Class and Certificate No.	Certificate issued by
	(Nationality:)	(No.)	
	(Nationality:)	(No.)	
	(Nationality:)	(No.)	

☆ *Check with "X" for the radio operator who is designated to have primary responsibility for radio-communications during distress incidents.*

2.2 Minimum number of persons with required qualifications to operate the radio installations:

....

INTERNATIONAL OIL POLLUTION PREVENTION CERTIFICATE

No CTG0/MSL/2013062119 p.m.

Issued under the provisions of the International Convention for the Prevention of Pollution from Ships, 1973 as modified by the Protocol of 1978 relating thereto, as amended, (hereinafter referred to as "the Convention") under the authority of the Government of

ANTIGUA AND BARBUDA

By BUREAU VERITAS

(Note : This Certificate shall be supplemented by a Record of Construction and Equipment.)

Name of Ship BV No : **36Y339**	Distinctive Number or Letters	Port of Registry	Gross Tonnage	IMO Number
SUZIE Q	V2ZK4	ST.JOHN'S	1980	8205204

Deadweight of ship (metric tons) *(for oil tankers)* : -

TYPE OF SHIP

☐ Oil tanker
☐ Ship other than oil tanker with cargo tanks coming under Regulation 2(2) of Annex I of the Convention
☒ Ship other than any of the above

THIS IS TO CERTIFY

1. That the ship has been surveyed in accordance with Regulation 6 of Annex I of the Convention; and
2. That the survey shows that the structure, equipment systems, fittings, arrangement and material of the ship and the condition thereof are in all respects satisfactory and that the ship complies with the applicable requirements of Annex I of the Convention.

This Certificate is valid until **21 May 2018 ***
subject to surveys in accordance with Regulation 6 of Annex I of the Convention.
Completion date of the survey on which this certificate is based : 24/06/2013

Issued at Cartagena, Colombia, on the 24 June 2013

Valid only when the Supplement No. CTG0/MSL/2013062108 p.m. is available for inspection.

The undersigned declares that he is duly authorized by the said Government to issue this certificate.

BUREAU VERITAS

BUREAU VERITAS PARIS 1828 CARTAGENA COLOMBIA REGISTRE INTERNATIONAL

Mauricio SALAZAR
By Order of the Secretary

BUREAU VERITAS 1828

*** *Insert the date of expiry as specified by the Administration in accordance with regulation 10(1) of Annex I of the Convention. The day and month of this date correspond to the anniversary date as defined in regulation 1(27) of annex I of the Convention, unless amended in accordance with regulation 10(8) of Annex I of the Convention.*

NE 7413D - Page 1/4

DNV·GL

Certificate No. 114984/128/14

INTERIM
SAFETY MANAGEMENT CERTIFICATE

Issued under the provisions of the
INTERNATIONAL CONVENTION FOR THE SAFETY OF LIFE AT SEA, 1974,
as amended

under the authority of the Government of the

HELLENIC REPUBLIC

by DNV GL

Name of Ship	Distinctive Number or Letters	Port of Registry	Gross Tonnage	IMO Number
HYUNDAI SMART	**SVBY2**	**Piraeus**	**141770**	**9475686**

Name and address of the Company (see paragraph 1.1.2 of the ISM Code)	Company identification number	Type of Ship *
Danaos Shipping Co. Ltd. **14, Akti Kondyli Street** **18545 Piraeus** **GREECE**	**0022438**	**Other cargo ship**

THIS IS TO CERTIFY THAT the requirements of paragraph 14.4 of the ISM Code have been met and that the Document of Compliance / Interim Document of Compliance of the Company is relevant to this ship.

This Interim Safety Management Certificate is valid until **7th November, 2014** subject to the Document of Compliance / Interim Document of Compliance remaining valid.

Issued at **Hamburg**, **8th May, 2014**

Seal

DNV GL Representative
(Reiner Großhäuser)

The validity of this Interim Safety Management Certificate is extended to:

Date of extension:

Seal

DNV GL Representative
( )

Insert the type of ship from: Passenger ship, passenger high-speed craft, cargo high-speed craft, bulk carrier, oil tanker, chemical tanker, gas carrier, mobile offshore drilling unit, other cargo ship.

ww.dnvgl.com

Form No. S772 / 2013-11 Page 1 of 1

PANAMA MARITIME AUTHORITY

Technical Office – Segumar Panama

Pan-Canal Building 4th fl., Omar Torrijos Herrera Ave. Albrook
Panama City, Panama

Tel: (507) 501-5358
Fax: (507) 501-5363/64
E-mail: msm@segumar.com

Application for Minimum Safe Manning Certificate

Please fill and Return by E-mail

Applicant Name / Address / e-mail:	**Name of Ship:** ______
	Type of Ship: ______
	Call Letters: ______
	IMO No.: ______
Operating Company Name: *(copy of Safety Management Certificate, shall be submitted if applicable)*	**Gross Tonnage:**
	ITC 69 ______
	National ______

GENERAL INFORMATION:

1. Have you ever applied for MSMC for this ship? **YES** ☐ **NO** ☐

If answer is Yes fill the following

MSMC Certificate No.: ______ Previous Tonnage: ______

MACHINERY:

1. Main engine's power (KW): **KW:** ______
2. Ship certified for UMS (unattended Machinery Space Operations)? **Yes** ☐ **No** ☐
3. Ship is fitted with GMDSS equipment? **Yes** ☐ **No** ☐

THE NATURE OF SERVICE AND TRADING AREA:

1. Distance between ports is less than 600 miles only? **Yes** ☐ **No** ☐
   If **yes,** describe the specific trading area: ______
2. Any other special condition or requirements? ______

PROPOSED MANNING:

DECK		ENGINE	
Capacity/regulation	Number of Persons	Capacity/regulation	Number of Persons
Master (II/2)		**Chief Engineer (III/2)**	
Master (II/3)		**2nd Engineer (III/2)**	
Chief Mate (II/2)		**Chief Engineer (III/3)**	
Chief Mate (II/3)		**2nd Engineer (III/3)**	
Deck Officer (II/1)		**Engineer Officer (III/1)**	
A.B. Seamen (II/4)		**Oiler (III/4)**	
Ordinary Seaman (VI/1)			

Fee for each certificate is USD$150.00 Payable to: "PANAMA MARITIME AUTHORITY" DRAWN ON A USA BANK

THE ROUTING & ABA NUMBERS OF THE USA BANK NEED TO BE MICRO-INCLUIDED ON THE BOTTOM OF THE CHECK (NO REGULAR TYPE WRITER)

DOCUMENT OF COMPLIANCE FOR THE CARRIAGE OF DANGEROUS GOODS

No. RINA No.

issued in pursuance of the provisions of Regulation II-2/54.3 of the
INTERNATIONAL CONVENTION FOR SAFETY OF LIFE AT SEA, 1974,
as amended,

under the authority of the Government of the

Republic of PHILIPPINES

by

RINA • REGISTRO ITALIANO NAVALE

Name of ship	Distinctive number or letters	Port of registry	Gross tonnage

IMO Number [1]	Type of ship

this is to Certify:

1. that the construction and equipment of the above mentioned ship were found to comply with the provisions of Regulation II-2/54 of the International Convention for the Safety of Life at Sea, 1974, as amended; and,

2. that the ship is suitable for the carriage of those classes of dangerous goods as specified on page 2 of this document, subject to any provisions in the International Maritime Dangerous Goods (IMDG) Code and the Code of Safe Practice for Solid Bulk Cargoes (BC Code) for individual substances also being complied with.

This Certificate is valid until:

Issued at: on:

RINA • REGISTRO ITALIANO NAVALE

1 In accordance with the IMO Ship Identification Number Scheme, adopted by the Organization by resolution A.600(15).

Form DGC PH - 02/2000

This certificate consists of 7 pages

SPACES IDENTIFIED ON HOLD PLAN OF PAGE 3

CLASS	CARGO SPACES					
	A	B	C	D	E	F
1.1+1.6 Esplosives	...	...	...	...	...	...
1.4 S Esplosives	...	...	...	...	...	...
2.1 Flammable gases	...	...	...	...	...	...
2.2 Not flammable gases	...	...	...	...	...	...
2.3 Toxic gases	...	...	...	...	...	...
3.1÷3.2 Flammable liquids (FP<23°C)	...	...	...	...	...	...
3.3 Flammable liquids (FP23°C÷61ºC)	...	...	...	...	...	...
4.1 Flammable solids	...	...	...	...	...	...
4.2 Spontaneus combustion substances	...	...	...	...	...	...
4.3 Substances reactiv with water	...	...	...	...	...	...
5.1 Oxidizing substances	...	...	...	...	...	...
5.2 Organic peroxides	...	...	...	...	...	...
6.1 Toxic substances (liquids)	...	...	...	...	...	...
6.1 Toxic substances (liquids FP<23°C)	...	...	...	...	...	...
6.1 Toxic substances (liquids FP23°C÷61°C)	...	...	...	...	...	...
6.1 Toxic substances (solids)	...	...	...	...	...	...
6.2 Infectious substances (*)	...	...	...	...	...	...
7 Radioactive materials (*)	...	...	...	...	...	...
8 Corrosives (liquids)	...	...	...	...	...	...
8 Corrosives (liquids FP<23°C)	...	...	...	...	...	...
8 Toxic substances (liquids FP23°C÷61 °C)	...	...	...	...	...	...
8 Corrosives (solids)	...	...	...	...	...	...
9 Miscellaneous dangerous substances	...	...	...	...	...	...
MHB	...	...	...	...	...	...

P = packaged goods; **B** = in bulk (**); **A** = packaged goods and in bulk (**);
T = portable tanks and/or tank vehicles; **X** = not allowed

(*) There are no special requirements in the above mentioned Regulation II-2/54 for the carriage of dangerous goods of classes 6.2 and 7, and for the carriage of dangerous goods in limited quantities, as required in Section 18 of the General Introduction of the IMDG Code.
(**) Cargoes in bulk are listed individually by name and class in the attached sheet.

Form DGC PH - 02/2000 RINA No.

IMO No. Name of ship Document No. Page 3/7

Name of ship Document No.

CARGO SPACES

Underdeck spaces

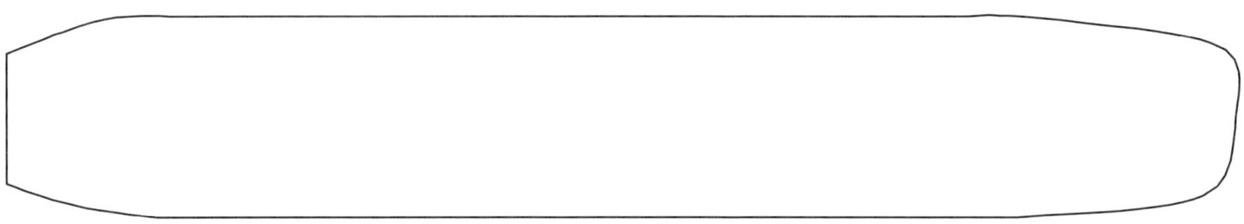

Weatherdeck spaces

Spaces	Description of cargo spaces
A	
B	
C	
D	
E	
F	

IMO No.	Name of ship	Document No.	Page 7/7

NOTES

THIS IS TO CERTIFY that at on the basis of a survey carried out on the occasion of the class intermediate survey, the ship was found to comply with the relevant provisions of the Convention.

Place Date	Signature and seal

York-Antwerp Rules 2016

Rule of Interpretation

In the adjustment of general average the following Rules shall apply to the exclusion of any law and practice inconsistent therewith.

Except as provided by the Rule Paramount and the numbered Rules, general average shall be adjusted according to the lettered Rules.

Rule Paramount

In no case shall there be any allowance for sacrifice or expenditure unless reasonably made or incurred.

Rule A

1. There is a general average act when, and only when, any extraordinary sacrifice or expenditure is intentionally and reasonably made or incurred for the common safety for the purpose of preserving from peril the property involved in a common maritime adventure.

2. General average sacrifices and expenditures shall be borne by the different contributing interests on the basis hereinafter provided.

Rule B

1. There is a common maritime adventure when one or more vessels are towing or pushing another vessel or vessels, provided that they are all involved in commercial activities and not in a salvage operation.

   When measures are taken to preserve the vessels and their cargoes, if any, from a common peril, these Rules shall apply.

2. If the vessels are in common peril and one is disconnected either to increase the disconnecting vessel's safety alone, or the safety of all vessels in the common maritime adventure, the disconnection will be a general average act.

3. Where vessels involved in a common maritime adventure resort to a port or place of refuge, allowances under these Rules may be made in relation to each of the vessels. Subject to the provisions of paragraphs 3 and 4 of Rule G, allowances in general average shall cease at the time that the common maritime adventure comes to an end.

Rule C

1. Only such losses, damages or expenses which are the direct consequence of the general average act shall be allowed as general average.

2. In no case shall there be any allowance in general average for losses, damages or expenses incurred in respect of damage to the environment or in consequence of the escape or release of pollutant substances from the property involved in the common maritime adventure.

3. Demurrage, loss of market, and any loss or damage sustained or expense incurred by reason of delay, whether on the voyage or subsequently, and any indirect loss whatsoever, shall not be allowed as general average.

Rule D

Rights to contribution in general average shall not be affected, though the event which gave rise to the sacrifice or expenditure may have been due to the fault of one of the parties to the common maritime adventure, but this shall not prejudice any remedies or defences which may be open against or to that party in respect of such fault.

Rule E

1. The onus of proof is upon the party claiming in general average to show that the loss or expense claimed is properly allowable as general average.

2. All parties to the common maritime adventure shall, as soon as possible, supply particulars of value in respect of their contributory interest and, if claiming in general average, shall give notice in writing to the average adjuster of the loss or expense in respect of which they claim contribution, and supply evidence in support thereof.

3. Failing notification, or if any party does not supply particulars in support of a notified claim, within 12 months of the termination of the common maritime adventure or payment of the expense, the average adjuster shall be at liberty to estimate the extent of the allowance on the basis of the information available to the adjuster. Particulars of value shall be provided within 12 months of the termination of the common maritime adventure, failing which the average adjuster shall be at liberty to estimate the contributory value on the same basis. Such estimates shall be communicated to the party in question in writing. Estimates may only be challenged within two months of receipt of the communication and only on the grounds that they are manifestly incorrect.

4. Any party to the common maritime adventure pursuing a recovery from a third party in respect of sacrifice or expenditure claimed in general average, shall so advise the average adjuster and, in the event that a recovery is achieved, shall supply to the average adjuster full particulars of the recovery within two months of receipt of the recovery.

Rule F

Any additional expense incurred in place of another expense which would have been allowable as general average shall be deemed to be general average and so allowed without regard to the saving, if any, to other interests, but only up to the amount of the general average expense avoided.

Rule G

1. General average shall be adjusted as regards both loss and contribution upon the basis of values at the time and place when and where the common maritime adventure ends.

2. This rule shall not affect the determination of the place at which the average adjustment is to be prepared.

3. When a ship is at any port or place in circumstances which would give rise to an allowance in general average under the provisions of Rules X and XI, and the cargo or part thereof is forwarded to destination by other means, rights and liabilities in general average shall, subject to cargo interests being notified if practicable, remain as nearly as possible the same as they would have been in the absence of such forwarding, as if the common maritime adventure had continued in the original ship for so long as justifiable under the contract of carriage and the applicable law.

4. The proportion attaching to cargo of the allowances made in general average by reason of applying the third paragraph of this Rule shall be limited to the cost which would have been borne by the owners of cargo if the cargo had been forwarded at their expense. This limit shall not apply to any allowances made under Rule F.

Rule I – Jettison of Cargo

No jettison of cargo shall be allowed as general average, unless such cargo is carried in accordance with the recognised custom of the trade.

Rule II – Loss or Damage by Sacrifices for the Common Safety

Loss of or damage to the property involved in the common maritime adventure by or in consequence of a sacrifice made for the common safety, and by water which goes down a ship's hatches opened or other opening made for the purpose of making a jettison for the common safety, shall be allowed as general average.

Rule III – Extinguishing Fire on Shipboard

Damage done to a ship and cargo, or either of them, by water or otherwise, including damage by beaching or scuttling a burning ship, in extinguishing a fire on board the ship, shall be allowed as general average; except that no allowance shall be made for damage by smoke however caused or by heat of the fire.

Rule IV – Cutting Away Wreck

Loss or damage sustained by cutting away wreck or parts of the ship which have been previously carried away or are effectively lost by accident shall not be allowed as general average.

Rule V – Voluntary Stranding

When a ship is intentionally run on shore for the common safety, whether or not she might have been driven on shore, the consequent loss or damage to the property involved in the common maritime adventure shall be allowed in general average.

Rule VI – Salvage Remuneration

(a) Expenditure incurred by the parties to the common maritime adventure in the nature of salvage, whether under contract or otherwise, shall be allowed in general average provided that the salvage operations were carried out for the purpose of preserving from peril the property involved in the common maritime adventure and subject to the provisions of paragraphs (b), (c) and (d)

(b) Notwithstanding (a) above, where the parties to the common maritime adventure have separate contractual or legal liability to salvors, salvage shall only be allowed should any of the following arise:

(i) there is a subsequent accident or other circumstances resulting in loss or damage to property during the voyage that results in significant differences between salved and contributory values,

(ii) there are significant general average sacrifices,

(iii) salved values are manifestly incorrect and there is a significantly incorrect apportionment of salvage expenses,

(iv) any of the parties to the salvage has paid a significant proportion of salvage due from another party,

(v) a significant proportion of the parties have satisfied the salvage claim on substantially different terms, no regard being had to interest, currency correction or legal costs of either the salvor or the contributing interest.

(c) Salvage expenditures referred to in paragraph (a) above shall include any salvage remuneration in which the skill and efforts of the salvors in preventing or minimising damage to the environment such as is referred to in Article 13 paragraph 1(b) of the International Convention on Salvage, 1989 have been taken into account.

(d) Special compensation payable to a salvor by the shipowner under Article 14 of the International Convention on Salvage, 1989 to the extent specified in paragraph 4 of that Article or under any other provision similar in substance (such as SCOPIC) shall not be allowed in general average and shall not be considered a salvage expenditure as referred to in paragraph (a) of this Rule.

Rule VII – Damage to Machinery and Boilers

Damage caused to any machinery and boilers of a ship which is ashore and in a position of peril, in endeavouring to refloat, shall be allowed in general average when shown to have arisen from an actual intention to float the ship for the common safety at the risk of such damage; but where a ship is afloat no loss or damage caused by working the propelling machinery and boilers shall in any circumstances be allowed as general average.

Rule VIII – Expenses Lightening a Ship when Ashore, and Consequent Damage

When a ship is ashore and cargo and ship's fuel and stores or any of them are discharged as a general average act, the extra cost of lightening, lighter hire and reshipping (if incurred), and any loss or damage to the property involved in the common maritime adventure in consequence thereof, shall be allowed as general average.

Rule IX – Cargo, Ship's Materials and Stores Used for Fuel

Cargo, ship's materials and stores, or any of them, necessarily used for fuel for the common safety at a time of peril shall be allowed as general average, but when such an allowance is made for the cost of ship's materials and stores the general average shall be credited with the estimated cost of the fuel which would otherwise have been consumed in prosecuting the intended voyage.

Rule X – Expenses at Port of Refuge, etc.

(a) (i) When a ship shall have entered a port or place of refuge or shall have returned to her port or place of loading in consequence of accident, sacrifice or other extraordinary circumstances which render that necessary for the common safety, the expenses of entering such port or place shall be allowed as general average; and when she shall have sailed thence with her original cargo, or a part of it, the corresponding expenses of leaving such port or place consequent upon such entry or return shall likewise be allowed as general average.

(ii) When a ship is at any port or place of refuge and is necessarily removed to another port or place because repairs cannot be carried out in the first port or place, the provisions of this Rule shall be applied to the second port or place as if it were a port or place of refuge and the cost of such removal including temporary repairs and towage shall be allowed as general average. The provisions of Rule XI shall be applied to the prolongation of the voyage occasioned by such removal.

(ii) Fuel and stores consumed during the extra period of detention shall be allowed as general average, except such fuel and stores as are consumed in effecting repairs not allowable in general average.

(iii) Port charges incurred during the extra period of detention shall likewise be allowed as general average except such charges as are incurred solely by reason of repairs not allowable in general average.

(iv) Provided that when damage to the ship is discovered at a port or place of loading or call without any accident or other extraordinary circumstance connected with such damage having taken place during the voyage, then the wages and maintenance of master, officers and crew and fuel and stores consumed and port charges incurred during the extra detention for repairs to damages so discovered shall not be allowable as general average, even if the repairs are necessary for the safe prosecution of the voyage.

(v) When the ship is condemned or does not proceed on her original voyage, the wages and maintenance of the master, officers and crew and fuel and stores consumed and port charges shall be allowed as general average only up to the date of the ship's condemnation or of the abandonment of the voyage or up to the date of completion of discharge of cargo if the condemnation or abandonment takes place before that date.

(c) (i) For the purpose of these Rules wages shall include all payments made to or for the benefit of the master, officers and crew, whether such payments be imposed by law upon the shipowners or be made under the terms of articles of employment.

(ii) For the purpose of these Rules, port charges shall include all customary or additional expenses incurred for the common safety or to enable a vessel to enter or remain at a port of refuge or call in the circumstances outlined in Rule XI(b)(i).

(d) The cost of measures undertaken to prevent or minimise damage to the environment shall be allowed in general average when incurred in any or all of the following circumstances:

(i) as part of an operation performed for the common safety which, had it been undertaken by a party outside the common maritime adventure, would have entitled such party to a salvage reward;

(ii) as a condition of entry into or departure from any port or place in the circumstances prescribed in Rule X(a);

(iii) as a condition of remaining at any port or place in the circumstances prescribed in Rule XI(b), provided that when there is an actual escape or release of pollutant substances, the cost of any additional measures required on that account to

(ii) Fuel and stores consumed during the extra period of detention shall be allowed as general average, except such fuel and stores as are consumed in effecting repairs not allowable in general average.

(iii) Port charges incurred during the extra period of detention shall likewise be allowed as general average except such charges as are incurred solely by reason of repairs not allowable in general average.

(iv) Provided that when damage to the ship is discovered at a port or place of loading or call without any accident or other extraordinary circumstance connected with such damage having taken place during the voyage, then the wages and maintenance of master, officers and crew and fuel and stores consumed and port charges incurred during the extra detention for repairs to damages so discovered shall not be allowable as general average, even if the repairs are necessary for the safe prosecution of the voyage.

(v) When the ship is condemned or does not proceed on her original voyage, the wages and maintenance of the master, officers and crew and fuel and stores consumed and port charges shall be allowed as general average only up to the date of the ship's condemnation or of the abandonment of the voyage or up to the date of completion of discharge of cargo if the condemnation or abandonment takes place before that date.

(c) (i) For the purpose of these Rules wages shall include all payments made to or for the benefit of the master, officers and crew, whether such payments be imposed by law upon the shipowners or be made under the terms of articles of employment.

(ii) For the purpose of these Rules, port charges shall include all customary or additional expenses incurred for the common safety or to enable a vessel to enter or remain at a port of refuge or call in the circumstances outlined in Rule XI(b)(i).

(d) The cost of measures undertaken to prevent or minimise damage to the environment shall be allowed in general average when incurred in any or all of the following circumstances:

(i) as part of an operation performed for the common safety which, had it been undertaken by a party outside the common maritime adventure, would have entitled such party to a salvage reward;

(ii) as a condition of entry into or departure from any port or place in the circumstances prescribed in Rule X(a);

(iii) as a condition of remaining at any port or place in the circumstances prescribed in Rule XI(b), provided that when there is an actual escape or release of pollutant substances, the cost of any additional measures required on that account to prevent or minimise pollution or environmental damage shall not be allowed as general average;

(iv) necessarily in connection with the handling on board, discharging, storing or reloading of cargo, fuel or stores whenever the cost of those operations is allowable as general average.

Rule XII – Damage to Cargo in Discharging, etc.

Damage to or loss of cargo, fuel or stores sustained in consequence of their handling, discharging, storing, reloading and stowing shall be allowed as general average, when and only when the cost of those measures respectively is allowed as general average.

Rule XIII – Deductions from Cost of Repairs

(a) Repairs to be allowed in general average shall not be subject to deductions in respect of "new for old" where old material or parts are replaced by new unless the ship is over fifteen years old in which case there shall be a deduction of one third. The deductions shall be regulated by the age of the ship from the 31st December of the year of completion of construction to the date of the general average act, except for insulation, life and similar boats, communications and navigational apparatus and equipment, machinery and boilers for which the deductions shall be regulated by the age of the particular parts to which they apply.

(b) The deductions shall be made only from the cost of the new material or parts when finished and ready to be installed in the ship. No deduction shall be made in respect of provisions, stores, anchors and chain cables. Drydock and slipway dues and costs of shifting the ship shall be allowed in full.

(c) The costs of cleaning, painting or coating of bottom shall not be allowed in general average unless the bottom has been painted or coated within the 24 months preceding the date of the general average act in which case one half of such costs shall be allowed.

Rule XIV – Temporary Repairs

(a) Where temporary repairs are effected to a ship at a port of loading, call or refuge, for the common safety, or of damage caused by general average sacrifice, the cost of such repairs shall be allowed as general average.

(b) Where temporary repairs of accidental damage are effected in order to enable the common maritime adventure to be completed, the cost of such repairs shall be allowed as general average without regard to the saving, if any, to other interests, but only up to the saving in expense which would have been incurred and allowed in general average if such repairs had not been effected there.

(c) No deductions "new for old" shall be made from the cost of temporary repairs allowable as general average.

Rule XV – Loss of Freight

Loss of freight arising from damage to or loss of cargo shall be allowed as general average, either when caused by a general average act, or when the damage to or loss of cargo is so allowed.

Deduction shall be made from the amount of gross freight lost, of the charges which the owner thereof would have incurred to earn such freight, but has, in consequence of the sacrifice, not incurred.

Rule XVI – Amount to be Allowed for Cargo Lost or Damaged by Sacrifice

(a) (i) The amount to be allowed as general average for damage to or loss of cargo sacrificed shall be the loss which has been sustained thereby based on the value at the time of discharge, ascertained from the commercial invoice rendered to the receiver or if there is no such invoice from the shipped value. Such commercial invoice may be deemed by the average adjuster to reflect the value at the time of discharge irrespective of the place of final delivery under the contract of carriage.

(ii) The value at the time of discharge shall include the cost of insurance and freight except insofar as such freight is at the risk of interests other than the cargo.

(b) When cargo so damaged is sold and the amount of the damage has not been otherwise agreed, the loss to be allowed in general average shall be the difference between the net proceeds of sale and the net sound value as computed in the first paragraph of this Rule.

Rule XVII – Contributory Values

(a) (i) The contribution to a general average shall be made upon the actual net values of the property at the termination of the common maritime adventure except that the value of cargo shall be the value at the time of discharge, ascertained from the commercial invoice rendered to the receiver or if there is no such invoice from the shipped value. Such commercial invoice may be deemed by the average adjuster to reflect the value at the time of discharge irrespective of the place of final delivery under the contract of carriage.

(ii) The value of the cargo shall include the cost of insurance and freight unless and insofar as such freight is at the risk of interests other than the cargo, deducting therefrom any loss or damage suffered by the cargo prior to or at the time of discharge. Any cargo may be excluded from contributing to general average should the average adjuster consider that the cost of including it in the adjustment would be likely to be disproportionate to its eventual contribution.

(iii) The value of the ship shall be assessed without taking into account the beneficial or detrimental effect of any demise or time charterparty to which the ship may be committed.

(b) To these values shall be added the amount allowed as general average for property sacrificed, if not already included, deduction being made from the freight and passage money at risk of such charges and crew's wages as would not have been incurred in earning the freight had the ship and cargo been totally lost at the date of the general average act and have not been allowed as general average; deduction being also made from the value of the property of all extra charges incurred in respect thereof subsequently to the general average act, except such charges as are allowed in general average. Where payment for salvage services has not been allowed as general average by reason of paragraph (b) of Rule VI, deductions in respect of payment for salvage services shall be limited to the amount paid to the salvors including interest and salvors' costs.

(c) In the circumstances envisaged in the third paragraph of Rule G, the cargo and other property shall contribute on the basis of its value upon delivery at original destination unless sold or otherwise disposed of short of that destination, and the ship shall contribute upon its actual net value at the time of completion of discharge of cargo.

(d) Where cargo is sold short of destination, however, it shall contribute upon the actual net proceeds of sale, with the addition of any amount allowed as general average.

(e) Mails, passengers' luggage and accompanied personal effects and accompanied private motor vehicles shall not contribute to general average.

Rule XVIII – Damage to Ship

The amount to be allowed as general average for damage or loss to the ship, her machinery and/or gear caused by a general average act shall be as follows:

(a) When repaired or replaced,

The actual reasonable cost of repairing or replacing such damage or loss, subject to deductions in accordance with Rule XIII;

(b) When not repaired or replaced,

The reasonable depreciation arising from such damage or loss, but not exceeding the estimated cost of repairs. But where the ship is an actual total loss or when the cost of repairs of the damage would exceed the value of the ship when repaired, the amount to be allowed as general average shall be the difference between the estimated sound value of the ship after deducting therefrom the estimated cost of repairing damage which is not general average and the value of the ship in her damaged state which may be measured by the net proceeds of sale, if any.

Rule XIX – Undeclared or Wrongfully Declared Cargo

(a) Damage or loss caused to goods loaded without the knowledge of the shipowner or his agent or to goods wilfully misdescribed at the time of shipment shall not be allowed as general average, but such goods shall remain liable to contribute, if saved.

(b) Where goods have been wrongfully declared at the time of shipment at a value which is lower than their real value, any general average loss or damage shall be allowed on the basis of their declared value, but such goods shall contribute on the basis of their actual value.

Rule XX – Provision of Funds

(a) The capital loss sustained by the owners of goods sold for the purpose of raising funds to defray general average disbursements shall be allowed in general average.

(b) The cost of insuring general average disbursements shall be allowed in general average.

Rule XXI – Interest on Losses Allowed in General Average

(a) Interest shall be allowed on expenditure, sacrifices and allowances in general average until three months after the date of issue of the general average adjustment, due allowance being made for any payment on account by the contributory interests or from the general average deposit fund.

(b) The rate for calculating interest accruing during each calendar year shall be the 12-month ICE LIBOR for the currency in which the adjustment is prepared, as announced on the first banking day of that calendar year, increased by four percentage points. If the adjustment is prepared in a currency for which no ICE LIBOR is announced, the rate shall be the 12-month US Dollar ICE LIBOR, increased by four percentage points.

Rule XXII – Treatment of Cash Deposits

(a) Where cash deposits have been collected in respect of general average, salvage or special charges, such sums shall be remitted forthwith to the average adjuster who shall deposit the sums into a special account, earning interest where possible, in the name of the average adjuster.

(b) The special account shall be constituted in accordance with the law regarding client or third party funds applicable in the domicile of the average adjuster. The account shall be held separately from the average adjuster's own funds, in trust or in compliance with similar rules of law providing for the administration of the funds of third parties.

(c) The sums so deposited, together with accrued interest, if any, shall be held as security for payment to the parties entitled thereto, of the general average, salvage or special charges in respect of which the deposits have been collected. Payments on account or refunds of deposits may only be made when such payments are certified in writing by the average adjuster and notified to the depositor requesting their approval. Upon the receipt of the depositor's approval, or in the absence of such approval within a period of 90 days, the average adjuster may deduct the amount of the payment on account or the final contribution from the deposit.

(d) All deposits and payments or refunds shall be without prejudice to the ultimate liability of the parties.

Rule XXIII – Time Bar for Contributing to General Average

(a) Subject always to any mandatory rule on time limitation contained in any applicable law:

(i) Any rights to general average contribution including any rights to claim under general average bonds and guarantees, shall be extinguished unless an action is brought by the party claiming such contribution within a period of one year after the date upon which the general average adjustment is issued. However, in no case shall such an action be brought after six years from the date of termination of the common maritime adventure.

(ii) These periods may be extended if the parties so agree after the termination of the common maritime adventure.

(b) This rule shall not apply as between the parties to the general average and their respective insurers.

The Hague Rules as Amended by the Brussels Protocol 1968

Commonly referred to as The Hague-Visby Rules

Article I

In these Rules the following words are employed, with the meanings set out below:

(a) 'Carrier' includes the owner or the charterer who enters into a contract of carriage with a shipper.

(b) 'Contract of carriage' applies only to contracts of carriage covered by a bill of lading or any similar document of title, in so far as such document relates to the carriage of goods by sea, including any bill of lading or any similar document as aforesaid issued under or pursuant to a charter party from the moment at which such bill of lading or similar document of title regulates the relations between a carrier and a holder of the same.

(c) 'Goods' includes goods, wares, merchandise, and articles of every kind whatsoever except live animals and cargo which by the contract of carriage is stated as being carried on deck and is so carried.

(d) 'Ship' means any vessel used for the carriage of goods by sea.

(e) 'Carriage of goods' covers the period from the time when the goods are loaded on to the time they are discharged from the ship.

Article II

Subject to the provisions of Article VI, under every contract of carriage of goods by sea the carrier, in relation to the loading, handling, stowage, carriage, custody, care and discharge of such goods, shall be subject to the responsibilities and liabilities and entitled to the rights and immunities hereinafter set forth.

Article III

1. The carrier shall be bound before and at the beginning of the voyage to exercise due diligence to:

(a) Make the ship seaworthy;

(b) Properly man, equip and supply the ship;

(c) Make the holds, refrigerating and cool chambers, and all other parts of the ship in which goods are carried, fit and safe for their reception, carriage and preservation.

2. Subject to the provisions of Article IV, the carrier shall properly and carefully load, handle, stow, carry, keep, care for, and discharge the goods carried.

3. After receiving the goods into his charge the carrier or the master or agent of the carrier shall, on demand of the shipper, issue to the shipper a bill of lading showing among other things:

(a) The leading marks necessary for identification of the goods as the same are furnished in writing by the shipper before the loading of such goods starts, provided such marks are stamped or otherwise shown clearly upon the goods if uncovered, or on the cases or coverings in which such goods are contained, in such a manner as should ordinarily remain legible until the end of the voyage.

(b) Either the number of packages or pieces, or the quantity, or weight, as the case may be, as furnished in writing by the shipper.

(c) The apparent order and condition of the goods.

Provided that no carrier, master or agent of the carrier shall be bound to state or show in the bill of lading any marks, number, quantity or weight which he has reasonable ground for suspecting not accurately to represent the goods actually received, or which he has had no reasonable means of checking.

4. Such a bill of lading shall be prima facie evidence of the receipt by the carrier of the goods as therein described in accordance with paragraph 3 (a), (b) and (c). However, proof to the contrary shall not be admissible when the bill of lading has been transferred to a third party acting in good faith.

5. The shipper shall be deemed to have guaranteed to the carrier the accuracy at the time of shipment of the marks, number, quantity and weight, as furnished by him, and the shipper shall indemnify the carrier against all loss, damages and expenses arising or resulting from inaccuracies in such particulars. The right of the carrier to such indemnity shall in no way limit his responsibility and liability under the contract of carriage to any person other than the shipper.

6. Unless notice of loss or damage and the general nature of such loss or damage be given in writing to the carrier or his agent at the port of discharge before or at the time of the removal of the goods into the custody of the person entitled to delivery thereof under the contract of carriage, or, if the loss or damage be not apparent, within three days, such removal shall be prima facie evidence of the delivery by the carrier of the goods as described in the bill of lading.

The notice in writing need not be given if the state of the goods has, at the time of their receipt, been the subject of joint survey or inspection.

Subject to paragraph 6bis the carrier and the ship shall in any event be discharged from all liability whatsoever in respect of the goods, unless suit is brought within one year of their delivery or of the date when they should have been delivered. This period, may however, be extended if the parties so agree after the cause of action has arisen.

In the case of any actual or apprehended loss or damage the carrier and the receiver shall give all reasonable facilities to each other for inspecting and tallying the goods.

6 bis. An action for indemnity against a third person may be brought even after the expiration of the year provided for in the preceding paragraph if brought within the time allowed by the law of the Court seized of the case. However, the time allowed shall be not less than three months, commencing from the day when the person bringing such action for indemnity has settled the claim or has been served with process in the action against himself.

7. After the goods are loaded the bill of lading to be issued by the carrier, master, or agent of the carrier, to the shipper shall, if the shipper so demands be a 'shipped' bill of lading, provided that if the shipper shall have previously taken up any document of title to such goods, he shall surrender the same as against the issue of the 'shipped' bill of lading, but at the option of the carrier such document of title may be noted at the port of shipment by the carrier, master, or agent with the name or names of the ship or ships upon which the goods have been shipped and the date or dates of shipment, and when so noted, if it shows the particulars mentioned in paragraph 3 of Article III, shall for the purpose of this article be deemed to constitute a 'shipped' bill of lading.

8. Any clause, covenant, or agreement in a contract of carriage relieving the carrier or the ship from liability for loss or damage to, or in connection with, goods arising from negligence, fault, or failure in the duties and obligations provided in this article or lessening such liability otherwise than as provided in these Rules, shall be null and void and of no effect. A benefit of insurance in favour of the carrier or similar clause shall be deemed to be a clause relieving the carrier from liability.

Article IV

1. Neither the carrier nor the ship shall be liable for loss or damage arising or resulting from unseaworthiness unless caused by want of due diligence on the part of the carrier to make the ship seaworthy, and to secure that the ship is properly manned, equipped and supplied, and to make the holds, refrigerating and cool chambers and all other parts of the ship in which goods are carried fit and safe for their reception, carriage and preservation in accordance with the provisions of paragraph 1 of Article III. Whenever loss or damage has resulted from unseaworthiness the burden of proving the exercise of due diligence shall be on the carrier or other person claiming exemption under this article.

2. Neither the carrier nor the ship shall be responsible for loss or damage arising or resulting from:

(a) Act, neglect, or default of the master, mariner, pilot, or the servants of the carrier in the navigation or in the management of the ship.

(b) Fire, unless caused by the actual fault or privity of the carrier.

(c) Perils, dangers and accidents of the sea or other navigable waters.

(d) Act of God.

(e) Act of war.

(f) Act of public enemies.

(g) Arrest or restraint of princes, rulers or people, or seizure under legal process.

(h) Quarantine restrictions.

(i) Act or omission of the shipper or owner of the goods, his agent or representative.

(j) Strikes or lockouts or stoppage or restraint of labour from whatever cause, whether partial or general.

(k) Riots and civil commotions.

(l) Saving or attempting to save life or property at sea.

(m) Wastage in bulk of weight or any other loss or damage arising from inherent defect, quality or vice of the goods.

(n) Insufficiency of packing.

(o) Insufficiency or inadequacy of marks.

(p) Latent defects not discoverable by due diligence.

(q) Any other cause arising without the actual fault or privity of the carrier, or without the fault or neglect of the agents or servants of the carrier, but the burden of proof shall be on the person claiming the benefit of this exception to show that neither the actual fault or privity of the carrier nor the fault or neglect of the agents or servants of the carrier contributed to the loss or damage.

3. The shipper shall not be responsible for loss or damage sustained by the carrier or the ship arising or resulting from any cause without the act, fault or neglect of the shipper, his agents or his servants.

4. Any deviation in saving or attempting to save life or property at sea or any reasonable deviation shall not be deemed to be an infringement or breach of these Rules or of the contract of carriage, and the carrier shall not be liable for any loss or damage resulting therefrom.

5 (a) Unless the nature and value of such goods have been declared by the shipper before shipment and inserted in the bill of lading, neither the carrier nor the ship shall in any event be or become liable for any loss or damage to or in connection with the goods in an amount exceeding the equivalent of 666.67 units of account per package or unit or 2 units of account per kilo of gross weight of the goods lost or damaged, whichever is the higher.

(b) The total amount recoverable shall be calculated by reference to the value of such goods at the place and time at which the goods are discharged from the ship in accordance with the contract or should have been so discharged.

The value of the goods shall be fixed according to the commodity exchange price, or, if there be no such price, according to the current market price, or, if there be no commodity exchange price or current market price, by reference to the normal value of goods of the same kind and quality.

(c) Where a container, pallet or similar article of transport is used to consolidate goods, the number of packages or units enumerated in the bill of lading as packed in such article of transport shall be deemed the number of packages or units for the purpose of this paragraph as far as these packages or units are concerned. Except as aforesaid such article of transport shall be considered the package or unit.

(d) The unit of account mentioned in this Article is the special drawing right as defined by the International Monetary Fund. The amounts mentioned in h_visby/art/art04_5asub-paragraph (a) of this paragraph shall be converted into national currency on the basis of the value of that currency on a date to be determined by the law of the Court seized of the case.

(e) Neither the carrier nor the ship shall be entitled to the benefit of the limitation of liability provided for in this paragraph if it is proved that the damage resulted from an act or omission of the carrier done with intent to cause damage, or recklessly and with knowledge that damage would probably result.

(f) The declaration mentioned in sub-paragraph (a) of this paragraph, if embodied in the bill of lading, shall be prima facie evidence, but shall not be binding or conclusive on the carrier.

(g) By agreement between the carrier, master or agent of the carrier and the shipper other maximum amounts than those mentioned in sub-paragraph (a) of this paragraph may be fixed, provided that no maximum amount so fixed shall be less than the appropriate maximum mentioned in that sub-paragraph.

(h) Neither the carrier nor the ship shall be responsible in any event for loss or damage to, or in connection with, goods if the nature or value thereof has been knowingly mis-stated by the shipper in the bill of lading.

6. Goods of an inflammable, explosive or dangerous nature to the shipment whereof the carrier, master or agent of the carrier has not consented with knowledge of their nature and character, may at any time before discharge be landed at any place, or destroyed or rendered innocuous by the carrier without compensation and the shipper of such goods shall be liable for all damages and expenses directly or indirectly arising out of or resulting from such shipment. If any such goods shipped with such knowledge and consent shall become a danger to the ship or cargo, they may in like manner be landed at any place, or destroyed or rendered innocuous by the carrier without liability on the part of the carrier except to general average, if any.

Article IV bis

1. The defences and limits of liability provided for in these Rules shall apply in any action against the carrier in respect of loss or damage to goods covered by a contract of carriage whether the action be founded in contract or in tort.

2. If such an action is brought against a servant or agent of the carrier (such servant or agent not being an independent contractor), such servant or agent shall be entitled to avail himself of the defences and limits of liability which the carrier is entitled to invoke under these Rules.

3. The aggregate of the amounts recoverable from the carrier, and such servants and agents, shall in no case exceed the limit provided for in these Rules.

4. Nevertheless, a servant or agent of the carrier shall not be entitled to avail himself of the provisions of this article, if it is proved that the damage resulted from an act or omission of the servant or agent done with intent to cause damage or recklessly and with knowledge that damage would probably result.

Article V

A carrier shall be at liberty to surrender in whole or in part all or any of his rights and immunities or to increase any of his responsibilities and obligations under these Rules, provided such surrender or increase shall be embodied in the bill of lading issued to the shipper. The provisions of these Rules shall not be applicable to charter parties, but if bills of lading are issued in the case of a ship under a charter party they shall comply with the terms of these Rules. Nothing in these Rules shall be held to prevent the insertion in a bill of lading of any lawful provision regarding general average.

Article VI

Notwithstanding the provisions of the preceding articles, a carrier, master or agent of the carrier and a shipper shall in regard to any particular goods be at liberty to enter into any agreement in any terms as to the responsibility and liability of the carrier for such goods, and as to the rights and immunities of the carrier in respect of such goods, or his obligation as to seaworthiness, so far as this stipulation is not contrary to public policy, or the care or diligence of his servants or agents in regard to the loading, handling, stowage, carriage, custody, care and discharge of the goods carried by sea, provided that in this case no bill of lading has been or shall be issued and that the terms agreed shall be embodie in a receipt which shall be a non-negotiable document and shall be marked as such.

An agreement so entered into shall have full legal effect.

Provided that this article shall not apply to ordinary commercial shipments made in the ordinary course of trade, but only to other shipments where the character or condition of the property to be carried or the circumstances, terms and conditions under which the carriage is to be performed are such as reasonably to justify a special agreement.

Article VII

Nothing herein contained shall prevent a carrier or a shipper from entering into any agreement, stipulation, condition, reservation or exemption as to the responsibility and liability of the carrier or the ship for the loss or damage to, or in connection with, the custody and care and handling of goods prior to the loading on, and subsequent to the discharge from, the ship on which the goods are carried by sea.

Article VIII

The provisions of these Rules shall not affect the rights and obligations of the carrier under any statute for the time being in force relating to the limitation of the liability of owners of sea-going vessels.

Article IX

These Rules shall not affect the provisions of any international Convention or national law governing liability for nuclear damage.

Article X

The provisions of these Rules shall apply to every bill of lading relating to the carriage of goods between ports in two different States if

(a) the bill of lading is issued in a contracting State, or

(b) the carriage is from a port in a contracting State, or

(c) the contract contained in or evidenced by the bill of lading provides that these Rules or legislation of any State giving effect to them are to govern the contract;

whatever may be the nationality of the ship, the carrier, the shipper, the consignee, or any other interested person.

(The last two paragraphs of this Article are not reproduced. They require contracting States to apply the Rules to bills of lading mentioned in the Article and authorise them to apply the Rules to other bills of lading).

(Article 11 to 16 of the International Convention for the unification of certain rules of law relating to bills of lading signed at Brussels on August 25, 1974 are not reproduced. They deal with the coming into force of the Convention, procedure for ratification, accession and denunciation and the right to call for a fresh conference to consider amendments to the Rules contained in the Convention).

PREAMBLE

THE STATES PARTIES TO THIS CONVENTION

HAVING RECOGNIZED the desirability of determining by agreement certain rules relating to the carriage of goods by sea,

HAVING DECIDED to conclude a convention for this purpose and have thereto agreed as follows:

PART I. GENERAL PROVISIONS

Article 1. Definitions

In this Convention:

1. "Carrier" means any person by whom or in whose name a contract of carriage of goods by sea has been concluded with a shipper.

2. "Actual carrier" means any person to whom the performance of the carriage of the goods, or of part of the carriage, has been entrusted by the carrier, and includes any other person to whom such performance has been entrusted.

3. "Shipper" means any person by whom or in whose name or on whose behalf a contract of carriage of goods by sea has been concluded with a carrier, or any person by whom or in whose name or on whose behalf the goods are actually delivered to the carrier in relation to the contract of carriage by sea.

4. "Consignee" means the person entitled to take delivery of the goods.

5. "Goods" includes live animals; where the goods are consolidated in a container, pallet or similar article of transport or where they are packed, goods includes such article of transport or packaging if supplied by the shipper.

6. "Contract of carriage by sea" means any contract whereby the carrier undertakes against payment of freight to carry goods by sea from one port to another; however, a contract which involves carriage by sea and also carriage by some other means is deemed to be a contract of carriage by sea for the purposes of this Convention only in so far as it relates to the carriage by sea.

7. "Bill of lading" means a document which evidences a contract of carriage by sea and the taking over or loading of the goods by the carrier, and by which the carrier undertakes to deliver the goods against surrender of the document. A provision in the document that the goods are to be delivered to the order of a named person, or to order, or to bearer, constitutes such an undertaking.

8. "Writing" includes, *inter alia*, telegram and telex.

Article 2. Scope of application

1. The provisions of this Convention are applicable to all contracts of carriage by sea between two different States, if:

(a) the port of loading as provided for in the contract of carriage by sea is located in a Contracting State, or

(b) the port of discharge as provided for in the contract of carriage by sea is located in a Contracting State, or

(c) one of the optional ports of discharge provided for in the contract of carriage by sea is the actual port of discharge and such port is located in a Contracting State, or

(d) the bill of lading or other document evidencing the contract of carriage by sea is issued in a Contracting State, or

(e) the bill of lading or other document evidencing the contract of carriage by sea provides that the provisions of this Convention or the legislation of any State giving effect to them are to govern the contract.

2. The provisions of this Convention are applicable without regard to the nationality of the ship, the carrier, the actual carrier, the shipper, the consignee or any other interested person.

3. The provisions of this Convention are not applicable to charter-parties. However, where a bill of lading is issued pursuant to a charter-party, the provisions of the Convention apply to such a bill of lading if it governs the relation between the carrier and the holder of the bill of lading, not being the charterer.

4. If a contract provides for future carriage of goods in a series of shipments during an agreed period, the provisions of this Convention apply to each shipment. However, where a shipment is made under a charter-party, the provisions of paragraph 3 of this article apply.

Article 3. Interpretation of the Convention

In the interpretation and application of the provisions of this Convention regard shall be had to its international character and to the need to promote uniformity.

PART II. LIABILITY OF THE CARRIER

Article 4. Period of responsibility

1. The responsibility of the carrier for the goods under this Convention covers the period during which the carrier is in charge of the goods at the port of loading, during the carriage and at the port of discharge.

2. For the purpose of paragraph 1 of this article, the carrier is deemed to be in charge of the goods

(a) from the time he has taken over the goods from:

(i) the shipper, or a person acting on his behalf; or

(ii) an authority or other third party to whom, pursuant to law or regulations applicable at the port of loading, the goods must be handed over for shipment;

(b) until the time he has delivered the goods:

(i) by handing over the goods to the consignee; or

(ii) in cases where the consignee does not receive the goods from the carrier, by placing them at the disposal of the consignee in accordance with the contract or with the law or with the usage of the particular trade, applicable at the port of discharge; or

(iii) by handing over the goods to an authority or other third party to whom, pursuant to law or regulations applicable at the port of discharge, the goods must be handed over.

3. In paragraphs 1 and 2 of this article, reference to the carrier or to the consignee means, in addition to the carrier or the consignee, the servants or agents, respectively of the carrier or the consignee.

Article 5. Basis of liability

1. The carrier is liable for loss resulting from loss of or damage to the goods, as well as from delay in delivery, if the occurrence which caused the loss, damage or delay took place while the goods were in his charge as defined in article 4, unless the carrier proves that he, his servants or agents took all measures that could reasonably be required to avoid the occurrence and its consequences.

2. Delay in delivery occurs when the goods have not been delivered at the port of discharge provided for in the contract of carriage by sea within the time expressly agreed upon or, in the absence of such agreement, within the time which it would be reasonable to require of a diligent carrier, having regard to the circumstances of the case.

3. The person entitled to make a claim for the loss of goods may treat the goods as lost if they have not been delivered as required by article 4 within 60 consecutive days following the expiry of the time for delivery according to paragraph 2 of this article.

4. *(a)* The carrier is liable

(i) for loss of or damage to the goods or delay in delivery caused by fire, if the claimant proves that the fire arose from fault or neglect on the part of the carrier, his servants or agents;

(ii) for such loss, damage or delay in delivery which is proved by the claimant to have resulted from the fault or neglect of the carrier, his servants or agents in taking all measures that could reasonably be required to put out the fire and avoid or mitigate its consequences.

(b) In case of fire onboard the ship affecting the goods, if the claimant or the carrier so desires, a survey in accordance with shipping practices must be held into the cause and circumstances of the fire, and a copy of the surveyors report shall be made available on demand to the carrier and the claimant.

5. With respect to live animals, the carrier is not liable for loss, damage or delay in delivery resulting from any special risks inherent in that kind of carriage. If the carrier proves that he has complied with any special instructions given to him by the shipper respecting the animals and that, in the circumstances of the case, the loss, damage or delay in delivery could be attributed to such risks, it is presumed that the loss, damage or delay in delivery was so caused, unless there is proof that all or a part of the loss, damage, or delay in delivery resulted from fault or neglect on the part of the carrier, his servants or agents.

6. The carrier is not liable, except in general average, where loss, damage or delay in delivery resulted from measures to save life or from reasonable measures to save property at sea.

7. Where fault or neglect on the part of the carrier, his servants or agents combines with another cause to produce loss, damage or delay in delivery, the carrier is liable only to the extent that the loss, damage or delay in delivery is attributable to such fault or neglect, provided that the carrier proves the amount of the loss, damage or delay in delivery not attributable thereto.

Article 6. Limits of liability

1. *(a)* The liability of the carrier for loss resulting from loss of or damage to goods according to the provisions of article 5 is limited to an amount equivalent to 835 units of account per package or other shipping unit or 2.5 units of account per kilogram of gross weight of the goods lost or damaged, whichever is the higher.

(b) The liability of the carrier for delay in delivery according to the provisions of article 5 is limited to an amount equivalent to two and a half times the freight payable for the goods delayed, but not exceeding the total freight payable under the contract of carriage of goods by sea.

(c) In no case shall the aggregate liability of the carrier, under both subparagraphs (a) and (b) of this paragraph, exceed the limitation which would be established under subparagraph (a) of this paragraph for total loss of the goods with respect to which such liability was incurred.

2. For the purpose of calculating which amount is the higher in accordance with paragraph 1 *(a)* of this article, the following rules apply:

(a) Where a container, pallet or similar article of transport is used to consolidate goods, the package or other shipping units enumerated in the bill of lading, if issued, or otherwise in any other document evidencing the contract of carriage by sea, as packed in such article of transport are deemed packages or shipping units. Except as aforesaid the goods in such article of transport are deemed one shipping unit.

(b) In cases where the article of transport itself has been lost or damaged, that article of transport, if not owned or otherwise supplied by the carrier, is considered one separate shipping unit.

3. Unit of account means the unit of account mentioned in article 26.

4. By agreement between the carrier and the shipper, limits of liability exceeding those provided for in paragraph 1 may be fixed.

Article 7. Application to non-contractual claims

1. The defences and limits of liability provided for in this Convention apply in any action against the carrier in respect of loss of or damage to the goods covered by the contract of carriage by sea, as well as of delay in delivery whether the action is founded in contract, in tort or otherwise.

2. If such an action is brought against a servant or agent of the carrier, such servant or agent, if he proves that he acted within the scope of his employment, is entitled to avail himself of the defences and limits of liability which the carrier is entitled to invoke under this Convention.

3. Except as provided in article 8, the aggregate of the amounts recoverable from the carrier and from any persons referred to in paragraph 2 of this article shall not exceed the limits of liability provided for in this Convention.

Article 8. Loss of right to limit responsibility

1. The carrier is not entitled to the benefit of the limitation of liability provided for in article 6 if it is proved that the loss, damage or delay in delivery resulted from an act or omission of the carrier done with the intent to cause such loss, damage or delay, or recklessly and with knowledge that such loss, damage or delay would probably result.

2. Notwithstanding the provisions of paragraph 2 of article 7, a servant or agent of the carrier is not entitled to the benefit of the limitation of liability provided for in article 6 if it is proved that the loss, damage or delay in delivery resulted from an act or omission of such servant or agent, done with the intent to cause such loss, damage or delay, or recklessly and with knowledge that such loss, damage or delay would probably result.

Article 9. Deck cargo

1. The carrier is entitled to carry the goods on deck only if such carriage is in accordance with an agreement with the shipper or with the usage of the particular trade or is required by statutory rules or regulations.

2. If the carrier and the shipper have agreed that the goods shall or may be carried on deck, the carrier must insert in the bill of lading or other document evidencing the contract of carriage by sea a statement to that effect. In the absence of such a statement the carrier has the burden of proving that an agreement for carriage on deck has been entered into; however, the carrier is not entitled to invoke such an agreement against a third party, including a consignee, who has acquired the bill of lading in good faith.

3. Where the goods have been carried on deck contrary to the provisions of paragraph 1 of this article or where the carrier may not under paragraph 2 of this article invoke an agreement for carriage on deck, the carrier, notwithstanding the provisions of paragraph 1 of article 5, is liable for loss of or damage to the goods, as well as for delay in delivery, resulting solely from the carriage on deck, and the extent of his liability is to be determined in accordance with the provisions of article 6 or article 8 of this Convention, as the case may be.

4. Carriage of goods on deck contrary to express agreement for carriage under deck is deemed to be an act or omission of the carrier within the meaning of article 8.

Article 10. Liability of the carrier and actual carrier

1. Where the performance of the carriage or part thereof has been entrusted to an actual carrier, whether or not in pursuance of a liberty under the contract of carriage by sea to do so, the carrier nevertheless remains responsible for the entire carriage according to the provisions of this Convention. The carrier is responsible, in relation to the carriage performed by the actual carrier, for the acts and omissions of the actual carrier and of his servants and agents acting within the scope of their employment.

2. All the provisions of this Convention governing the responsibility of the carrier also apply to the responsibility of the actual carrier for the carriage performed by him. The provisions of paragraphs 2 and 3 of article 7 and of paragraph 2 of article 8 apply if an action is brought against a servant or agent of the actual carrier.

3. Any special agreement under which the carrier assumes obligations not imposed by this Convention or waives rights conferred by this Convention affects the actual carrier only if agreed to by him expressly and in writing. Whether or not the actual carrier has so agreed, the carrier nevertheless remains bound by the obligations or waivers resulting from such special agreement.

4. Where and to the extent that both the carrier and the actual carrier are liable, their liability is joint and several.

5. The aggregate of the amounts recoverable from the carrier, the actual carrier and their servants and agents shall not exceed the limits of liability provided for in this Convention.

6. Nothing in this article shall prejudice any right of recourse as between the carrier and the actual carrier.

Article 11. Through carriage

1. Notwithstanding the provisions of paragraph 1 of article 10, where a contract of carriage by sea provides explicitly that a specified part of the carriage covered by the said contract is to be performed by a named person other than the carrier, the contract may also provide that the carrier is not liable for loss, damage or delay in delivery caused by an occurrence which takes place while the goods are in the charge of the actual carrier during such part of the carriage. Nevertheless, any stipulation limiting or excluding such liability is without effect if no judicial proceedings can be instituted against the actual carrier in a court competent under paragraph 1 or 2 of article 21. The burden of proving that any loss, damage or delay in delivery has been caused by such an occurrence rests upon the carrier.

2. The actual carrier is responsible in accordance with the provisions of paragraph 2 of article 10 for loss, damage or delay in delivery caused by an occurrence which takes place while the goods are in his charge.

PART III. LIABILITY OF THE SHIPPERS

Article 12. General rule

The shipper is not liable for loss sustained by the carrier or the actual carrier, or for damage sustained by the ship, unless such loss or damage was caused by the fault or neglect of the shipper, his servants or agents. Nor is any servant or agent of the shipper liable for such loss or damage unless the loss or damage was caused by fault or neglect on his part.

Article 13. Special rules on dangerous goods

1. The shipper must mark or label in a suitable manner dangerous goods as dangerous.

2. Where the shipper hands over dangerous goods to the carrier or an actual carrier, as the case may be, the shipper must inform him of the dangerous character of the goods and, if necessary, of the precautions to be taken. If the shipper fails to do so and such carrier or actual carrier does not otherwise have knowledge of their dangerous character:

(a) the shipper is liable to the carrier and any actual carrier for the loss resulting from the shipment of such goods, and

(b) the goods may at any time be unloaded, destroyed or rendered innocuous, as the circumstances may require, without payment of compensation.

3. The provisions of paragraph 2 of this article may not be invoked by any person if during the carriage he has taken the goods in his charge with knowledge of their dangerous character.

4. If, in cases where the provisions of paragraph 2, subparagraph *(b)*, of this article do not apply or may not be invoked, dangerous goods become an actual danger to life or property, they may be unloaded, destroyed or rendered innocuous, as the circumstances may require, without payment of compensation except where there is an obligation to contribute in general average or where the carrier is liable in accordance with the provisions of article 5.

PART IV. TRANSPORT DOCUMENTS

Article 14. Issue of bill of lading

1. When the carrier or the actual carrier takes the goods in his charge, the carrier must, on demand of the shipper, issue to the shipper a bill of lading.

2. The bill of lading may be signed by a person having authority from the carrier. A bill of lading signed by the master of the ship carrying the goods is deemed to have been signed on behalf of the carrier.

3. The signature on the bill of lading may be in handwriting, printed in facsimile, perforated, stamped, in symbols, or made by any other mechanical or electronic means, if not inconsistent with the law of the country where the bill of lading is issued.

Article 15. Contents of bill of lading

1. The bill of lading must include, Inter alia, the following particulars:

(a) the general nature of the goods, the leading marks necessary for identification of the goods, an express statement, if applicable, as to the dangerous character of the goods, the number of packages or pieces, and the weight of the goods or their quantity otherwise expressed, all such particulars as furnished by the shipper;

(b) the apparent condition of the goods;

(c) the name and principal place of business of the carrier;

(d) the name of the shipper;

(e) the consignee if named by the shipper;

(f) the port of loading under the contract of carriage by sea and the date on which the goods were taken over by the carrier at the port of loading;

(g) the port of discharge under the contract of carriage by sea;

(h) the number of originals of the bill of lading, if more than one;

(i) the place of issuance of the bill of lading;

(j) the signature of the carrier or a person acting on his behalf;

(k) the freight to the extent payable by the consignee or other indication that freight is payable by him;

(l) the statement referred to in paragraph 3 of article 23;

(m) the statement, if applicable, that the goods shall or may be carried on deck;

(n) the date or the period of delivery of the goods at the port of discharge if expressly agreed upon between the parties; and

(o) any increased limit or limits of liability where agreed in accordance with paragraph 4 of article 6.

2. After the goods have been loaded onboard, if the shipper so demands, the carrier must issue to the shipper a "shipped" bill of lading which, in addition to the particulars required under paragraph 1 of this article, must state that the goods are onboard a named ship or ships, and the date or dates of loading. If the carrier has previously issued to the shipper a bill of lading or other document of title with respect to any of such goods, on request of the carrier the shipper must surrender such document in exchange for a "shipped" bill of lading. The carrier may amend any previously issued document in order to meet the shippers demand for a "shipped" bill of lading if, as amended, such document includes all the information required to be contained in a "shipped" bill of lading.

3. The absence in the bill of lading of one or more particulars referred to in this article does not affect the legal character of the document as a bill of lading provided that it nevertheless meets the requirements set out in paragraph 7 of article 1.

Article 16. Bills of lading: reservations and evidentiary effect

1. If the bill of lading contains particulars concerning the general nature, leading marks, number of packages of pieces, weight or quantity of the goods which the carrier or other person issuing the bill of lading on his behalf knows or has reasonable grounds to suspect do not accurately represent the goods actually taken over or, where a "shipped" bill of lading is issued, loaded, or if he had no reasonable means of checking such particulars, the carrier or such other person must insert in the bill of lading a reservation specifying these inaccuracies, grounds of suspicion or the absence of reasonable means of checking.

2. If the carrier or other person issuing the bill of lading on his behalf fails to note on the bill of lading the apparent condition of the goods, he is deemed to have noted on the bill of lading that the goods were in apparent good condition.

3. Except for particulars in respect of which and to the extent to which a reservation permitted under paragraph 1 of this article has been entered:

(a) the bill of lading is *prima facie* evidence of the taking over or, where a "shipped" bill of lading is issued, loading, by the carrier of the goods as described in the bill of lading; and

(b) proof to the contrary by the carrier is not admissible if the bill of lading has been transferred to a third party, including a consignee, who in good faith has acted in reliance on the description of the goods therein.

4. A bill of lading which does not, as provided in paragraph 1, subparagraph *(k)*, of article 15, set forth the freight or otherwise indicate that freight is payable by the

consignee or does not set forth demurrage incurred at the port of loading payable by the consignee, is *prima facie* evidence that no freight or such demurrage is payable by him. However, proof to the contrary by the carrier is not admissible when the bill of lading has been transferred to a third party, including a consignee, who in good faith has acted in reliance on the absence in the bill of lading of any such indication.

Article 17. Guarantees by the shipper

1. The shipper is deemed to have guaranteed to the carrier the accuracy of particulars relating to the general nature of the goods, their marks, number, weight and quantity as furnished by him for insertion in the bill of lading. The shipper must indemnify the carrier against the loss resulting from inaccuracies in such particulars. The shipper remains liable even if the bill of lading has been transferred by him. The right of the carrier to such indemnity in no way limits his liability under the contract of carriage by sea to any person other than the shipper.

2. Any letter of guarantee or agreement by which the shipper undertakes to indemnify the carrier against loss resulting from the issuance of the bill of lading by the carrier, or by a person acting on his behalf, without entering a reservation relating to particulars furnished by the shipper for insertion in the bill of lading, or to the apparent condition of the goods, is void and of no effect as against any third party, including a consignee, to whom the bill of lading has been transferred.

3. Such a letter of guarantee or agreement is valid as against the shipper unless the carrier or the person acting on his behalf, by omitting the reservation referred to in paragraph 2 of this article, intends to defraud a third party, including a consignee, who acts in reliance on the description of the goods in the bill of lading. In the latter case, if the reservation omitted relates to particulars furnished by the shipper for insertion in the bill of lading, the carrier has no right of indemnity from the shipper pursuant to paragraph 1 of this article.

4. In the case of intended fraud referred to in paragraph 3 of this article, the carrier is liable, without the benefit of the limitation of liability provided for in this Convention, for the loss incurred by a third party, including a consignee, because he has acted in reliance on the description of the goods in the bill of lading.

Article 18. Documents other than bills of lading

Where a carrier issues a document other than a bill of lading to evidence the receipt of the goods to be carried, such a document is *prima facie* evidence of the conclusion of the contract of carriage by sea and the taking over by the carrier of the goods as therein described.

PART V. CLAIMS AND ACTIONS

Article 19. Notice of loss, damage or delay

1. Unless notice of loss or damage, specifying the general nature of such loss or damage, is given in writing by the consignee to the carrier not later than the working day after the day when the goods were handed over to the consignee, such handing over is *prima facie* evidence of the delivery by the carrier of the goods as described in the document of transport or, if no such document has been issued, in good condition.

2. Where the loss or damage is not apparent, the provisions of paragraph 1 of this article apply correspondingly if notice in writing is not given within 15 consecutive days after the day when the goods were handed over to the consignee.

3. If the state of the goods at the time they were handed over to the consignee has been the subject of a joint survey or inspection by the parties, notice in writing need not be given of loss or damage ascertained during such survey or inspection.

4. In the case of any actual or apprehended loss or damage, the carrier and the consignee must give all reasonable facilities to each other for inspecting and tallying the goods.

5. No compensation shall be payable for loss resulting from delay in delivery unless a notice has been given in writing to the carrier within 60 consecutive days after the day when the goods were handed over to the consignee.

6. If the goods have been delivered by an actual carrier, any notice given under this article to him shall have the same effect as if it had been given to the carrier; and any notice given to the carrier shall have effect as if given to such actual carrier.

7. Unless notice of loss or damage, specifying the general nature of the loss or damage, is given in writing by the carrier or actual carrier to the shipper not later than 90 consecutive days after the occurrence of such loss or damage or after the delivery of the goods in accordance with paragraph 2 of article 4, whichever is later, the failure to give such notice is *prima facie* evidence that the carrier or the actual carrier has sustained no loss or damage due to the fault or neglect of the shipper, his servants or agents.

8. For the purpose of this article, notice given to a person acting on the carriers or the actual carriers behalf, including the master or the officer in charge of the ship, or to a person acting on the shippers behalf is deemed to have been given to the carrier, to the actual carrier or to the shipper, respectively.

Article 20. Limitation of actions

1. Any action relating to carriage of goods under this Convention is time-barred if judicial or arbitral proceedings have not been instituted within a period of two years.

2. The limitation period commences on the day on which the carrier has delivered the goods or part thereof or, in cases where no goods have been delivered, on the last day on which the goods should have been delivered.

3. The day on which the limitation period commences is not included in the period.

4. The person against whom a claim is made may at any time during the running of the limitation period extend that period by a declaration in writing to the claimant. This period may be further extended by another declaration or declarations.

5. An action for indemnity by a person held liable may be instituted even after the expiration of the limitation period provided for in the preceding paragraphs if instituted within the time allowed by the law of the State where proceedings are instituted. However, the time allowed shall not be less than 90 days commencing from the day when the person instituting such action for indemnity has settled the claim or has been served with process in the action against himself.

Article 21. Jurisdiction

1. In judicial proceedings relating to carriage of goods under this Convention the plaintiff, at his option, may institute an action in a court which according to the law of the State where the court is situated, is competent and within the jurisdiction of which is situated one of the following places:

(a) the principal place of business or, in the absence thereof, the habitual residence of the defendant; or

(b) the place where the contract was made, provided that the defendant has there a place of business, branch or agency through which the contract was made; or

(c) the port of loading or the port of discharge; or

(d) any additional place designated for that purpose in the contract of carriage by sea.

2. *(a)* Notwithstanding the preceding provisions of this article, an action may be instituted in the courts of any port or place in a Contracting State at which the carrying vessel or any other vessel of the same ownership may have been arrested

in accordance with applicable rules of the law of that State and of international law. However, in such a case, at the petition of the defendant, the claimant must remove the action, at his choice, to one of the jurisdictions referred to in paragraph 1 of this article for the determination of the claim, but before such removal the defendant must furnish security sufficient to ensure payment of any judgement that may subsequently be awarded to the claimant in the action.

(b) All questions relating to the sufficiency or otherwise of the security shall be determined by the court of the port or place of the arrest.

3. No judicial proceedings relating to carriage of goods under this Convention may be instituted in a place not specified in paragraph 1 or 2 of this article. The provisions of this paragraph do not constitute an obstacle to the jurisdiction of the Contracting States for provisional or protective measures.

4. *(a)* Where an action has been instituted in a court competent under paragraphs 1 or 2 of this article or where judgement has been delivered by such a court, no new action may be started between the same parties on the same grounds unless the judgement of the court before which the first action was instituted is not enforceable in the country in which the new proceedings are instituted;

(b) For the purpose of this article, the institution of measures with a view to obtaining enforcement of a judgement is not to be considered as the starting of a new action;

(c) For the purpose of this article, the removal of an action to a different court within the same country, or to a court in another country, in accordance with paragraph 2 *(a)* of this article, is not to be considered as the starting of a new action.

5. Notwithstanding the provisions of the preceding paragraphs, an agreement made by the parties, after a claim under the contract of carriage by sea has arisen, which designates the place where the claimant may institute an actions, is effective.

Article 22. Arbitration

1. Subject to the provisions of this article, parties may provide by agreement evidenced in writing that any dispute that may arise relating to carriage of goods under this Convention shall be referred to arbitration.

2. Where a charter-party contains a provision that disputes arising thereunder shall be referred to arbitration and a bill of lading issued pursuant to the charterparty does not contain special annotation providing that such provision shall be binding upon the holder of the bill of lading, the carrier may not invoke such provision as against a holder having acquired the bill of lading in good faith.

3. The arbitration proceedings shall, at the option of the claimant, be instituted at one of the following places:

(a) a place in a State within whose territory is situated:

(i) the principal place of business of the defendant or, in the absence thereof, the habitual residence of the defendant; or

(ii) the place where the contract was made, provided that the defendant has there a place of business, branch or agency through which the contract was made; or

(iii) the port of loading or the port of discharge; or

(b) any place designated for that purpose in the arbitration clause or agreement.

4. The arbitrator or arbitration tribunal shall apply the rules of this Convention.

5. The provisions of paragraphs 2 and 4 of this article are deemed to be part of every arbitration clause or agreement, and any term of such clause or agreement which is inconsistent therewith is null and void.

6. Nothing in this article affects the validity of an agreement relating to arbitration made by the parties after the claim under the contract of carriage by sea has arisen.

PART VI. SUPPLEMENTARY PROVISIONS

Article 23. Contractual stipulations

1. Any stipulation in a contract of carriage by sea, in a bill of lading, or in any other document evidencing the contract of carriage by sea is null and void to the extent that it derogates, directly or indirectly, from the provisions of this Convention. The nullity of such a stipulation does not affect the validity of the other provisions of the contract or document of which it forms a part. A clause assigning benefit of insurance of goods in favour of the carrier, or any similar clause, is null and void.

2. Notwithstanding the provisions of paragraph 1 of this article, a carrier may increase his responsibilities and obligations under this Convention.

3. Where a bill of lading or any other document evidencing the contract of carriage by sea is issued, it must contain a statement that the carriage is subject to the provisions of this Convention which nullify any stipulation derogating therefrom to the detriment of the shipper or the consignee.

4. Where the claimant in respect of the goods has incurred loss as a result of a stipulation which is null and void by virtue of the present article, or as a result of the omission of the statement referred to in paragraph 3 of this article, the carrier must pay compensation to the extent required in order to give the claimant compensation

in accordance with the provisions of this Convention for any loss of or damage to the goods as well as for delay in delivery. The carrier must, in addition, pay compensation for costs incurred by the claimant for the purpose of exercising his right, provided that costs incurred in the action where the foregoing provision is invoked are to be determined in accordance with the law of the State where proceedings are instituted.

Article 24. General average

1. Nothing in this Convention shall prevent the application of provisions in the contract of carriage by sea or national law regarding the adjustment of general average.

2. With the exception of article 20, the provisions of this Convention relating to the liability of the carrier for loss of or damage to the goods also determine whether the consignee may refuse contribution in general average and the liability of the carrier to indemnify the consignee in respect of any such contribution made or any salvage paid.

Article 25. Other conventions

1. This Convention does not modify the rights or duties of the carrier, the actual carrier and their servants and agents provided for in international conventions or national law relating to the limitation of liability of owners of seagoing ships.

2. The provisions of articles 21 and 22 of this Convention do not prevent the application of the mandatory provisions of any other multilateral convention already in force at the date of this Convention relating to matters dealt with in the said articles, provided that the dispute arises exclusively between parties having their principal place of business in States members of such other convention. However, this paragraph does not affect the application of paragraph 4 of article 22 of this Convention.

3. No liability shall arise under the provisions of this Convention for damage caused by a nuclear incident if the operator of a nuclear installation is liable for such damage:

(a) under either the Paris Convention of 29 July 1960 on Third Party Liability in the Field of Nuclear Energy as amended by the Additional Protocol of 28 January 1964, or the Vienna Convention of 21 May 1963 on Civil Liability for Nuclear Damage, or

(b) by virtue of national law governing the liability for such damage, provided that such law is in all respects as favourable to persons who may suffer damage as is either the Paris Convention or the Vienna Convention.

4. No liability shall arise under the provisions of this Convention for any loss of or damage to or delay in delivery of luggage for which the carrier is responsible under

any international convention or national law relating to the carriage of passengers and their luggage by sea.

5. Nothing contained in this Convention prevents a Contracting State from applying any other international convention which is already in force at the date of this Convention and which applies mandatorily to contracts of carriage of goods primarily by a mode of transport other than transport by sea. This provision also applies to any subsequent revision or amendment of such international convention.

Article 26. Unit of account

1. The unit of account referred to in article 6 of this Convention is the special drawing right as defined by the International Monetary Fund. The amounts mentioned in article 6 are to be converted into the national currency of a State according to the value of such currency at the date of judgement or the date agreed upon by the parties. The value of a national currency, in terms of the special drawing right, of a Contracting State which is a member of the International Monetary Fund is to be calculated in accordance with the method of valuation applied by the International Monetary Fund in effect at the date in question for its operations and transactions. The value of a national currency, in terms of the special drawing right, of a Contracting State which is not a member of the International Monetary Fund is to be calculated in a manner determined by that State.

2. Nevertheless, those States which are not members of the International Monetary Fund and whose law does not permit the application of the provisions of paragraph 1 of this article may, at the time of signature, or at the time of ratification, acceptance, approval or accession or at any time thereafter, declare that the limits of liability provided for in this Convention to be applied in their territories shall be fixed as 12,500 monetary units per package or other shipping unit or 37.5 monetary units per kilogram of gross weight of the goods.

3. The monetary unit referred to in paragraph 2 of this article corresponds to sixty-five and a half milligrams of gold of millesimal fineness nine hundred. The conversion of the amounts referred to in paragraph 2 into the national currency is to be made according to the law of the State concerned.

4. The calculation mentioned in the last sentence of paragraph 1 and the conversion mentioned in paragraph 3 of this article is to be made in such a manner as to express in the national currency of the Contracting State as far as possible the same real value for the amounts in article 6 as is expressed there in units of account. Contracting States must communicate to the depositary the manner of calculation pursuant to paragraph 1 of this article, or the result of the conversion mentioned in paragraph 3 of this article, as the case may be, at the time of signature or when

depositing their instruments of ratification, acceptance, approval or accession, or when availing themselves of the option provided for in paragraph 2 of this article and whenever there is a change in the manner of such calculation or in the result of such conversion.

(Part VII 'Final Clauses' is not reproduced here as this is only concerned with ratification and renunciation procedures and is not relevant to this course.)

Common understanding adopted by the United Nations Conference on the Carriage of Goods by Sea.

It is the common understanding that the liability of the carrier under this Convention is based on the principle of presumed fault or neglect. This means that, as a rule, the burden of proof rests on the carrier but, with respect to certain cases, the provisions of thc Convention modify this rule.

United Nations A/RES/63/122

General Assembly

Distr.: General
2 February 2009

Sixty-third session
Agenda item 74

Resolution adopted by the General Assembly

[*on the report of the Sixth Committee (A/63/438)*]

63/122. United Nations Convention on Contracts for the International Carriage of Goods Wholly or Partly by Sea

The General Assembly,

Recalling its resolution 2205 (XXI) of 17 December 1966, by which it established the United Nations Commission on International Trade Law with a mandate to further the progressive harmonization and unification of the law of international trade and in that respect to bear in mind the interests of all peoples, in particular those of developing countries, in the extensive development of international trade,

Concerned that the current legal regime governing the international carriage of goods by sea lacks uniformity and fails to adequately take into account modern transport practices, including containerization, door-to-door transport contracts and the use of electronic transport documents,

Noting that the development of international trade on the basis of equality and mutual benefit is an important element in promoting friendly relations among States,

Convinced that the adoption of uniform rules to modernize and harmonize the rules that govern the international carriage of goods involving a sea leg would enhance legal certainty, improve efficiency and commercial predictability in the international carriage of goods and reduce legal obstacles to the flow of international trade among all States,

Believing that the adoption of uniform rules to govern international contracts of carriage wholly or partly by sea will promote legal certainty, improve the efficiency of international carriage of goods and facilitate new access opportunities for previously remote parties and markets, thus playing a fundamental role in promoting trade and economic development, both domestically and internationally,

Noting that shippers and carriers do not have the benefit of a binding and balanced universal regime to support the operation of contracts of carriage involving various modes of transport,

Recalling that, at its thirty-fourth and thirty-fifth sessions, in 2001 and 2002, the Commission decided to prepare an international legislative instrument governing door-to-door transport operations that involve a sea leg,[1]

Recognizing that all States and interested international organizations were invited to participate in the preparation of the draft Convention on Contracts for the International Carriage of Goods Wholly or Partly by Sea and in the forty-first session of the Commission, either as members or as observers, with a full opportunity to speak and make proposals,

Noting with satisfaction that the text of the draft Convention was circulated for comment to all States Members of the United Nations and intergovernmental organizations invited to attend the meetings of the Commission as observers, and that the comments received were before the Commission at its forty-first session,[2]

Taking note with satisfaction of the decision of the Commission at its forty-first session to submit the draft Convention to the General Assembly for its consideration,[3]

Taking note of the draft Convention approved by the Commission,[4]

Expressing its appreciation to the Government of the Netherlands for its offer to host a signing ceremony for the Convention in Rotterdam,

1. *Commends* the United Nations Commission on International Trade Law for preparing the draft Convention on Contracts for the International Carriage of Goods Wholly or Partly by Sea;

2. *Adopts* the United Nations Convention on Contracts for the International Carriage of Goods Wholly or Partly by Sea, contained in the annex to the present resolution;

3. *Authorizes* a ceremony for the opening for signature to be held on 23 September 2009 in Rotterdam, the Netherlands, and recommends that the rules embodied in the Convention be known as the "Rotterdam Rules";

4. *Calls upon* all Governments to consider becoming party to the Convention.

67th plenary meeting
11 December 2008

Annex

United Nations Convention on Contracts for the International Carriage of Goods Wholly or Partly by Sea

The States Parties to this Convention,

Reaffirming their belief that international trade on the basis of equality and mutual benefit is an important element in promoting friendly relations among States,

---

[1] *Official Records of the General Assembly, Fifty-sixth Session, Supplement No. 17* and corrigendum (A/56/17 and Corr.3), paras. 319–345; and ibid., *Fifty-seventh Session, Supplement No. 17* (A/57/17), paras. 210–224.

[2] A/CN.9/658 and Add.1–14 and Add.14/Corr.1.

[3] *Official Records of the General Assembly, Sixty-third Session, Supplement No. 17* and corrigendum (A/63/17 and Corr.1), para. 298.

[4] Ibid., annex I.

Convinced that the progressive harmonization and unification of international trade law, in reducing or removing legal obstacles to the flow of international trade, significantly contributes to universal economic cooperation among all States on a basis of equality, equity and common interest, and to the well-being of all peoples,

Recognizing the significant contribution of the International Convention for the Unification of Certain Rules of Law relating to Bills of Lading, signed in Brussels on 25 August 1924, and its Protocols, and of the United Nations Convention on the Carriage of Goods by Sea, signed in Hamburg on 31 March 1978, to the harmonization of the law governing the carriage of goods by sea,

Mindful of the technological and commercial developments that have taken place since the adoption of those conventions and of the need to consolidate and modernize them,

Noting that shippers and carriers do not have the benefit of a binding universal regime to support the operation of contracts of maritime carriage involving other modes of transport,

Believing that the adoption of uniform rules to govern international contracts of carriage wholly or partly by sea will promote legal certainty, improve the efficiency of international carriage of goods and facilitate new access opportunities for previously remote parties and markets, thus playing a fundamental role in promoting trade and economic development, both domestically and internationally,

Have agreed as follows:

Chapter 1
General provisions

Article 1
Definitions

For the purposes of this Convention:

1. "Contract of carriage" means a contract in which a carrier, against the payment of freight, undertakes to carry goods from one place to another. The contract shall provide for carriage by sea and may provide for carriage by other modes of transport in addition to the sea carriage.

2. "Volume contract" means a contract of carriage that provides for the carriage of a specified quantity of goods in a series of shipments during an agreed period of time. The specification of the quantity may include a minimum, a maximum or a certain range.

3. "Liner transportation" means a transportation service that is offered to the public through publication or similar means and includes transportation by ships operating on a regular schedule between specified ports in accordance with publicly available timetables of sailing dates.

4. "Non-liner transportation" means any transportation that is not liner transportation.

5. "Carrier" means a person that enters into a contract of carriage with a shipper.

6. (*a*) "Performing party" means a person other than the carrier that performs or undertakes to perform any of the carrier's obligations under a contract of carriage with respect to the receipt, loading, handling, stowage, carriage, care, unloading or

delivery of the goods, to the extent that such person acts, either directly or indirectly, at the carrier's request or under the carrier's supervision or control.

(*b*) "Performing party" does not include any person that is retained, directly or indirectly, by a shipper, by a documentary shipper, by the controlling party or by the consignee instead of by the carrier.

7. "Maritime performing party" means a performing party to the extent that it performs or undertakes to perform any of the carrier's obligations during the period between the arrival of the goods at the port of loading of a ship and their departure from the port of discharge of a ship. An inland carrier is a maritime performing party only if it performs or undertakes to perform its services exclusively within a port area.

8. "Shipper" means a person that enters into a contract of carriage with a carrier.

9. "Documentary shipper" means a person, other than the shipper, that accepts to be named as "shipper" in the transport document or electronic transport record.

10. "Holder" means:

(*a*) A person that is in possession of a negotiable transport document; and (i) if the document is an order document, is identified in it as the shipper or the consignee, or is the person to which the document is duly endorsed; or (ii) if the document is a blank endorsed order document or bearer document, is the bearer thereof; or

(*b*) The person to which a negotiable electronic transport record has been issued or transferred in accordance with the procedures referred to in article 9, paragraph 1.

11. "Consignee" means a person entitled to delivery of the goods under a contract of carriage or a transport document or electronic transport record.

12. "Right of control" of the goods means the right under the contract of carriage to give the carrier instructions in respect of the goods in accordance with chapter 10.

13. "Controlling party" means the person that pursuant to article 51 is entitled to exercise the right of control.

14. "Transport document" means a document issued under a contract of carriage by the carrier that:

(*a*) Evidences the carrier's or a performing party's receipt of goods under a contract of carriage; and

(*b*) Evidences or contains a contract of carriage.

15. "Negotiable transport document" means a transport document that indicates, by wording such as "to order" or "negotiable" or other appropriate wording recognized as having the same effect by the law applicable to the document, that the goods have been consigned to the order of the shipper, to the order of the consignee, or to bearer, and is not explicitly stated as being "non-negotiable" or "not negotiable".

16. "Non-negotiable transport document" means a transport document that is not a negotiable transport document.

17. "Electronic communication" means information generated, sent, received or stored by electronic, optical, digital or similar means with the result that the information communicated is accessible so as to be usable for subsequent reference.

18. "Electronic transport record" means information in one or more messages issued by electronic communication under a contract of carriage by a carrier, including information logically associated with the electronic transport record by attachments or otherwise linked to the electronic transport record contemporaneously with or subsequent to its issue by the carrier, so as to become part of the electronic transport record, that:

(*a*) Evidences the carrier's or a performing party's receipt of goods under a contract of carriage; and

(*b*) Evidences or contains a contract of carriage.

19. "Negotiable electronic transport record" means an electronic transport record:

(*a*) That indicates, by wording such as "to order", or "negotiable", or other appropriate wording recognized as having the same effect by the law applicable to the record, that the goods have been consigned to the order of the shipper or to the order of the consignee, and is not explicitly stated as being "non-negotiable" or "not negotiable"; and

(*b*) The use of which meets the requirements of article 9, paragraph 1.

20. "Non-negotiable electronic transport record" means an electronic transport record that is not a negotiable electronic transport record.

21. The "issuance" of a negotiable electronic transport record means the issuance of the record in accordance with procedures that ensure that the record is subject to exclusive control from its creation until it ceases to have any effect or validity.

22. The "transfer" of a negotiable electronic transport record means the transfer of exclusive control over the record.

23. "Contract particulars" means any information relating to the contract of carriage or to the goods (including terms, notations, signatures and endorsements) that is in a transport document or an electronic transport record.

24. "Goods" means the wares, merchandise, and articles of every kind whatsoever that a carrier undertakes to carry under a contract of carriage and includes the packing and any equipment and container not supplied by or on behalf of the carrier.

25. "Ship" means any vessel used to carry goods by sea.

26. "Container" means any type of container, transportable tank or flat, swapbody, or any similar unit load used to consolidate goods, and any equipment ancillary to such unit load.

27. "Vehicle" means a road or railroad cargo vehicle.

28. "Freight" means the remuneration payable to the carrier for the carriage of goods under a contract of carriage.

29. "Domicile" means (*a*) a place where a company or other legal person or association of natural or legal persons has its (i) statutory seat or place of incorporation or central registered office, whichever is applicable, (ii) central administration or (iii) principal place of business, and (*b*) the habitual residence of a natural person.

30. "Competent court" means a court in a Contracting State that, according to the rules on the internal allocation of jurisdiction among the courts of that State, may exercise jurisdiction over the dispute.

Article 2
Interpretation of this Convention

In the interpretation of this Convention, regard is to be had to its international character and to the need to promote uniformity in its application and the observance of good faith in international trade.

Article 3
Form requirements

The notices, confirmation, consent, agreement, declaration and other communications referred to in articles 19, paragraph 2; 23, paragraphs 1 to 4; 36, subparagraphs 1 (*b*), (*c*) and (*d*); 40, subparagraph 4 (*b*); 44; 48, paragraph 3; 51, subparagraph 1 (*b*); 59, paragraph 1; 63; 66; 67, paragraph 2; 75, paragraph 4; and 80, paragraphs 2 and 5, shall be in writing. Electronic communications may be used for these purposes, provided that the use of such means is with the consent of the person by which it is communicated and of the person to which it is communicated.

Article 4
Applicability of defences and limits of liability

1. Any provision of this Convention that may provide a defence for, or limit the liability of, the carrier applies in any judicial or arbitral proceeding, whether founded in contract, in tort, or otherwise, that is instituted in respect of loss of, damage to, or delay in delivery of goods covered by a contract of carriage or for the breach of any other obligation under this Convention against:

(*a*) The carrier or a maritime performing party;

(*b*) The master, crew or any other person that performs services on board the ship; or

(*c*) Employees of the carrier or a maritime performing party.

2. Any provision of this Convention that may provide a defence for the shipper or the documentary shipper applies in any judicial or arbitral proceeding, whether founded in contract, in tort, or otherwise, that is instituted against the shipper, the documentary shipper, or their subcontractors, agents or employees.

Chapter 2
Scope of application

Article 5
General scope of application

1. Subject to article 6, this Convention applies to contracts of carriage in which the place of receipt and the place of delivery are in different States, and the port of loading of a sea carriage and the port of discharge of the same sea carriage are in different States, if, according to the contract of carriage, any one of the following places is located in a Contracting State:

(*a*) The place of receipt;

(*b*) The port of loading;

(*c*) The place of delivery; or

(*d*) The port of discharge.

2. This Convention applies without regard to the nationality of the vessel, the carrier, the performing parties, the shipper, the consignee, or any other interested parties.

Article 6
Specific exclusions

1. This Convention does not apply to the following contracts in liner transportation:

(*a*) Charter parties; and

(*b*) Other contracts for the use of a ship or of any space thereon.

2. This Convention does not apply to contracts of carriage in non-liner transportation except when:

(*a*) There is no charter party or other contract between the parties for the use of a ship or of any space thereon; and

(*b*) A transport document or an electronic transport record is issued.

Article 7
Application to certain parties

Notwithstanding article 6, this Convention applies as between the carrier and the consignee, controlling party or holder that is not an original party to the charter party or other contract of carriage excluded from the application of this Convention. However, this Convention does not apply as between the original parties to a contract of carriage excluded pursuant to article 6.

Chapter 3
Electronic transport records

Article 8
Use and effect of electronic transport records

Subject to the requirements set out in this Convention:

(*a*) Anything that is to be in or on a transport document under this Convention may be recorded in an electronic transport record, provided the issuance and subsequent use of an electronic transport record is with the consent of the carrier and the shipper; and

(*b*) The issuance, exclusive control, or transfer of an electronic transport record has the same effect as the issuance, possession, or transfer of a transport document.

Article 9
Procedures for use of negotiable electronic transport records

1. The use of a negotiable electronic transport record shall be subject to procedures that provide for:

(*a*) The method for the issuance and the transfer of that record to an intended holder;

(*b*) An assurance that the negotiable electronic transport record retains its integrity;

(*c*) The manner in which the holder is able to demonstrate that it is the holder; and

(*d*) The manner of providing confirmation that delivery to the holder has been effected, or that, pursuant to articles 10, paragraph 2, or 47, subparagraphs 1 (*a*) (ii) and (*c*), the electronic transport record has ceased to have any effect or validity.

2. The procedures in paragraph 1 of this article shall be referred to in the contract particulars and be readily ascertainable.

Article 10
Replacement of negotiable transport document or negotiable electronic transport record

1. If a negotiable transport document has been issued and the carrier and the holder agree to replace that document by a negotiable electronic transport record:

(*a*) The holder shall surrender the negotiable transport document, or all of them if more than one has been issued, to the carrier;

(*b*) The carrier shall issue to the holder a negotiable electronic transport record that includes a statement that it replaces the negotiable transport document; and

(*c*) The negotiable transport document ceases thereafter to have any effect or validity.

2. If a negotiable electronic transport record has been issued and the carrier and the holder agree to replace that electronic transport record by a negotiable transport document:

(*a*) The carrier shall issue to the holder, in place of the electronic transport record, a negotiable transport document that includes a statement that it replaces the negotiable electronic transport record; and

(*b*) The electronic transport record ceases thereafter to have any effect or validity.

Chapter 4
Obligations of the carrier

Article 11
Carriage and delivery of the goods

The carrier shall, subject to this Convention and in accordance with the terms of the contract of carriage, carry the goods to the place of destination and deliver them to the consignee.

Article 12
Period of responsibility of the carrier

1. The period of responsibility of the carrier for the goods under this Convention begins when the carrier or a performing party receives the goods for carriage and ends when the goods are delivered.

2. (*a*) If the law or regulations of the place of receipt require the goods to be handed over to an authority or other third party from which the carrier may collect them, the period of responsibility of the carrier begins when the carrier collects the goods from the authority or other third party.

(*b*) If the law or regulations of the place of delivery require the carrier to hand over the goods to an authority or other third party from which the consignee may collect them, the period of responsibility of the carrier ends when the carrier hands the goods over to the authority or other third party.

3. For the purpose of determining the carrier's period of responsibility, the parties may agree on the time and location of receipt and delivery of the goods, but a provision in a contract of carriage is void to the extent that it provides that:

(*a*) The time of receipt of the goods is subsequent to the beginning of their initial loading under the contract of carriage; or

(*b*) The time of delivery of the goods is prior to the completion of their final unloading under the contract of carriage.

Article 13
Specific obligations

1. The carrier shall during the period of its responsibility as defined in article 12, and subject to article 26, properly and carefully receive, load, handle, stow, carry, keep, care for, unload and deliver the goods.

2. Notwithstanding paragraph 1 of this article, and without prejudice to the other provisions in chapter 4 and to chapters 5 to 7, the carrier and the shipper may agree that the loading, handling, stowing or unloading of the goods is to be performed by the shipper, the documentary shipper or the consignee. Such an agreement shall be referred to in the contract particulars.

Article 14
Specific obligations applicable to the voyage by sea

The carrier is bound before, at the beginning of, and during the voyage by sea to exercise due diligence to:

(*a*) Make and keep the ship seaworthy;

(*b*) Properly crew, equip and supply the ship and keep the ship so crewed, equipped and supplied throughout the voyage; and

(*c*) Make and keep the holds and all other parts of the ship in which the goods are carried, and any containers supplied by the carrier in or upon which the goods are carried, fit and safe for their reception, carriage and preservation.

Article 15
Goods that may become a danger

Notwithstanding articles 11 and 13, the carrier or a performing party may decline to receive or to load, and may take such other measures as are reasonable, including unloading, destroying, or rendering goods harmless, if the goods are, or reasonably appear likely to become during the carrier's period of responsibility, an actual danger to persons, property or the environment.

Article 16
Sacrifice of the goods during the voyage by sea

Notwithstanding articles 11, 13, and 14, the carrier or a performing party may sacrifice goods at sea when the sacrifice is reasonably made for the common safety or for the purpose of preserving from peril human life or other property involved in the common adventure.

Chapter 5
Liability of the carrier for loss, damage or delay

Article 17
Basis of liability

1. The carrier is liable for loss of or damage to the goods, as well as for delay in delivery, if the claimant proves that the loss, damage, or delay, or the event or circumstance that caused or contributed to it took place during the period of the carrier's responsibility as defined in chapter 4.

2. The carrier is relieved of all or part of its liability pursuant to paragraph 1 of this article if it proves that the cause or one of the causes of the loss, damage, or delay is not attributable to its fault or to the fault of any person referred to in article 18.

3. The carrier is also relieved of all or part of its liability pursuant to paragraph 1 of this article if, alternatively to proving the absence of fault as provided in paragraph 2 of this article, it proves that one or more of the following events or circumstances caused or contributed to the loss, damage, or delay:

(*a*) Act of God;

(*b*) Perils, dangers, and accidents of the sea or other navigable waters;

(*c*) War, hostilities, armed conflict, piracy, terrorism, riots, and civil commotions;

(*d*) Quarantine restrictions; interference by or impediments created by governments, public authorities, rulers, or people including detention, arrest, or seizure not attributable to the carrier or any person referred to in article 18;

(*e*) Strikes, lockouts, stoppages, or restraints of labour;

(*f*) Fire on the ship;

(*g*) Latent defects not discoverable by due diligence;

(*h*) Act or omission of the shipper, the documentary shipper, the controlling party, or any other person for whose acts the shipper or the documentary shipper is liable pursuant to article 33 or 34;

(*i*) Loading, handling, stowing, or unloading of the goods performed pursuant to an agreement in accordance with article 13, paragraph 2, unless the carrier or a performing party performs such activity on behalf of the shipper, the documentary shipper or the consignee;

(*j*) Wastage in bulk or weight or any other loss or damage arising from inherent defect, quality, or vice of the goods;

(*k*) Insufficiency or defective condition of packing or marking not performed by or on behalf of the carrier;

(*l*) Saving or attempting to save life at sea;

(*m*) Reasonable measures to save or attempt to save property at sea;

(*n*) Reasonable measures to avoid or attempt to avoid damage to the environment; or (*o*) Acts of the carrier in pursuance of the powers conferred by articles 15 and 16.

4. Notwithstanding paragraph 3 of this article, the carrier is liable for all or part of the loss, damage, or delay:

(*a*) If the claimant proves that the fault of the carrier or of a person referred to in article 18 caused or contributed to the event or circumstance on which the carrier relies; or

(*b*) If the claimant proves that an event or circumstance not listed in paragraph 3 of this article contributed to the loss, damage, or delay, and the carrier cannot prove that this event or circumstance is not attributable to its fault or to the fault of any person referred to in article 18.

5. The carrier is also liable, notwithstanding paragraph 3 of this article, for all or part of the loss, damage, or delay if:

(*a*) The claimant proves that the loss, damage, or delay was or was probably caused by or contributed to by (i) the unseaworthiness of the ship; (ii) the improper crewing, equipping, and supplying of the ship; or (iii) the fact that the holds or other parts of the ship in which the goods are carried, or any containers supplied by the carrier in or upon which the goods are carried, were not fit and safe for reception, carriage, and preservation of the goods; and

(*b*) The carrier is unable to prove either that: (i) none of the events or circumstances referred to in subparagraph 5 (*a*) of this article caused the loss, damage, or delay; or (ii) it complied with its obligation to exercise due diligence pursuant to article 14.

6. When the carrier is relieved of part of its liability pursuant to this article, the carrier is liable only for that part of the loss, damage or delay that is attributable to the event or circumstance for which it is liable pursuant to this article.

Article 18
Liability of the carrier for other persons

The carrier is liable for the breach of its obligations under this Convention caused by the acts or omissions of:

(*a*) Any performing party;

(*b*) The master or crew of the ship;

(*c*) Employees of the carrier or a performing party; or

(*d*) Any other person that performs or undertakes to perform any of the carrier's obligations under the contract of carriage, to the extent that the person acts, either directly or indirectly, at the carrier's request or under the carrier's supervision or control.

Article 19
Liability of maritime performing parties

1. A maritime performing party is subject to the obligations and liabilities imposed on the carrier under this Convention and is entitled to the carrier's defences and limits of liability as provided for in this Convention if:

(*a*) The maritime performing party received the goods for carriage in a Contracting State, or delivered them in a Contracting State, or performed its activities with respect to the goods in a port in a Contracting State; and (*b*) The occurrence that caused the loss, damage or delay took place: (i) during the period between the arrival of the goods at the port of loading of the ship and their departure from the port of discharge from the ship; (ii) while the maritime performing party had custody of the goods; or (iii) at any other time to the extent that it was participating in the performance of any of the activities contemplated by the contract of carriage.

2. If the carrier agrees to assume obligations other than those imposed on the carrier under this Convention, or agrees that the limits of its liability are higher than the limits specified under this Convention, a maritime performing party is not bound by this agreement unless it expressly agrees to accept such obligations or such higher limits.

3. A maritime performing party is liable for the breach of its obligations under this Convention caused by the acts or omissions of any person to which it has entrusted the performance of any of the carrier's obligations under the contract of carriage under the conditions set out in paragraph 1 of this article.

4. Nothing in this Convention imposes liability on the master or crew of the ship or on an employee of the carrier or of a maritime performing party.

Article 20
Joint and several liability

1. If the carrier and one or more maritime performing parties are liable for the loss of, damage to, or delay in delivery of the goods, their liability is joint and several but only up to the limits provided for under this Convention.

2. Without prejudice to article 61, the aggregate liability of all such persons shall not exceed the overall limits of liability under this Convention.

Article 21
Delay

Delay in delivery occurs when the goods are not delivered at the place of destination provided for in the contract of carriage within the time agreed.

Article 22
Calculation of compensation

1. Subject to article 59, the compensation payable by the carrier for loss of or damage to the goods is calculated by reference to the value of such goods at the place and time of delivery established in accordance with article 43.

2. The value of the goods is fixed according to the commodity exchange price or, if there is no such price, according to their market price or, if there is no commodity exchange price or market price, by reference to the normal value of the goods of the same kind and quality at the place of delivery.

3. In case of loss of or damage to the goods, the carrier is not liable for payment of any compensation beyond what is provided for in paragraphs 1 and 2 of this article except when the carrier and the shipper have agreed to calculate compensation in a different manner within the limits of chapter 16.

Article 23
Notice in case of loss, damage or delay

1. The carrier is presumed, in absence of proof to the contrary, to have delivered the goods according to their description in the contract particulars unless notice of

loss of or damage to the goods, indicating the general nature of such loss or damage, was given to the carrier or the performing party that delivered the goods before or at the time of the delivery, or, if the loss or damage is not apparent, within seven working days at the place of delivery after the delivery of the goods.

2. Failure to provide the notice referred to in this article to the carrier or the performing party shall not affect the right to claim compensation for loss of or damage to the goods under this Convention, nor shall it affect the allocation of the burden of proof set out in article 17.

3. The notice referred to in this article is not required in respect of loss or damage that is ascertained in a joint inspection of the goods by the person to which they have been delivered and the carrier or the maritime performing party against which liability is being asserted.

4. No compensation in respect of delay is payable unless notice of loss due to delay was given to the carrier within twenty-one consecutive days of delivery of the goods.

5. When the notice referred to in this article is given to the performing party that delivered the goods, it has the same effect as if that notice was given to the carrier, and notice given to the carrier has the same effect as a notice given to a maritime performing party.

6. In the case of any actual or apprehended loss or damage, the parties to the dispute shall give all reasonable facilities to each other for inspecting and tallying the goods and shall provide access to records and documents relevant to the carriage of the goods.

Chapter 6
Additional provisions relating to particular stages of carriage

Article 24
Deviation

When pursuant to applicable law a deviation constitutes a breach of the carrier's obligations, such deviation of itself shall not deprive the carrier or a maritime performing party of any defence or limitation of this Convention, except to the extent provided in article 61.

Article 25
Deck cargo on ships

1. Goods may be carried on the deck of a ship only if:

(*a*) Such carriage is required by law;

(*b*) They are carried in or on containers or vehicles that are fit for deck carriage, and the decks are specially fitted to carry such containers or vehicles; or

(*c*) The carriage on deck is in accordance with the contract of carriage, or the customs, usages or practices of the trade in question.

2. The provisions of this Convention relating to the liability of the carrier apply to the loss of, damage to or delay in the delivery of goods carried on deck pursuant to paragraph 1 of this article, but the carrier is not liable for loss of or damage to such goods, or delay in their delivery, caused by the special risks involved in their carriage on deck when the goods are carried in accordance with subparagraphs 1 (*a*) or (*c*) of this article.

3. If the goods have been carried on deck in cases other than those permitted pursuant to paragraph 1 of this article, the carrier is liable for loss of or damage to the goods or delay in their delivery that is exclusively caused by their carriage on deck, and is not entitled to the defences provided for in article 17.

4. The carrier is not entitled to invoke subparagraph 1 (*c*) of this article against a third party that has acquired a negotiable transport document or a negotiable electronic transport record in good faith, unless the contract particulars state that the goods may be carried on deck.

5. If the carrier and shipper expressly agreed that the goods would be carried under deck, the carrier is not entitled to the benefit of the limitation of liability for any loss of, damage to or delay in the delivery of the goods to the extent that such loss, damage, or delay resulted from their carriage on deck.

Article 26
Carriage preceding or subsequent to sea carriage

When loss of or damage to goods, or an event or circumstance causing a delay in their delivery, occurs during the carrier's period of responsibility but solely before their loading onto the ship or solely after their discharge from the ship, the provisions of this Convention do not prevail over those provisions of another international instrument that, at the time of such loss, damage or event or circumstance causing delay:

(*a*) Pursuant to the provisions of such international instrument would have applied to all or any of the carrier's activities if the shipper had made a separate and direct contract with the carrier in respect of the particular stage of carriage where the loss of, or damage to goods, or an event or circumstance causing delay in their delivery occurred;

(*b*) Specifically provide for the carrier's liability, limitation of liability, or time for suit; and

(*c*) Cannot be departed from by contract either at all or to the detriment of the shipper under that instrument.

Chapter 7
Obligations of the shipper to the carrier

Article 27
Delivery for carriage

1. Unless otherwise agreed in the contract of carriage, the shipper shall deliver the goods ready for carriage. In any event, the shipper shall deliver the goods in such condition that they will withstand the intended carriage, including their loading, handling, stowing, lashing and securing, and unloading, and that they will not cause harm to persons or property.

2. The shipper shall properly and carefully perform any obligation assumed under an agreement made pursuant to article 13, paragraph 2.

3. When a container is packed or a vehicle is loaded by the shipper, the shipper shall properly and carefully stow, lash and secure the contents in or on the container or vehicle, and in such a way that they will not cause harm to persons or property.

Article 28
Cooperation of the shipper and the carrier in providing information and instructions

The carrier and the shipper shall respond to requests from each other to provide information and instructions required for the proper handling and carriage of the goods if the information is in the requested party's possession or the instructions are within the requested party's reasonable ability to provide and they are not otherwise reasonably available to the requesting party.

Article 29
Shipper's obligation to provide information, instructions and documents

1. The shipper shall provide to the carrier in a timely manner such information, instructions and documents relating to the goods that are not otherwise reasonably available to the carrier, and that are reasonably necessary:

(*a*) For the proper handling and carriage of the goods, including precautions to be taken by the carrier or a performing party; and

(*b*) For the carrier to comply with law, regulations or other requirements of public authorities in connection with the intended carriage, provided that the carrier notifies the shipper in a timely manner of the information, instructions and documents it requires.

2. Nothing in this article affects any specific obligation to provide certain information, instructions and documents related to the goods pursuant to law, regulations or other requirements of public authorities in connection with the intended carriage.

Article 30
Basis of shipper's liability to the carrier

1. The shipper is liable for loss or damage sustained by the carrier if the carrier proves that such loss or damage was caused by a breach of the shipper's obligations under this Convention.

2. Except in respect of loss or damage caused by a breach by the shipper of its obligations pursuant to articles 31, paragraph 2, and 32, the shipper is relieved of all or part of its liability if the cause or one of the causes of the loss or damage is not attributable to its fault or to the fault of any person referred to in article 34.

3. When the shipper is relieved of part of its liability pursuant to this article, the shipper is liable only for that part of the loss or damage that is attributable to its fault or to the fault of any person referred to in article 34.

Article 31
Information for compilation of contract particulars

1. The shipper shall provide to the carrier, in a timely manner, accurate information required for the compilation of the contract particulars and the issuance of the transport documents or electronic transport records, including the particulars referred to in article 36, paragraph 1; the name of the party to be identified as the shipper in the contract particulars; the name of the consignee, if any; and the name of the person to whose order the transport document or electronic transport record is to be issued, if any.

2. The shipper is deemed to have guaranteed the accuracy at the time of receipt by the carrier of the information that is provided according to paragraph 1 of this

article. The shipper shall indemnify the carrier against loss or damage resulting from the inaccuracy of such information.

Article 32
Special rules on dangerous goods

When goods by their nature or character are, or reasonably appear likely to become, a danger to persons, property or the environment:

(*a*) The shipper shall inform the carrier of the dangerous nature or character of the goods in a timely manner before they are delivered to the carrier or a performing party. If the shipper fails to do so and the carrier or performing party does not otherwise have knowledge of their dangerous nature or character, the shipper is liable to the carrier for loss or damage resulting from such failure to inform; and

(*b*) The shipper shall mark or label dangerous goods in accordance with any law, regulations or other requirements of public authorities that apply during any stage of the intended carriage of the goods. If the shipper fails to do so, it is liable to the carrier for loss or damage resulting from such failure.

Article 33
Assumption of shipper's rights and obligations by the documentary shipper

1. A documentary shipper is subject to the obligations and liabilities imposed on the shipper pursuant to this chapter and pursuant to article 55, and is entitled to the shipper's rights and defences provided by this chapter and by chapter 13.

2. Paragraph 1 of this article does not affect the obligations, liabilities, rights or defences of the shipper.

Article 34
Liability of the shipper for other persons

The shipper is liable for the breach of its obligations under this Convention caused by the acts or omissions of any person, including employees, agents and subcontractors, to which it has entrusted the performance of any of its obligations, but the shipper is not liable for acts or omissions of the carrier or a performing party acting on behalf of the carrier, to which the shipper has entrusted the performance of its obligations.

Chapter 8
Transport documents and electronic transport records

Article 35
Issuance of the transport document or the electronic transport record

Unless the shipper and the carrier have agreed not to use a transport document or an electronic transport record, or it is the custom, usage or practice of the trade not to use one, upon delivery of the goods for carriage to the carrier or performing party, the shipper or, if the shipper consents, the documentary shipper, is entitled to obtain from the carrier, at the shipper's option:

(*a*) A non-negotiable transport document or, subject to article 8, subparagraph (*a*), a non-negotiable electronic transport record; or

(*b*) An appropriate negotiable transport document or, subject to article 8, subparagraph (*a*), a negotiable electronic transport record, unless the shipper and the carrier have agreed not to use a negotiable transport document or negotiable electronic transport record, or it is the custom, usage or practice of the trade not to use one.

Article 36
Contract particulars

1. The contract particulars in the transport document or electronic transport record referred to in article 35 shall include the following information, as furnished by the shipper:

(*a*) A description of the goods as appropriate for the transport;

(*b*) The leading marks necessary for identification of the goods;

(*c*) The number of packages or pieces, or the quantity of goods; and

(*d*) The weight of the goods, if furnished by the shipper.

2. The contract particulars in the transport document or electronic transport record referred to in article 35 shall also include:

(*a*) A statement of the apparent order and condition of the goods at the time the carrier or a performing party receives them for carriage;

(*b*) The name and address of the carrier;

(*c*) The date on which the carrier or a performing party received the goods, or on which the goods were loaded on board the ship, or on which the transport document or electronic transport record was issued; and

(*d*) If the transport document is negotiable, the number of originals of the negotiable transport document, when more than one original is issued.

3. The contract particulars in the transport document or electronic transport record referred to in article 35 shall further include:

(*a*) The name and address of the consignee, if named by the shipper;

(*b*) The name of a ship, if specified in the contract of carriage;

(*c*) The place of receipt and, if known to the carrier, the place of delivery; and

(*d*) The port of loading and the port of discharge, if specified in the contract of carriage.

4. For the purposes of this article, the phrase "apparent order and condition of the goods" in subparagraph 2 (*a*) of this article refers to the order and condition of the goods based on:

(*a*) A reasonable external inspection of the goods as packaged at the time the shipper delivers them to the carrier or a performing party; and

(*b*) Any additional inspection that the carrier or a performing party actually performs before issuing the transport document or electronic transport record.

Article 37
Identity of the carrier

1. If a carrier is identified by name in the contract particulars, any other information in the transport document or electronic transport record relating to the identity of the carrier shall have no effect to the extent that it is inconsistent with that identification.

2. If no person is identified in the contract particulars as the carrier as required pursuant to article 36, subparagraph 2 (*b*), but the contract particulars indicate that the goods have been loaded on board a named ship, the registered owner of that ship is presumed to be the carrier, unless it proves that the ship was under a bareboat charter at the time of the carriage and it identifies this bareboat charterer and indicates its address, in which case this bareboat charterer is presumed to be the carrier. Alternatively, the registered owner may rebut the presumption of being the carrier by identifying the carrier and indicating its address. The bareboat charterer may rebut any presumption of being the carrier in the same manner.

3. Nothing in this article prevents the claimant from proving that any person other than a person identified in the contract particulars or pursuant to paragraph 2 of this article is the carrier.

Article 38
Signature

1. A transport document shall be signed by the carrier or a person acting on its behalf.

2. An electronic transport record shall include the electronic signature of the carrier or a person acting on its behalf. Such electronic signature shall identify the signatory in relation to the electronic transport record and indicate the carrier's authorization of the electronic transport record.

Article 39
Deficiencies in the contract particulars

1. The absence or inaccuracy of one or more of the contract particulars referred to in article 36, paragraphs 1, 2 or 3, does not of itself affect the legal character or validity of the transport document or of the electronic transport record.

2. If the contract particulars include the date but fail to indicate its significance, the date is deemed to be:

(*a*) The date on which all of the goods indicated in the transport document or electronic transport record were loaded on board the ship, if the contract particulars indicate that the goods have been loaded on board a ship; or

(*b*) The date on which the carrier or a performing party received the goods, if the contract particulars do not indicate that the goods have been loaded on board a ship.

3. If the contract particulars fail to state the apparent order and condition of the goods at the time the carrier or a performing party receives them, the contract particulars are deemed to have stated that the goods were in apparent good order and condition at the time the carrier or a performing party received them.

Article 40
Qualifying the information relating to the goods in the contract particulars

1. The carrier shall qualify the information referred to in article 36, paragraph 1, to indicate that the carrier does not assume responsibility for the accuracy of the information furnished by the shipper if:

(*a*) The carrier has actual knowledge that any material statement in the transport document or electronic transport record is false or misleading; or (*b*) The carrier has reasonable grounds to believe that a material statement in the transport document or electronic transport record is false or misleading.

2. Without prejudice to paragraph 1 of this article, the carrier may qualify the information referred to in article 36, paragraph 1, in the circumstances and in the manner set out in paragraphs 3 and 4 of this article to indicate that the carrier does not assume responsibility for the accuracy of the information furnished by the shipper.

3. When the goods are not delivered for carriage to the carrier or a performing party in a closed container or vehicle, or when they are delivered in a closed container or vehicle and the carrier or a performing party actually inspects them, the carrier may qualify the information referred to in article 36, paragraph 1, if:

(*a*) The carrier had no physically practicable or commercially reasonable means of checking the information furnished by the shipper, in which case it may indicate which information it was unable to check; or

(*b*) The carrier has reasonable grounds to believe the information furnished by the shipper to be inaccurate, in which case it may include a clause providing what it reasonably considers accurate information.

4. When the goods are delivered for carriage to the carrier or a performing party in a closed container or vehicle, the carrier may qualify the information referred to in:

(*a*) Article 36, subparagraphs 1 (*a*), (*b*), or (*c*), if:

(i) The goods inside the container or vehicle have not actually been inspected by the carrier or a performing party; and

(ii) Neither the carrier nor a performing party otherwise has actual knowledge of its contents before issuing the transport document or the electronic transport record; and

(*b*) Article 36, subparagraph 1 (*d*), if:

(i) Neither the carrier nor a performing party weighed the container or vehicle, and the shipper and the carrier had not agreed prior to the shipment that the container or vehicle would be weighed and the weight would be included in the contract particulars; or

(ii) There was no physically practicable or commercially reasonable means of checking the weight of the container or vehicle.

Article 41
Evidentiary effect of the contract particulars

Except to the extent that the contract particulars have been qualified in the circumstances and in the manner set out in article 40:

(*a*) A transport document or an electronic transport record is prima facie evidence of the carrier's receipt of the goods as stated in the contract particulars;

(*b*) Proof to the contrary by the carrier in respect of any contract particulars shall not be admissible, when such contract particulars are included in:

(i) A negotiable transport document or a negotiable electronic transport record that is transferred to a third party acting in good faith; or

(ii) A non-negotiable transport document that indicates that it must be surrendered in order to obtain delivery of the goods and is transferred to the consignee acting in good faith;

(*c*) Proof to the contrary by the carrier shall not be admissible against a consignee that in good faith has acted in reliance on any of the following contract particulars included in a non-negotiable transport document or a non-negotiable electronic transport record:

(i) The contract particulars referred to in article 36, paragraph 1, when such contract particulars are furnished by the carrier;

(ii) The number, type and identifying numbers of the containers, but not the identifying numbers of the container seals; and

(iii) The contract particulars referred to in article 36, paragraph 2.

Article 42
"Freight prepaid"

If the contract particulars contain the statement "freight prepaid" or a statement of a similar nature, the carrier cannot assert against the holder or the consignee the fact that the freight has not been paid. This article does not apply if the holder or the consignee is also the shipper.

Chapter 9
Delivery of the goods

Article 43
Obligation to accept delivery

When the goods have arrived at their destination, the consignee that demands delivery of the goods under the contract of carriage shall accept delivery of the goods at the time or within the time period and at the location agreed in the contract of carriage or, failing such agreement, at the time and location at which, having regard to the terms of the contract, the customs, usages or practices of the trade and the circumstances of the carriage, delivery could reasonably be expected.

Article 44
Obligation to acknowledge receipt

On request of the carrier or the performing party that delivers the goods, the consignee shall acknowledge receipt of the goods from the carrier or the performing party in the manner that is customary at the place of delivery. The carrier may refuse delivery if the consignee refuses to acknowledge such receipt.

Article 45
Delivery when no negotiable transport document or negotiable electronic transport record is issued

When neither a negotiable transport document nor a negotiable electronic transport record has been issued:

(*a*) The carrier shall deliver the goods to the consignee at the time and location referred to in article 43. The carrier may refuse delivery if the person claiming to be the consignee does not properly identify itself as the consignee on the request of the carrier;

(*b*) If the name and address of the consignee are not referred to in the contract particulars, the controlling party shall prior to or upon the arrival of the goods at the place of destination advise the carrier of such name and address;

(*c*) Without prejudice to article 48, paragraph 1, if the goods are not deliverable because (i) the consignee, after having received a notice of arrival, does not, at the time or within the time period referred to in article 43, claim delivery of the goods from the carrier after their arrival at the place of destination, (ii) the carrier refuses delivery because the person claiming to be the consignee does not properly identify itself as the consignee, or (iii) the carrier is, after reasonable effort, unable to locate the consignee in order to request delivery instructions, the carrier may so advise the controlling party and request instructions in respect of the delivery of the goods. If, after reasonable effort, the carrier is unable to locate the controlling party, the carrier may so advise the shipper and request instructions in respect of the delivery of the goods. If, after reasonable effort, the carrier is unable to locate the shipper, the carrier may so advise the documentary shipper and request instructions in respect of the delivery of the goods;

(*d*) The carrier that delivers the goods upon instruction of the controlling party, the shipper or the documentary shipper pursuant to subparagraph (*c*) of this article is discharged from its obligations to deliver the goods under the contract of carriage.

Article 46
Delivery when a non-negotiable transport document that requires surrender is issued

When a non-negotiable transport document has been issued that indicates that it shall be surrendered in order to obtain delivery of the goods:

(*a*) The carrier shall deliver the goods at the time and location referred to in article 43 to the consignee upon the consignee properly identifying itself on the request of the carrier and surrender of the non-negotiable document. The carrier may refuse delivery if the person claiming to be the consignee fails to properly identify itself on the request of the carrier, and shall refuse delivery if the non-negotiable document is not surrendered. If more than one original of the non-negotiable document has been issued, the surrender of one original will suffice and the other originals cease to have any effect or validity;

(*b*) Without prejudice to article 48, paragraph 1, if the goods are not deliverable because (i) the consignee, after having received a notice of arrival, does not, at the time or within the time period referred to in article 43, claim delivery of the goods from the carrier after their arrival at the place of destination, (ii) the carrier refuses delivery because the person claiming to be the consignee does not properly identify itself as the consignee or does not surrender the document, or (iii) the carrier is, after reasonable effort, unable to locate the consignee in order to request delivery instructions, the carrier may so advise the shipper and request instructions in respect of the delivery of the goods. If, after reasonable effort, the carrier is unable to locate the shipper, the carrier may so advise the documentary shipper and request instructions in respect of the delivery of the goods;

(*c*) The carrier that delivers the goods upon instruction of the shipper or the documentary shipper pursuant to subparagraph (*b*) of this article is discharged from its obligation to deliver the goods under the contract of carriage, irrespective of whether the non-negotiable transport document has been surrendered to it.

Article 47
Delivery when a negotiable transport document or negotiable electronic transport record is issued

1. When a negotiable transport document or a negotiable electronic transport record has been issued:

(*a*) The holder of the negotiable transport document or negotiable electronic transport record is entitled to claim delivery of the goods from the carrier after they have arrived at the place of destination, in which event the carrier shall deliver the goods at the time and location referred to in article 43 to the holder:

(i) Upon surrender of the negotiable transport document and, if the holder is one of the persons referred to in article 1, subparagraph 10 (*a*) (i), upon the holder properly identifying itself; or

(ii) Upon demonstration by the holder, in accordance with the procedures referred to in article 9, paragraph 1, that it is the holder of the negotiable electronic transport record;

(*b*) The carrier shall refuse delivery if the requirements of subparagraph (*a*) (i) or (*a*) (ii) of this paragraph are not met;

(*c*) If more than one original of the negotiable transport document has been issued, and the number of originals is stated in that document, the surrender of one original will suffice and the other originals cease to have any effect or validity. When a negotiable electronic transport record has been used, such electronic transport record ceases to have any effect or validity upon delivery to the holder in accordance with the procedures required by article 9, paragraph 1.

2. Without prejudice to article 48, paragraph 1, if the negotiable transport document or the negotiable electronic transport record expressly states that the goods may be delivered without the surrender of the transport document or the electronic transport record, the following rules apply:

(*a*) If the goods are not deliverable because (i) the holder, after having received a notice of arrival, does not, at the time or within the time period referred to in article 43, claim delivery of the goods from the carrier after their arrival at the place of destination, (ii) the carrier refuses delivery because the person claiming to be a holder does not properly identify itself as one of the persons referred to in article 1, subparagraph 10 (*a*) (i), or (iii) the carrier is, after reasonable effort, unable to locate the holder in order to request delivery instructions, the carrier may so advise the shipper and request instructions in respect of the delivery of the goods. If, after reasonable effort, the carrier is unable to locate the shipper, the carrier may so advise the documentary shipper and request instructions in respect of the delivery of the goods;

(*b*) The carrier that delivers the goods upon instruction of the shipper or the documentary shipper in accordance with subparagraph 2 (*a*) of this article is discharged from its obligation to deliver the goods under the contract of carriage to the holder, irrespective of whether the negotiable transport document has been surrendered to it, or the person claiming delivery under a negotiable electronic transport record has demonstrated, in accordance with the procedures referred to in article 9, paragraph 1, that it is the holder;

(*c*) The person giving instructions under subparagraph 2 (*a*) of this article shall indemnify the carrier against loss arising from its being held liable to the holder under subparagraph 2 (*e*) of this article. The carrier may refuse to follow those instructions if the person fails to provide adequate security as the carrier may reasonably request;

(*d*) A person that becomes a holder of the negotiable transport document or the negotiable electronic transport record after the carrier has delivered the goods pursuant to subparagraph 2 (*b*) of this article, but pursuant to contractual or other arrangements made before such delivery acquires rights against the carrier under the contract of carriage, other than the right to claim delivery of the goods;

(*e*) Notwithstanding subparagraphs 2 (*b*) and 2 (*d*) of this article, a holder that becomes a holder after such delivery, and that did not have and could not reasonably have had knowledge of such delivery at the time it became a holder, acquires the rights incorporated in the negotiable transport document or negotiable electronic transport record. When the contract particulars state the expected time of arrival of the goods, or indicate how to obtain information as to whether the goods have been delivered, it is presumed that the holder at the time that it became a holder had or could reasonably have had knowledge of the delivery of the goods.

Article 48
Goods remaining undelivered

1. For the purposes of this article, goods shall be deemed to have remained undelivered only if, after their arrival at the place of destination:

(*a*) The consignee does not accept delivery of the goods pursuant to this chapter at the time and location referred to in article 43;

(*b*) The controlling party, the holder, the shipper or the documentary shipper cannot be found or does not give the carrier adequate instructions pursuant to articles 45, 46 and 47;

(*c*) The carrier is entitled or required to refuse delivery pursuant to articles 44, 45, 46 and 47;

(*d*) The carrier is not allowed to deliver the goods to the consignee pursuant to the law or regulations of the place at which delivery is requested; or

(*e*) The goods are otherwise undeliverable by the carrier.

2. Without prejudice to any other rights that the carrier may have against the shipper, controlling party or consignee, if the goods have remained undelivered, the carrier may, at the risk and expense of the person entitled to the goods, take such action in respect of the goods as circumstances may reasonably require, including:

(*a*) To store the goods at any suitable place;

(*b*) To unpack the goods if they are packed in containers or vehicles, or to act otherwise in respect of the goods, including by moving them; and

(*c*) To cause the goods to be sold or destroyed in accordance with the practices or pursuant to the law or regulations of the place where the goods are located at the time.

3. The carrier may exercise the rights under paragraph 2 of this article only after it has given reasonable notice of the intended action under paragraph 2 of this article to the person stated in the contract particulars as the person, if any, to be notified of the arrival of the goods at the place of destination, and to one of the following persons in the order indicated, if known to the carrier: the consignee, the controlling party or the shipper.

4. If the goods are sold pursuant to subparagraph 2 (*c*) of this article, the carrier shall hold the proceeds of the sale for the benefit of the person entitled to the goods, subject to the deduction of any costs incurred by the carrier and any other amounts that are due to the carrier in connection with the carriage of those goods.

5. The carrier shall not be liable for loss of or damage to goods that occurs during the time that they remain undelivered pursuant to this article unless the claimant proves that such loss or damage resulted from the failure by the carrier to take steps that would have been reasonable in the circumstances to preserve the goods and that the carrier knew or ought to have known that the loss or damage to the goods would result from its failure to take such steps.

Article 49
Retention of goods

Nothing in this Convention affects a right of the carrier or a performing party that may exist pursuant to the contract of carriage or the applicable law to retain the goods to secure the payment of sums due.

Chapter 10
Rights of the controlling party

Article 50
Exercise and extent of right of control

1. The right of control may be exercised only by the controlling party and is limited to:

(*a*) The right to give or modify instructions in respect of the goods that do not constitute a variation of the contract of carriage;

(*b*) The right to obtain delivery of the goods at a scheduled port of call or, in respect of inland carriage, any place en route; and

(*c*) The right to replace the consignee by any other person including the controlling party.

2. The right of control exists during the entire period of responsibility of the carrier, as provided in article 12, and ceases when that period expires.

Article 51
Identity of the controlling party and transfer of the right of control

1. Except in the cases referred to in paragraphs 2, 3 and 4 of this article:

(*a*) The shipper is the controlling party unless the shipper, when the contract of carriage is concluded, designates the consignee, the documentary shipper or another person as the controlling party;

(*b*) The controlling party is entitled to transfer the right of control to another person. The transfer becomes effective with respect to the carrier upon its notification of the transfer by the transferor, and the transferee becomes the controlling party; and

(*c*) The controlling party shall properly identify itself when it exercises the right of control.

2. When a non-negotiable transport document has been issued that indicates that it shall be surrendered in order to obtain delivery of the goods:

(*a*) The shipper is the controlling party and may transfer the right of control to the consignee named in the transport document by transferring the document to that person without endorsement. If more than one original of the document was issued, all originals shall be transferred in order to effect a transfer of the right of control; and

(*b*) In order to exercise its right of control, the controlling party shall produce the document and properly identify itself. If more than one original of the document was issued, all originals shall be produced, failing which the right of control cannot be exercised.

3. When a negotiable transport document is issued:

(*a*) The holder or, if more than one original of the negotiable transport document is issued, the holder of all originals is the controlling party;

(*b*) The holder may transfer the right of control by transferring the negotiable transport document to another person in accordance with article 57. If more than one original of that document was issued, all originals shall be transferred to that person in order to effect a transfer of the right of control; and

(*c*) In order to exercise the right of control, the holder shall produce the negotiable transport document to the carrier, and if the holder is one of the persons referred to in article 1, subparagraph 10 (*a*) (i), the holder shall properly identify itself. If more than one original of the document was issued, all originals shall be produced, failing which the right of control cannot be exercised.

4. When a negotiable electronic transport record is issued:

(*a*) The holder is the controlling party;

(*b*) The holder may transfer the right of control to another person by transferring the negotiable electronic transport record in accordance with the procedures referred to in article 9, paragraph 1; and

(*c*) In order to exercise the right of control, the holder shall demonstrate, in accordance with the procedures referred to in article 9, paragraph 1, that it is the holder.

Article 52
Carrier's execution of instructions

1. Subject to paragraphs 2 and 3 of this article, the carrier shall execute the instructions referred to in article 50 if:

(*a*) The person giving such instructions is entitled to exercise the right of control;

(*b*) The instructions can reasonably be executed according to their terms at the moment that they reach the carrier; and (*c*) The instructions will not interfere with the normal operations of the carrier, including its delivery practices.

2. In any event, the controlling party shall reimburse the carrier for any reasonable additional expense that the carrier may incur and shall indemnify the carrier against loss or damage that the carrier may suffer as a result of diligently executing any instruction pursuant to this article, including compensation that the carrier may become liable to pay for loss of or damage to other goods being carried.

3. The carrier is entitled to obtain security from the controlling party for the amount of additional expense, loss or damage that the carrier reasonably expects will arise in connection with the execution of an instruction pursuant to this article. The carrier may refuse to carry out the instructions if no such security is provided.

4. The carrier's liability for loss of or damage to the goods or for delay in delivery resulting from its failure to comply with the instructions of the controlling party in breach of its obligation pursuant to paragraph 1 of this article shall be subject to articles 17 to 23, and the amount of the compensation payable by the carrier shall be subject to articles 59 to 61.

Article 53
Deemed delivery

Goods that are delivered pursuant to an instruction in accordance with article 52, paragraph 1, are deemed to be delivered at the place of destination, and the provisions of chapter 9 relating to such delivery apply to such goods.

Article 54
Variations to the contract of carriage

1. The controlling party is the only person that may agree with the carrier to variations to the contract of carriage other than those referred to in article 50, subparagraphs 1 (*b*) and (*c*).

2. Variations to the contract of carriage, including those referred to in article 50, subparagraphs 1 (*b*) and (*c*), shall be stated in a negotiable transport document or in a non-negotiable transport document that requires surrender, or incorporated in a negotiable electronic transport record, or, upon the request of the controlling party, shall be stated in a non-negotiable transport document or incorporated in a non-negotiable electronic transport record. If so stated or incorporated, such variations shall be signed in accordance with article 38.

Article 55
Providing additional information, instructions or documents to carrier

1. The controlling party, on request of the carrier or a performing party, shall provide in a timely manner information, instructions or documents relating to the goods not yet provided by the shipper and not otherwise reasonably available to the carrier that the carrier may reasonably need to perform its obligations under the contract of carriage.

2. If the carrier, after reasonable effort, is unable to locate the controlling party or the controlling party is unable to provide adequate information, instructions or documents to the carrier, the shipper shall provide them. If the carrier, after reasonable effort, is unable to locate the shipper, the documentary shipper shall provide such information, instructions or documents.

Article 56
Variation by agreement

The parties to the contract of carriage may vary the effect of articles 50, subparagraphs 1 (*b*) and (*c*), 50, paragraph 2, and 52. The parties may also restrict or exclude the transferability of the right of control referred to in article 51, subparagraph 1 (*b*).

Chapter 11
Transfer of rights

Article 57
When a negotiable transport document or negotiable electronic transport record is issued

1. When a negotiable transport document is issued, the holder may transfer the rights incorporated in the document by transferring it to another person:

(*a*) Duly endorsed either to such other person or in blank, if an order document; or

(*b*) Without endorsement, if: (i) a bearer document or a blank endorsed document; or (ii) a document made out to the order of a named person and the transfer is between the first holder and the named person.

2. When a negotiable electronic transport record is issued, its holder may transfer the rights incorporated in it, whether it be made out to order or to the order of a named person, by transferring the electronic transport record in accordance with the procedures referred to in article 9, paragraph 1.

Article 58
Liability of holder

1. Without prejudice to article 55, a holder that is not the shipper and that does not exercise any right under the contract of carriage does not assume any liability under the contract of carriage solely by reason of being a holder.

2. A holder that is not the shipper and that exercises any right under the contract of carriage assumes any liabilities imposed on it under the contract of carriage to the extent that such liabilities are incorporated in or ascertainable from the negotiable transport document or the negotiable electronic transport record.

3. For the purposes of paragraphs 1 and 2 of this article, a holder that is not the shipper does not exercise any right under the contract of carriage solely because:

(*a*) It agrees with the carrier, pursuant to article 10, to replace a negotiable transport document by a negotiable electronic transport record or to replace a negotiable electronic transport record by a negotiable transport document; or

(*b*) It transfers its rights pursuant to article 57.

Chapter 12
Limits of liability

Article 59
Limits of liability

1. Subject to articles 60 and 61, paragraph 1, the carrier's liability for breaches of its obligations under this Convention is limited to 875 units of account per package or other shipping unit, or 3 units of account per kilogram of the gross weight of the

goods that are the subject of the claim or dispute, whichever amount is the higher, except when the value of the goods has been declared by the shipper and included in the contract particulars, or when a higher amount than the amount of limitation of liability set out in this article has been agreed upon between the carrier and the shipper.

2. When goods are carried in or on a container, pallet or similar article of transport used to consolidate goods, or in or on a vehicle, the packages or shipping units enumerated in the contract particulars as packed in or on such article of transport or vehicle are deemed packages or shipping units. If not so enumerated, the goods in or on such article of transport or vehicle are deemed one shipping unit.

3. The unit of account referred to in this article is the Special Drawing Right as defined by the International Monetary Fund. The amounts referred to in this article are to be converted into the national currency of a State according to the value of such currency at the date of judgement or award or the date agreed upon by the parties. The value of a national currency, in terms of the Special Drawing Right, of a Contracting State that is a member of the International Monetary Fund is to be calculated in accordance with the method of valuation applied by the International Monetary Fund in effect at the date in question for its operations and transactions. The value of a national currency, in terms of the Special Drawing Right, of a Contracting State that is not a member of the International Monetary Fund is to be calculated in a manner to be determined by that State.

Article 60
Limits of liability for loss caused by delay

Subject to article 61, paragraph 2, compensation for loss of or damage to the goods due to delay shall be calculated in accordance with article 22 and liability for economic loss due to delay is limited to an amount equivalent to two and one-half times the freight payable on the goods delayed. The total amount payable pursuant to this article and article 59, paragraph 1, may not exceed the limit that would be established pursuant to article 59, paragraph 1, in respect of the total loss of the goods concerned.

Article 61
Loss of the benefit of limitation of liability

1. Neither the carrier nor any of the persons referred to in article 18 is entitled to the benefit of the limitation of liability as provided in article 59, or as provided in the contract of carriage, if the claimant proves that the loss resulting from the breach of the carrier's obligation under this Convention was attributable to a personal act or omission of the person claiming a right to limit done with the intent to cause such loss or recklessly and with knowledge that such loss would probably result.

2. Neither the carrier nor any of the persons mentioned in article 18 is entitled to the benefit of the limitation of liability as provided in article 60 if the claimant proves that the delay in delivery resulted from a personal act or omission of the person claiming a right to limit done with the intent to cause the loss due to delay or recklessly and with knowledge that such loss would probably result.

Chapter 13
Time for suit

Article 62
Period of time for suit

1. No judicial or arbitral proceedings in respect of claims or disputes arising from a breach of an obligation under this Convention may be instituted after the expiration of a period of two years.

2. The period referred to in paragraph 1 of this article commences on the day on which the carrier has delivered the goods or, in cases in which no goods have been delivered or only part of the goods have been delivered, on the last day on which the goods should have been delivered. The day on which the period commences is not included in the period.

3. Notwithstanding the expiration of the period set out in paragraph 1 of this article, one party may rely on its claim as a defence or for the purpose of set-off against a claim asserted by the other party.

Article 63
Extension of time for suit

The period provided in article 62 shall not be subject to suspension or interruption, but the person against which a claim is made may at any time during the running of the period extend that period by a declaration to the claimant. This period may be further extended by another declaration or declarations.

Article 64
Action for indemnity

An action for indemnity by a person held liable may be instituted after the expiration of the period provided in article 62 if the indemnity action is instituted within the later of:

(*a*) The time allowed by the applicable law in the jurisdiction where proceedings are instituted; or

(*b*) Ninety days commencing from the day when the person instituting the action for indemnity has either settled the claim or been served with process in the action against itself, whichever is earlier.

Article 65
Actions against the person identified as the carrier

An action against the bareboat charterer or the person identified as the carrier pursuant to article 37, paragraph 2, may be instituted after the expiration of the period provided in article 62 if the action is instituted within the later of:

(*a*) The time allowed by the applicable law in the jurisdiction where proceedings are instituted; or

(*b*) Ninety days commencing from the day when the carrier has been identified, or the registered owner or bareboat charterer has rebutted the presumption that it is the carrier, pursuant to article 37, paragraph 2.

Chapter 14
Jurisdiction

Article 66
Actions against the carrier

Unless the contract of carriage contains an exclusive choice of court agreement that complies with article 67 or 72, the plaintiff has the right to institute judicial proceedings under this Convention against the carrier:

(*a*) In a competent court within the jurisdiction of which is situated one of the following places:

(i) The domicile of the carrier;

(ii) The place of receipt agreed in the contract of carriage;

(iii) The place of delivery agreed in the contract of carriage; or

(iv) The port where the goods are initially loaded on a ship or the port where the goods are finally discharged from a ship; or

(*b*) In a competent court or courts designated by an agreement between the shipper and the carrier for the purpose of deciding claims against the carrier that may arise under this Convention.

Article 67
Choice of court agreements

1. The jurisdiction of a court chosen in accordance with article 66, subparagraph *b*), is exclusive for disputes between the parties to the contract only if the parties so agree and the agreement conferring jurisdiction:

(*a*) Is contained in a volume contract that clearly states the names and addresses of the parties and either (i) is individually negotiated or (ii) contains a prominent statement that there is an exclusive choice of court agreement and specifies the sections of the volume contract containing that agreement; and

(*b*) Clearly designates the courts of one Contracting State or one or more specific courts of one Contracting State.

2. A person that is not a party to the volume contract is bound by an exclusive choice of court agreement concluded in accordance with paragraph 1 of this article only if:

(*a*) The court is in one of the places designated in article 66, subparagraph (*a*);

(*b*) That agreement is contained in the transport document or electronic transport record;

(*c*) That person is given timely and adequate notice of the court where the action shall be brought and that the jurisdiction of that court is exclusive; and

(*d*) The law of the court seized recognizes that that person may be bound by the exclusive choice of court agreement.

Article 68
Actions against the maritime performing party

The plaintiff has the right to institute judicial proceedings under this Convention against the maritime performing party in a competent court within the jurisdiction of which is situated one of the following places:

(*a*) The domicile of the maritime performing party; or

(*b*) The port where the goods are received by the maritime performing party, the port where the goods are delivered by the maritime performing party or the port in which the maritime performing party performs its activities with respect to the goods.

Article 69
No additional bases of jurisdiction

Subject to articles 71 and 72, no judicial proceedings under this Convention against the carrier or a maritime performing party may be instituted in a court not designated pursuant to article 66 or 68.

Article 70
Arrest and provisional or protective measures

Nothing in this Convention affects jurisdiction with regard to provisional or protective measures, including arrest. A court in a State in which a provisional or protective measure was taken does not have jurisdiction to determine the case upon its merits unless:

(*a*) The requirements of this chapter are fulfilled; or

(*b*) An international convention that applies in that State so provides.

Article 71
Consolidation and removal of actions

1. Except when there is an exclusive choice of court agreement that is binding pursuant to article 67 or 72, if a single action is brought against both the carrier and the maritime performing party arising out of a single occurrence, the action may be instituted only in a court designated pursuant to both article 66 and article 68. If there is no such court, such action may be instituted in a court designated pursuant to article 68, subparagraph (*b*), if there is such a court.

2. Except when there is an exclusive choice of court agreement that is binding pursuant to article 67 or 72, a carrier or a maritime performing party that institutes an action seeking a declaration of non-liability or any other action that would deprive a person of its right to select the forum pursuant to article 66 or 68 shall, at the request of the defendant, withdraw that action once the defendant has chosen a court designated pursuant to article 66 or 68, whichever is applicable, where the action may be recommenced.

Article 72
Agreement after a dispute has arisen and jurisdiction when the defendant has entered an appearance

1. After a dispute has arisen, the parties to the dispute may agree to resolve it in any competent court.

2. A competent court before which a defendant appears, without contesting jurisdiction in accordance with the rules of that court, has jurisdiction.

Article 73
Recognition and enforcement

1. A decision made in one Contracting State by a court having jurisdiction under this Convention shall be recognized and enforced in another Contracting State in accordance with the law of such latter Contracting State when both States have made a declaration in accordance with article 74.

2. A court may refuse recognition and enforcement based on the grounds for the refusal of recognition and enforcement available pursuant to its law.

3. This chapter shall not affect the application of the rules of a regional economic integration organization that is a party to this Convention, as concerns the recognition or enforcement of judgements as between member States of the regional economic integration organization, whether adopted before or after this Convention.

Article 74
Application of chapter 14

The provisions of this chapter shall bind only Contracting States that declare in accordance with article 91 that they will be bound by them.

Chapter 15
Arbitration

Article 75
Arbitration agreements

1. Subject to this chapter, parties may agree that any dispute that may arise relating to the carriage of goods under this Convention shall be referred to arbitration.

2. The arbitration proceedings shall, at the option of the person asserting a claim against the carrier, take place at:

(*a*) Any place designated for that purpose in the arbitration agreement; or

(*b*) Any other place situated in a State where any of the following places is located:

(i) The domicile of the carrier;

(ii) The place of receipt agreed in the contract of carriage;

(iii) The place of delivery agreed in the contract of carriage; or

(iv) The port where the goods are initially loaded on a ship or the port where the goods are finally discharged from a ship.

3. The designation of the place of arbitration in the agreement is binding for disputes between the parties to the agreement if the agreement is contained in a volume contract that clearly states the names and addresses of the parties and either:

(*a*) Is individually negotiated; or

(*b*) Contains a prominent statement that there is an arbitration agreement and specifies the sections of the volume contract containing the arbitration agreement.

4. When an arbitration agreement has been concluded in accordance with paragraph 3 of this article, a person that is not a party to the volume contract is bound by the designation of the place of arbitration in that agreement only if:

(*a*) The place of arbitration designated in the agreement is situated in one of the places referred to in subparagraph 2 (*b*) of this article;

(*b*) The agreement is contained in the transport document or electronic transport record;

(*c*) The person to be bound is given timely and adequate notice of the place of arbitration; and

(*d*) Applicable law permits that person to be bound by the arbitration agreement.

5. The provisions of paragraphs 1, 2, 3 and 4 of this article are deemed to be part of every arbitration clause or agreement, and any term of such clause or agreement to the extent that it is inconsistent therewith is void.

Article 76
Arbitration agreement in non-liner transportation

1. Nothing in this Convention affects the enforceability of an arbitration agreement in a contract of carriage in non-liner transportation to which this Convention or the provisions of this Convention apply by reason of:

(*a*) The application of article 7; or

(*b*) The parties' voluntary incorporation of this Convention in a contract of carriage that would not otherwise be subject to this Convention.

2. Notwithstanding paragraph 1 of this article, an arbitration agreement in a transport document or electronic transport record to which this Convention applies by reason of the application of article 7 is subject to this chapter unless such a transport document or electronic transport record:

(*a*) Identifies the parties to and the date of the charter party or other contract excluded from the application of this Convention by reason of the application of article 6; and

(*b*) Incorporates by specific reference the clause in the charter party or other contract that contains the terms of the arbitration agreement.

Article 77
Agreement to arbitrate after a dispute has arisen

Notwithstanding the provisions of this chapter and chapter 14, after a dispute has arisen the parties to the dispute may agree to resolve it by arbitration in any place.

Article 78
Application of chapter 15

The provisions of this chapter shall bind only Contracting States that declare in accordance with article 91 that they will be bound by them.

Chapter 16
Validity of contractual terms

Article 79
General provisions

1. Unless otherwise provided in this Convention, any term in a contract of carriage is void to the extent that it:

(*a*) Directly or indirectly excludes or limits the obligations of the carrier or a maritime performing party under this Convention;

(*b*) Directly or indirectly excludes or limits the liability of the carrier or a maritime performing party for breach of an obligation under this Convention; or

(*c*) Assigns a benefit of insurance of the goods in favour of the carrier or a person referred to in article 18.

2. Unless otherwise provided in this Convention, any term in a contract of carriage is void to the extent that it:

(*a*) Directly or indirectly excludes, limits or increases the obligations under this Convention of the shipper, consignee, controlling party, holder or documentary shipper; or

(*b*) Directly or indirectly excludes, limits or increases the liability of the shipper, consignee, controlling party, holder or documentary shipper for breach of any of its obligations under this Convention.

Article 80
Special rules for volume contracts

1. Notwithstanding article 79, as between the carrier and the shipper, a volume contract to which this Convention applies may provide for greater or lesser rights, obligations and liabilities than those imposed by this Convention.

2. A derogation pursuant to paragraph 1 of this article is binding only when:

(*a*) The volume contract contains a prominent statement that it derogates from this Convention;

(*b*) The volume contract is (i) individually negotiated or (ii) prominently specifies the sections of the volume contract containing the derogations;

(*c*) The shipper is given an opportunity and notice of the opportunity to conclude a contract of carriage on terms and conditions that comply with this Convention without any derogation under this article; and

(*d*) The derogation is neither (i) incorporated by reference from another document nor (ii) included in a contract of adhesion that is not subject to negotiation.

3. A carrier's public schedule of prices and services, transport document, electronic transport record or similar document is not a volume contract pursuant to paragraph 1 of this article, but a volume contract may incorporate such documents by reference as terms of the contract.

4. Paragraph 1 of this article does not apply to rights and obligations provided in articles 14, subparagraphs (*a*) and (*b*), 29 and 32 or to liability arising from the breach thereof, nor does it apply to any liability arising from an act or omission referred to in article 61.

5. The terms of the volume contract that derogate from this Convention, if the volume contract satisfies the requirements of paragraph 2 of this article, apply between the carrier and any person other than the shipper provided that:

(*a*) Such person received information that prominently states that the volume contract derogates from this Convention and gave its express consent to be bound by such derogations; and

(*b*) Such consent is not solely set forth in a carrier's public schedule of prices and services, transport document or electronic transport record.

6. The party claiming the benefit of the derogation bears the burden of proof that the conditions for derogation have been fulfilled.

Article 81
Special rules for live animals and certain other goods

Notwithstanding article 79 and without prejudice to article 80, the contract of carriage may exclude or limit the obligations or the liability of both the carrier and a maritime performing party if:

(*a*) The goods are live animals, but any such exclusion or limitation will not be effective if the claimant proves that the loss of or damage to the goods, or delay in delivery, resulted from an act or omission of the carrier or of a person referred to in article 18, done with the intent to cause such loss of or damage to the goods or such loss due to delay or done recklessly and with knowledge that such loss or damage or such loss due to delay would probably result; or

(*b*) The character or condition of the goods or the circumstances and terms and conditions under which the carriage is to be performed are such as reasonably to justify a special agreement, provided that such contract of carriage is not related to ordinary commercial shipments made in the ordinary course of trade and that no negotiable transport document or negotiable electronic transport record is issued for the carriage of the goods.

Chapter 17
Matters not governed by this convention

Article 82
International conventions governing the carriage of goods by other modes of transport

Nothing in this Convention affects the application of any of the following international conventions in force at the time this Convention enters into force, including any future amendment to such conventions, that regulate the liability of the carrier for loss of or damage to the goods:

(*a*) Any convention governing the carriage of goods by air to the extent that such convention according to its provisions applies to any part of the contract of carriage;

(*b*) Any convention governing the carriage of goods by road to the extent that such convention according to its provisions applies to the carriage of goods that remain loaded on a road cargo vehicle carried on board a ship;

(*c*) Any convention governing the carriage of goods by rail to the extent that such convention according to its provisions applies to carriage of goods by sea as a supplement to the carriage by rail; or (*d*) Any convention governing the carriage of goods by inland waterways to the extent that such convention according to its provisions applies to a carriage of goods without trans-shipment both by inland waterways and sea.

Article 83
Global limitation of liability

Nothing in this Convention affects the application of any international convention or national law regulating the global limitation of liability of vessel owners.

Article 84
General average

Nothing in this Convention affects the application of terms in the contract of carriage or provisions of national law regarding the adjustment of general average.

Article 85
Passengers and luggage

This Convention does not apply to a contract of carriage for passengers and their luggage.

Article 86
Damage caused by nuclear incident

No liability arises under this Convention for damage caused by a nuclear incident if the operator of a nuclear installation is liable for such damage:

(*a*) Under the Paris Convention on Third Party Liability in the Field of Nuclear Energy of 29 July 1960 as amended by the Additional Protocol of 28 January 1964 and by the Protocols of 16 November 1982 and 12 February 2004, the Vienna Convention on Civil Liability for Nuclear Damage of 21 May 1963 as amended by the Joint Protocol Relating to the Application of the Vienna Convention and the Paris Convention of 21 September 1988 and as amended by the Protocol to Amend the 1963 Vienna Convention on Civil Liability for Nuclear Damage of 12 September 1997, or the Convention on Supplementary Compensation for Nuclear Damage of 12 September 1997, including any amendment to these conventions and any future convention in respect of the liability of the operator of a nuclear installation for damage caused by a nuclear incident; or

(*b*) Under national law applicable to the liability for such damage, provided that such law is in all respects as favourable to persons that may suffer damage as either the Paris or Vienna Conventions or the Convention on Supplementary Compensation for Nuclear Damage.

Chapter 18
Final clauses

Article 87
Depositary

The Secretary-General of the United Nations is hereby designated as the depositary of this Convention.

Article 88
Signature, ratification, acceptance, approval or accession

1. This Convention is open for signature by all States at Rotterdam, the Netherlands, on 23 September 2009, and thereafter at the Headquarters of the United Nations in New York.

2. This Convention is subject to ratification, acceptance or approval by the signatory States.

3. This Convention is open for accession by all States that are not signatory States as from the date it is open for signature.

4. Instruments of ratification, acceptance, approval and accession are to be deposited with the Secretary-General of the United Nations.

Article 89
Denunciation of other conventions

1. A State that ratifies, accepts, approves or accedes to this Convention and is a party to the International Convention for the Unification of certain Rules of Law relating to Bills of Lading signed at Brussels on 25 August 1924, to the Protocol to amend the International Convention for the Unification of certain Rules of Law relating to Bills of Lading, signed at Brussels on 23 February 1968, or to the Protocol to amend the International Convention for the Unification of certain Rules of Law relating to Bills of Lading as Modified by the Amending Protocol of 23 February 1968, signed at Brussels on 21 December 1979, shall at the same time denounce that Convention and the protocol or protocols thereto to which it is a party by notifying the Government of Belgium to that effect, with a declaration that the denunciation is to take effect as from the date when this Convention enters into force in respect of that State.

2. A State that ratifies, accepts, approves or accedes to this Convention and is a party to the United Nations Convention on the Carriage of Goods by Sea concluded at Hamburg on 31 March 1978 shall at the same time denounce that Convention by notifying the Secretary-General of the United Nations to that effect, with a declaration that the denunciation is to take effect as from the date when this Convention enters into force in respect of that State.

3. For the purposes of this article, ratifications, acceptances, approvals and accessions in respect of this Convention by States parties to the instruments listed in paragraphs 1 and 2 of this article that are notified to the depositary after this Convention has entered into force are not effective until such denunciations as may be required on the part of those States in respect of these instruments have become effective. The depositary of this Convention shall consult with the Government of Belgium, as the depositary of the instruments referred to in paragraph 1 of this article, so as to ensure necessary coordination in this respect.

Article 90
Reservations

No reservation is permitted to this Convention.

Article 91
Procedure and effect of declarations

1. The declarations permitted by articles 74 and 78 may be made at any time. The initial declarations permitted by article 92, paragraph 1, and article 93, paragraph 2,

shall be made at the time of signature, ratification, acceptance, approval or accession. No other declaration is permitted under this Convention.

2. Declarations made at the time of signature are subject to confirmation upon ratification, acceptance or approval.

3. Declarations and their confirmations are to be in writing and to be formally notified to the depositary.

4. A declaration takes effect simultaneously with the entry into force of this Convention in respect of the State concerned. However, a declaration of which the depositary receives formal notification after such entry into force takes effect on the first day of the month following the expiration of six months after the date of its receipt by the depositary.

5. Any State that makes a declaration under this Convention may withdraw it at any time by a formal notification in writing addressed to the depositary. The withdrawal of a declaration, or its modification where permitted by this Convention, takes effect on the first day of the month following the expiration of six months after the date of the receipt of the notification by the depositary.

Article 92
Effect in domestic territorial units

1. If a Contracting State has two or more territorial units in which different systems of law are applicable in relation to the matters dealt with in this Convention, it may, at the time of signature, ratification, acceptance, approval or accession, declare that this Convention is to extend to all its territorial units or only to one or more of them, and may amend its declaration by submitting another declaration at any time.

2. These declarations are to be notified to the depositary and are to state expressly the territorial units to which the Convention extends.

3. When a Contracting State has declared pursuant to this article that this Convention extends to one or more but not all of its territorial units, a place located in a territorial unit to which this Convention does not extend is not considered to be in a Contracting State for the purposes of this Convention.

4. If a Contracting State makes no declaration pursuant to paragraph 1 of this article, the Convention is to extend to all territorial units of that State.

Article 93
Participation by regional economic integration organizations

1. A regional economic integration organization that is constituted by sovereign States and has competence over certain matters governed by this Convention may similarly sign, ratify, accept, approve or accede to this Convention. The regional economic integration organization shall in that case have the rights and obligations of a Contracting State, to the extent that that organization has competence over matters governed by this Convention. When the number of Contracting States is relevant in this Convention, the regional economic integration organization does not count as a Contracting State in addition to its member States which are Contracting States.

2. The regional economic integration organization shall, at the time of signature, ratification, acceptance, approval or accession, make a declaration to the depositary specifying the matters governed by this Convention in respect of which competence

has been transferred to that organization by its member States. The regional economic integration organization shall promptly notify the depositary of any changes to the distribution of competence, including new transfers of competence, specified in the declaration pursuant to this paragraph.

3. Any reference to a "Contracting State" or "Contracting States" in this Convention applies equally to a regional economic integration organization when the context so requires.

Article 94
Entry into force

1. This Convention enters into force on the first day of the month following the expiration of one year after the date of deposit of the twentieth instrument of ratification, acceptance, approval or accession.

2. For each State that becomes a Contracting State to this Convention after the date of the deposit of the twentieth instrument of ratification, acceptance, approval or accession, this Convention enters into force on the first day of the month following the expiration of one year after the deposit of the appropriate instrument on behalf of that State.

3. Each Contracting State shall apply this Convention to contracts of carriage concluded on or after the date of the entry into force of this Convention in respect of that State.

Article 95
Revision and amendment

1. At the request of not less than one third of the Contracting States to this Convention, the Secretary-General of the United Nations shall convene a conference of the Contracting States for revising or amending it.

2. Any instrument of ratification, acceptance, approval or accession deposited after the entry into force of an amendment to this Convention is deemed to apply to the Convention as amended.

Article 96
Denunciation of this Convention

1. A Contracting State may denounce this Convention at any time by means of a notification in writing addressed to the depositary.

2. The denunciation takes effect on the first day of the month following the expiration of one year after the notification is received by the depositary. If a longer period is specified in the notification, the denunciation takes effect upon the expiration of such longer period after the notification is received by the depositary.

DONE at New York, this eleventh day of December two thousand and eight, in a single original, of which the Arabic, Chinese, English, French, Russian and Spanish texts are equally authentic.

IN WITNESS WHEREOF the undersigned plenipotentiaries, being duly authorized by their respective Governments, have signed this Convention.

BUDGET ESTIMATE

PROFORMA BUDGET ESTIMATE		Dry Cargo Vessel
COST CATEGORY	Annual Cost US $	Notes & Assumptions
		Exchange rates: GBP 0.65/USD1. 00
		In Rp 40/USD 1.00
Officers' earnings and leave pay	270,000	4 European, 5 Indian
Ratings earnings and leave pay	90,000	18, All Indian
Ratings overtime	0	Consolidated in basic pay
Pension and Insurance Contributions	72.00	
Crew establishment costs	18,000	Reliefs - Europeans 5 months, Indians 9 months
Crew travel expenses	36,000	
Sundry/unrecoverable medical	3,000	
TOTAL CREW COSTS	**424,200**	Victualling rate $3.60 per man/day plus extra meals
Provisions	36,000	
Deck stores & general	9,000	No allowance for dry dock paints
Engine stores-general	27,000	One wire & one polyprop per year
Paint	12,000	Assumes 280 days at sea
Cordage	4,800	
Lubricants	63,000	
Cabin stores/laundry	9,000	
Fresh Water	4,800	
TOTAL STORING COSTS	**165,000**	
Deck repairs and spares	54,000	
Engine repairs and spare	90,000	CSM cycle maintained, SSH not due this year
Electronics and nav. aids	18,000	
Surveys	9,000	
TOTAL MAINTENANCE COSTS	**171,000**	Hull valuation $18 million
		Allows 25% for supplementary call
Insurance - hull & machinery	82,500	
P&I calls	52,500	Daily indemnity basis $10000, terms 14/90/180
Insurance - War risks	1,500	Deductibles: 1 hull $3000, 1 P&I $15000
Insurance - Loss of earnings	18,000	
Deductible allowance	45,000	
TOTAL INSURANCE COSTS	**199,500**	
Communication expenses	9,000	
Owners' port costs	13,500	
Sundries	9,000	
Management fee	90,000	
TOTAL ADMINISTRATION COSTS	**121,500**	
SUB TOTAL	**1,081,800**	Total estimated cost drydock next year $400,000
		including hull special survey
Annual drydocking allowance	200,000	
GRAND TOTAL	**1,281,8000**	
	$3512 per day	

1. Agents	**STANDARD STATEMENT OF FACTS** RECOMMENDED BY THE BALTIC AND INTERNATIONAL MARITIME CONFERENCE (BIMCO) AND THE FEDERATION OF NATIONAL ASSOCIATIONS OF SHIP BROKERS AND AGENTS (FONASBA)
2. Vessel's name	3. Port
4. Owners/Disponent Owners	5. Vessel berthed 6. Loading commenced / 7. Loading completed
8. Cargo	9. Discharging commenced / 10. Discharging completed 11. Cargo documents on board / 12. Vessel sailed
13. Charter Party * 15. Bill of Lading weight/quantity / 16. Outturn weight/quantity	14. Working hours/meal hours of the port *
17. Vessel arrived on roads	18.
19. Notice of readiness tendered	20.
21. Next tide available	22.

DETAILS OF DAILY WORKING*

Date	Day	Hours worked		Hours stopped		No. of gangs	Quantity load./disch.	Remarks*
		From	To	From	To			

General remarks*	
Place and date	Name and signature (Master)*
Name and signature (Agents)	Name and Signature (for the Charteres/Shippers/Receivers)*

1. Agents	**STANDARD STATEMENT OF FACTS** RECOMMENDED BY THE BALTIC AND INTERNATIONAL MARITIME CONFERENCE (BIMCO) AND THE FEDERATION OF NATIONAL ASSOCIATIONS OF SHIP BROKERS AND AGENTS (FONASBA)
2. Vessel's name	3. Port
4. Owners/Disponent Owners	5. Vessel berthed
	6. Loading commenced / 7. Loading completed
8. Cargo	9. Discharging commenced / 10. Discharging completed
	11. Cargo documents on board / 12. Vessel sailed
13. Charter Party *	14. Working hours/meal hours of the port *
15. Bill of Lading weight/quantity / 16. Outturn weight/quantity	
17. Vessel arrived on roads	18.
19. Notice of readiness tendered	20.
21. Next tide available	22.

DETAILS OF DAILY WORKING*

Date	Day	Hours worked		Hours stopped		No. of gangs	Quantity load./disch.	Remarks*
		From	To	From	To			

General remarks*	
Place and date	Name and signature (Master)*
Name and signature (Agents)	Name and Signature (for the Charteres/Shippers/Receivers)*

INSTRUCTIONS FOR FILLING IN THE BOXES

General

It is recommended to fill in the boxes with a short text. When it is a matter of figures to be inserted as is the case in most of the boxes, this should be done as follows:

6. Loading commenced
1975-03-15-0800

the figures being mentioned in the following order: year-month-date-time.

Boxes Calling for Special Attention

Charter Party*:

Insert name and date of charter, for instance, "Gencon" dated 1975-03-01.

Working hours/meal hours of the port*:

Indicate normal working hours/meal hours of the port and not the actual hours worked on board the vessel which may be longer or shorter than the hours normally worked in the port. Such day-by-day figures should be indicated in the box provided for under "Details of Daily Working".

Some empty boxes are made available in which other relevant information applying to the particular port or vessel could be inserted, such as, time of granting free pratique, if applicable, etc.

Details of Daily Working*:

Insert day-by-day figures and indicate in the vertical column marked "Remarks *" all relevant details as to reasons for stoppages such as bad weather, strikes, breakdown of winches/cranes, shortage of cargo, etc.

General Remarks*:

This box should be used for insertion of such general observations which are not covered in any of the boxes provided for in the first main group of boxes, for instance, reasons for berthing delay or other general observations.

Signatures*:

It is of importance that the boxes provided for signatures are duly signed by the parties concerned.

1. Agents	**STANDARD TIME SHEET (SHORT FORM)** RECOMMENDED BY THE BALTIC AND INTERNATIONAL MARITIME CONFERENCE (BIMCO) AND THE FEDERATION OF NATIONAL ASSOCIATIONS OF SHIP BROKERS AND AGENTS (FONSABA)
2. Vessel's name	3. Port
4. Owners/Disponent Owners	5. Vessel berthed
	6. Loading commenced / 7. Loading completed
8. Cargo	9. Discharging commenced / 10. Discharging completed
	11. Cargo documents on board / 12. Vessel
13. Charter Party*	14. Working hours/meal hours of the port*
15. Bill of Lading weight/quantity / 16. Outturn weight/quantity	
17. Vessel arrived on roads	18. Time to count from
19. Notice of readiness tendered	20. Rate of demurrage / 21. Rate of despatch money
22. Next tide available	23.
24. Laytime allowed for loading / 25. Laytime allowed for discharging	26.

LAYTIME

Date	Day	Time worked		Laytime used			Time saved on demurrage			Remarks*
		From	to	days	hours	minutes	days	hours	minutes	

General remarks*		
Place	and	date
Signature*		Signature*

* See Explanatory Notes overleaf for filling in the boxes

STANDARD TIME SHEET (SHORT FORM)
RECOMMENDED BY
THE BALTIC AND INTERNATIONAL MARITIME CONFERENCE (BIMCO)
AND THE FEDERATION OF NATIONAL ASSOCIATIONS
OF SHIP BROKERS AND AGENTS (FONSABA)

1. Agents

2. Vessel's name

3. Port

4. Owners/Disponent Owners

5. Vessel berthed

6. Loading commenced

7. Loading completed

8. Cargo

9. Discharging commenced

10. Discharging completed

11. Cargo documents on board

12. Vessel

13. Charter Party*

14. Working hours/meal hours of the port*

15. Bill of Lading weight/quantity

16. Outturn weight/quantity

17. Vessel arrived on roads

18. Time to count from

19. Notice of readiness tendered

20. Rate of demurrage

21. Rate of despatch money

22. Next tide available

23.

24. Laytime allowed for loading

25. Laytime allowed for discharging

26.

LAYTIME

Date	Day	Time worked		Laytime used			Time saved on demurrage			Remarks*
		From	to	days	hours	minutes	days	hours	minutes	

General remarks*

Place and date

Signature*

Signature*

* See Explanatory Notes overleaf for filling in the boxes

INSTRUCTIONS FOR FILLING IN THE BOXES

General

It is recommended to fill in the boxes with a short text. When it is a matter of figures to be inserted as is the case in most of the boxes, this should be done as follows:

6. Loading commenced
1975-03-15-0800

the figures being mentioned in the following order: year–month–date–time.

Boxes Calling for Special Attention

Charter Party*:

Insert name and date of charter, for instance, "Gencon" dated 1975-03-01.

Working hours/meal hours of the port*:

Indicate normal working hours/meal hours of the port and not the actual hours worked on board the vessel which may be longer or shorter than the hours normally worked in the port. Such day-by-day figures should be indicated in the box provided for under "Laytime Computation".

Some empty boxes are made available in which other relevant information applying to the particular port or vessel could be inserted, such as, time of granting free pratique, if applicable, etc.

Laytime Computation*:

Insert day-by-day figures and indicate in the vertical column marked "Remarks*" all relevant details as to reasons for stoppages such as bad weather, strikes, breakdown of winches/cranes, shortage of cargo, etc.

General Remarks*:

This box should be used for insertion of such general observations which are not covered in any of the boxes provided for in the first main group of boxes, for instance, reasons for berthing delay or other general observations.

Signatures*:

It is of importance that the boxes provided for signatures are duly signed by the parties concerned.

BIMCO Standard Bunker Contract
CONFIRMATION NOTE

Sellers and Buyers hereby confirm the bunker nomination as follows:

1. Place of Nomination	2. Date of Nomination
3. Sellers (Cl. 1)	4. Buyers (Cl. 1)
5. Vessel	6. Port or Place of Delivery/ETA (Cl. 5)
7. Product(s)/Specifications (Cl. 2)	
8. Grade(s)/Quantities (Cl. 2 and Cl. 3)	
9. Price(s)/Currency (Cl. 7)	
10. Delivery Means and Additional Charges (Cl. 7)	
11. Payment (Cl. 8)	
12. Min. Hourly Pumping Rate (Cl. 9(c)(ii)))	13. Compensation Rates for Delay (Cl. 9(c))
14. Dispute Resolution Alternative Agreed (Cl. 15)	
15. Additional Clauses, if any	

All terms and conditions of the "BIMCO Standard Bunker Contract", which the Buyers have had the opportunity to familiarise themselves with, and any agreed amendments thereto, including the Dispute Resolution Clause, are herewith incorporated and shall apply to the delivery of Marine Fuels contracted for above.

"BIMCO Standard Bunker Contract" General Terms and Conditions

Preamble

These General Terms and Conditions shall apply to all deliveries contracted for unless the Sellers expressly confirm otherwise in the Confirmation Note. Each delivery shall constitute a separate contract.

1. Definitions

Throughout this Contract, except where the context otherwise requires, the following definitions shall be applied:

"*Marine Fuels*" means products, derived from crude oil, delivered or to be delivered to the Vessel.

"*Sellers*" means the party contracting to sell and deliver Marine Fuels, and

"*Buyers*" means the party contracting to purchase, take delivery and pay for the Marine Fuels.

"*Bunker Tanker*" means bunker barge or tanker or tank truck supplying Marine Fuels to the Vessel.

2. Grades/Quality

(a) The Buyers shall have the sole responsibility for the nomination of the grades of Marine Fuels fit for use by the Vessel.

(b) The Sellers warrant that the Marine Fuels shall be of a homogeneous and stable nature, shall comply with the grades nominated by the Buyers and be of satisfactory quality. Unless otherwise agreed in the Confirmation Note, the Marine Fuels shall in all respects comply with ISO Standard 8217:1996 or any subsequent amendments thereof.

3. Quantities/Measurements

(a) Subject to the provisions of sub-clause 6(c) and Clause 9 hereunder the quantities of Marine Fuels delivered shall be determined from the official gauge or meter of the Bunker Tanker effecting delivery, or in case of delivery ex wharf, of the shore-meter.

(b) The Buyers and the Sellers shall both have the right to be present or represented when such measurements are taken and shall be given sufficient information and access to the official gauge or meter of the Bunker Tanker or shore-meter and relevant documentation to verify the volume delivered.

(c) The Marine Fuels to be delivered under this Contract shall be measured and calculated in accordance with the ISO-ASTM-API-IP Petroleum Measurement Tables.

4. Sampling

(a) The Sellers shall arrange for a representative sample of each grade of Marine Fuels to be drawn throughout the entire bunkering operation and that sample shall be thoroughly mixed and carefully divided into four (4) identical samples. The sampling shall be performed in the presence of both the Sellers and the Buyers or their respective representatives. The absence of the Buyers or their representatives shall not prejudice the validity of the samples taken.

(b) The sample shall be drawn at a point, to be mutually agreed between the Sellers and the Buyers or their respective representatives, closest to the receiving Vessel's bunker manifold.

(c) The sample shall be drawn using a mutually accepted sampling device which shall be constructed, secured and sealed in such a way so as to prevent the sampling device and the sample being tampered with throughout the transfer period.

(d) The four (4) identical samples referred to in sub-clause 4(a) shall be securely sealed and provided with labels showing the Vessel's name, identity of delivery facility, product name, delivery date and place and point of sampling and seal number, authenticated with the Vessel's stamp and signed by the Sellers' representative and the Master of the Vessel or his authorised representative.

(e) Two (2) samples shall be retained by the Sellers for minimum sixty (60) days after delivery of the Marine Fuels to the Vessel or, on being requested in writing by the Buyers, for as long as the Buyers may reasonably require, and the other two (2) samples shall be retained by the Vessel.

(f) If the quantity is delivered by more than one Bunker Tanker, the sampling procedure shall be repeated as outlined in this Clause 4.

5. Delivery

(a) Delivery of the Marine Fuels shall be made day and night, Sundays and holidays included, at the port or place of delivery, subject always to the custom of that port or place.

(b) The Buyers, or their agents at the port or place of delivery, shall give the Sellers or their representatives at the port or place of delivery, 72 and 48 hours approximate and 24 hours definite notice of the Vessel's arrival and the location and time at which deliveries are required.

(c) The Sellers shall:

(i) be in possession of all permits required to comply with all relevant regulations pertaining to delivery of Marine Fuels at the port or place of delivery, and;

(ii) subject to local laws, render all necessary assistance which may be reasonably required to make connections and disconnections between the delivery hose(s) and the Vessel's bunker manifold.

(d) The Buyers shall be responsible for making all connections and disconnections between the delivery hose(s) and the Vessel's bunker manifold and to ensure that the hose(s) are properly connected to the Vessel's bunker manifold prior to the commencement of delivery.

(e) The Buyers shall ensure that the Vessel is in possession of all certificates required to comply with all relevant regulations pertaining to delivery of the Marine Fuels at the port or place of delivery and that the Master of the Vessel shall:

(i) advise the Sellers in writing, prior to delivery, of the maximum allowable pumping rate and pressure and agree on communication and emergency shut-down procedures;

(ii) notify the Sellers in writing prior to delivery, of any special conditions, difficulties, peculiarities, deficiencies or defects in respect of and particular to the Vessel which might adversely affect the delivery of the Marine Fuels, and;

(iii) provide a free side to receive the Marine Fuels and render all necessary assistance which may reasonably be required to moor or unmoor the Bunker Tanker, as applicable.

6. Documentation

(a) Before commencement of delivery the Sellers shall present for written acknowledgement by the Master of the Vessel or his authorised representative, a bunker requisition form or similar document, duly signed by the Sellers or their representative, which shall contain the quantities to be delivered and all information required in accordance with ISO/TR 13739:1998 or any subsequent amendments thereof, including, in particular, the values for:

- viscosity
- density

"BIMCO Standard Bunker Contract"
General Terms and Conditions

- sulphur content
- flash point
- delivery temperature

In addition, and if available, similar information shall be provided for vanadium, ash content, water content and pour point.

(b) Once the delivery is completed and quantities measured, a receipt shall be signed and stamped by the Master of the Vessel or his authorised representative, and returned to the Sellers, or their representative, as acknowledgement of the actual volume and the actual delivery temperature only and a duplicate copy shall be retained by the Master of the Vessel. This receipt shall contain the following minimum information which is warranted by the Sellers:

- delivered quantity in volume units
- density in kg/m^3 at 15° C as per ISO 3675
- delivery temperature
- flash point
- sulphur content in % m/m as per ISO 8754
- viscosity

(c) In the event the Master of the Vessel is not satisfied with the sampling, quality, quantity or any other matter concerning the Marine Fuels or their delivery, he shall make appropriate remarks in the receipt either detailing the complaints or referring to a separate letter of protest to be issued and delivered immediately. Verification of the information provided under sub-clause 6(b) may be obtained by analysis of the Vessel's retained sample.

7. Price

(a) The price of the Marine Fuels shall be in the amount expressed per unit and in the currency stated in the Confirmation Note for each grade of Marine Fuels delivered into the Vessel's tanks free delivered/ex wharf as applicable and stated in the Confirmation Note.

In the event the price is quoted in volume units, conversion to standard volume shall be at 60 degrees Fahrenheit or at fifteen (15) degrees Celsius.

(b) Any and all additional charges, if applicable, shall be specified in the Sellers' quotation and in the Confirmation Note and shall include but not be limited to:

(i) Wharfage charges, barging charges or other similar charges;

(ii) Mooring charges or port dues incurred by the Sellers which are for Buyers' account, and;

(iii) Duties, taxes, charges or other costs in the country where delivery takes place, for which the Sellers are accountable but which are for the Buyers' account.

8. Payment

(a) Payment for the Marine Fuels shall be made by the Buyers within thirty (30) days or, if otherwise agreed, within the number of days stated in the Confirmation Note after the completion of delivery.

In the event payment has been made in advance of delivery, same shall be adjusted on the basis of the actual quantities of Marine Fuels delivered and additional payment and/or refund shall be made within thirty (30) days after the completion of delivery.

(b) Payment shall be made in full, without set-off, counterclaim, deduction and/or discount, free of bank charges.

(c) Payment shall be deemed to have been made on the date the payment is credited to the counter of the bank designated by the Sellers. If payment falls on a non-business day, then payment shall be made on or before the business day nearest to the due date. If the preceding and succeeding business day are equally near to the due date, then payment shall be made on or before the preceding business day.

(d) Any delay in payment and/or refund shall entitle either party to interest at the rate of two (2) per cent. per month or any part thereof.

(e) In the event of non-payment, the Sellers reserve the right to pursue such legal remedies as may be available to them to recover the amount owed.

9. Claims

(a)(i) Any dispute as to the quantity delivered must be noted at the time of delivery in the receipt or in the letter of protest referred to in sub-clause 6(c). Any claim as to short delivery shall be presented by the Buyers in writing within fifteen (15) days from the date of delivery, failing which any such claim shall be deemed to be waived and barred.

(ii) The Buyers shall be charged for all proven additional expenses incurred by the Sellers in connection with the Buyers' failure to take delivery of the full quantity of the Marine Fuels ordered by the Buyers.

(b)(i) Any claim as to the quality or description of the Marine Fuels must be notified in writing, as per sub-clause 6(c) or promptly after the circumstances giving rise to such claim have been discovered. If the Buyers do not notify the Sellers of any such claim within thirty (30) days of the date of delivery, such claim shall be deemed to be waived and barred.

(ii) In the event a claim is raised pursuant to sub-clause 9(b)(i), the parties hereto shall have the quality of the Marine Fuels analysed by a mutually agreed, qualified and independent laboratory. The Sellers shall provide the laboratory with one of the samples retained by them as per sub-clause 4(e). If ISO grades have been specified the analysis shall be established by tests in accordance with ISO Standard 8217:1996 and ISO 4259 or any subsequent amendments thereof. If non-ISO grades have been agreed, tests will be made in accordance with standards corresponding to the aforementioned ISO standards. Unless otherwise agreed the expenses of the analysis shall be for the account of the party whose claim is found wrong by the analysis.

(c) In the event of any delay resulting from:

(i) the Buyers' failure to give proper notices and/or to comply with the notices given pursuant to sub-clause 5(b) and/or the Buyers' Vessel failing to receive Marine Fuels at the pumping rate referred to in sub-clause 5(e)(i), or;

(ii) the Sellers' failure to commence delivery of the Marine Fuels promptly in accordance with the Buyers' required delivery time as notified pursuant to sub-clause 5(b) and/or the Sellers' failure to deliver the Marine Fuels in accordance with the minimum hourly pumping rate referred to in the Confirmation Note,

then the party suffering such delay shall be entitled to compensation from the other party for that delay, at the agreed rates per day, or pro rata, stated in the Confirmation Note.

(d) Neither party hereto shall be liable for indirect or consequential loss and/or damage arising from this Contract.

10. Risk/Title

Risk in the Marine Fuels shall pass to the Buyers once the Marine Fuels have passed the Sellers' flange connecting the Vessel's bunker manifold with the delivery facilities provided by the Sellers. Title to the Marine Fuels shall pass to the Buyers upon payment for the value of the Marine Fuels delivered, pursuant to the terms of Clause 8 hereof. Until such time as payment is made, on behalf of themselves and the Vessel, the Buyers agree that they are in possession of the Marine Fuels

"BIMCO Standard Bunker Contract"
General Terms and Conditions

solely as Bailee for the Sellers. If, prior to payment, the Sellers' Marine Fuels are commingled with other marine fuels on board the Vessel, title to the Marine Fuels shall remain with the Sellers corresponding to the quantity of the Marine Fuels delivered. The above is without prejudice to such other rights as the Sellers may have under the laws of the governing jurisdiction against the Buyers or the Vessel in the event of non-payment.

11. Termination

Without prejudice to accrued rights hereunder, either party hereto shall be entitled to terminate this Contract in the event of:

(a) any application being made or any proceedings being commenced, or any order or judgement being given by any court, for

(i) the liquidation, winding up, bankruptcy, insolvency, dissolution, administration or re-organisation or similar, or

(ii) the appointment of a receiver, liquidator, trustee, administrator, administrative receiver or similar functionary

of the other party of all or a substantial part of its assets (otherwise than for the purpose of a reconstruction or amalgamation);

(b) the other party suspending payment, ceasing to carry on business or compounding or making any special arrangement with its creditors, or;

(c) any act being done or event occurring which, under the applicable law thereof, has a substantially similar effect to any of the said acts or events described above.

12. Indemnity

(a) Without prejudice to any other claims arising hereunder or in connection herewith and notwithstanding the provisions of sub-clause 9(d), if loss is suffered or a liability is incurred by either party hereto as a direct result of compliance with directions given by the other party, during or for the purposes of the parties' obligations hereunder, then the injured party is to be indemnified by the other in respect of such loss or liability.

(b) Where claims arise under sub-clause 9(c) and sub-clause 12(a), compensation payable in accordance with sub-clause 9(c) shall be taken into account in assessing sums payable under sub-clause 12(a).

13. Force Majeure

Neither party hereto shall be responsible for any loss, damage, delay or failure in performance under this Contract resulting from an act of God, or the port of delivery being affected by war, civil commotion, riot, quarantine, strike, stoppage, lock-out, arrest, restraint of princes, rulers and people, or any other event whatsoever which cannot be avoided or guarded against by the exercise of due diligence.

14. Safety and the Environment

(a) In the event of any spillage (which for the purpose of this Clause shall mean any leakage, escape, spillage or overflow of the Marine Fuels) causing or likely to cause pollution occurring at any stage of the bunkering operation, the Buyers and the Sellers shall jointly, and regardless as to whether the Buyers or the Sellers are responsible, immediately take such actions as are reasonably necessary to effect clean up and which shall always be conducted in accordance with such local laws and regulations which may compulsorily apply.

(b) Where it is a compulsory requirement of the law of the port or place of delivery of the Marine Fuels that the Sellers shall have in place their own oil spill contingency plans, the Sellers shall ensure that valid oil spill contingency plans approved by the relevant authorities are in effect to the extent that is so required.

(c) The Sellers hereby guarantee payment of and/or agree to indemnify and hold the Buyers harmless for any claims, losses, damages, expenses, penalties or other liabilities incurred by the Buyers under the United States Oil Pollution Act of 1990, or other state, national or international oil pollution legislation, as a result of any spillage occurring whilst the Marine Fuels are being transported directly or indirectly to or from the Vessel's bunker manifold except to the extent that such spillage is caused by any fault on the part of the Buyers. The Buyers shall similarly indemnify the Sellers where any such spillage occurs once risk in the Marine Fuels has passed to the Buyers except to the extent that such spillage is caused by any fault on the part of the Sellers.

(d) The Sellers shall use their best endeavours to ensure that the bunker supplying company is fully insured for oil spill liabilities as required by statutory rules or regulations. If such coverage or insurance is not obtained by the bunker supplying company it shall be the sole responsibility of the Sellers to establish such coverage for their account. Proof and conditions of such coverage, whether established by the bunker supplying company or by the Sellers shall be made available to the Buyers at their request, as soon as practically possible.

(e) The Buyers hereby advise the Sellers that they enforce a company drug and alcohol policy on board their vessels, whereby the Sellers' personnel must not be intoxicated at any time on board. It is understood and agreed that the selling, possession, distribution, use or being under the influence of any controlled substance or dangerous drugs other than those medically prescribed is prohibited.

(f) The Sellers hereby advise the Buyers that they enforce a company drug and alcohol policy in their facilities and on board their vessels, which the Buyers' personnel must comply with while in such facilities or on board such vessels. It is understood and agreed that the selling, possession, distribution, use or being under the influence of alcohol or any controlled substance or dangerous drugs other than those medically prescribed is prohibited.

15. Dispute Resolution

*) **(a)** This Contract shall be governed by and construed in accordance with English law and any dispute arising out of or in connection with this Contract shall be referred to arbitration in London in accordance with the Arbitration Act 1996 or any statutory modification or re-enactment thereof save to the extent necessary to give effect to the provisions of this Clause.

The arbitration shall be conducted in accordance with the London Maritime Arbitrators Association (LMAA) Terms current at the time when the arbitration proceedings are commenced.

The reference shall be to three arbitrators. A party wishing to refer a dispute to arbitration shall appoint its arbitrator and send notice of such appointment in writing to the other party requiring the other party to appoint its own arbitrator within 14 calendar days of that notice and stating that it will appoint its arbitrator as sole arbitrator unless the other party appoints its own arbitrator and gives notice that it has done so within the 14 days specified. If the other party does not appoint its own arbitrator and give notice that it has done so within the 14 days specified, the party referring a dispute to arbitration may, without the requirement of any further prior notice to the other party, appoint its arbitrator as

"BIMCO Standard Bunker Contract"
General Terms and Conditions

sole arbitrator and shall advise the other party accordingly. The award of a sole arbitrator shall be binding on both parties as if he had been appointed by agreement.

Nothing herein shall prevent the parties agreeing in writing to vary these provisions to provide for the appointment of a sole arbitrator.

In cases where neither the claim nor any counterclaim exceeds the sum of US$50,000 (or such other sum as the parties may agree) the arbitration shall be conducted in accordance with the LMAA Small Claims Procedure current at the time when the arbitration proceedings are commenced.

*) **(b)** This Contract shall be governed by and construed in accordance with Title 9 of the United States Code and the Maritime Law of the United States and any dispute arising out of or in connection with this Contract shall be referred to three persons at New York, one to be appointed by each of the parties hereto, and the third by the two so chosen; their decision or that of any two of them shall be final, and for the purposes of enforcing any award, judgement may be entered on an award by any court of competent jurisdiction. The proceedings shall be conducted in accordance with the rules of the Society of Maritime Arbitrators, Inc.

In cases where neither the claim nor any counterclaim exceeds the sum of US$50,000 (or such other sum as the parties may agree) the arbitration shall be conducted in accordance with the Shortened Arbitration Procedure of the Society of Maritime Arbitrators, Inc. current at the time when the arbitration proceedings are commenced.

*) **(c)** This Contract shall be governed by and construed in accordance with the laws of the place mutually agreed by the parties and any dispute arising out of or in connection with this Contract shall be referred to arbitration at a mutually agreed place, subject to the procedures applicable there.

(d) Notwithstanding (a), (b) or (c) above, the parties may agree at any time to refer to mediation any difference and/or dispute arising out of or in connection with this Contract.

In the case of a dispute in respect of which arbitration has been commenced under (a), (b) or (c) above, the following shall apply:-

(i) Either party may at any time and from time to time elect to refer the dispute or part of the dispute to mediation by service on the other party of a written notice (the "Mediation Notice") calling on the other party to agree to mediation.

(ii) The other party shall thereupon within fourteen (14) calendar days of receipt of the Mediation Notice confirm that they agree to mediation, in which case the parties shall thereafter agree a mediator within a further fourteen (14) calendar days, failing which on the application of either party a mediator will be appointed promptly by the Arbitration Tribunal ("the Tribunal") or such person as the Tribunal may designate for that purpose. The mediation shall be conducted in such place and in accordance with such procedure and on such terms as the parties may agree or, in the event of disagreement, as may be set by the mediator.

(iii) If the other party does not agree to mediate, that fact may be brought to the attention of the Tribunal and may be taken into account by the Tribunal when allocating the costs of the arbitration as between the parties.

(iv) The mediation shall not affect the right of either party to seek such relief or take such steps as it considers necessary to protect its interest.

(v) Either party may advise the Tribunal that they have agreed to mediation. The arbitration procedure shall continue during the conduct of the mediation but the Tribunal may take the mediation timetable into account when setting the timetable for steps in the arbitration.

(vi) Unless otherwise agreed or specified in the mediation terms, each party shall bear its own costs incurred in the mediation and the parties shall share equally the mediator's costs and expenses.

(vii) The mediation process shall be without prejudice and confidential and no information or documents disclosed during it shall be revealed to the Tribunal except to the extent that they are disclosable under the law and procedure governing the arbitration.

(Note: The parties should be aware that the mediation process may not necessarily interrupt time limits.)

*) *Sub-clauses (a), (b) and (c) are alternatives; if this Clause has been incorporated into the Contract without an express choice of law and arbitration forum chosen from sub-clauses (a), (b) and (c), then sub-clause (a) of this Clause shall apply. Sub-clause (d) shall apply in all cases.*

Voyage Calculation Blank Form

A.

		SPEED	DIST PD	BUNKERS	FO	DO	PORT
	L						
	B						

B.

VOYAGE DETAIL	

C.

VOYAGE LEGS	MILES	DAYS	LSFO	FO	DO
TOTALS					

D.

		MT		
CARGO CALC				dwat
RESTRICTION?			less	cons
BUNKER CONSTRAINT				
COST OF BUNKERS				Disc
cu cap	max dwt cubically		**CARGO TO LOAD**	LSFO
				Max-Cargo

No safety margin is mentioned but ___ MT LSFO is available.

F.

VOY EXPENSES			
FO ROB ___ * $price			
FO ROB ___*$price			
LOAD PORT			
DISC PORT			
OTHER			
LSFO ___ *$price			
TOTAL EXP			

E. BUNKER QUICK CALC

Option Bunker ___ and/or _____.
Not at ____. ____?? Yes No.

If Bunker at _____ to get to ____ then benefit is only $_____ in extra freight. Deviation is ___ NM + 0.5 days plus bunker time + call cost $__ + $____ extra usage of bunkers. Take all at ____.

G.

CARGO	RATE	COMM	NET	
		5%	0	FREIGHT
			0	EXPENSES
TOT EXPENSES			0	EARNINGS
				VOY LENGTH*DRC
				PROFIT
				EARNING PER DAY

ANSWER A	**CARGO TO LOAD**	**_____ MT**		
ANSWER B	**BUNKER**	**Bunker ____ to take ____MT**		
ANSWER C	**DAILY NET PROFIT**	**$**	**Total Earnings for Voyage**	**£**

MINIMUM SAFE MANNING CERTIFICATE

Issued in compliance with the International Convention for the Safety of Life at Sea 1974 Chapter V Regulation 14(2), and the Merchant Shipping (Safe Manning and Watchkeeping) Regulations 2003

This is to certify that in accordance with the principles and guidelines set out in Resolution A .890 (21) of the International Maritime Organisation the ship named in this certificate will be considered to be safely manned, when it proceeds to sea with not less than the numbers and grades of the personnel shown in this document, subject to any conditions stated hereunder.

Vessel

Name of Ship

Port of Registry

Official Number

IMO Number

Type of Ship

Gross Tonnage

Registered Power

Trading Area

Personnel

Grade/Capacity	Minimum STCW Reg	Number of Persons
Master		
Chief Mate		
OOW Navigational		
Chief Engineer		
Second Engineer		
OOW Engineering		
Deck Rating		
Deck Rating		
Engine Rating		
Engine Rating		

Minimum Qualifications and Requirements: *All Deck and Engine Room officers, are to be in possession of a Certificate of Competence and an Endorsement issued by the appropriate authority in compliance with the STCW Convention 78, as amended.*
Furthermore all officers are required to be holders of an Endorsement issued under Regulation I/10, by the Malta Maritime Authority; stating that the holder is competent to serve in a capacity on board ship with trading patterns, tonnage and registered power indicated.
Any shortages from the specified number of personnel should be referred to the Merchant Shipping Directorate, Malta Maritime Authority for approval.

Special Conditions

Issued at Valletta Malta on the

This Certificate is valid until the

Merchant Shipping Directorate

Merchant Shipping Directorate Malta Maritime Authority Maritime House Lascaris Wharf Valletta VLT 01 Malta
Voice: +356 21250360, 99494317 Fax: +356 21241460 E-mail: mership.malta@mma.gov.mt

Ofcom
OFFICE OF COMMUNICATIONS

Ship Radio Licence / Ship Portable Radio Licence

United Kingdom of Great Britain & Northern Ireland, the Channel Islands & the Isle of Man
Royaume–Uni de Grande Bretagne et d'Irlande du Nord, les Iles Anglo-Normandes et l'Ile de Man
Vereinigte Königreich von Großbritannien und Nordirland, die Kanalinseln und die Isle of Man

Wireless Telegraphy Act 2006

Note: This Licence is valid only if the vessel and Licensee accord with the details of the Licence and shall continue in force until the Licence is surrendered by the Licensee or revoked by Ofcom.

Section 1

Licence details

Licence Class	
Licence number	
Licensee's name	
Licensee's address	
Mailing address	
Name of vessel *(Applicable only for a Ship Radio Licence)*	
Call sign *(Applicable only for a Ship Radio Licence)*	
MMSI *(Applicable only for a Ship Radio Licence)*	
MMSI for VHF DSC portable radio	
"T" number identification *(Applicable only for a Ship Portable Radio Licence)*	
Date of issue	

Where this is a **Ship Radio Licence**, this Licence, granted by the Office of Communications ("Ofcom"), authorises the Licensee to establish, install and use radio transmitting and receiving equipment as indicated in the table below and subject to the terms set out in Section 2, on board the vessel detailed above.

Where this is a **Ship Portable Radio Licence**, this Licence, granted by the Office of Communications ("Ofcom") and intended for use in United Kingdom territorial waters, authorises the Licensee to establish, install and use radio transmitting and receiving equipment as indicated in the table below and subject to the terms set out in Section 2.

Radio Equipment

Quantity	Type; International Telecommunication Union ("ITU") category; Ship frequency or band permitted in accordance with the relevant ITU Radio Regulations[1]; ITU-R Recommendations[1]

This Licence, the relevant Maritime Radio Operator's Certificate of Competence and valid Authority to Operate, and any notices of variation to the Licence shall be kept with or near to the radio equipment at all times, where it is physically practicable to do so.

Issued by:

Ofcom Licensing Centre
Riverside House
2a Southwark Bridge Road
London, SE1 9HA
UK
Tel. +44 (0)20 7981 3131
Fax. +44 (0)20 7981 3333

[1] Extracts from the ITU Radio Regulations and Recommendations ITU-R are published by the ITU in "Manual for use by the Maritime Mobile and Maritime Mobile - Satellite Services", available from the ITU in Geneva, Telephone: +41 22 730 6141 or e-mail sales@itu.int
(Coast station radio frequency assignments are detailed in the Admiralty List of Radio Signals, published by the UK Hydrographic Office, Admiralty Way, Taunton Somerset, Telephone: +44(0)1823 337900 Fax +44(0)1823 284077 - www.ukho.gov.uk)

Section 2

Terms

Licence term

1 This Licence shall continue in force unless revoked by Ofcom or surrendered by the Licensee.

Licence variation and revocation

2 Ofcom may exercise their power to vary or revoke this Licence in accordance with the Wireless Telegraphy Act 2006 ("the WT Act").

3 The Licensee shall be notified of any variation or revocation of this Licence in writing or by a general notice applicable to holders of this class of Licence.

Interpretation

4 In this Licence:

(a) the establishment, installation and use of the "radio equipment" shall be interpreted as establishment and use of stations and installation and use of apparatus for wireless telegraphy as specified in the WT Act;

(b) the terms used shall have the same meaning as they have in the WT Act;

(c) the schedules form part of this Licence together with any subsequent schedules which Ofcom may issue as a variation to this Licence at a later date;

(d) an Authority to Operate means an authority issued by the Secretary of State pursuant to the WT Act;

(e) a Maritime Radio Operator's Certificate of Competence is a certificate issued by the Secretary of State pursuant to the WT Act;

(f) "Licence details" means all information provided by the Licensee in the Licence application or in any application to amend the Licence and all information recorded in the Licence;

(g) the terms 'ship' and 'vessel' also include:

(i) a hovercraft;

(ii) a light station;

(iii) installations to which the Continental Shelf Act 1964 applies;

(iv) other structures within the United Kingdom's territorial (external) waters; and

(v) a survival craft.

(h) the Interpretation Act 1978 shall apply to this Licence as it applies to an Act of Parliament.

Licence changes and confirmation of licence details

5 This Licence is not transferable.

6 The Licensee must give prior or immediate notice to Ofcom of any change in the Licence details.

7 The Licensee must provide confirmation to Ofcom that the Licence details are correct at least once every ten (10) years where the Licence details have not changed during that period.

Fees

8 The Licensee shall pay to Ofcom the relevant fee as provided in the WT Act and the Regulations made under the WT Act on or before the date of issue of the Licence or any other date which may be made in the Regulations, failing which Ofcom may revoke the Licence.

Radio equipment use

9 The Licensee must ensure that the radio equipment covered by this Licence is constructed and used only in accordance with the terms specified in the schedules relevant to this Licence.

10 The Licensee must ensure that the radio equipment is used only by persons:

(a) who have been authorised by the Licensee to do so and who have been made aware of, and comply with, the terms of the Licence; and

(b) who hold, or are under the direct personal supervision of a person who holds a relevant Maritime Radio Operator's Certificate of Competence and valid Authority to Operate.

11 Clause 10 (b) shall not apply to persons using channels M (157.850 MHz) and M2 (161.425 MHz).

12 Notwithstanding the terms set out in Clause 10 above, in the event of an emergency where there is a risk to life, the radio equipment may be used by any person to summon assistance.

Access and inspection

13 The Licensee shall permit a person authorised by Ofcom:

(a) to have access to the radio equipment; and

(b) to inspect the Licence, the relevant Maritime Radio Operator's Certificate of Competence and valid Authority to Operate and any notices of variation to the Licence, and the radio equipment at any and all reasonable times or, when in the opinion of that person an urgent situation exists, at any time, to ensure that the radio equipment is being used in accordance with the terms of the Licence.

Modification, restriction and close down

14 A person authorised by Ofcom may require the radio equipment to be modified in operation, restricted, or either temporarily or permanently closed down with immediate effect if in the opinion of the person authorised by Ofcom:

(a) a breach of the Licence has occurred; or

(b) the use of the radio equipment is causing or contributing to undue interference to the use of other authorised radio equipment.

15 Ofcom may require the radio equipment to be modified in operation, restricted or either temporarily or permanently closed down either immediately or on the expiry of such period as Ofcom may specify:

(a) in the interests of long term spectrum planning; or

(b) in the event of a national or local state of emergency being declared.

16 Ofcom may exercise the power set out in clause 15 by a written notice served on the Licensee or by a general notice applicable to holders of this class of Licence.

Schedule 1 – applicable to a Ship Radio Licence

Radio equipment use

1 The Licensee shall ensure that the radio equipment is only used:

(a) to send messages to other ship stations, coast stations, aircraft stations and satellite stations from radio stations used on-board;

(b) to receive messages intended for general reception or for specific reception by the radio equipment from other ship stations, coast stations, aircraft stations, satellite stations, special service stations, radio navigation stations and from radio stations used on board;

(c) to send to and to receive from any radio station any message which is necessary for the safety of life or for navigational safety reasons; or

(d) to send "public correspondence" messages from the vessel indicated in the Licence to stations linked to a public telecommunication system and to receive messages from such stations which are intended to be received by this vessel.

2 The radio equipment must be used on board the vessel indicated in the Licence except in the case of an emergency when the radio equipment may be used anywhere.

Keeping and display of licence documents

3 This Licence, the relevant Maritime Radio Operator's Certificate of Competence and valid Authority to Operate, and any notices of variation to the Licence shall be kept with or near to the licensed radio equipment at all times, where it is physically practicable to do so.

4 This Licence, the relevant Maritime Radio Operator's Certificate of Competence and valid Authority to Operate and any notices of variation to the Licence shall accompany the radio equipment to which it relates, when the vessel is taken abroad.

Identification of transmissions

5 The Licensee shall use one of the following methods of identification for all transmissions:

(a) the vessel call sign indicated in the Licence;

(b) a Maritime Mobile Service Identity ("MMSI") indicated in the Licence;

(c) the Hovercraft Registration Mark;

(d) the vessel's name and, where necessary, the name of the owner of the vessel or the vessel registration number or port of registry providing this would not delay distress, urgency or safety communications.

6 None of the information referred to in clause 5 shall be sent in code.

7 The call sign as described in clause 5(a) shall remain with the vessel, and shall if necessary be surrendered on the sale, transfer, destruction or loss of the vessel.

8 The MMSI as described in clause 5(b) shall if necessary be surrendered on change of ownership, transfer, destruction or loss of the vessel.

Radio equipment and conformity requirements

9 Radio equipment[2] intended for use on board United Kingdom licensed vessels shall;

(a) comply with the Merchant Shipping (Marine Equipment Regulations 1999); or

(b) comply with the applicable UK Radio Interface Requirements (published by Ofcom); or

(c) have been previously type approved in accordance with Section 84 of the Telecommunications Act 1984 and with the provision that the equipment has been placed on the market before 8 April 2001. (After 7 April 2000 type approval certificates are not applicable); or

(d) have been previously type approved in accordance with the Merchant Shipping Notice MSN 1735 (M+F) published by the Maritime and Coastguard Agency.

10 Where included in Section 1, the radio equipment used on board the ship shall only be used on ship frequencies and to the maximum powers and classes of emission allocated in accordance with the relevant International Telecommunication Union (ITU) Radio Regulations[3], and ITU-R Recommendations[3] within the frequency bands indicated below:

[2] Clauses 9(a) to 9(d) are not intended to specify particular radio equipment conformance or approval requirements that would apply to particular types of vessel. Information relating to mandatory requirements may be obtained from: The Maritime and Coastguard Agency, Telephone +44(0)2380 329100.

[3] Extracts from the ITU Radio Regulations and Recommendations ITU-R are published by the ITU in "Manual for use by the Maritime Mobile and Maritime Mobile - Satellite Services", available from the ITU in Geneva, Telephone: +41 22 730 6141 or e-mail sales@itu.int
(Coast station radio frequency assignments are detailed in the Admiralty List of Radio Signals, published by the UK Hydrographic Office, Admiralty Way, Taunton Somerset, Telephone: +44(0)1823 337900 Fax +44(0)1823 284077 - www.ukho.gov.uk)

Frequency bands applicable to a Ship Radio Licence:

Radiotelegraphy (including DSC for frequency bands as applicable)

Frequency/band	415 kHz - 535 kHz	1,605 kHz – 4,000 kHz	4,000 kHz - 27,500 kHz
ITU frequency/band designation	X	Y	Z

Radiotelephony (including AIS, DSC for frequency bands as applicable)

Frequency/band	1,605 kHz-4,000 kHz	4,000 kHz-27,500 kHz	156 MHz-174[4] MHz,
ITU frequency/band designation	T	U	V

Frequency/band	457.525[5] MHz 467.525[5] MHz 457.550[5] MHz 467.550[5] MHz 457.575[5] MHz 467.575[5] MHz 457.5375[6] MHz 457.5625[6] MHz 467.5375[6] MHz 467.5625[6] MHz	Channel "M" (157.850[4] MHz) for use in UK territorial waters only.	Channel "M2" (161.425[4] MHz) for use in UK territorial waters only.
ITU frequency/band designation	–	–	–

Other Frequencies:

Frequency/band	EPIRB 2,182 kHz	EPIRB (PLB) 121.5 MHz,	EPIRB (PLB) 243 MHz
ITU frequency/band designation	A	B	C

[4] 25 kHz channel spacing
[5] 12.5 or 25 kHz channel spacing
[6] 12.5 kHz channel spacing

Frequency/band	Satellite EPIRB(PLB) 406 MHz - 406.1 MHz	Satellite EPIRB operation within 1,645.5 MHz - 1,646.5 MHz	SART 9,200 MHz - 9,500 MHz
ITU frequency/band designation	E	F	G

Frequency/band	Mobile satellite 1,626.5 MHz – 1,660.5 MHz and Receive frequency band 1,525 MHz - 1,559 MHz	Ship to aircraft on scene communications 121.5, 123.1 MHz	Radar/radar target enhancer 2,900 MHz - 3,100 MHz
ITU frequency/band designation	S	–	–

Frequency/band	Radar/radar target enhancer 9,300 MHz - 9,500 MHz
ITU frequency/band designation	–

Schedule 2 – applicable to a Ship Portable Radio Licence

Radio equipment use

1 This Licence covers the use of the radio equipment in UK territorial waters.

2 The Licensee shall ensure that the radio equipment, which may be used on any vessel, is only used:

(a) to send messages to other ship stations, coast stations, aircraft stations;

(b) to receive messages intended for general reception or for specific reception by the radio equipment from other ship stations, coast stations and aircraft stations; or

(c) to send to and to receive from any radio station any message which is necessary for the safety of life or for navigational safety reasons.

3 The radio equipment listed in Section 1 of this Licence may consist of one or more of the following:

(a) one (1) hand held portable VHF radio transceiver with an integral antenna and power supply, which is not designed to be permanently installed on a vessel;

(b) the equipment described in clause 3(a), with the additional functionality of VHF/DSC transmissions;

(c) one (1) Emergency Position Indicating Radio Beacon (EPIRB) and/or one (1) Personal Locator Beacon (PLB) operating on 121.5 MHz, 243 MHz, 406 MHz band or 1.6 GHz band; or

(d) one (1) piece of aeronautical search and rescue equipment with frequencies 121.5 and 123.1 MHz;

which comply with the radio equipment and conformity requirements in clauses 10 and 11 of this schedule.

4 The radio equipment shall be used on board a vessel or its tender except in the case of an emergency when the radio equipment may be used anywhere.

Keeping and display of licence documents

5 This Licence, the relevant Maritime Radio Operator's Certificate of Competence and valid Authority to Operate, and any notices of variation to the Licence shall be kept with or near to the licensed radio equipment at all times, where it is physically practicable to do so.

Identification of transmissions

6 The Licensee shall use one of the following methods of identification for all transmissions:

(a) the "T" reference number indicated in the Licence;

(b) a Maritime Mobile Service Identity ("MMSI") indicated in the Licence;

(c) the Hovercraft Registration Mark;

(d) the vessel's name and, where necessary, the name of the owner of the vessel or th vessel registration number or port of registry providing this would not delay distress, urgency or safety communications.

7 None of the information referred to in clause 6 shall be sent in code.

8 The "T" reference number as described in clause 6(a) shall if necessary be surrendered on change of ownership, transfer, destruction or loss of the radio equipment.

9 The MMSI number as described in clause 6(b) shall remain with the radio equipment ar shall, if necessary, be surrendered on destruction or loss of the radio equipment.

Radio equipment and conformity requirements

10 Radio equipment[7] intended for use on board any vessel shall;

(a) comply with the Merchant Shipping (Marine Equipment Regulations 1999); or

(b) comply with the applicable UK Radio Interface Requirements (published by Ofcom); or

(c) have been previously type approved in accordance with Section 84 of the Telecommunications Act 1984 and with the provision that the equipment has been placed on the market before 8 April 2001. (After 7 April 2000 type approval certificates are not applicable); or

(d) have been previously type approved in accordance with the Merchant Shipping Notice MSN 1735 (M+F) published by the Maritime and Coastguard Agency.

---

[7] Clauses 10(a) to 10(d) are not intended to specify particular radio equipment conformance or approval requirements that would apply to particular types of vessel. Information relating to mandato requirements may be obtained from: The Maritime and Coastguard Agency, Telephone +44(0)2380 329100.

11 Where included in Section 1, the radio equipment used shall only be used on ship frequencies and to the maximum powers and classes of emission allocated in accordance with the relevant International Telecommunication Union (ITU) Radio Regulations[8], and ITU-R Recommendations[8] within the frequency bands indicated below:

Frequency bands applicable to a Ship Portable Radio Licence:

Radiotelephony (including DSC for frequency bands as applicable)

Frequency/band	156 MHz - 174[9] MHz	Channel "M" (157.850[9]) MHz for use in UK territorial waters only.	Channel "M2" (161.425[9]) MHz for use in UK territorial waters only.
ITU frequency/band designation	V	–	–

Other Frequencies

Frequency/band	EPIRB (PLB) 121.5 MHz,	EPIRB (PLB) 243 MHz	Satellite EPIRB(PLB) 406 MHz - 406.1 MHz
ITU frequency/band designation	B	C	E

Frequency/band	Satellite EPIRB operation within 1,645.5 MHz - 1,646.5 MHz	Ship to aircraft on scene communications 121.5, 123.1 MHz
ITU frequency/band designation	F	–

Issued by:
Ofcom Licensing Centre
Riverside House
2a Southwark Bridge Road
London, SE1 9HA
Tel. +44 (0)20 7981 3131

[8] Extracts from the ITU Radio Regulations and Recommendations ITU-R are published by the ITU in "Manual for use by the Maritime Mobile and Maritime Mobile - Satellite Services", available from the ITU in Geneva, Telephone: +41 22 730 6141 or e-mail sales@itu.int
(Coast station radio frequency assignments are detailed in the Admiralty List of Radio Signals, published by the UK Hydrographic Office, Admiralty Way, Taunton Somerset, Telephone: +44(0)1823 337900 Fax +44(0)1823 284077 - www.ukho.gov.uk)
[9] 25 kHz channel spacing

Fax. +44 (0)20 7981 3333

Certificate no: **ANO 0300057/LL5**
Page 1 of 4

International Load Line Certificate

Issued under the provisions of the International Convention on Load Lines, 1966, as modified by the Protocol of 1988 relating thereto,
under the authority of the Government of the Commonwealth of The Bahamas by Lloyd's Register Asia

	Particulars of Ship
Name of ship	**SAMPLE LL5 (OIL TANKER)(MULTIPLE LL'S)**
Distinctive number or letters	**X1XX1**
Port of registry	**NASSAU**
Length (L) as defined in article 2(8) (metres)	**220.990**
IMO number	**1234567**
Freeboard assigned as	**A new ship**
Type of ship	**Type A**

Freeboard from deck line [1]			Load line	
Tropical	**9469**	mm (T)	**0**	mm above (S)
Summer	**9469**	mm (S)	Upper edge of line through centre of ring	
Winter	**9469**	mm (W)	**0**	mm below (S)
Winter North Atlantic	**Not required**	mm (WNA)	**Not required**	mm below (S)
Timber tropical	-	mm (LT)	-	mm above (LS)
Timber summer	-	mm (LS)	-	mm above (S)
Timber winter	-	mm (LW)	-	mm below (LS)
Timber winter North Atlantic	-	mm (LWNA)	-	mm below (LS)

Allowance for fresh water for all freeboards other than timber	**261**	mm
Allowance for fresh water for timber freeboards	-	mm
The upper edge of the deck line from which these freeboards are measured is	**0**	mm

below the top of steel upper deck at side

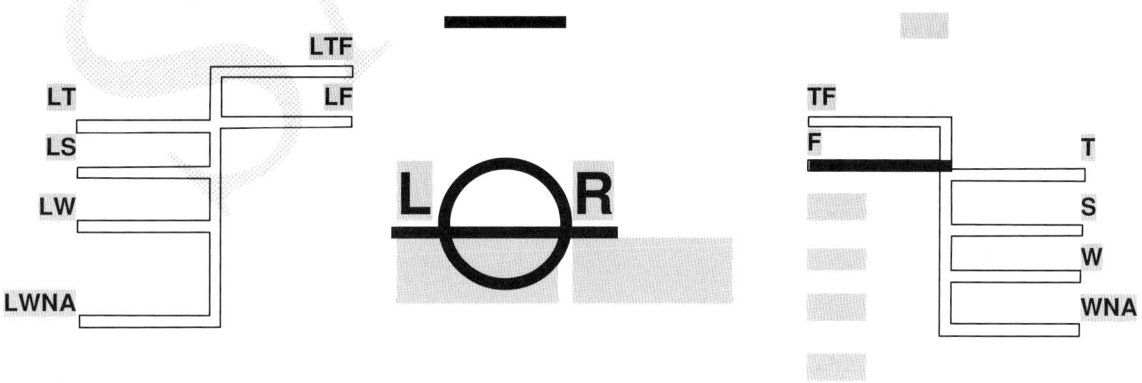

[1] *Freeboards and load lines which are not applicable need not be entered on the certificate. Subdivision load lines may be entered on the certificate on a voluntary basis.*

Form 2210zz1-5 (2014.12)

Certificate no: **ANO 0300057/LL5**
Page 2 of 4

This is to certify:

1. that the ship has been surveyed in accordance with the requirements of article 14 of the Convention;
2. that the survey showed that the freeboards have been assigned and load lines shown on page 1 have been marked in accordance with the Convention.

This certificate is valid until[2] **06 November 2010** subject to annual surveys in accordance with article 14(1) (c) of the Convention.

Completion date of the survey on which this certificate is based **07 November 2005**

Issued at **Another Place** on **07 November 2005**

A N Other
Surveyor to Lloyd's Register Asia

A subsidiary of Lloyd's Register Group Limited

Notes:

1. When a ship departs from a port situated on a river or inland waters, deeper loading shall be permitted corresponding to the weight of fuel and all other materials required for consumption between the point of departure and the sea.
2. When a ship is in fresh water of unit density the appropriate load line may be submerged by the amount of fresh water allowance shown above. Where the density is other than unity, the allowance shall be made proportional to the difference between 1.025 and the actual density.

[2] *Insert the date of expiry as specified by the Administration in accordance with article 19 (1) of the Convention. The day and the month of this date correspond to the anniversary date as defined in article 2 (9) of the Convention, unless amended in accordance with article 19 (8) of the Convention.*
**Delete as appropriate*

Form 2210zz1-5 (2014.12)

Certificate no: **ANO 0300057/LL5**
Page 3 of 4

Endorsement for annual surveys

This is to certify that, at an annual survey required by article 14(1)(c) of the Convention, the ship was found to comply with the relevant requirements of the Convention.

Annual survey
Signed:
Place of survey
Date

Annual survey
Signed:
Place of survey
Date

Annual survey
Signed:
Place of survey
Date

Annual survey
Signed:
Place of survey
Date

Annual survey in accordance with article 19(8)(c)

This is to certify that, at a survey in accordance with article 19(8)(c) of the Convention, the ship was found to comply with the relevant requirements of the Convention.

Annual survey
Signed:
Place of survey
Date

Form 2210zz1-5 (2014.12)

Certificate no: **ANO 0300057/LL5**
Page 4 of 4

Endorsement to extend the certificate if valid for less than 5 years where article 19(3) applies

The ship complies with the relevant requirements of the Convention, and this certificate shall, in accordance with article 19(3) of the Convention, be accepted as valid until

Signed:
Place of survey
Date

Endorsement where the renewal survey has been completed and article 19(4) applies

The ship complies with the relevant requirements of the Convention, and this certificate shall, in accordance with article 19(4) of the Convention, be accepted as valid until

Signed:
Place of survey
Date

Endorsement to extend the validity of the certificate until reaching the port of survey or for a period of grace where article 19(5) or 19(6) applies

This certificate shall in accordance with article 19(5)/19(6)* of the Convention, be accepted as valid until

Signed:
Place of survey
Date

Endorsement for advancement of anniversary date where article 19(8) applies

In accordance with article 19(8) of the Convention, the new anniversary date is

Signed:
Place of survey
Date

In accordance with article 19(8) of the Convention, the new anniversary date is

Signed:
Place of survey
Date

**Delete as appropriate*

Form 2210zz1-5 (2014.12)

Cargo Ship Safety Construction Certificate

Issued under the provisions of the International Convention for the Safety of Life at Sea, 1974, as modified by the Protocol of 1988 relating thereto,

under the authority of the Government of the Commonwealth of The Bahamas by Lloyd's Register EMEA

	Particulars of Ship
Name of ship	**SAMPLE (OIL TANKER)(MULTIPLE LL's)**
Distinctive number or letters	**X1XX1**
Port of registry	**NASSAU**
Gross tonnage	**42,433**
Deadweight of ship (metric tons) [1]	**74,999***
IMO number	**1234567**
Type of ship [*]	~~Bulk carrier~~ **Oil tanker** ~~Chemical tanker~~ ~~Gas carrier~~ ~~Cargo ship other than any of the above~~
Date of build:[2]	
Date of building contract	**15 July 2003**
Date on which keel was laid or ship was at similar stage of construction	**21 October 2004**
Date of delivery	**07 November 2005**
Date on which the work for a conversion or an alteration or modification of a major character was commenced (where applicable)	**Not Applicable**

This is to certify:

1. that the ship has been surveyed in accordance with the requirements of regulation I/10 of the Convention;
2. that the survey showed that the condition of the structure, machinery and equipment as defined in the above regulation was satisfactory and the ship complied with the relevant requirements of chapters II-1 and II-2 of the Convention (other than those relating to fire safety systems and appliances and fire control plans) ;
3. that the last two inspections of the outside of the ship's bottom took place on **02 October 2008** and **07 November 2010**;
4. that an Exemption Certificate **has not** been issued.
5. that the ship **was not** subjected to an alternative design and arrangements in pursuance of regulation(s) **II-1/55 / II-2/17** of the Convention;
6. a Document of approval of alternative design and arrangements for **machinery and electrical installations/fire protection is not** appended to this Certificate.

This certificate is valid until[3] **06 November 2015** subject to the annual and intermediate surveys and inspections of the outside of the ship's bottom in accordance with regulation I/10 of the Convention.

Completion date of the survey on which this certificate is based **07 November 2010**

Issued at **Another Place** on **07 November 2010**

***Valid for a range of deadweights to a maximum of 74,999 metric tons.**

A.N. Other
Surveyor to Lloyd's Register EMEA
a member of the Lloyd's Register group.

[1] *For oil tankers, chemical tankers and gas carriers only.*
[*] *Delete as appropriate*
[2] *All applicable dates shall be completed.*
[3] *Insert the date of expiry as specified by the Administration in accordance with regulation I/14(a) of the Convention. The day and the month of this date correspond to the anniversary date as defined in regulation I/2(n) of the Convention, unless amended in accordance with regulation I/14(h).*

Form 2221zz1 (2015.03)

Certificate no: **ANO 1000175**
Page 2 of 4

Endorsement for annual and intermediate surveys

This is to certify that, at a survey required by regulation I/10 of the Convention, the ship was found to comply with the relevant requirements of the Convention.

Annual survey

Signed: ______________________
Place of survey
Date

Annual / Intermediate * survey

Signed: ______________________
Place of survey
Date

Annual / Intermediate* survey

Signed: ______________________
Place of survey
Date

Annual survey

Signed: ______________________
Place of survey
Date

Annual/intermediate survey in accordance with regulation I/14(h)(iii)

This is to certify that, at an **annual / intermediate*** survey in accordance with regulation I/14(h)(iii) of the Convention, this ship was found to comply with the relevant requirements of the Convention.

Signed: ______________________
Place of survey
Date

* *Delete as appropriate*

Form 2221zz1 (2015.03)

Certificate no: **ANO 1000175**
Page 3 of 4

Endorsement for inspections of the outside of the ship's bottom[4]

This is to certify that, at an inspection required by regulation I/10 of the Convention, the ship was found to comply with the relevant requirements of the Convention.

First inspection

Signed:
Place of survey
Date

Second inspection

Signed:
Place of survey
Date

Endorsement to extend the certificate if valid for less than 5 years where regulation I/14(c) applies

The ship complies with the relevant requirements of the Convention, and this certificate shall, in accordance with regulation I/14(c) of the Convention, be accepted as valid until

Signed:
Place of survey
Date

Endorsement where the renewal survey has been completed and regulation I/14(d) applies

The ship complies with the relevant requirements of the Convention, and this certificate shall, in accordance with regulation I/14(d) of the Convention, be accepted as valid until

Signed:
Place of survey
Date

Endorsement to extend the validity of the certificate until reaching the port of survey or for a period of grace where regulation I/14(e) or I/14(f) applies

The certificate shall, in accordance with regulation **I/14(e) / I/14(f) *** of the Convention, be accepted as valid until

Signed:
Place of survey
Date

[4] *Provision may be made for additional inspections.*

* *Delete as appropriate*

Form 2221zz1 (2015.03)

Certificate no: **ANO 1000175**
Page 4 of 4

Endorsement for advancement of anniversary date where regulation I/14(h) applies

In accordance with regulation I/14(h) of the Convention, the new anniversary date is .

Signed: ______________________________

Place of survey

Date

In accordance with regulation I/14(h) of the Convention, the new anniversary date is .

Signed: ______________________________

Place of survey

Date

Form 2221zz1 (2015.03)